# Analyzing
# American Corrections

**Other Titles of Related Interest in Sociology**

*Research Methods and Statistics*

Earl Babbie, *The Practice of Social Research,* 4th
Earl Babbie, *Observing Ourselves: Essays in Social Research*
Earl Babbie, *Survey Research Methods*
Anthony Capon, *Statistics for the Social Sciences*
Margaret Jendrek, *Through the Maze: Statistics with Computer Applications*
John Lofland/Lyn Lofland, *Analyzing Social Settings: A Guide to Qualitative
 Observation and Analysis,* 2d
Joseph Healey, *Statistics: A Tool for the Social Sciences*
June True, *Finding Out: Conducting and Evaluating Social Research*
John Hedderson, *SPSS-X Made Simple*

*Criminology and Deviance*

Joseph Sheley, *America's "Crime Problem"*
Ronald Akers, *Deviance: A Social Learning Approach,* 3d
Erdwin Pfuhl, *The Deviance Process,* 2d
James Skipper et al., *Deviance: Voices from the Margin*
Joseph Sheley, *Exploring Crime: An Anthology*

*Specialized Texts*

James Spates/John Macionis, *Sociology of Cities,* 2d
Martin Marger, *Elites and Masses,* 2d
Martin Marger, *Race and Ethnic Relations: American and Global Perspectives*
Arnold Sherman/Aliza Kolker, *The Social Bases of Politics*
Robert Atchley, *Social Forces in Aging,* 5th
Robert Atchley, *Aging: Continuity and Change,* 2d
Donald Cowgill, *Aging Around the World*
Judith Perrolle, *Computers and Social Change: Information, Property, and Power*
John Weeks, *Population,* 3d
David Miller, *Introduction to Collective Behavior*
Frederic Wolinsky, *Sociology of Health and Medicine*

# Analyzing American Corrections

**NEAL SHOVER**
*University of Tennessee*

**WERNER J. EINSTADTER**
*Eastern Michigan University*

**Wadsworth Publishing Company**
Belmont, California
A Division of Wadsworth, Inc.

*Sociology Editor:* Sheryl Fullerton
*Production Editor:* Leland Moss
*Managing Designer:* MaryEllen Podgorski
*Designer:* Joy Dickinson
*Print Buyer:* Barbara Britton
*Copy Editor:* Anne Montague
*Technical Illustrator:* Alan Noyes
*Compositor:* G & S Typesetters, Inc.
*Cover:* Charles Fuhrman Design
*Signing Representative:* Mark Francisco

*Analyzing American Corrections* is a substantially revised version of Neal Shover's *A Sociology of American Corrections*, originally published by the Dorsey Press in 1979.

Printed in the United States of America  19

1  2  3  4  5  6  7  8  9  10—92  91  90  89  88

**Library of Congress Cataloging-in-Publication Data**

Shover, Neal.
   Analyzing American corrections.

   Bibliography: p.
   Includes index.
   1. Corrections—United States.  I. Einstadter, Werner J.  II. Title.
   HV9471.S54  1988      365.'973      87-16764
   ISBN 0-534-08551-2

**To Jeanie**

—Neal Shover

**To the Memory of my Parents**

—Werner Einstadter

# Contents

# *Preface*

The 1970s and 1980s have been good times for criminologists and other scholars concerned with criminal justice. State funding for criminal justice activities increased dramatically. Researchers discovered new opportunities as consultants to criminal justice agencies, and research support became plentiful. Criminal justice curricula and programs were established at hundreds of American universities with thousands of students—undergraduate and graduate alike—electing criminology or criminal justice as their major field of study. These developments were matched by an outpouring of new instructional materials and textbooks.

We believe that the bulk of these materials and books share three tendencies. To begin with, they are primarily descriptive in their approach and do not sufficiently stimulate students to think about and to analyze correctional issues and problems. Second, they reflect an apolitical, technical approach to corrections. The premises and priorities of state managers, including the fundamental importance of controlling crime, are taken as legitimate and pressing. The fundamental approach to correctional problems and processes emphasizes the development and ap-

plication of workable, effective correctional *techniques*. In short, much of the pedagogical literature in corrections is technocratic in approach. Finally, most are designed primarily for introductory courses in the curriculum, largely ignoring courses for intermediate or advanced students.

We have tried to avoid these tendencies in this book. Our aims are twofold: to focus on the social and political contours that affect correctional practice, and to discuss some of the controversy that embroils and impinges on the correctional enterprise. In both ways we hope to enable students to make informed and critical judgments about corrections.

Although both of us now hold academic positions, we have had more than 20 combined years of employment experience in correctional agencies. This includes work in prison classification and counseling, as a probation and parole officer and a parole district supervisor, and as director of a program for violent offenders. Both of us found the day-to-day realities of the correctional enterprise very different from what we envisioned as neophytes. Our correctional employment experiences find expression in an insistence that students must be taught how to look behind the public face of corrections for an understanding of its day-to-day reality. Largely because of our correctional experiences, we maintain a skeptical, even critical, stance toward the claims made by state managers and correctional publicists.

## Organization of the Book

There are 14 chapters in the book. Chapter 1 is a brief overview of the correctional apparatus in America, its size, and its location in the criminal justice system. Chapter 2 lays out a simple framework for thinking about correctional processes. It focuses primarily on two components of corrections, strategies and structures. The concept of constraints is defined and discussed, along with the principle of emergence. We illustrate how constraints shape corrections and influence the outcome of correctional planning. The impact of macrosocial forces on the correctional enterprise are considered as well. Chapter 2 concludes with some comments on the day-to-day work of correctional personnel.

In Chapter 3 we consider correctional ideologies. We distinguish three ideologies on the basis of the political philosophies they embody: conservative, liberal, and radical. We show how each draws different conclusions as to the nature of corrections.

Chapter 4 deals with the problems and processes of criminal sentencing. Sentencing is presented as a social process involving interaction between representatives of different offices in the criminal justice system. Problems of sentencing disparity and discrimination are discussed. Chapter 4 concludes with materials on the sentencing reform movement of recent years, especially the trend toward determinate sentencing.

Chapters 5 through 10 summarize much of what is known about correctional organizations, strategies, and processes. Separate chapters are devoted to the jail and detention home, prisons for males, prisons for females, and probation and parole. Chapter 10 examines the process of correctional change and some contemporary developments in corrections.

Chapters 11 through 13 deal with the evaluation of correctional strategies. We suggest that three different evaluation modes can be applied to corrections: humaneness, legality/due process, and efficiency-effectiveness. Chapter 12 is a detailed presentation of the elements of evaluation research. Chapter 13 briefly summarizes some of the results of correctional evaluation research and interprets the debate over research as inevitable political and social process.

The final chapter deals with the future implications of current and evolving correctional ideology and practice.

## Acknowledgments

We benefited from the help and suggestions of many people in the course of completing this book. Carole Haimelin and Loretta McHan expertly typed the manuscript. Susan Caringella-MacDonald, Western Michigan University; Ben M. Crouch, Texas A&M University; John Irwin, San Francisco State University; Joseph E. Jacoby, Bowling Green State University; and Joseph G. Weis, University of Washington read and commented on earlier drafts of the manuscript. Although we incorporated many of their suggestions, we are responsible for any remaining problems. Our editor Sheryl Fullerton provided expert guidance and support throughout the project. We especially appreciate her characteristic and unfailing good humor. We wish to thank Leland Moss for his kind advice, patience, and overall coordination of the project. Special thanks to Constance Einstadter for her editorial assistance, advice, and support.

# 1

# Introduction: Criminal Justice and Corrections

*F*ollowing more than two decades of tumult and debate, the system of criminal justice in America is in a state of readjustment. During the 1960s and 1970s, many challenges were brought against the correctional system. One group attacked it for being ineffective in the "war against crime," for being preoccupied with the legal rights and rehabilitation of offenders to the detriment of victims and law-abiding citizens. These critics—the "new realists" (Platt and Takagi, 1977)—called for a renewed emphasis on swift and certain punishment to deal with what they believed to be a small group of "serious" or "dangerous" offenders. Others indicted the criminal justice system for placing too much emphasis on punishment and the repression of offenders. Many of these critics espoused a radical political–economic interpretation of correctional issues. These conflicting perspectives have produced considerable ferment in the components of criminal justice, ideological changes in the way the treatment of correctional populations is justified, and altered the role that corrections plays in the broader framework of criminal justice.

The clientele of correctional agencies were not idle during this period of ferment. Mounting court challenges to the treatment they received at the hands of the correctional apparatus, offenders won decisions forcing correctional administrators to modify some procedures they had taken for granted. In addition, a wave of prisoner rebellions swept the American correctional scene in the early 1970s, during which a number of offenders and correctional employees were killed. Clearly, these were times of turmoil and incipient change.

While the controversies have not subsided, their intensity has diminished somewhat. The stance of the "new realists" appears to have taken hold and become the dominant position in criminal justice circles. This philosophical reversal of the earlier emphasis on rehabilitation has brought changes whose implications are still uncertain. These controversies, changes, and differences in approach to criminal justice make it important to develop an understanding of the nature of the criminal justice system.

This book aims at an understanding of the past, present, and likely future conditions of one component of the criminal justice system: *corrections*, by which we mean all the officially organized and sanctioned actions to which offenders are subjected as a result of their conviction of crime(s). Dealing with American correctional structures and practices, we use sociological knowledge and analysis to understand and to highlight the day-to-day realities of correctional structures and processes.

## The Place of Corrections

Offenders enter the criminal justice system when they are taken into custody as suspected perpetrators of criminal acts. They enter the correctional system upon conviction and sentencing by a court of proper jurisdiction. Prior to reaching the correctional stage of the system, offenders have contact with its other components: the *police*, the *prosecutor's office*, perhaps the *public defender*, and the *court*.

Depending on their age and the type of crime they are charged with committing, offenders arrive at the correctional stage via somewhat different routes. Figure 1.1 (pp. 4–5) illustrates a schematic overview of the entire criminal justice process. It shows a three-

part flow of criminal cases, one each for felons, misdemeanants, and juvenile offenders. Note that offenders may be dropped out at several points in the criminal justice process, and thus do not progress to subsequent stages.

Although Figure 1.1 presents a schematic overview of criminal justice, the components of criminal justice often do not work as predictably or harmoniously as a mechanical system. However, implicit in the very notion of criminal justice as a *system* is the fact that the activities of each component do affect the activities of the others. This concept is built on three assumptions:

**1.** An institution or process that represents a totality in its own right is, at the same time, comprised of distinguishable parts or subsystems.

**2.** These components of the larger system exist in a state of interdependence. The state or condition of any one component influences the state or condition of the other components.

**3.** Changes in the state or condition of any system component modifies the other components in patterned, predictable ways.

Although we lack a well-developed understanding of the systemic properties of criminal justice, it is not difficult to see that the correctional subsystem is affected by the activities of other components of the system. For example, the current "get tough" policy of many courts has had an impact on corrections: Between 1978 and 1983, the number of persons confined in the nation's jails and prisons increased by 42 percent (DeWitt, 1986). Correctional programs and facilities have struggled to cope as prison populations escalated to unprecedented levels.

## Some Parameters of the Correctional Subsystem

For many years, both the number of correctional employees and public expenditures for corrections grew slowly. This pattern has changed dramatically in recent years. The past two decades have seen a steady increase in criminal justice spending. Spending for corrections alone increased 115 percent between 1960 and 1980 (DeWitt, 1980). In 1981, state and local correctional employees numbered 270,957, at a payroll of more than $380,000,000 a month. At the federal level, there were around 10,000 employees (McGarrell and Flanagan, 1985). Total expenditures for state corrections in 1980 amounted to more than $4 billion.

Correctional agencies, like military installations and factories, often contribute substantially to the economy of the local communities where they are located. They represent the principal employer in many communities in the United States. Clearly, corrections is a large enterprise that employs thousands of people and spends substantial public revenues.

How many people are "served" by the various components of corrections? Panel 1.1 gives a summary picture of the correctional population in 1985. A brief glance should indicate that the correctional mandate covers considerable numbers. These numbers are estimates, and the real numbers fluctuate constantly; however, they are large—and, more important, they are increasing.

In a very real sense, those employed in the correctional subsystem owe their jobs and sustenance to the existence of this offender population. We are reminded of Marx's comment—only half-facetious—that "the criminal . . . appears as one of those 'natural equilibrating forces' which establish a just balance and open up a whole perspective of 'useful' occupations" (1964: 159–160). Given the size, importance, and controversy that surrounds American corrections, an analysis of it is timely and needed.

---

**PANEL 1.1**

*Correctional Populations—1985*

---

**M**ore than 1 percent of the U.S. population is under some form of correctional supervision:

*Persons under correctional supervision*

|  | Number | Percent |
|---|---|---|
| Probation | 1,502,000 | 65 |
| Parole | 252,000 | 11 |
| Prison | 464,000 | 19 |
| Jail (sentenced only) | 107,600 | 5 |
| Total | 2,325,600 | 100 |

The number of persons under each type of correctional supervision is at an all-time high.

- The nation's adult probation population grew by 10.7 percent (nearly 145,000 persons) in 1983.

- During 1983, the parole population grew by 12.1 percent (more than 27,000 persons).

- The prison population grew by more than 6 percent during 1984, adding 26,618 more prisoners.

- Local jail populations including convicted and unconvicted inmates grew by more than 40 percent between 1978 and 1983, rising from 76 to 98 jail inmates per 100,000 U.S. residents.

SOURCE: U.S. Department of Justice (1986c).

FIGURE 1.1   **The Criminal Justice System and the Flow of Criminal Cases**

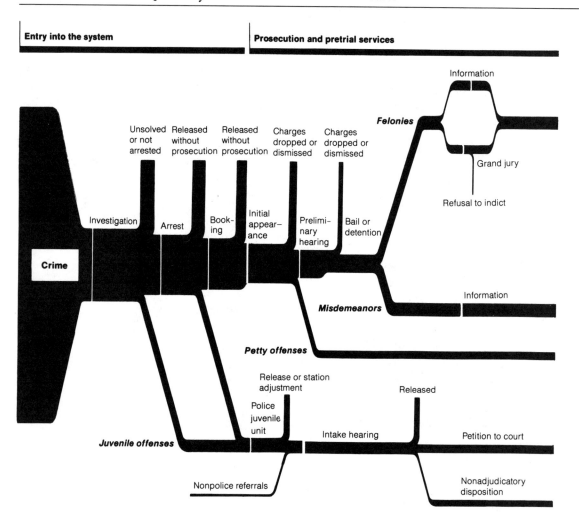

| Entry into the system | Prosecution and pretrial services |

SOURCE: U.S. Department of Justice (1983b: 42–43)

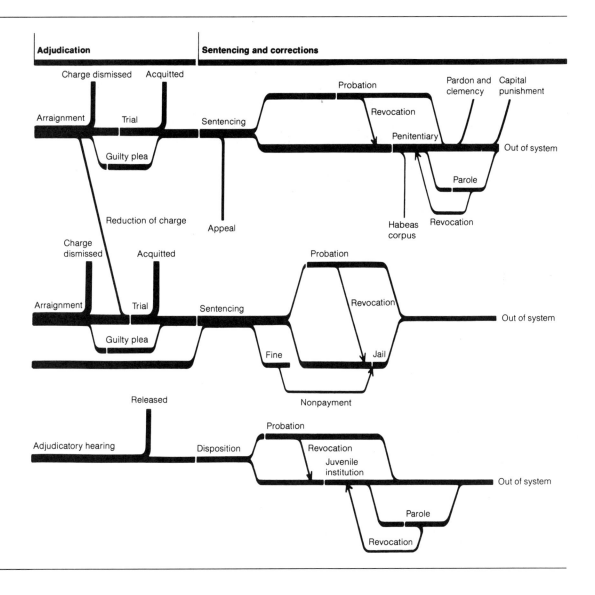

**Adjudication** | **Sentencing and corrections**

Charge dismissed    Acquitted

Arraignment    Trial

Guilty plea

Reduction of charge

Sentencing

Probation

Revocation

Penitentiary

Pardon and clemency    Capital punishment

Out of system

Parole

Appeal    Habeas corpus    Revocation

Charge dismissed    Acquitted

Arraignment    Trial

Guilty plea

Sentencing

Probation

Revocation

Fine    Jail

Out of system

Nonpayment

Released

Adjudicatory hearing    Disposition

Probation

Revocation    Juvenile institution

Out of system

Parole

Revocation

# 2

# Correctional Strategies
# and Structures
# as Social Process

*O*ur principal objective in this book is an enhanced ability to think analytically and critically about the correctional system and process. To achieve this objective, we must become familiar with what at first may appear a bewildering landscape of institutions, policies, and practices. Let's begin by sorting them out.

Many of the most important questions about corrections are about ideologies, strategies, structures, and interactions. Correctional *ideologies* are broad, abstract assumptions and beliefs about crime and how best to deal with it. They provide a way of perceiving and interpreting crime and crime control efforts. Doctrines of deterrence and incapacitation are examples. These ideologies acquire specificity and focus in state-sponsored correctional *strategies* such as probation, imprisonment, and execution. Such strategies

are entrusted to a network of bureaucracies. These bureaucratic *structures* include the jail, the training school, the prison, and parole agencies. The routine day-to-day *interactions* between correctional personnel and offenders are the focus of these correctional ideologies, strategies, and structures.

An example here may help to clarify the distinctions between the four components of corrections. Consider the ideology of deterrence, which includes the assumption that punishing offenders reduces the likelihood that they and others will commit further crime. The correctional strategy of the death penalty is one expression of this ideology. Traditionally, executions in the United States are carried out by prison employees in an area of the prison typically known as death row. Condemned to death, isolated from the rest of the prison population, and denied even the minimal mobility permitted other inmates, death row inmates live in a distinctive social and interactional world.

Based on interviews with 35 men confined on Alabama's death row, Robert Johnson concludes that "the death sentence dramatically affects the human environment of death row, polarizing guards and inmates and otherwise contributing to an atmosphere of violence and fear" (1981: 80). Consequently, interaction on death row, especially between inmates and guards, is guarded and brief. In fact, Johnson's research led him to conclude that confinement on death row is a form of torture (1987: 51). It amounts to a "living death." This is the case precisely because of the structure of death row. The same lesson applies to other correctional strategies and structures; the nature of day-to-day life and interaction is shaped by the organizational context in which they take place.

In the broadest terms, we want to gain a better understanding of the social forces that mold and sometimes transform the four components of corrections. This chapter discusses and provides examples of those forces. Because correctional ideologies both are shaped by social contexts and, in turn, shape correctional strategies and structures, they are treated separately, in Chapter 3.

## Constraints and the Principle of Emergence

As we encounter them at any given time, correctional ideologies, strategies, and structures are the cumulative products of countless decisions by political figures and correctional personnel. These discrete decisions by legislators, judges, correctional administrators, probation officers, and others occur over a long period of time. In the final analysis, if we are to understand the forms and

functioning of corrections, we must understand the decision-making processes of those who construct and reconstruct them day to day.

When confronted with the need to make a decision, what process do we follow? When legislators must decide to vote for or against a bill to increase the severity of threatened penalties for some crime, how do they reach a decision? How can we describe the decision-making process of parole board members? The concept of *constraint* is helpful here. Constraints are forces that shape decision making by causing us: (1) not to "see" some options that, objectively, are open to us; (2) to perceive some options as unworkable, inappropriate or in other ways unacceptable; and (3) to interpret other options as worthy of consideration, possessing merit, or viable. If we can learn about the constraints under which correctional decisions are made, we can improve our understanding of those decisions.

At least four kinds of forces independently constrain and thereby shape correctional decision making and the components of corrections: ideological constraints, contextual constraints, interorganizational process constraints, and bureaucratic process constraints. All four are *emergent* forces, meaning that the nature and impact of any one of them cannot be understood in terms of or reduced to any of the others. Each type must be analyzed in its own right.

To understand the *principle of emergence,* consider the example of water. When a specific combination of the two chemical elements hydrogen and oxygen occurs, water results. However, water has a property or quality—liquidity—that is not found in its constituent parts. In other words, water has an emergent property that cannot be grasped or understood by analyzing its parts. The same principle applies in the social realm.

The behaviors and interactions we observe in institutional settings cannot be understood by analyzing the characteristics or qualities of the individuals we find there. Rather, the institutional setting itself significantly shapes the ways people behave and interact, regardless of age, gender, education, personality, or social class.

The presumed social, educational, or psychological shortcomings of the employees of correctional agencies are often cited to explain problems in those agencies. For example, the suspicion, distrust, and brutality that characterize some interactions between guards and inmates oftentimes are attributed to differences in their social backgrounds. Thus many people mistakenly believe that prison violence, brutality and dehumanization

> can be traced to some innate or acquired characteristic of the correctional or inmate population. Thus, on the one hand, there is the contention that [these problems] exist . . . because guards are sadistic, uneducated, and insensitive people. . . . Or, from other quarters comes the argument that violence and brutality in prison are the logical and predictable result of the involuntary confinement of a collective of individuals whose life histories have been characterized by disregard for law, order and social convention and a concurrent propensity for impulsivity and aggression (Haney *et al.*, 1973: 70).

Put the two together, the argument goes, and misunderstanding and violence are the natural result.

The New York State Special Commission on Attica adopted this type of interpretation when it investigated the 1971 inmate uprising at Attica, New York, during which 43 persons were killed. Prior to the riot, the commission charged, "the relationship between most officers and inmates was characterized by fear, hostility, and mistrust, nurtured by racism." The commission further suggested that this "was probably inevitable when predominantly poor, urban, black, and Spanish-speaking inmates were placed under the supervision of white officers from rural areas equipped with only three weeks of training" (1972: 80). Interpreted this way, the solution to prison problems is to change the characteristics of guards, inmates, or both. Use women as guards, or insist on a higher level of education for guards.

Interpretations of organizational problems that focus on the characteristics of individuals are flawed logically because they violate the principle of emergence—they ignore the fact that *organizational* structures and dynamics generate and shape the behavior of the members. Replacing "old-style" guards with different ones simply may not work; the same kinds of problems that prompted reform may emerge again unless the organization itself is modified.

Recognizing the emergent qualities of organizations and their effects on the member individuals was a key point of departure for the well-known Stanford University study of simulated imprisonment (Haney *et al.*, 1973). The researchers created an artificial prison, using undergraduate students as guards and inmates. By staffing and populating the prison this way, the investigators sought to create a setting in which any subsequent pathological conduct could be attributed solely to the structural and cultural components of prison organization. The study was so successful that the researchers terminated it earlier than planned because of the extreme pathological processes that developed in the experimental "prison." For example, some "guards" became callous and overbearing in their behavior toward "inmates," some of whom wept or showed other signs of emotional distress and begged to be permitted to terminate their participation earlier than scheduled. This research provides important evidence of the power of organizational forces on individual behavior and interactional dynamics.

A review of some recent research on female employees of male correctional institutions also may help to clarify the principle of emergence and the need to distinguish different types of causal forces. The fact that very few women were employed in corrections until recent years fed speculation that the pathologies and peculiar dynamics of correctional agencies resulted from their employees' masculinity. Now that increasing numbers of women are finding employment in corrections, researchers have examined their responses to and impact on correctional agencies. Generally, the research findings reinforce the importance of organizational variables and processes in shaping correctional work performance. When John Whitehead examined role conflict, job satisfaction, and job burnout among 700 probation officers in several states, he found very few differences by gender. He concluded that "policymakers . . . should devote attention to the job problems facing all probation officers, female and male alike, rather than mistakenly [assuming] that gender is a critical variable" (1986: 51). Nancy Jurik studied 179 correctional officers to determine whether better-educated, female, and minority officers hold more positive attitudes toward inmates. Her analysis demonstrates that minority officers do hold somewhat more positive attitudes, but that education and gender are unrelated to these attitudes. Like Whitehead, Jurik concluded:

> correctional reforms that focus primarily on changing the demographic composition of correctional officers are quite unlikely to ameliorate significantly the tension in today's prisons. It is necessary for both reformers and social scientists to develop more sophisticated analyses of the interplay between individual attributes and work organization characteristics and their joint effects on behavior (1985: 52).

## Social and Political– Economic Context

Corrections does not exist in a vacuum. It is situated in and shaped by its social and political–economic context. True to the principle of emergence, we cannot analyze this context adequately by examining the properties of the units that make it up. Determining which aspects of the context exert the greatest impact on corrections is crucial. We then should explore the precise nature of the links between these variables and characteristics of the correctional system and process, and the circumstances under which these constraints operate.

Just as corrections does not exist in a vacuum, it does not change only in response to its own internal dynamics. It also responds to changes in its social and political–economic context. In Chapter 10 we discuss the problem of interpreting historical correctional change. For the moment, we concentrate on the problem of interpreting static relationships between corrections and its context(s).

Studies of the relationships between contextual variables and corrections have been pursued at different levels of abstraction or distance. We arbitrarily distinguish two sets of environmental forces that shape corrections: *macrosocial* forces and *community-level* forces. Sociologists employ the former concept to refer to the characteristics of large systems or units such as states or nation-states. Consequently, when we discuss the macrosocial context of corrections, we refer to something broader than simply the local community and the network of agencies that encompass any particular correctional bureaucracy. Instead, we focus on the characteristics of large social settings such as states or nations that seemingly produce variation in their correctional ideologies, strategies, and structures. By contrast, analyses of the community context of corrections usually focus on differences among smaller geographical units, such as cities. However, both types of explanations generally highlight the importance of broad social, cultural, or economic factors.

### Corrections in Macrosocial Context

As in many areas of social scientific theory and inquiry, there is little scholarly agreement on either the types of forces that shape corrections or their relative importance. However, there are at least two distinct theoretical approaches to these problems. Although social scientists in both camps agree that corrections is shaped by the context in which it operates, they present an interesting contrast.

On one hand, scholars of a *radical* persuasion have devoted much of their time and attention to *theoretical analyses* of the context–corrections link. The result is a sizable body of theory that interprets the relationship between macro-level political–economic forces and social control, primarily in capitalist societies. For the most part, radical scholars have neglected empirical research to test their theoretical interpretations of static relationships. On the other hand, *liberal* scholars oftentimes tend toward low-level, even ad hoc theoretical analyses of corrections, devoting much of their energies to studies of noncontextual variables.

The hallmark of radical analyses of corrections is an insistence that, in the final analysis, macro-level economic structures and dynamics are the most powerful forces that shape corrections. Class conflict occupies a central place in the radical interpretation. Economic systems based on private ownership of the means of production and private accumulation of profit produces a system of social classes with unequal power and wealth. Corrections is seen as one of the processes used to maintain the structural integrity of the economy and existing class relations.

It does this in large part by managing those segments of the population who either are superfluous for the capitalist economy or who appear as potential disruptive threats to existing arrangements. Such threats escalate during periods of economic crisis. This doesn't mean that those who staff correctional bureaucracies consciously and willfully employ corrections to manage subordinate classes. Rather, it means that the ultimate result of their efforts is the maintenance of a system of class inequity. In turn, this benefits those classes who occupy dominant positions.

Whereas agreement on the primacy of economic relationships and class conflict as decision-making constraints is the hallmark of radical scholarship, liberal interpretations of corrections come in a variety of shapes and sizes. Some liberal scholars agree with radicals that macro-level structural forces and dynamics exert powerful constraints on corrections, but they reject the notion that all of these can be reduced to economic forces or relationships. Typically, liberals argue that cultural variation, public sentiment about crime and offenders, and pluralist political processes mold corrections. And while many liberal scholars agree that correctional strategies and structures are employed to manage social conflict in the wider society, they reject the assumption that class conflict is the most important—or even the only noteworthy—type.

Since radical theorists argue that corrections is used to regulate conflicts that often result from economic crises, some radical analyses of corrections use variation in the rate of unemployment as a measure of economic crisis. Matthew Yeager's research (1979) on annual fluctuation in the American prison population during 1951–77 shows that fluctuation in the unemployment rate is a strong predictor of fluctuations in the size of the American prison population. He examined the predictive power of other contextual variables as well, but the results did not change.

But how does an increase in the level of unemployment change the decisions of criminal justice officials and produce increases in the rate of imprisonment? Steven Box and Chris Hale suggest that when the rate of unemployment increases dramatically, how unemployed male criminal defendants are perceived by criminal justice officials changes as well. If a defendant is unemployed,

> the judiciary is more likely to view him as potentially more likely to commit other, particularly economic offenses, and consequently pass an immediate prison sentence. This severe sentence is imposed partly because members of the judiciary believe it will incapacitate him, and thus marginally reduce the crime rate, but also because this sentence may deter other unemployed males tempted by the possible economic gains of crime (1985: 215).

So during periods of high unemployment, the appearance in court of unemployed male property offenders escalates "judicial anxiety" about a potentially eroding social order (Box and Hale, 1982). In turn, this causes them to increase their use of imprisonment as a correctional strategy.

Research on the historical use of the death penalty exemplifies a liberal approach to the problem of explaining macro-level variation in correctional strategies. Between 1930, when data on executions were first collected by the federal government, and the end of 1984, 3,891 persons were executed in the U.S. However, there is substantial regional variation in the use of executions. Of the total number of executions, 2,012, or 51.7 percent, occurred in the 11 states of the former Confederacy. This pattern of extreme geographic imbalance in the use of the death penalty continues today. On December 31, 1984, 1,405 persons were under sentence of death in the United States. Of this total, 788,

or 56.1 percent, were on death rows in the Southern states (U.S. Department of Justice, 1985a).

For all the states, Daniel Glaser and Max Zeigler (1974) show that there is an inverse relationship historically between the rate of execution and the average length of time in confinement of male homicide offenders who were *not* executed. States with the highest rates of execution also are the states in which unexecuted offenders serve the shortest periods of confinement. Although Glaser and Zeigler did not collect any state-level data to interpret their findings, they speculate that these twin phenomena reflect a generally low valuation of human life by residents of Southern states. Doubtless it is easy to see how executions show a low regard for the lives of offenders. Glaser and Zeigler suggest that the short sentences served by unexecuted homicide offenders imply a low regard for the lives of victims as well. Thus they posit a cultural interpretation of state-level variation in executions and the average confinement period for homicide.

Research by G. T. Broach, P. D. Jackson, and V. H. Ascolillo shows similar characteristics. They examined contextual determinants of the severity of sentences rendered in 1970 in cases involving violations of the Selective Service Act. They began by suggesting that differences in correctional strategies of this type probably result from state-level differences in "socioeconomic environment" (1978: 374). They also assumed that the severity of sentences imposed on Selective Service defendants would vary with several state-level policymaking and political structure variables. The data analysis confirmed their predictions. States with liberal political traditions and policymaking processes which also are "more economically developed and income equitable" have more lenient sentencing practices.

## Corrections in Community Context

Three studies illustrate how community-level processes interact with and help to shape criminal justice structures and strategies. For present purposes we do not restrict ourselves to research on *correctional* agencies, but draw from studies of the police as well. Based on a study of several police departments in the United States, James Q. Wilson (1968) suggests there are three distinctive styles of policing: *watchman, legalistic,* and *service.* Wilson's evidence suggests that these differences result from differences in the communities and citizens served by a police department. In other words, watchman-style police departments typically are found in communities with similar characteristics. The same is true of the other styles.

John Hagan and Ilene Bernstein analyzed and interpreted changes in the sentences imposed on draft resisters in a large American city during the period 1963–76. Noting the importance of examining the effects of context, they suggest that "context can vary . . . by time *and* place. . . . We hold place constant and consider the influence of time" (1979: 111). To measure changes in context, they systematically examined editorials in the city's major newspapers for the 14-year period. The analysis showed that

> editorials up to 1969 . . . [expressed the view] that those who opposed the [Vietnam] war had a right to protest publicly, [but] they also had an obligation to accept whatever punishment the state deemed appropriate. . . . By 1969, however, . . . editorials [sounded the theme] that imprisonment was a wasteful and ineffectual response to the principled protests of many draft resisters (1979: 112).

The percentage of draft resisters sentenced to prison decreased from 76.8 during 1963–68 to 33.7 during 1969–76.

It seems plausible to argue that there were two distinct contexts in which the sentencing of draft resisters occurred. . . . [T]he period from 1963 to 1968 [was] an era of *coercive control.* . . . In contrast, . . . the period from 1969 to 1976 [was] an era of *cooptive control* (1979: 113).

Hagan and Bernstein conclude that "control strategies are shaped by the [contexts] in which they occur" (1979: 118).

The Vienna Correctional Center (VCC), located in rural southern Illinois, is a minimum-security, reform-oriented correctional facility housing inmates who do not differ appreciably from those housed in other Illinois prisons. The institution enjoys harmonious relationships with residents in its rural, conservative environment and has little of the staff–inmate conflict characteristic of most prisons. According to James B. Jacobs, the reasons for the institution's success are found in the: (1) strategies pursued by local elites; (2) community's economic dependence on the institution as a source of jobs and income; and (3) cultural emphasis on interpersonal informality and personal trust that are characteristic of southern Illinois.

While these community characteristics helped to establish and reinforce the community's stake in the institution, the warden's success in tying the prison's reform programs to the needs of the community also have been important. A native of the region, the warden enjoys a personal friendship with the local newspaper editor, and established cooperative relationships with a local junior college. Citizens are permitted to fish in the prison's well-stocked lake, outsiders enter the prison to attend church services, and the prison expanded its reform programs to respond to the community's need for services. Specifically, the prison volunteered labor on several community projects, established an emergency medical technician program that provides an ambulance service to the community that is manned by 18 trained inmates, and permitted the community to use its landfill temporarily after the U.S. Environmental Protection Agency closed the local facility. Jacobs claims that

> [t]he growth of VCC and the expansion of its reform program, highlighted by the continuous movement of local citizens into the prison and of prisoners out into the surrounding community, has occurred because of, not in spite of, the unique requirements of the surrounding environment (1983: 106).

He suggests it is "ironic and instructive" that the best prospects for establishing experimental, flexible, and humane prisons may be in rural areas traditionally disdained by social scientists.

## Interorganizational Processes

Correctional agencies, their programs, and their personnel operate in an interorganizational web of agencies—the criminal justice system. The police are responsible for investigating crimes that come to their attention and gathering evidence for use in subsequent processing. Prosecutors represent the state in bringing the accused to trial. In most jurisdictions, public defenders represent defendants who are indigent—meaning the vast majority of them. Judges are charged with providing both the state and the accused with an impartial, procedurally correct disposition of formal criminal charges.

Criminal justice has been called a "loosely coupled system" because few formal lines of authority tie together its component parts (for example, Hagan, Hewitt, and Alwin, 1979). Nevertheless, while each of the organizations and individuals that make up the criminal justice system has a separate function to fulfill, they must interact frequently

and routinely with one another. Some of this interaction occurs in formally designated, public areas such as the courtroom, but most of it occurs behind the scenes. In day-to-day interactions, routinized relationships develop and assume a form of their own. Over time, these relationships constrain the operations of the separate agencies and their respective personnel. What is the nature of some of these relationships among the agencies of criminal justice?

Generally, some agencies in the criminal justice system hold positions of dominance while others tend to be subordinate. For the most part, correctional agencies and their personnel are among the latter. Unlike the police, prosecutors, and the courts, correctional agencies have virtually no control over the cases they accept for processing. In this respect and in others as well, correctional agencies function as "backup institutions" (Emerson, 1969). This means that the operating procedures and case decisions of correctional managers and functionaries often are influenced by their subordinate relationships with other criminal justice agencies.

The interdependence of law enforcement and correctional agencies is apparent in studies of parole supervision. More often than not, parole supervision bureaucracies and parole agents learn about difficulties encountered by parolees only after the parolees have been arrested and jailed (Studt, 1973). The agents' ability to intervene largely hinges on whether police officials routinely and expeditiously notify them when parolees are jailed. However, a study of parole supervision in California shows that

> although agents located in small-town, suburban areas often cultivate relationships with the police, district offices in large metropolitan areas seem to have few lines of communication with police at the precinct level; and the maze of red tape with which agents [are] required to contend in the large central police offices [is]

clearly frustrating to [agents] in [their] efforts to help [jailed parolees] (Studt, 1973: 135).

Relations between correctional bureaucracies and other agencies in the criminal justice apparatus also may constrain the correctional decision makers. Consider the presentence recommendations of probation officers. Research over the past 20 years has shown a high rate of agreement between probation officers' recommendations and judges' sentences (Carter and Wilkins, 1967; Hagan, 1975; Curry, 1975; Kingsworth and Rizzo, 1979). The meaning of this high level of agreement has been unclear. It could mean that probation officers play an important role in determining defendants' sentences, or it could mean that probation officers learn over a period of time to anticipate judicial sentencing decisions and to provide them with concordant recommendations. Research by John Rosecrance suggests that the latter may be the case. Based on 15 years' experience as a probation officer and interviews with court personnel, he argues that probation officers' sentence recommendations frequently "serve only to endorse prearranged judicial agreements." He suggests that probation officers make their decisions within narrow parameters by "responding to cues provided by (1) judges, (2) prosecuting attorneys, and (3) probation supervisors" (1985: 539).

Rosecrance's finding that probation officers' decisions are influenced by their supervisors' cues brings us to the third category of forces that shape corrections: bureaucratic structure and process.

## Bureaucratic Structure and Process

The day-to-day work of corrections takes place in agencies that have many of the characteristics of what Max Weber called the *bureaucratic* form of organization. These in-clude a formalized division of labor (specialized tasks), a formal hierarchy of authority, and formalized channels of communication between superiors and subordinates. Weber argued that the dominance of bureaucracy in the modern world is due to its superiority in goal achievement as compared with other forms of organization. Decades of social research have shown, however, that the technical superiority of the bureaucratic form of organization carries with it a variety of potential shortcomings as well. Who among us has not encountered bureaucratic officials so determined to follow procedure that they are unable or unwilling to respond to nonroutine problems or situations? We are familiar as well with organizational functionaries who let their loyalty to superiors or to the organization override ethical or legal principles. It is clear that the very act of creating a bureaucracy sets in motion forces that can produce distortions of the work process. In correctional bureaucracies, these forces can work at cross-purposes with the provision of services in the ideologically or professionally "purest" manner.

The importance of research on these organizational forces is underscored by Robert Martinson *et al.* in their critique of research on parole and parolee behavior:

> An organizational approach would regard the agent–parolee relationship as perhaps changeable, but only within limits set on a much larger canvas. The parole agent has discretion within the complex limits set by operational manuals, by district officer supervision, and by career concerns (1964: 36).

Richard McCleary's research in a parole supervision agency showed that case decisions were "often determined by organizational demands not necessarily related to the rehabilitation of parolees or to the protection of society" (1975: 209). Robert Prus and John

Stratton (1976) found a similar pattern in their study of parole officers and their decision making.

### Differential Authority

In the same way that bureaucracies are built on task specialization and a division of labor, they incorporate a formal distribution of authority. In other words, personnel at some levels or in some positions are granted—and exercise—substantially greater control over the work process than do personnel at other levels. Typically, for example, management has greater authority than do blue-collar employees. This differential authority is one of the ways that bureaucratic forces affect the work performance of correctional personnel. Research by Paul Takagi and James Robison shows this process at work. Using questionnaires with hypothetical descriptions of parolees, they focused on the factors that influence parole officers' decisions to revoke parole. They found that the decision was affected in part by the parole officers' perceptions of their supervisors' likely response. Thus in pondering whether to revoke parole, a powerful influence

> appeared to be at the district supervisor level, where there is a high degree of correspondence between district supervisors and their subordinates on the case-recommendation task. This finding suggests that the selective enforcement of some [parole] rules is as much a characteristic of the officials as selective adherence to rules is a characteristic of the [parolee] (1969: 85–86).

Whenever a complex task is divided into discrete tasks for individuals, subordinates tend to focus on accomplishing immediate goals, thereby demonstrating their competence to superiors. Occasionally they even lose sight of larger goals. Studies of the prison have shown that when guards are expected primarily to avoid creating problems for their supervisors, "corruption of authority" can result (Sykes, 1956). Similar processes have been reported in other correctional agencies. Thus white-collar personnel devote an inordinate amount of their time to those kinds of activities that are most visible to their superiors. Probation and parole officers spend the bulk of their time preparing reports.

Sociological research suggests a relationship between managerial style and workers' feelings of alienation and dissatisfaction in the workplace (Etzioni, 1964). Traditionally, prison guards have been organized on a paramilitary model and correctional administrators have relied primarily on monetary and punitive sanctions to secure compliant, predictable behavior from them. In fact, prison guards have been managed in much the same way that inmates have been controlled. However, research suggests that this is the most alienative style of management. Other management styles do not produce as many negative side effects (Burns and Stalker, 1961). The lesson for correctional managers and employees is clear: Substantial improvements in employee morale and loyalty can be achieved not by trying to change the employees as individuals but instead by modifying an aspect of the organization—management style.

We must not exaggerate the importance of and control exerted by designated authorities in bureaucracies. To do so is to suggest that bureaucratic organizations are free of internal dissension. The truth is something different. Despite what may appear to the outsider as a monolithic and calm appearance, many organizations are shot through with conflicts and disagreements over many aspects of organizational life. The conflict between bureaucratic norms of loyalty and the norms of employees who regard themselves as professionals exemplifies this process.

Peter Blau and W. Richard Scott (1962) have shown that groups of self-defined professionals often chafe under the rules and regulations of the organizations that employ them. Similarly, David T. Stanley suggests that the "conscientious, professionally minded parole officer, particularly if educated as a social worker, is painfully aware of the conflicts between his professional values and the goals and practices of the parole organization" (1976: 130). Jacobs (1976) showed that the marginality and demoralization of a group of counselors newly introduced into a maximum-security prison stemmed from their belief that their job responsibilities did not meet their self-definition as professionals. And a study of probation officers noted that "their lack of genuine professional status in the court [was] a constant source of personal anxiety, work alienation, and general dissatisfaction" (Blumberg, 1967: 130).

### Emergent Goals and Equilibrating Processes

Bureaucracies owe much of their superiority in goal attainment to the fact that they routinize work flow. They thrive on routine. Research has shown that faced with exceptional circumstances or cases, organizational personnel creatively modify procedures in order to maintain a smooth flow of resources and work. The maintenance of a smooth work flow gives rise to *equilibrating processes,* which function to ensure that the organization continues to operate with only minimal disruptions to daily routines. R. A. Berk *et al.* (1981) show that California prison officials historically used parole as a mechanism to regulate prison populations. The pattern was the same for men's and women's prisons (Berk *et al.,* 1983). By using parole as an equilibrating mechanism, officials managed to avoid the unsettling consequences of large, sudden increases in prison populations.

The organizational tendency to maintain smooth operating procedures is only one of several *emergent goals* in bureaucracies' day-to-day operations. Another emergent goal of considerable importance is the desire to avoid public criticism or "heat." Correctional administrators are highly sensitive to public criticism or ridicule for decisions they make in specific cases. Parole boards are known to be quite susceptible to pressures of this type (Dawson, 1966). Consequently, they often reach decisions to parole or not parole with an eye toward the likely public reaction in the event something goes wrong.

A related process is the need on the part of organizational managers to deliver evidence of success to their superiors. For example, political leaders generally expect police officials and employees to control or even to reduce the level of street crime in their cities. David Seidman and Michael Couzens show how this generated problems of interpreting and using crime statistics—which are collected and disseminated by these police departments—during the 1970s:

> As the role of the police in the society became a matter of increased interest, crime statistics were used to evaluate the performance of police departments. . . . [This] creates pressures to have the statistics show certain things. Sometimes the pressure is to show that crime is being reduced. . . . These pressures impinge upon the data-generating system, the police departments, and in some cases affect the statistics, entirely apart from the effects of the number of crimes which are actually committed (1974: 484).

Correctional employees labor under the same need to show evidence of success. This may cause correctional administrators to devote excessive resources to activities that are visible to outsiders. These can be pointed to as evidence of success, even if this occurs at the expense of other staff activities. An example is found in research on the California Department of Corrections. During the 1950s and early 1960s, department officials claimed that reduced parole caseloads would lead to improved parolee behavior (as evidenced by lower rates of recidivism). The department randomly assigned parolees to 35- and 70-man caseloads:

> [A] preliminary evaluation showed no difference [in recidivism rates]. According to Takagi, high [Department of Corrections] officials decided at this point that a no-difference finding would be politically unacceptable. The POs assigned to the small caseloads were consequently told that they would be promoted strictly on the basis of their caseload recidivism rates. . . . A subsequent reevaluation of the program found that the smaller caseloads were more effective than the larger caseloads in reducing recidivism. . . . [However,] the change was due entirely to a shift in the structural dynamic of the parole agency (McCleary, 1975: 224).

In later chapters we demonstrate how knowledge of emergent goals helps us understand some day-to-day correctional processes.

### Organizational Culture and Typifications

Earlier we pointed to the fallacy of citing the characteristics of individuals to explain the problems of correctional bureaucracies. This *dispositional hypothesis* (Haney, Banks, and Zimbardo, 1973) fails as well because it ignores the fact that employees of organizations usually employ organizationally based perspectives in their work performance; the origins of their attitudes and fundamental approaches to work lie in an organizational culture. Consequently, if we wish to understand the individual, we must look to the collective as well. This means that we must understand the perspectives of organizational employees, especially as these are rooted in an organizational culture. For example, Clem-

ens Bartollas *et al.* (1976) found that they could understand the dynamics of juvenile correctional institutions only if they took account of the code of youth leaders, a part of the cultural life of the institution.

One aspect of organizational culture, *typifications*, is an especially important key to understanding the dynamics of decision making in complex organizations. Typifications are the stock ways that employees learn to perceive and interpret people and routine events in their daily work. These typifications simultaneously structure employees' perceptions of clients and shape their decision-making process (Schur, 1971). As Robert M. Emerson notes, the use of typifications provides workers with "pre-existing formulas for allocating time and other resources among cases" (1983: 437).

Victoria Lynn Swigert and Ronald A. Farrell examined how the staff of a diagnostic clinic attached to a criminal court evaluated and processed homicide defendants. The clinic was responsible for providing information that the court could use in its sentencing decisions. The investigators found that the clinic staff employed a conceptualization of the typical homicide offender as a "normal primitive."

> The normal primitive is seen as one whose social and cultural background predisposes him to violent behavior. Living under disorganized primitive conditions, his response to any situation of personal challenge is aggression (1976: 101).

In their day-to-day diagnostic work, clinic staff use this conception as the basis of their recommendations to the court. Normal primitives receive dispositions more severe than those meted out to other types of homicide offenders.

Like correctional workers, police officers acquire and apply a complex of typifications to order and make sense of citizens and criminal suspects they encounter in their daily work. One type of person is the "asshole":

> The asshole—creep, bigmouth, bastard, animal, mope, rough, jerkoff, clown, scumbag, wiseguy, phony, idiot, shithead, bum, fool, or any of a number of anatomical, oral, or incestuous terms—is a part of every policeman's world (Van Maanen, 1978: 221).

The label "asshole" is applied to those "who would question, limit, or otherwise attempt to control the police" (Van Maanen, 1978: 235). Police officers consider them fair game for impolite or even abusive treatment.

## Thinking about Corrections

We have distinguished and illustrated three of the four emergent forces that constrain correctional strategies and structures. We conclude this chapter with some suggestions as to how these materials can be used to interpret and understand some potentially puzzling aspects of correctional performance.

We begin with the problem of interpreting variation in (a) the use of specific correctional strategies, or (b) performance measures. We can illustrate the former with data on racial disparity in the median length of prison sentences imposed on defendants admitted to state prisons in the U.S. during 1983. For the ten states that reported data, the median sentence for newly admitted white inmates was 66.3 months, while the rate for blacks was 73.7 months (U.S. Department of Justice, 1986e: 5). We could just as easily have cited the substantial variation among the states in the *rate* of imprisonment, or the use of parole as a strategy for managing prison release. As an example of the latter, consider that in 1984, 63.7 percent of all parolees in the U.S. who exited parole did so by completing parole successfully; however, the success rate varied from 19.0 percent of Maine parolees to 91.5 percent of parolees in North Dakota (U.S. Department of Justice, 1986g).

Variations such as these cannot be explained solely by attributing them to the behavior of individuals. There is no reason to believe that North Dakota parolees behave so differently from Maine parolees as to explain the vast difference in parole success rates in these two states. Instead, a major part of the explanation can be found in the differential interaction of context and the criminal justice system in the two states, and in the rate-producing dynamics of their correctional bureaucracies (Kitsuse and Cicourel, 1963). Earlier we reviewed research by Hagan and Bernstein (1979) on the sanctioning of draft resisters during two different time periods. Recall that prison sentences were used more often in 1963–68 than in 1969–76. The investigators also found that black resisters were more likely than white resisters to be imprisoned during the former period. In contrast, they found that white resisters were considerably more likely than black resisters to be imprisoned during the latter period. In other words, the interaction of time period, race, and other variables influenced sanctioning.

It is easy for students and correctional employees to become frustrated by their seeming inability to reform corrections as they would like. There may be obstacles and problems at every turn that defy description and comprehension. The materials we have presented in this chapter should suggest some of the reasons that rationally constructed reforms are so difficult to put in place. Some changes simply cannot be implemented easily in certain types of macrosocial or community contexts. They are incompatible with the structures and culture of the wider context. Given a different context or a change in context, the same reforms might find ready acceptance and implementation.

It is frustrating as well to see that reforms often fail to achieve their intended goals. In the process of implementation, they become distorted and function in ways very different from those envisioned by their supporters. Incompatibility with macrosocial structures and cultural biases may explain some of this. But it can be explained also by the fact that the criminal justice system and the bureaucracies that compose it tend to implement reforms in ways that are compatible with or serve their own ends.

## Corrections As Interaction

Characteristically, supporters of most ideologies argue that their pet ideas, if implemented in correctional strategies and structures, will change the behavior of offenders and thereby reduce the rate of street crime. Most of these ideological entrepreneurs believe that face-to-face contacts between offenders and correctional personnel are especially important for changing offenders. For this reason, many correctional ideologies contain, somewhere within them, a theory of interpersonal change. For this reason, we treat correctional interaction as an autonomous component of corrections, albeit one that does not constrain correctional decision makers nearly as much as correctional ideologies, strategies, and structures. Consequently, we devote little attention to it.

There is considerable intuitive appeal in interpersonal theories of correction. As individuals, we know that contacts with others can be one of the most powerful sources of change in our lives. Researchers have found that contacts with individual correctional employees, usually guards or work supervisors, have greater impact on inmates than formal programs created specifically to change them (Glaser, 1964). Moreover, ex-offenders may remember these contacts for years (Shover, 1985).

The interpersonal aspects of corrections can be appealing especially to students, who assume that correctional employment offers a chance to go one-on-one with offenders to help rehabilitate them. This assumption tends to generate an exaggerated view of the options and latitude available to correctional personnel in their encounters with offenders. The behavior and decisions of correctional personnel are affected by a variety of considerations, only some of which are under their immediate control. The structure and dynamics of the organizations that employ them, typifications and perspectives learned on the job, and their interactions with offenders all affect their behavior and decisions. Consequently, if we want to understand why correctors behave as they do, we must have a better understanding of these diverse determinants.

How do some of the constraints we have discussed find expression in interaction between correctors and offenders? Let's take the case of interaction between prison inmates and parole board members at the parole board hearing. Parole board members decide whether an inmate is ready or suitable for parole largely on the basis of their perceptions of the kind of person the inmate is believed to be. Awareness of this inevitably leads offenders to accentuate those aspects of their biography, identity, and activities that are most favorable. This is a rational response in such situations. Correctors are aware of this calculated quality of interaction, which gives rise to the pervasive worry on their part that offenders are trying to "con" them:

> Parole [board] members experience . . . a universal fear of being "conned." The parole board shows considerable concern about the inmate who is too glib, who seems to have everything down pat and is so smooth that every detail of his story fits neatly into place. The board members resent inmates who seem

**Chapter 2**

to be trying to "con" them or to "take them in" (Dawson, 1966: 255).

Awareness of this "fear-of-being-conned" syndrome places offenders in an awkward and unenviable position: Many do not know exactly how to interact with correctors. On one hand, if they appear too contrite or changed, they may be accused of trying to perpetrate a con job. Should they, on the other hand, be overly candid and forthcoming about their activities—for example, the crimes they committed for which they were not arrested—this information may be used against them. The fear-of-being-conned syndrome explains why much of the interaction between offenders and correctional employees is shallow and rarely comes to grips with the fundamental concerns or problems of offenders.

# 3

# Correctional
# Ideologies

We noted in Chapter 2 that correctional ideologies are assumptions about the causes of crime, the nature of offenders, and how best to deal with them to reduce criminal behavior. As one part of the belief systems that we accept uncritically, correctional ideologies serve to structure our perceptions and interpretations of crime and correctional matters. They provide an integrated interpretation of the totality of correctional strategies within a specific historical context.

We intentionally omitted discussion of correctional ideologies in Chapter 2 and focused instead on correctional strategies and structures, and the forces that shape them. We did so in large part because correctional ideologies differ in at least one important way from the components of corrections discussed there: Correctional ideologies are powerful forces in their own right, helping to rationalize and shape correctional strategies and structures.

But the importance of understanding correctional ideologies goes beyond their impact on strategies and structures. Consider that on any given day in the United States, state employees routinely impose extraordinary deprivations on some citizens. Those singled out for this correctional attention may be separated involuntarily from their homes and families, removed to and confined in penal reservations, or even put to death. The vast majority of citizens either take little notice of these activities or simply acquiesce in the face of the state's efforts. When executions occur, few citizens raise a word of protest. Most accept them as evidence that the state is proceeding appropriately in the correctional realm and that "everything is under control." The fact that we routinely overlook the pain and deprivation imposed on officially designated criminal offenders is due in part to the impact of correctional ideologies. They rationalize and thereby provide *justification* for state correctional efforts.

A cursory review of some popular correctional ideologies of the past 100 years shows great substantive variation. For example, a view of offenders as essentially *undeveloped human beings* enjoyed great currency in the United States between the end of the Civil War and 1900. It was argued that offenders were persons who had not acquired the discipline and training to adequately develop their higher faculties. As a result, they employed criminal means to solve their problems and meet their needs. Writing in 1893, the economist Carroll D. Wright declared that the criminal

> is an undeveloped man in all his elements, whether you think of him as a worker or as a moral and intellectual being. His faculties are all underdeveloped, not only those which enable him to labor honestly and faithfully for the care and support of himself and his family, but also all his moral and intellectual faculties. He is not a fallen being; he is an undeveloped individual (quoted in Currie, 1973: 22).

In 1888, another writer declared that the criminal is less than whole. In other words, he

> is what he is, not primarily in virtue of that which he has acquired, but of that which he has missed. The fundamental truth regarding him is not that he has become a criminal, but that he has not become, in the full sense, a man. All that he has been is but the vicious exhibition of that which he has failed to be (quoted in Currie, 1973: 28).

This correctional ideology played a major part in the armament of the American reformatory movement.

Prescriptions for reducing recidivism show great diversity as well. In an earlier era, military drill and calisthenics were a standard part of the correctional program in many institutions, on the assumption that these could instill discipline and orderly habits, the absence of which had probably led offenders to transgress. Religious instruction has at various times been pointed to as the key to offender restoration. Now academic and vocational training are seen as ripe with reformative potential.

Many scholars and correctional practitioners distinguish between *punitive* and *rehabilitative* ideologies. A punitive ideology justifies the intentional use of strategies that impose pain, suffering, or prolonged discomfort on offenders. As with all correctional ideologies, this includes guidelines—typically these are crude and ambiguous—for determining when punishments are used appropriately. Think, for example, about the ritualistic procedures employed to execute condemned prisoners. Rehabilitative ideologies justify intentional modifications of the conditions of offenders' lives in the belief that these will help them. Because they want to assist and improve offenders, those who accept and campaign for rehabilitative strategies oftentimes are ridiculed as "do-gooders."

While the distinction between punitive and rehabilitative can be made hypothetically, in reality it seems to blur. Irrespective of the intent underlying them, punitive and rehabilitative actions both are types of *social control*. "The first difficulty in meshing treatment with a correctional effort is that the treatment can be forced on offenders" (Lerman, 1975: 11). Indeed, those who receive correctional treatment often feel that what they are required to submit to in the name of rehabilitation, rhetoric and intentions notwithstanding, is punishment.

> In correctional practice, treatment and punishment generally coexist and cannot appro-

priately be viewed as mutually exclusive. Correctional activities (treatments) are undertaken in settings established as places of punishment. Restriction of freedom is a punishment, no matter whether it is imposed by physical confinement (jail or prison) or by surveillance of movement in the community (probation or parole) (Robison and Smith, 1971: 80).

As a matter of fact, correctional programs whose ostensible purpose is *either* treatment or punishment usually include elements of both. Consider the Community Treatment Project. A part of the "treatment" given to youths in this experimental program was a series of graded punishments. Those youths in the program who did not behave or who disobeyed their youth officers temporarily were confined in jail (Lerman, 1975). Punishment itself is thought by some to have a rehabilitative impact on offenders.

Punitive and rehabilitative ideologies can be thought of as partially overlapping circles, as in Figure 3.1. Both circles have a distinctive nature, represented by their unshaded portions. But they also share something: Each provides a justification for state intervention in the lives of offenders and state

FIGURE 3.1 **The Relationship between Punishment and Rehabilitative Ideologies**

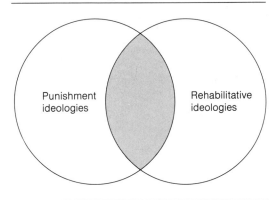

imposition of restraints on their life conditions. These restraints can range from small fines or probation to imprisonment or even death. In sum, "the real choice in correction . . . is not between treatment on one hand and punishment on the other but between one treatment–punishment alternative and another" (Robison and Smith, 1971: 80).

As in the past, today there is great variation in and controversy surrounding correctional ideologies. This variation is apparent in three areas. Some correctional ideologies aim at reducing the *incidence* of crime by reducing the numbers of crimes that known offenders will commit in the future. Others promise to control the *prevalence* of crime by reducing the numbers of people committing crime at any given time. Correctional ideologies also differ in their targets for change. Some focus on the individual offender, others focus on the offender's interpersonal environment, on the criminal justice system itself, on the larger economy and social structure. But one of the most important types of variation in correctional ideologies is the political philosophy they're built on. The mandate of the corrections system, to manage only some types of criminal offenders, primarily those who commit street crimes, is a product of the political process. Correction structures and strategies are constructed and periodically reconstructed by political figures—legislators and state managers. State employees—examples include judges and parole board members—control entry and exit from the process. And the state itself staffs and operates correctional structures such as the jail and the prison.

The political nature of corrections is obscured or even disguised entirely, in part because citizens are encouraged to think of crime control as a purely technical and managerial process. To keep this awareness of the politics of corrections squarely in the foreground, we group and discuss correctional ideologies on the basis of the political philosophies and derivative theories of state functioning they embody (Miller, 1973; Currie, 1985; Cohen, 1985).

## Liberal Ideologies

Liberals believe that most of the defects of human behavior have their origins in the social environment. The key to changing people lies in learning how to manipulate either these environments or their psychological consequences. Unlike conservatives, who are obsessed with social defense and the repression of offenders, liberals focus their efforts on improving offenders and the social situations that produce them. In a word, liberals are *reformers*.

It was liberal correctional ideologies that spawned the post–World War II movement to supplant punishment with *treatment*. As an influential basis of correctional practice, liberalism reached its peak during the 1950s and 1960s. Subsequent decades saw conservative ideologies gain in prominence and official favor as rationales for changing correctional strategies.

Appalled by evidence of increasing correctional harshness in the 1970s, some liberals launched a counterattack on conservative ideologies and correctional strategies (Cullen and Wozniak, 1982). Some have called for a return to rehabilitative ideologies. Francis Cullen and Karen Gilbert (1982) argue that such a movement holds the best prospects for alleviating the misery and suffering of prisoners.

### The Medical Model

Historically, one of the most popular liberal correctional beliefs is the medical model (or individual treatment model). Although the medical model has fallen into official disfavor, there is no denying its long standing as

an influential set of beliefs about offenders and what should be done with them. Its basic assumptions:

**1.** Criminal behavior is symptomatic of something wrong with the emotional makeup or psyche of offenders.

**2.** The nature of these underlying deficiencies or problems can be diagnosed by an intensive, expertly conducted examination of offenders' symptoms.

---

**PANEL 3.1**

### On the Medical Model

We quickly learned we were expected to view this journey through prison as a quest, and the object of our quest was to discover our problem. It was assumed we were here because of psychological problems, and our task now, by which we could expect to be judged, was to isolate and come to terms with them. Boys who had stolen cars were thought to be acting out a symbolic return to the womb and once they had been helped to understand their true motivation and recognize its utter futility they would be free of the compulsion. I mock this now, even if I didn't mock it then, but it's not the most basic notion at which I will invite you to laugh with me, but simply at the grotesque extensions which sometimes flourished here in the California Department of Corrections. And no matter what your private opinion, when the Adult Authority, the remote body authorized to grant parole, asked in tones of high seriousness if you had come to grips with your problem, you were willing to concede you might have a problem even if you had to invent one on the spot.

SOURCE: Malcolm Braly, *False Starts* (Boston: Little, Brown, 1976), pp. 157–58.

**3.** Identifiable external symptoms and identifiable underlying pathologies covary in patterned, predictable ways.

**4.** Preventive or treatment efforts should be directed not toward the external symptoms but toward the underlying deficiency or pathology (that is, the underlying causes).

**5.** Therapeutic efforts that concentrate only on the symptoms of a problem, while leaving the problem itself unaffected, will only result in the appearance of some other type of symptomatic behavior (the principle of the interchangeability of symptoms).

**6.** There are appropriate treatments for particular kinds of underlying problems or pathologies.

**7.** It is impossible to specify in advance just how much time will be required before offenders respond to treatment.

In its heyday, the individual treatment model was used as justification for an array of popular correctional strategies. The sentencing codes of many states provided for indeterminate sentences with broad ranges so that correctional experts would have sufficient time to work their cures. Many states operated prison classification programs where newly admitted inmates spent the first few weeks of confinement. During this time they were studied by correctional staff, ostensibly to determine the nature of the problems that presumably caused them to transgress. At the end of the classification process, individualized *treatment plans* were recommended for inmates in hopes of reversing the psychic forces that triggered their criminal behavior. Once the inmates were released into the general prison population, these plans presumably would be im-

plemented through periodic counseling sessions with treatment personnel. The reality of this process bore little resemblance to the ideology (Shover, 1974).

Whereas the medical model aims its correctional efforts at the individual offender, other liberal ideologies focus on the small social groups in which the offender is enmeshed. They are alike in emphasizing that the seed of criminal behavior is found in the significant relationships that offenders establish and maintain in their everyday lives. We discuss two very different versions of a small-groups approach to corrections: *behavior modification* and *group dynamics*.

### Behavior Modification

Behavior modification represents the confluence of experimental psychology and psychological learning theory. Behavior therapists argue that behavior is learned and controlled by the nature of individuals' interactions with others.

Behavior therapy advocates generally contrast their approach with traditional evocative or psychoanalytically based therapy. These and other contrasts are evident in the assumptions that underlie behavior therapy:

**1.** Criminal behavior is not symptomatic of anything dysfunctional in the offender's psyche. In fact, it is not symptomatic of anything.

**2.** Criminal behavior itself is the target of change, not something within the offender. If treatment efforts successfully change the offender's overt, observable criminal behavior, a new aberrant behavior such as bedwetting will not appear.

**3.** Offensive behavior is learned according to the laws of operant learning. It can be unlearned by employing the same principles. Behavior is a function of the results it produces in the environment (that is, the result of environmental contingencies); modify these and you can modify behavior.

Behavior of any kind, whether social or antisocial, is learned. Supporters of behavior modification claim that knowledge of how behavior is learned can be employed systematically to extinguish or "unlearn" undesirable behavior. In short, punishments and rewards can be used to modify offenders' behaviors so the likelihood of further criminal acts is reduced or eradicated.

Supporters of behavior therapy claim that it is more scientific than the medical model, because it deals only with observable phenomena (units of behavior) rather than hypothesized psychic problems and processes. Thus it does not rely on the unique observational skills of individual therapists with many years of advanced training—a stricture that makes traditional "talk therapy" unavailable for most persons. Behavior therapy can be conducted by lay citizens with short periods of specialized training.

In the words of one enthusiast, "Behavior modification techniques are remarkably well suited for integration into the criminal justice system" (Schwitzgebel, 1971: 63). Among the correctional programs touted as consistent with behavior modification are token economies in correctional institutions, contract programming for inmates and parolees, and a variety of experimental programs.

To critics, however, behavior modification programs evoke surrealistic images of mind control and the tyranny of social scientists. Some correctional strategies grounded in behavior therapy have been successfully challenged in court as violations of the Eighth Amendment to the Constitution, which prohibits cruel and unusual punishment. Many groups and individuals concerned about the human and legal rights of offenders have supported these challenges. They see the appearance of behavior modification as a disturbing sign of the increasing willingness to ignore fundamental offender rights in the technocratic quest for results in the "war against crime."

The proposals and programs of some behavior therapists have done little to allay these suspicions and fears. One proposal, for example, involved drugs that induce prolonged vomiting. Some psychologists argue for creating new social environments that inhibit the development of social problems by incorporating appropriate contingencies, role models, and incentives.

## Group Dynamics

Precursors of the group dynamics approach to corrections can be seen in the pioneering research of Kurt Lewin and his students (Cartwright, 1951). In a series of studies, they found that the behavior and attitudes of individuals could be changed most effectively if they were dealt with as members of small groups rather than on a one-to-one basis. For instance, they found that women change their eating habits more easily if informed of the advantages of the new diets in group settings and permitted to discuss them than if lectured and simply advised of the advantages.

As with most correctional ideologies, early discussions of group treatment methods were optimistic. Claiming that "opinion is almost unanimous that group therapy is an effective technique for treating mental patients," Donald Cressey urged criminologists to develop a theory for using group treatment methods that would draw upon and employ the expertise of ex-offenders (1965: 55). This was said to be "the most difficult and crucial task that criminologists will face during the remainder of this century" (1965: 50). Like Cressey, Marshall Clinard argued that "individual clinical methods of treating potential or actual delinquency . . . have not demonstrated any marked success" (1949: 260). He felt this was because the etiology of criminal behavior lies not primarily in "the conventional individualistic, early childhood explanation of psychiatry and psychoanalysis, but may develop out of a much more extensive process of group interaction" (1949: 260). Cressey articulated this argument:

> The person or personality is . . . a part of the kinds of social relationships and values in which he participates; he obtains his essence from the rituals, values, norms, rules, schedules, customs, and regulations of various kinds which surround him; he is not separable from the social relationships in which he lives. The person behaves according to the rules (which are sometimes contradictory) of the social organizations in which he participates; he cannot

---

**PANEL 3.2**

*An Inmate Comments on Group Therapy*

[T]he official big gig offered by the authorities in their modern penology bag is Group Therapy. Spell that in capitals and color it sacred.

For me there was never any escape from group therapy, since I was always quite candid in admitting that I was a thief because I enjoyed the stimulation of crime and because I had a marked aversion to the 40-hour week. This didn't go over at all well in a system geared to the premise that a thief is never a thief through preference, but through the workings of a warped id. Nature's abhorrence of a vacuum, I tell you, is as nothing compared to the psychologist's loathing of a simple and direct explanation.

SOURCE: John MacIsaac, *Half the Fun Was Getting There* (Englewood Cliffs, N.J.: Prentice-Hall, 1968), p. 69.

---

behave any other way. This is to say that criminal or noncriminal behavior is—like other behaviors, attitudes, beliefs, and values which a person exhibits—the property of groups, not of individuals. Criminal and delinquent behavior is not just a product of an individual's contacts with certain kinds of groups; it is in a very real sense "owned" by groups rather than by individuals, just as a language is owned by a collectivity rather than by any individual (1965: 51).

Therefore, "if [the] behavior of an individual is an intrinsic part of groups to which he belongs, attempts to change the behavior must be directed at groups" (1955: 117).

Although there are a variety of approaches to the group treatment of offenders, advocates of group methods generally agree on some core assumptions (Kassebaum *et al.,* 1971):

**1.** An open, permissive group setting helps individuals learn what effect they have on others and how others perceive them. This knowledge can lead to a more accurate and realistic understanding of self.

**2.** The permissive nature of small groups and the processes of group development and interaction are such that members may feel a degree of uncritical acceptance that they have not experienced before.

**3.** In the process of discussing and trying to resolve the problems of others within the group, members necessarily assume a therapeutic role and learn to view themselves differently.

**4.** Because the members of the group have similar backgrounds and problems, they are best able to deal with one another's problems. Moreover, the similarity of the members serves as a check on the behavior of individual members, because the group will not permit the individual to play "treatment games" with the group leader.

**5.** In the process of group interaction and discussion, the individual may learn more constructive means of handling personal problems from the experiences and suggestions of others.

Despite its substantial theoretical underpinnings and the urgent pleas of its supporters, group treatment methods did not take firm root in American correctional ideologies and practice. Most American political leaders and correctional managers have shown distinct biases in favor of correctional ideologies that focus on the individual offender. Group treatment methods were, however, used in some places to justify experimental programs such as Highfields (Weeks, 1958) and in the California Department of Corrections.

## *The System As the Problem*

The 1960s was a time of great theoretical ferment in the social sciences, especially in criminology and the sociology of deviance. *Labeling theory,* a synthesis of earlier work by a number of scholars, increasingly found acceptance as an explanation for deviant behavior. This theory maintains that social control agencies and processes unwittingly shape the problems that are their mandates. Supporters of labeling theory pointed to a number of ways that social control processes may exacerbate the problems of offenders and thereby promote further crime. These beliefs underlie the core assumptions:

**1.** Official processing by criminal justice agencies "hardens" many offenders by (a) dramatizing their misconduct; (b) eroding their self-concepts; and (c) exposing them to criminal peers and definitions favorable to violation of the law.

**2.** Official processing stigmatizes many offenders, thereby hindering them from finding acceptance and reintegration in conventional social networks and institutions, escalating delinquent and criminal careers.

**3.** Traditional social control institutions such as training schools and prisons are so segregated from the outside world that they generate artificial internal worlds that undermine rehabilitative efforts.

**4.** The best way to avoid processes of career escalation is to provide the least intrusive intervention in offenders' lives. This may necessitate using alternative procedures for processing many offenders, and also minimizing the use of segregative controls.

Liberals called for a variety of criminal justice reforms to rectify these problems. Correctional programs such as juvenile diversion, deinstitutionalization, and community-based corrections all found shelter under this ideological umbrella. The movement to establish community-based correctional programs merits additional comment.

A belief in the rehabilitative powers of the local community was briefly popular during the late 1960s and 1970s. It gained strong support in much the same way that belief in military drill and religious instruction did in earlier eras. The irony of this fact was wryly noted by James Q. Wilson (1975: 170): "Today we smile in amusement at the naiveté of those early prison reformers who imagined that religious instruction while in solitary confinement would lead to moral regeneration. How they would now smile at us at our presumption that . . . a return to the community could achieve the same end." Nevertheless, the ideology of community corrections breathed new fires of justification into some traditional correctional strategies (probation; parole), was embraced by advocates of more recent innovations (halfway houses), and was used to justify some entirely new ones (community correctional centers).

John Irwin interpreted this movement to develop community corrections programs. According to him, by 1970 the growing criticism of other rehabilitative ideologies

took full shape and spread among criminologists and criminal justice experts. For a short period of several years there was an intense effort to quickly substitute a new ideology—community corrections—for the old, which would leave most of the basic structures, par-

ticularly the discretionary decision-making systems, intact. However, flaws in this system were quickly recognized, and the same type of criticisms which were aimed at the [other rehabilitative ideologies] were turned toward it. . . . The movement toward community corrections still continues, but it has had its rationale seriously damaged and will probably not succeed in supplanting the dying [rehabilitative ideologies] (1977: 31).

The community corrections movement quickly lost momentum in the 1970s when it was overwhelmed by the swelling conservative tide among political leaders.

---

**PANEL 3.3**

*A Skeptical View of Official Handling*

Official action may actually help to fix and perpetuate delinquency in the child through a process in which the individual begins to think of himself as delinquent and organizes his behavior accordingly. That process itself is further reinforced by the effect of the labeling upon the child's family, neighbors, teachers, and peers, whose reactions communicate to the child in subtle ways a kind of expectation of delinquent conduct. The undesirable consequences of official treatment are maximized in programs that rely on institutionalizing the child. The most informed and benign official treatment of the child therefore contains within it the seeds of its own frustration and itself may often feed the very disorder it is designed to cure. . . .

The formal sanctioning system and pronouncement of delinquency should be used only as a last resort. In place of the formal system, dispositional alternatives to adjudication must be developed for dealing with juveniles, including agencies to provide and coordinate services and procedures to

achieve necessary control without unnecessary stigma. Alternatives already available, such as those related to court intake, should be more fully exploited.

The range of conduct for which court intervention is authorized should be narrowed.

The cases that fall within the narrowed jurisdiction of the court and filter through the screen of prejudicial, informal disposition modes would largely involve offenders for whom more vigorous measures seem necessary. . . .

*The Commission recommends:*

The movement for narrowing the juvenile court's jurisdiction should be continued. . . .

Juvenile courts should make fullest feasible use of preliminary conferences to dispose of cases short of adjudication.

SOURCE: President's Commission on Law Enforcement and Administration of Justice (1967a: 80–85).

## PANEL 3.4

### *Breaking the Criminal Cycle*

Thanks to a program being funded by the Law Enforcement Assistance Administration, at least several thousand potential crimes will not be committed during at least the next several years.

The program is an effort to crack down on "career criminals" by assisting local prosecutors to identify repeat offenders as they are arrested for new crimes, to speed such cases through the courts and to obtain stiff prison sentences.

Begun in 22 cities in May 1975, the program resulted in the identification of 5,107 career criminals through August 1, 1977. More than 4,700 of them were convicted of a variety of crimes, mostly serious, and were given prison sentences averaging 14.3 years.

About half of these career criminals were free on bond or were on probation or parole for previous offenses. Indeed, the 5,107 criminals had a total of 30,000 prior convictions.

James Gregg, acting administrator of the agency, calls the program "one of LEAA's most worthwhile undertakings." We agree.

So effective has the approach been, in fact, that many cities and counties are financing their own programs with their own money.

More and more people involved in the justice system are coming around to the belief that there is such a thing as the career criminal and that there really isn't a great deal that can be done to rehabilitate him. Some studies have indicated that merely growing older is the surest cure for criminal tendencies.

It follows then that the best thing both for society and for the repeat offender is to keep him out of circulation as long as possible.

The nation's war on crime finally may have found the enemy.

SOURCE: *Knoxville News-Sentinel* (Tennessee). November 26, 1977, p. 6.

## Conservative Ideologies

The importance of maintaining social order plays a prominent part in conservative correctional ideologies. Because conservatives see criminal offenders as a threat to public order, they offer them little sympathy. Instead, conservative writings usually sound a sympathetic note for the victims of crime.

From the conservative point of view, the primary cause of crime is insufficient control over a fundamentally flawed human nature. Despite their higher faculties, human beings are believed to be animalistic by nature (Currie, 1985). Perhaps they can be polished through social engineering, but they cannot be made perfect. Not surprisingly, conservatives reject all interpretations of crime that attribute it to social or environmental conditions. Rather, inadequate social controls are the problem. Tolerance of deviance and permissiveness are thought to explain high levels of crime.

The conservative approach to corrections tends to emphasize the need to repress crime through the use of swift, sure, and measured punishment (Van den Haag, 1977; Wilson, 1983). Crime results from individual, rational choices to break the law. The key to controlling crime is to ensure that the consequences of criminal acts are so unpleasant that individuals will choose not to engage in them. Conservatives generally support the liberal use of imprisonment to control crime. If offenders are exposed to rehabilitative programs while incarcerated, so be it; but it is imprisonment itself, with its attendant deprivations, that must be primarily relied on to prevent crime and recidivism. Correctional treatment may be all well and good but it is not considered necessary.

Acceptance of retribution as grounds for punishment is characteristic of conservatism. *Retribution* is the belief that it is only proper for those who break the law to be punished for their transgression. It is proper because the law expressly informs those who would violate it that they must expect punishment if they do so:

> We must have the courage to give our criminals the punishment they deserve. We must not shirk our responsibility. . . . For crimes of violence, the offenders should suffer punishments of violence. . . . Those who risk the lives of others (and this includes white-collar criminals) surely deserve to have their own put at risk. . . . Those who kill should be killed (Newman, 1983: 22–23).

The same observer extended this assumption to a call for measured infliction of corporal punishment on offenders as "just deserts" for their crimes.

But most supporters of the notion of retribution insist that it must not be confused with vengeance. Rather, punishment is good because it serves utilitarian purposes as well:

> Prescribed by the law broken, and proportioned to the gravity of the offense committed, retribution [is inflicted] . . . to enforce the law and to vindicate the legal order. . . . Retribution is to restore an objective order rather than to satisfy a subjective craving for revenge. . . . Whatever its origin, a transpersonal social order objectively does exist. If it is to continue, it must be vindicated through the punishment of offenders (Van den Haag, 1975: 11–12).

In this view, punishment is not only proper but necessary. It reinforces the legal order. On this common base of support for retributive correctional strategies, we distinguish two conservative correctional ideologies: *deterrence* and *incapacitation*.

### Deterrence

Deterrence is the belief that punishing offenders for their misdeeds will reduce both the likelihood of their repeating the act (*specific deterrence*) and the likelihood of others committing the same act (*general deterrence*). Thus deterrence theory suggests that deterrence may work differently on those who actually are punished and those who only observe it from afar. Analytically, the specific effects of a correctional measure or punishment may be minimal even while its general effects are considerable.

Like other conservative ideologies, deterrence doctrine sketches the criminal as a rational being who can be dissuaded from lawless ways by a judicious use of punishments. In the law-and-order climate of the 1970s and 1980s, interest in deterrence grew rapidly (Zimring and Hawkins, 1973; Tittle and Logan, 1973; Gibbs, 1975; Tittle, 1980).

If offenders are rational, what makes them choose to commit crime? At least three answers have been proposed. One emphasizes that offenders' commitments to legitimate others and legitimate lines of conduct are so weak that these represent no real control on their behavior (Hirschi, 1969). Offenders such as these exist at the margin of society (Zimring and Hawkins, 1968). Lacking the controls of a stake in conformity, they engage in illicit behavior whenever it appears propitious to them. The second answer is that offenders differ psychologically from the law-abiding portion of the population. For example, their risk perception or their criminal calculus may differ from those of most people (Claster, 1967; Zimring and Hawkins, 1973: 96–128). Finally, offenders commit crime when the benefits they expect to gain from crime exceed their anticipated losses from doing so. When viewed through the prism of deterrence theory, offenders respond either to increasing costs of criminal behavior or to increases in the benefits expected from lawful conduct. This means that the state need not rely exclusively on punitive programs; offenders can be dissuaded from crime by programs that increase the attractiveness of and payoffs from noncriminal behavior (Nagel and Neef, 1981). Conservatives, however, focus their efforts almost exclusively on punitive strategies to increase the threatened costs of unlawful conduct.

Regardless of the answer one adopts, supporters of the deterrence ideology believe it is the state's inefficient response and ineffectual punishment that prompt individuals to commit crime. Therefore, if we would deter them from criminality, we must judiciously employ punishments that are swift, sure, and sufficiently severe.

> There is scarcely any evidence to support the proposition that would-be criminals are indifferent to the risks associated with a proposed course of action. Criminals may be willing to run greater risks (or they may have a weaker sense of morality) than the average citizen, but if the expected cost of crime goes up without a corresponding increase in the expected benefits, then the would-be criminal—unless he or she is among that small fraction of criminals who are utterly irrational—engages in less crime (Wilson, 1975: 175–76).

For supporters of deterrence, the task ahead for social scientists is clear. They should conduct research on the deterrent effectiveness of various types and levels of punishments, and develop theoretical knowledge about deterrence. This knowledge can be used by policymakers to maximize both the general and specific deterrent effects for particular types of crime.

### Incapacitation

An especially pessimistic view of offenders and what can be done with them is held by supporters of the ideology of *incapacitation*. The concept of incapacitation is simple: Offenders cannot commit further crimes— at least crimes against people outside of prison—while they are incarcerated. By defi-

nition, locking up people known to be criminals will reduce the level of crime. The reason for this unmincing approach to incarceration and other forms of punishment is equally simple: Certain types of individuals are believed to be especially prone to engage in crime, and little can be done about it other than to isolate them until they have passed through their crime-prone years.

Supporters of incapacitation generally argue that a high percentage of "serious," that is, street, crime is committed by a small proportion of the American population. The key to a successful strategy of incapacitation is to identify and incapacitate this group of "career criminals." The task of developing techniques to accomplish this objective has been entrusted to social scientists.

Ignoring the effects of other variables, a policy of incapacitation leads to increases in the size of the prison population. In time, there is no room for additional inmates. Unless new prisons can be constructed quickly, extraordinary measures must be taken to stabilize or reduce the prison population. Thus the incapacitation, if pursued too vigorously, undermines its own effectiveness. Consequently, adherents concede that incapacitative strategies must be pursued judiciously via *selective incapacitation*. We will comment on these proposals at greater length in Chapter 13.

Many investigators are doubtful that significant reductions in street crime can be achieved by a strategy of selective incapacitation (Gottfredson and Hirschi, 1986). Other critics of incapacitation charge that it is a violation of fundamental moral and legal precepts. They maintain that extraordinary punishments should be used only when a person's *behavior* warrants it, not because of past crimes or crimes he may commit in the future.

## Radical Ideologies

Both conservative and liberal ideologies lend themselves to campaigns for limited reforms of correctional strategies and structures. Rarely do their supporters call into question the premises of the entire criminal justice system. Moreover, most of their reformist zeal is spent on efforts to reduce the incidence of crime by offenders who are known to criminal justice personnel. Radical correctional ideologies, with their unique conception of the causes of crime, present a marked contrast.

Discussions of radical correctional ideologies are difficult because of the many points of disagreement among their supporters. For present purposes we limit our comments to radical ideologies heavily influenced by neo-Marxist interpretations of the capitalist state and its crime control policies (Gibbons, 1979; Beirne and Quinney, 1982; Greenberg, 1981; Bohm, 1982).

Radicals argue that the nature and rate of crime in America are inevitable results of the structure and dynamics of its capitalist economy. Private ownership and control of the means of production, vast inequity in income, and the dynamics of class conflict are the key to understanding America's crime problem. Radicals are not so naive as to believe that crime can be eradicated. But they do argue that the level of crime generally and its distribution among the various types could be modified substantially by changes in the political economy.

Because of their focus on the larger social structure and economy as the key to crime control, historically radicals devoted little if any effort to correctional programs aimed at individual offenders. The arrival of a socialist economy, they argued, holds the only real hope for making significant inroads against crime in America. Also, radicals charged that the rhetoric and substance of correctional re-

form are part of the process by which public consciousness and understanding of crime and criminals are manipulated and mystified. And to the extent that reforms actually are adopted, they only enhance the ability of the correctional apparatus to control problem populations (underclasses). This led most radicals to view official reform efforts as a form of collaboration with an oppressive social control apparatus.

For both these reasons, then, radicals traditionally eschewed discussions of practical programs for controlling or reducing the level of crime in the United States. In fact, they generally scoffed at those who offered short-term proposals for correctional programs intended to reduce crime:

> It is as if we merely [have] to change our ideas or consciousness to create changes in prisons. [Reformers] do not see that there are objective material conditions that support the process of imprisonment as it is. Until those conditions are changed, prisons and parole will not change (Schmidt, 1977: 118).

Like most social scientists, supporters of radical correctional ideologies were taken by surprise by the speed and ease with which conservative correctional ideologies gained ascendancy in the past 15 years. Too late they realized that a disdainful stance toward practical crime control programs leaves a clear field for the supporters of conservative strategies. So, faced with the rapid acceptance of punitive ideologies and controls, and the expansion of official control networks, radicals offered a variety of short-term proposals for crime control (Gross, 1982; Platt, 1982, 1984; Michalowski, 1983). Although there are some differences, for the most part these are similar to liberal proposals (Cullen and Wozniak, 1982). Radicals hope that their support for practical reforms will at least retard the spread of conservative correctional strategies. Progressive proposals may function as a "holding action" until altered economic circumstances arrive, bringing with them renewed prospects for fundamental changes.

## Some Dynamics of Correctional Ideologies

In the Marxist view, *ideology* is a body of ideas or beliefs that is inextricably linked to a particular sociohistorical context, even though its supporters and promoters are ignorant of this tie. In other words, ideologies are socially determined and relative, although they often are thought to have an objective, transituational validity and application. In fact, people of every historical era imbue the ideologies of their era with general validity.

Plamenatz (1970: 15) notes that the concept of ideology generally is used "to refer to a set of closely related beliefs or ideas, or even attitudes, characteristic of a group or community." This definition leads us to three fundamental characteristics of ideologies. First, they reflect the social and political contexts in which they are formulated or "discovered." Second, to some extent they reflect the common social and economic characteristics of the groups that create and promote them. And third, they are instruments by means of which groups pursue their collective interests. In sum, ideologies are one of the means by which groups struggle to advance their material and symbolic interests.

The foregoing review of some contemporary ideological competitors shows that there is no shortage of competing correctional ideologies. Why, then, do some ideologies receive official support while others are rejected? Why, for example, do rehabilitative ideologies dominate public debate about offenders and corrections during some periods whereas punitive ideologies gain official and broad popular support during others?

Because their appeal is influenced by changes in social context, the substance of dominant correctional ideologies varies systematically in time and place. At present we have only the crudest understanding of the relationships between contextual variables and the nature of correctional ideologies. It seems apparent, however, that changes in social and economic contexts may lead to a "need for" and, therefore, a discovery of "new" ideologies. It was Max Weber who pointed out that "the structure of basic socio-economic relations among men does not lead directly to intellectual orientations; its influence lies in producing differential receptivities to the various intellectual systems" (Portes, 1971: 311).

The rapid ascendance of ideologies of deterrence and incapacitation in recent years begs interpretation. Traditional explanations emphasize the causative role of purely intellectual variables, such as accumulating research findings or theoretical breakthroughs in correctional techniques. We suggest, however, that such explanations for changing correctional ideologies may be incomplete and misleading.

What changes in the social context of corrections or the social position of correctional theorists may account for the recent popularity of deterrence and incapacitative ideologies? Tony Platt and Paul Takagi (1977) have interpreted this new conservative strain produced by scholars whom they call the "new realists." Platt and Takagi argue that crime has continued to increase in recent years, and that the reasons for this are political and economic, especially the crises of world monopoly capitalism. Massive government expenditures have failed to stem the rising rate of street crime. This, they argue, necessitates newer and more severe forms of repression and control, which demand new ideological rationales and legitimation. Enter the new realists.

Their theories of deterrence and incapacitation provide the ideological rationale for the new stringent state policies. According to Platt and Takagi, one reason for this is "the social sciences in North American universities have *always* legitimated the ruling ideology of monopoly capitalism. . . . Criminology, with its particularly close ties to the state apparatus, was originally developed as a science of repression." However, in recent years this "long-standing collaboration between criminology and the state has been even more strongly cemented . . . with the help of massive investments and subsidies from the federal government and corporate think tanks" (1977: 10).

One other development has encouraged the new realists to come forward with theoretical justification for increased state controls: their own increasingly precarious class position. The crisis of world capitalism has produced more street crime and has threatened their own economic security. Platt and Takagi claim that "the ideological repertoire of the new 'realists' is typical of the petty bourgeoisie in crisis. Faced on the one side by an increasingly militant and organized working class, and on the other by the pressures of inflation and rising unemployment in the professional strata, the 'new middle class' feels itself 'beleaguered and pressed from all sides'" (1977: 13).

Other evidence supports the view that rehabilitative ideologies gain support during economic good times while pessimistic, punitive ideologies dominate during economic crises and downturns (Reiman and Headlee,

1981; Greenberg, 1982; Reiman, 1982). This does not mean that one must accept a one-sided political–economic explanation of changing correctional ideologies. Rather, we suggest an interpretation closely akin to the one taken by Elliott Currie in his analysis of the American reformatory movement:

> In emphasizing the social and economic context surrounding the rise of the Reformatory Movement (and its alteration after 1900), I do not mean to imply a crude "economic determinism." I will not be suggesting that the political economy of post–Civil War capitalism somehow directly elicited in mysterious fashion an appropriate ideology of penal treatment. I am suggesting that the post-war political economy formed the general framework within which the theorists of the Reformatory Movement worked, and that their acceptance of that framework both stimulated certain lines of thought and excluded others (1973: 5).

Contrary to conventional wisdom, changes in the correctional knowledge base may be largely epiphenomenal in efforts to understand historical transformations of correctional structures and practices. Instead, changes in public opinion and scientific knowledge may be "discovered" whenever necessary; that is, when changes in the economy mandate a modified correctional structure. Consequently, we must ask to what extent correctional ideologies exert a substantial, independent influence on the operations of the correctional industry.

# 4

# Sentencing

The part of a state's criminal law that stipulates the range and types of sentences a judge may impose on convicted offenders is known as the *sentencing code*. It represents one of the most important correctional strategies employed by the state and its functionaries. While sentences can and do vary greatly in their severity, the types of sentences imposed on those convicted of crimes are few. We begin with a brief discussion of the variety of criminal sentences.

## Basic Terms

*Indeterminate sentences,* such as one to three years, specify both a minimum and a maximum term of confinement. Defendants who receive indeterminate sentences ordinarily cannot tell, at the time of sentencing, exactly when they will be released. There are varying degrees of indeterminateness. Perhaps the epitome of a truly indeterminate sentence is one day to life. Such sentences are rare. In most states, indeterminate sentences specify a longer minimum, say, two years, and a maximum far short of life, such as ten years. Under such sentences, parole eligibility is provided for by law. Usually, inmates may be released to community supervision after a statutorily determined portion of the minimum sentence has been served.

*Determinate sentences* specify a fixed term of confinement, such as five years or one year and one day. Such sentences let defendants know at the time of sentencing how long they will be imprisoned. Ordinarily, a determinate sentence enables them to calculate their release date within a few moments after receiving their sentence.

Sometimes a sentence that is technically an indeterminate one may function in reality as a flat sentence. In such cases, the time between the minimum and maximum terms of imprisonment is so short that it effectively precludes any possibility of conditional release before the expiration of the maximum term. A sentence of ten years to ten years and one day is an example. In such a case, the inmate's eligibility date for conditional release literally would arrive within hours of the time he or she would be released from confinement at the expiration of sentence.

In most jurisdictions, a fixed sentence does not mean that a defendant actually must spend as much time in prison as the sentence stipulates. Instead, many states have "good time" laws stipulating that sentences be reduced a certain amount for each month or year of the sentence, as long as an inmate's conduct is good. A typical law requires that an inmate serve, say, 3 years and 9 months in prison on a 5-year sentence, or 11 years and 3 months on a 20-year sentence.

Many defendants appear in court charged with multiple offenses or with multiple counts of one offense. In such cases, the prosecutor and judge have great discretion in deciding how to sentence. Although the court often elects to dismiss all charges but one, in other cases the defendant will be sentenced for more than one offense.

In such cases, the court can impose either consecutive or concurrent sentences. *Consecutive sentences* must be served "back to back"; only after one sentence has been served does the offender begin serving the next one. An offender who is sent to prison with consecutive sentences of two to five years and one to three years would have to serve at least three years before release on parole. *Concurrent sentences* are served together, or at the same time. In the example cited here, the offender's sentence of one to

three years would be "eaten up" by the two-to-five-year sentence and he or she would be eligible for conditional release after serving two years.

Sentencing codes distinguish between permissible felony and misdemeanor sentences. Typically, a *misdemeanor sentence* cannot exceed one year, or a fine of, say, $1,000. *Felony sentences* do not have these upper limits.

## Importance of the Sentencing Process

"There is no decision in the criminal process that is as complicated and difficult as the one made by the sentencing judge" (President's Commission, 1967a: 141). There is also no decision that is more important to the defendant. For this reason, no discussion of the correctional apparatus and process can ignore conviction and sentencing, the offender's beliefs about them, and the potential constraints these may pose for the correctional process generally. In short, the sentencing process directly affects several aspects of the correctional process.

To individual offenders, the sentence they receive directly determines the degree of unpleasantness they must suffer for having been convicted. Since parole eligibility is tied directly to the type and length of criminal sentences, the sentence determines, with some precision, the amount of time inmates must spend in confinement.

Defendants' perceptions and evaluations of how the criminal process treats them may influence their beliefs about its legitimacy (Casper, 1978a, 1978b). In the collective body of inmates, the sentence each has received helps determine collective perceptions of the fairness or unfairness of the entire criminal justice system. These shared perceptions influence individual offenders, and may make the task of dissuading them from further law violation that much more difficult. To the correctional system as a whole, the configuration of sentences that its clientele receive determines the total drain on resources and in other ways constrains the action of its personnel. For example, if an inordinately large number of offenders receive lengthy prison sentences, an unusually recalcitrant prison population may result, since long-term inmates may feel they have little to gain by being cooperative with prison authorities. Furthermore, if increasing numbers of offenders are funneled into any particular part of the correctional system, there may be serious repercussions for other components of the apparatus. Since the early 1970s the prison population in the United States has increased dramatically, putting severe strains upon the prison system of the various states. Many states have been hard pressed to find secure housing for the influx of prisoners as local courts continue to sentence offenders to the penitentiary at high rates. The states have resorted to several extraordinary practices, including early-release programs, to make room for new prisoners (Austin, 1986).

## Adult Sentencing As Social Process

Figure 1.1 (pages 4–5) shows the flow of cases through the criminal justice system. What it does not show is the high rate of attrition of cases as they proceed through the system. Beginning with arrest and at every subsequent step, some cases are dropped from the process. Those felony defendants who arrive in court for sentencing represent less than half of all those that began with a formal police request for prosecution. Figure 4.1 represents typical outcomes for every 100 felony charges filed by the police in 37 cities in the United States in 1981.

While the rate of attrition is substantial in nearly all jurisdictions, it varies considerably for the 50 states, and by regions of the U.S. (U.S. Department of Justice, 1983d). Contrary to popular belief, however, rates of attrition are lowest for crimes most feared by the public (U.S. Department of Justice, 1983d).

### *The Myth of Trial by Jury*

Adults charged with felonies are guaranteed the right to a trial by their peers (a jury trial). Crime shows on television usually show

FIGURE 4.1 **Typical Outcome of 100 Felony Defendants Brought by the Police for Prosecution, 37 Jurisdictions—1981**

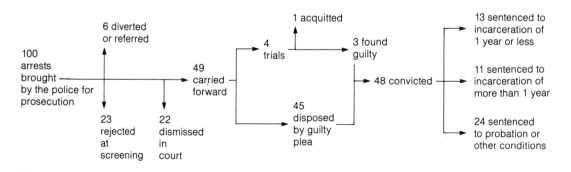

SOURCE: Boland (1986: 2)

defendants locked in dramatic courtroom battles before alert, discerning juries. But few real-life defendants exercise their constitutional right to a jury trial. For them the question of guilt or innocence is moot once they reach the trial stage of the justice process, because the overwhelming majority of criminal charges in America that reach the court are settled by guilty pleas. Of the total of 35,591 defendants convicted in U.S. district courts in the year ending June 30, 1984, 87.1 percent had entered pleas of guilty or nolo contendere (Flanagan and McGarrell, 1986: 476). The proportion varies considerably from one district to another. It is even higher in some states and state courts. A study of felony case handling in 37 local jurisdictions during 1981 found that the percentage of convictions that followed guilty pleas ranged from 42 to 97 percent, with an average of 84 percent (Boland, 1986: Table 19).

## The Myth of the Judge As a Solitary Decision Maker

It would be a serious mistake to think of the sentence as a product of the efforts of only one person, the judge. In truth, the sentence is a product of a complex network of relationships between representatives of different offices, including the police, prosecutor's office, and the court. Typically, the judge merely ratifies sentencing decisions that have already been made in private. Taken together, these offices make up what is commonly referred to as the criminal justice system, but each of them has goals that are only partially like those of other offices in the system. Each is also an organization, and the characteristic goals and activities of its varied personnel are affected by this fact as well. Consequently, the criminal justice system is actually a largely routinized series of working relationships between representatives of bureaucratic offices or agencies. Sentencing

decisions are negotiated between the defendant and these offices. In return for a guilty plea the defendant receives some consideration in sentencing.

## Routinization of Judgment

Investigators have called attention to this negotiated aspect of the sentencing process. According to Abraham Blumberg, the result has been the creation of a new model of the criminal process. The old model "is couched in constitutional–ideological terms of due process and rule of law; it is the one we think we have, or ought to have." The model that has supplanted it, he says, emphasizes efficiency and rationality in processing criminal cases. It is an "administrative, ministerial, rational–bureaucratic one" (1967: 189).

> The official goals of the criminal courts, based on ancient values, remain; due process, justice, and rule of law are necessary ideologies. But concerns of secularism and rationality, based on modern values of efficiency, maximum production, and career enhancement, have deflected and perhaps displaced those goals (1967: 78).

Similarly, Herbert L. Packer distinguishes two models of the criminal justice process: the Due Process Model and the Crime Control Model. They represent two distinctive value systems that influence the day-to-day operation of the criminal justice process. The value system that underlies the Due Process Model emphasizes the importance of protecting the factually innocent as well as convicting the factually guilty. As a result, each successive stage of the criminal process is designed to present formidable impediments to carrying suspects any further along.

> Considerations of this kind all lead to the rejection of informal [procedures] and to the insis-

tence on formal, adjudicative, adversary fact-finding processes in which the factual case against the accused is publicly heard by an impartial tribunal and is evaluated only after the accused has had a full opportunity to discredit the case against him (1964: 14).

Efficient handling of criminal cases is considered less important than preventing official oppression of the individual.

By contrast, the value system that underlies the Crime Control Model springs from the proposition that

> the repression of criminal conduct is by far the most important function to be performed by the criminal process. . . . [This value system] requires that primary attention be paid to the efficiency with which the . . . process operates to screen suspects, determine guilt, and secure appropriate dispositions of [convicted offenders] (1964: 9–10).

There is a strong presumption of guilt that underlies this process. Criminal justice employees use informal, routine, and stereotyped procedures to produce speedy resolutions of cases, usually in the form of a high proportion of guilty pleas. Packer argues that "the criminal process as it actually operates in the large majority of cases probably approximates fairly closely the dictates of the Crime Control Model. . . . The real-world criminal process tends to be far more administrative and managerial than it does adversarial and judicial" (1964: 61).

Although the significance of bureaucratic influences and concerns on the sentencing process is substantial, the personal characteristics of judges—their background, political philosophies, and demographic characteristics—may influence their decisions as well. In an illustrative study, S. Wheeler *et al.* (1966) found that Boston juvenile court judges who identified with a treatment doctrine tended to commit children to institutions more frequently than those primarily concerned with

punishment. John Hogarth (1971) employed personal interviews and an attitude questionnaire to collect data on 70 Canadian magistrates. These data were used to examine and explain variation in the magistrates' sentences in a sample of 2,500 criminal cases from 1965–67. Differences in the magistrates' attitudes and social background were related to their definitions of "the facts" in criminal cases. In turn, variations in definitions of the facts were related to differences in sentencing severity. Further, Hogarth found that magistrates appeared to use information in sentencing selectively, so as to keep their original attitudes intact. "Magistrates tended to seek information consistent with their preconceptions (which are the essence of their attitudes). At the same time, they tended to avoid information which was likely to present a picture of the offender that was in conflict with their expectations" (1971: 374).

### Misdemeanor Courts

For many defendants, the everyday world of America's criminal courts is not inspiring. Ensnared in the court process, they discover that the discrepancy between the expectations we acquire in high school civics and their experiences is substantial. The limited ethnographic research conducted in the lowest-level criminal courts points to a general disregard for procedural rights in these courts (Robertson, 1974). This seems to be especially true of the courts that routinely process our least powerful citizens (for example, chronic drunkenness offenders). Noting that these problems have long been known, the President's Crime Commission observed in 1967 that "the inescapable conclusion is that . . . conditions of inequity, indignity, and ineffectiveness previously deplored [are] . . . widespread" (President's Commission, 1967a: 29).

Maureen Mileski systematically observed how 417 cases were handled in one urban lower criminal courtroom. She began this study of courtroom encounters by noting: "The processing of defendants through court can be seen simply as a task for courtroom personnel—the cases presenting not only occasions for moral outrage or legal acumen, but also presenting problems for the legal bureaucracy as such" (1971: 473). Thus "the control of crime is as much a bureaucratic as it is a moral enterprise" (1971: 533). During courtroom observation, Mileski noted that judges occasionally engaged in "situational sanctioning" of defendants by lecturing to or chastising them, or by manifesting a firm or harsh demeanor. In part, judges appeared to use these sanctions as a mechanism for maintaining the informal rules of the court. Defendants who created minor disruptions in the courtroom, or who showed disrespect for its personnel, were likely to be sanctioned in this manner. There was little relationship between the seriousness of defendants' charges and whether or not they were the object of situational sanctions. The use of such sanctions is one mechanism that court personnel—in this case the judge—employ to reinforce and maintain a smooth flow of cases.

Malcolm Feeley (1979) observed the daily work performed in the lower criminal courts in New Haven, Connecticut. He claims that the entire court process alternatively is demeaning and indifferent to defendants. Nonetheless, the minor sanctions that the court imposes are less damaging than the pretrial process. For most defendants, according to Feeley, the process is costly both in time and in money. He concludes that "the process is the punishment." In two respects, John Paul Ryan's research in the Columbus, Ohio, municipal court offers an interesting contrast. First, the process of adjudication is not very costly in Columbus. Assigned counsel is used liberally and few defendants are held in jail while awaiting trial. And second, penalties are more severe; substantial fines, incarceration, and suspension of driving privileges are common. Ryan observes:

The Columbus misdemeanor court views the variety of sanctions available in a relatively punitive, rather than ameliorative, light. Instead of choosing which one sanction to employ against convicted defendants, this court often chooses *how much* of several sanctions. In this regard, the court is quite different from New Haven, where fines are used much less frequently, and where combinations of probation and suspended sentence often serve as punishment. No wonder, perhaps, that Feeley viewed the process [as] the primary punishment. In Columbus, the outcome is the punishment (1980: 99–100).

Ryan offers several possible explanations for these differences in court processing between New Haven and Columbus. Among them he suggests that political culture and relationships between the police and the courts are significant:

Differences in the political culture and structure of the two communities . . . clearly play a key role. The political culture of Columbus breeds a climate of severity. This is manifested in the institutional domination of the police in the lower court, in the Columbus police department's orientation to law enforcement . . . and in the community's expectations that traffic laws will be enforced (1980: 105).

Although Ryan did not collect systematic data on these variables, his findings and interpretations point to the importance of contextual and interorganizational forces in the operation of misdemeanor courts.

## Persistent Doubts about Sentencing

Armed with the medical model as justification, for 50 years judges wielded great discretion in sentencing. Sentencing statutes gave them great latitude, and they were permitted to take into account various extra-legal characteristics of defendants. They were encouraged to dispense unequal sentences. The possible discrimination that resulted was justified on the basis of defendants' different "needs" and the likelihood that they would commit crime in the future. But even as the medical model and the indeterminate sentence grew in popularity, nagging questions about some of their potentially harmful effects were not far behind. The questions and concerns clustered in three areas.

## Plea Bargaining

Plea bargaining is the process of negotiation—typically between a defendant or his attorney and the prosecuting attorney—over the sentence the defendant will receive in return for a plea of guilty. Once defendants are arrested and indicted for crimes, a variety of pressures and inducements come into play which influence them to avoid a trial and to "cop a plea" instead. Most defendants cannot afford a competent private lawyer. This means that they must make use of a public defender or other assigned counsel that are

provided in most states (Spangenberg *et al.*, 1986). Defendants may be held in jail for a protracted period before their cases come to trial. The jail experience leaves one poorly prepared to wage an effective courtroom battle even as it saps one's resistance to pleading guilty (Irwin, 1985). The apparatus must process defendants routinely and therefore efficiently. Defendants who insist on a trial may be threatened by the prosecutor with lengthy sentences if they are found guilty.

Criminal-court functionaries don't rely on the heavy hand alone to elicit guilty pleas. They offer a variety of inducements as well:

**1.** For defendants with multiple charges, concurrent as opposed to consecutive sentences.

**2.** A promise to drop any additional charges that may be pending.

**3.** A reduction of the charged offense to a lesser offense, such as armed robbery to simple robbery.

**4.** A recommendation to the judge for shorter sentences, or even for probation.

It should not be supposed that control over the sentencing decision is used only to promote the goal of efficiency in case handling. The discretion to be lenient can be made to serve a host of officials and purposes. Negotiated pleas of guilty are "frequently called upon to serve law enforcement needs by agreements through which leniency is exchanged for information, assistance, and testimony about other serious offenders" (President's Commission 1967b: 135). During the trial of the Watergate burglars in the mid-1970s, federal judge John Sirica used his control over the sentencing process to pressure defendants to divulge more about the offense than they previously were willing to reveal.

---

### PANEL 4.1

### *The Criminal Justice System: An Offender's View*

[**D**ealing] is the backbone of American justice. It doesn't matter if you've killed your kindly old parents, robbed the orphans' fund, or criminally molested an entire Sunday school class; if you have something to deal with, you can disentangle yourself from the law without earning a single gray hair behind bars. . . . The whole thing is marvelously flexible.

SOURCE: John MacIsaac, *Half the Fun Was Getting There* (Englewood Cliffs, N.J.: Prentice-Hall, 1968), pp. 204–5.

Plea bargaining has long been a matter of controversy among lawyers and social scientists. Critics see it as a potential threat to defendants who insist on exercising their right to a trial. They argue that defendants often are threatened with sentences considerably more severe than the ones they are offered in return for a plea of guilty.

The threat of a jury trial is one of the subtleties employed by the prosecution to reduce a defendant's resistance. Jury trials are discouraged in any event, because they are time-consuming, expensive, and introduce an altogether cumbersome dimension into a system which is otherwise characterized by regularity, supreme rationality, and efficiency. Indeed, at the time of sentence, whether one was convicted after a trial or by way of a plea becomes a basis for invidious comparison (Blumberg, 1967: 31).

On the whole, defendants who plead guilty receive shorter sentences than defendants who plead not guilty (U.S. Department of Justice, 1985b). However, opinion is divided on the issue of whether defendants who insist on pleading not guilty are intentionally punished by the court for insisting on a trial (LaFree, 1986).

Regardless, critics charge that the over-

---

**PANEL 4.2**

*An Experience with the Public Defender*

Our P.D. was a kindly and fatherly man who approached us with apparent sympathy. Yes, he acknowledged, you might beat them in a trial, but why take the chance when you could lose? Then they'll jam it into you. Take the middle course. Cop out. Save time, theirs and yours, save money. Cop out and do it the way that's easiest for everyone. There was, he said, little chance, considering the time we had already served, we would be sent to San Quentin.

Bob was convinced, and, with some reluctance, I agreed. As soon as we entered our pleas of guilty, we were routinely processed and swiftly sentenced to the California Department of Corrections at San Quentin for a period of not less than one year and not more than life.

This official process was marked by another irony. We had been sentenced and returned to the crowded bull pen to await return to our tanks. Bob seemed stunned. "San Quentin isn't Carson City," he told me. I knew that. Everyone had heard horror stories set in San Quentin. But I had also heard they had a school there, and I was telling myself how hard I would study, how much I would learn, how hard I would try, and what was another year or two. I was still young.

The P.D. came in to say a few consoling words to us, but he happened to sit down next to two other kids, even younger, and began to father away at them, telling them of the opportunities to be found in Quentin, and one of the boys burst into tears. They were juveniles who had not yet been sentenced. They were sitting there waiting to go home and here was this strange man telling them they were being sent to San Quentin.

The P.D. rose in some confusion and finally recognizing his mistake began to look around for us. I turned away and rested my head on my arms. He had advised us badly, failed his promise, cost us several years of our lives, and now he didn't even remember what we looked like.

SOURCE: Malcolm Braly, *False Starts* (Boston: Little, Brown, 1976), pp. 147–48.

whelming reliance on plea bargaining in the courts of our largest cities has fundamentally altered our adversary system, producing in its place a system of justice by negotiation—a *bureaucratic due process* (Blumberg, 1967). The courts' dependence on plea bargaining to manage their workload is criticized for leading to haphazard, sloppy police investigative work and case preparation by prosecutors. Knowing that a defendant may be induced to plead guilty in return for favorable treatment by the court, they are less likely to put forth the kind of rigorous and thorough efforts that would be required were the case to go to trial.

The defenders of plea bargaining claim there is no other way understaffed and overloaded criminal courts could effectively deal with the volume of criminal cases that comes before them. In this view, plea bargaining is an inevitable and necessary mechanism for coping with a staggering workload. They

also charge that plea bargaining, far from being an abridgement of offenders' legal rights, in truth enables defendants to avoid the expensive and risky trial process. Defendants who have little chance at trial of winning a not-guilty verdict may emerge with a better deal. Finally, defenders of plea bargaining contend that it provides a degree of indispensable flexibility in the sentencing process. This

> imports a degree of certainty and flexibility into a rigid, yet frequently erratic, system. The guilty plea is used to mitigate the harshness of mandatory sentencing provisions and to fix a punishment that more accurately reflects the specific circumstances of the case than otherwise would be possible under inadequate penal codes (President's Commission, 1967a: 135).

Although liberals skeptical of traditional sentencing practices have generated the lion's share of publicity, conservatives long have had misgivings about the medical model and indeterminate sentencing as well.

Traditionally most of the publicly expressed doubts about and attacks on the sentencing process have been generated by liberal social scientists. However, conservatives also have been critical of sentencing practices inspired by the medical model. For example, conservatives have attacked the use of plea bargaining. They fear that the flexibility of the plea-bargaining process, when coupled with what they assume is the inefficiency of public bureaucracies, produces lenient sentences for "dangerous offenders" and "career criminals":

> Conservatives traditionally have been opposed to the discretion inherent in the indeterminate sentence because of the freedom it provides judges to be "soft on criminals." Moreover, according to this perspective, judicial discretion undermines the deterrent value of punishment because offenders are never certain

---

**PANEL 4.3**

*Aftermath of a Broken Plea Agreement*

The only thing I resent and resent deeply is that I was promised by my lawyer and the DA that if I copped a guilty plea I'd get probation. I waived all my rights before the court—they say "no one promised you anything . . . this or that" . . . and you swear to it. When I went to court for the sentencing, the judge sentenced me to prison, not to probation. I have cancer of the abdomen and need radium treatments. The judge stipulated I get whatever I need in here . . . but I haven't yet. The judge said he figured I had cancer when I committed the crime, so I should have considered it.

SOURCE: Kathryn Watterson Burkhart, *Women in Prison* (New York: Popular Library, 1976), p. 24.

whether they will be punished or, if punished, how severe the punishment will be (Goodstein, 1984: 12).

Conservatives could not have been happy with the findings from research by Isaac Balbus, who studied the responses of the criminal courts in Chicago, Detroit, and Los Angeles to defendants arrested during the urban "riots" of the 1960s. He found that during the early stages of processing these defendants, the courts generally took a hard line and seemed to be concerned with helping maintain order in the streets. Extremely high bail was set in many cases, in an apparent effort to "keep them off the streets." However, during later stages of processing, especially at sentencing, the courts became much more preoccupied with managing the flow of cases smoothly, so they would not overwhelm or in other ways disrupt the court's operating procedures. In all three cities, by the time the defendants came to trial, the "sheer volume of cases" compelled court authorities "to offer lenient sentences in return for the assurance of a predictable and efficient disposition of cases" (1973: 239). In other words, those defendants who were willing to plead guilty, often to reduced charges, received very light sentences in return for their cooperation.

We are left, then, with the seemingly paradoxical conclusion that a participant in a full-scale ghetto revolt involving widespread participation and destruction of life and property is likely to incur less concrete deprivation from the criminal courts than one arrested for a comparable offense during "normal" conditions (1973: 252).

## Disparity and Discrimination

In 1974, the 50 federal district judges of the Second Circuit (New York, Vermont, and Connecticut) took part in a study of differences in sentencing (Partridge and Eldridge, 1974). Copies of 20 presentence reports were mailed to the judges and each was asked to decide on a sentence for the defendants described in the reports. The 20 hypothetical defendants were selected from actual cases that previously were sentenced by judges in the Second Circuit, and were selected so as to be representative of the kinds of cases handled by the courts. For the purpose of the study, sentence disparity was defined as "dissimilar treatment by different judges of similarly situated defendants." The results revealed substantial disparity in the sentences meted out in the 20 cases. In 16 of the 20 cases, there was no unanimity on whether any incarceration was appropriate. Moreover, even when a prison sentence was imposed, there were large differences in the length of the term. It is doubtful that these findings surprised anyone. As one observer notes, "Whatever their intention, whatever their purposes, disparity . . . is documented anew with each new researcher in each new generation" (Gaylin, 1974: 13).

Sentencing disparity is a significant problem. It may, for example, breed inmate bitterness and resistance and thereby make the correctional task more difficult. Nevertheless, disparity may be less of a problem than *discrimination*. While disparity has an individual referent, the referent for discrimination is the aggregate. Discrimination is dissimilar sentences imposed by judges on the basis of defendants' social class, sex, or race. The difference between disparity and discrimination is similar to the distinction between statistical errors and bias. Errors are assumed to be random occurrences; over a period of time they cancel one another. Bias is systematic, one-directional, and constant.

Scholarly evidence on the issue of sentencing discrimination is mixed and confusing. John Hagan reviewed the findings from 20 studies of sentencing discrimination and concluded that "while there may be evidence of differential sentencing, knowledge of extra-legal offender characteristics [such as sex or race] contributes relatively little to our ability to predict judicial dispositions" (1974: 379). A second analysis gave him no cause to revise those conclusions (1983). This is the dominant view of the sentencing process and sentencing discrimination.

In 1980, the National Institute of Justice requested that the National Academy of Sciences establish a panel to review research on criminal sentencing and its impact. The panel was composed of specialists representing a variety of academic disciplines, methodological approaches, and criminal justice expertise. The determinants of criminal sentencing, and sentencing disparity, was one focus of the investigations. The panel reviewed research on the issue and also commissioned papers by experts. Drawing from this review process, the panel concluded that social scientists have a very limited understanding of the forces that influence the severity of criminal sentences: "Despite the number and diversity of factors investigated as determinants of sentences, two-thirds or more of the variance in sentence outcomes remains unexplained" (Blumstein *et al.*, 1983a: 10). But the National Academy panel also adopted another conclusion, one that supports the dominant position on sentencing discrimination: "Using a variety of different indicators, offense seriousness and offender's prior record emerge consistently as the key determinants of sentences" (Blumstein *et al.*, 1983a: 11). Some readers may see a contradiction in the panel's conclusions; it is difficult to see how both can be correct. Such is the state of knowledge about sentencing discrimination.

We point out, however, that the possible absence of discrimination at the sentencing stage of the criminal process says nothing about its existence at earlier stages. It is possible the criminal process discriminates so much against the poor and minorities that by the time of sentencing there is little of it in evidence. Suppose a sample of university students is drawn for purposes of studying the relationship between height and scoring ability in basketball. However, all those over 5'6" are excluded from the sample at the outset. The study then concludes that there is no appreciable relationship between height and scoring ability. This may be true for the sample studied, but only because it contains no tall persons. In Chapter 13 we will return to the problem of interpreting research on correctional processing.

## The Influence of Probation Officers

Although the growth of indeterminate sentencing strategies in the early decades of the 20th century did not provide the original opportunity to incorporate probation officers in the criminal courts, it lent strong support to probation officers' claims for a voice in the sentencing process. Today probation officers and programs are an integral part of the criminal justice process in America.

One of the principal duties of probation officers is to prepare presentence investigations for judges, to assist them in sentencing decisions. There is a long-held suspicion that probation officers exacerbate the problem of sentencing disparity and discrimination. To what extent is this true? To what extent do so-called professional staff either ameliorate or contribute to sentencing disparity? Robert M. Carter and Leslie T. Wilkins show that, both in the federal courts and in the California superior courts, there is a close relationship between probation officers' recommendations and the sentence of the court. In short, when probation officers recommend defendants for probation, the court usually complies; when probation officers recommend against granting probation, the court usually sentences to imprisonment.

Carter and Wilkins next examined the characteristics of criminal defendants that seemed to be associated with the decisions of both probation officers and judges. "These data indicate that there is considerable agreement between probation officers and judges as to the significance of certain factors and characteristics for decisions relating to probation or imprisonment recommendations and dispositions" (1967: 511). Both groups assigned major importance to such factors as the defendant's prior criminal record, the nature of the offense, and the number of previous arrests. These two findings led Carter and Wilkins to conclude that "disparities in sentencing are supported, at least in terms of recommendations, by the parole office member of the judicial 'influence group'" (1967: 514). In other words, probation officers' recommendations contribute to sentencing disparities.

These findings are supported and the analysis is extended in a study by Hagan of the presentencing behavior of probation officers in 17 cities in a western Canadian province. Questionnaires containing descriptions of hypothetical defendants were mailed to the probation officers, who were asked to complete a presentence report on each defendant. Hagan found that the 765 responding probation officers tended to be somewhat influenced in their decisions by extra-legal attributes of offenders such as race and sex. This was especially true in those courts where judges specifically request the probation officer's sentencing recommendations. Thus "the organizational arrangements that give the probation officer an advisory role in the court process may also introduce a channel of extra-legal influence." Hagan speculates that "the more traditional judges seem to be serving the interests of offenders best by resisting the expanding role of the probation officer" (1975: 635).

## The Juvenile Sentencing Process

Whereas adults are tried in criminal courts, juveniles usually are tried in a juvenile court. Typically, they are sentenced by the court to an indeterminate term of confinement not to exceed their minority. After sentencing, juveniles typically become wards of a state department of corrections (or youth commission), which retains custody of them until they are discharged. While wards of the state, juveniles may spend one or more periods of time in confinement, interspersed with other periods of *aftercare* (parole).

In 1982, juvenile courts in the United States handled an estimated 1,292,500 delinquency cases, a rate of 43.2 cases per 1,000 children 10 through 17 years of age (Nimick *et al.,* 1985: 8). This represents a substantial increase from the estimated rate of 19.8 in 1957. As with all measures of performance of correctional bureaucracies, the rate of cases handled by the juvenile court varies substantially among the 50 states. In 1982 it ranged from a low of 21.4 cases per 1,000 children in Pennsylvania to 84.6 in New Mexico. The reasons for this state-level variation are not clear, although it apparently has little to do with variation in the level of juvenile crime.

Most state sentencing codes provide that juvenile and adult courts have *concurrent jurisdiction* of juveniles charged with designated crimes. This means that beyond a certain age, juveniles who are charged with any of these crimes may, at the discretion of the court, be tried as adults in criminal court. For example, in some states a juvenile of 15 or older who is charged with murder or rape may be tried as an adult.

Not only are adults and juveniles ordinarily sentenced by different types of courts, but the types of sentences they receive vary as well. Because the state extends its *parens patriae* powers to the realm of juvenile justice, many claim that juveniles do not have a

"trial" in the literal sense of that term. Instead, a "friendly hearing" is held to determine what is in the best interests of "the
child." It is widely believed that since rules of
evidence and procedure and guarantees of
due process could interfere with this process,
they are abbreviated or dispensed with entirely. The judge is permitted to proceed in a
"parental fashion," to probe for the facts and
to arrive at a decision that meets the "needs
of the child."

In most respects, the research on juvenile
courts and court decision making parallels
research on adult criminal courts. Besides a
handful of excellent case studies of court
processing (for example, Emerson, 1969;
Bortner, 1982), there are dozens of statistical
analyses of sentencing variation (for example, Thomas and Cage, 1977; Liska and
Tausig, 1979; Horwitz and Wasserman, 1980;
Bailey and Peterson, 1981). Also, much of
the research on juvenile court dispositions is
informed by modest, low-level theoretical
propositions; studies based on theoretical
models of the state and criminal justice are
less common (for example, Carter and Clelland, 1979). As in the area of research on
adult courts, research on juvenile sentencing
shows considerable variation by community
context (for example, Cohen and Kluegel,
1978; Thomson and Zingraff, 1981; Dannefer and Schutt, 1982; Hasenfeld and Cheung,
1985). Like adult courts, juvenile court judges
became more punitive in sentencing during
the 1970s and 1980s (Nimick *et al.*, 1985;
Thomas and Bilchik, 1985; Bortner, 1986).
And finally, the results of research on juvenile sentencing are equally difficult to interpret. In fact, the cumulative lessons of
dozens of studies seem to defy theoretical
explanation and summary (McCarthy and
Smith, 1986). This continues to stimulate efforts to develop a refined theoretical understanding of sentencing processes (for example, Thornberry and Christenson, 1984;
Henretta *et al.*, 1986).

## The Attack on Official Discretion

Against this backdrop of persisting doubts
about sentencing, some parts of the state apparatus began to respond. These initial inroads appeared first in the area of juvenile
sentencing. Beginning in 1965, U.S. Supreme Court decisions abrogated the states'
arbitrary powers to deal with juvenile offenders without protection of due process
rights.

The Court also took a critical look at the
adult sentencing process, especially the use
of the death penalty (Bowers, 1984). Of the
3,859 persons executed by civil authorities in
the United States between 1930 and 1967, 54
percent were black. Of the 455 executed for
rape, 89 percent were black (U.S. Department of Justice, 1982). Although there are
dissenting assessments (for example, Kleck,
1981), many see this as evidence of massive
discrimination. A number of studies showed,
moreover, that the death penalty was much
more likely to be imposed in cases of black
offenders and white victims than in cases of
white offenders and black victims. One investigator, who has documented over 12,000
executions in the United States since 1622,
records only two cases in which a white was
executed for killing a black (Espy, 1980a:
172, 1980b). Marvin Wolfgang and Marc Reidel (1973) analyzed 1,265 rape convictions in
seven Southern states between 1945 and
1965. They found that 13 percent of the 823
blacks convicted of rape were sentenced to
death while only 2 percent of the 442 convicted white rapists received the death penalty. "Of the 317 black defendants with white
victims, 113 were sentenced to death (36%),
compared to only 19 of the 921 defendants
(2%) with all other victim–defendant racial
combinations" (Radelet and Vandiver, 1986:
103).

In 1972, in the landmark case of *Furman
v. Georgia* [408 U.S. (1971: 238)], the U.S.
Supreme Court ruled that the death penalty

was applied arbitrarily and therefore consti-tuted cruel and unusual punishment, a vio-lation of the Eighth Amendment to the Con-stitution. The Court split 5–4 and each of the nine justices wrote a separate opinion. In his opinion, Justice William O. Douglas observed:

> We know that the discretion of judges and juries in imposing the death penalty enables the penalty to be selectively applied, feeding prejudices against the accused if he is poor and despised, and lacking political clout, or if he is a member of a suspect or unpopular minority, and saving those who by social position may be in a more protected position (p. 255).

The 633 persons then condemned to death in 32 states, 58 percent of whom were black, had their sentences reduced to life imprison-ment (Radelet and Vandiver, 1986: 99–100).

Criticism of the sentencing process was not limited to use of the death penalty. In a broader context of calls for greater account-ability by public officials, attacks on unfet-tered judicial discretion gained new strength and momentum. A federal judge charged that "the almost unchecked and sweeping powers we give to judges in the fashioning of sentences are terrifying and intolerable for a society that professes devotion to the rule of law" (Frankel, 1973: 5). An anecdote may be instructive here. One of the authors recalls a day when a county sheriff delivered a pris-oner to the penitentiary reception center and presented the court papers to the custodial officer in charge. The prisoner had been sen-tenced to a flat two years, an impermissible sentence in Illinois at that time. Reluctantly, the captain told the sheriff that he could not accept the prisoner. Without recourse, the sheriff returned the prisoner to the county jail. When he was told what had transpired, the sentencing judge became angry. He had the prisoner returned to court immediately

and imposed a sentence of two years to two years and one minute. The next day the pris-oner was sent to the penitentiary and, this time, he was accepted. One can only wonder about the judge's temperament and knowl-edge of the state sentencing code.

Led by a coalition of prisoners, activist lawyers, and liberal academics, the attack on official discretion focused on three areas: the indeterminate sentence and parole, and their impacts on the prisoner and on the prison world. Until recent years, great dis-cretion and power over release was vested in state parole boards. In such states—Califor-nia was the outstanding example—judges gave offenders the sentence prescribed by statute, and the Adult Authority (parole board) met with them after their arrival in prison to make whatever reductions in the maximum sentence it deemed appropriate. An offender might go to prison with a sen-tence of 5 years to life only later to have the parole board cut the maximum sentence to 15 years.

The medical model and indeterminate sentencing practices were criticized for the anxiety and hostility they created in inmates who did not know their release date. Believ-ing that the key to release was in program-ming, many prisoners cynically participated in treatment programs of dubious value, in the hope their record would impress the pa-role board.

Some critics saw more subtle consequences of these sentencing practices. They argued that the indeterminate sentence under-mined inmate solidarity and thereby made it easier for prison officials to manage inmates. For instance, John Irwin claimed that the in-determinate sentence

> has [had] an important impact upon the con-vict in respect to his prison behavior. Generally, the inmate desires to present a favorable view of his progress in prison and/or remain largely inconspicuous to the prison administration.

[The indeterminate sentence,] among other things, has driven a wedge into convict solidarity (1970: 65).

### The Justice Model and Just Deserts

Liberal critics of unchecked official discretion and traditional sentencing practices proposed specific alternatives aimed at (1) the destruction of the individual treatment model of corrections; (2) the creation of a system of shorter, mandatory sentences; and (3) the extension of the sanction of imprisonment to a wider range of crimes—so that corporate and white-collar offenders also would face the threat of confinement. The purpose of these suggested reforms was to minimize or eliminate disparities and discrimination in criminal sentences (American Friends Service Committee, 1971). Liberal reformers called for precise, rigorous guidelines to structure and reduce judicial sentencing.

Several of these proposals were similar and found expression in what came to be known as the "justice model" of corrections (Fogel, 1975; Twentieth Century Fund, 1976). Like most liberal critics, proponents of the justice model were outraged by the gap between the rhetoric and reality of the indeterminate sentence and rehabilitation. They charged that "the deliberate masking of brutal practice with the rhetoric of rehabilitation is cruel and inhumane" (Fogel and Hudson, 1981: v). Professed goals of rehabilitation promised more than the state could deliver and were used as instruments of coercion as well. Under the justice model, imprisonment would be a form of "just deserts" for lawbreaking. Prisoners would be treated humanely and fairly, and would forfeit only those citizenship rights required to maintain order in the prison. Rehabilitation, if retained at all, would be limited to voluntary programs. Establishment of a justice model of corrections would mean that "prisons [would] better serve a democratic society

by operating under lawful constitutional standards of humaneness and prisoner involvement than by seeking their guidance from the latest psychological, medical and/or religious fad" (Fogel and Hudson, 1981: x).

Together with supporters of the justice model, liberals called for a drastic reduction in the use of imprisonment generally, while maintaining that it should be used primarily for those who committed "serious offenses." The backbone of their proposals was a system of presumptive, mandatory sentences.

A typical reform proposal begins by grading all felonies into categories on the basis of their seriousness, followed by statutory provision of presumptive terms of imprisonment for each type. Judges would be required to impose these *presumptive sentences* on defendants convicted of designated crimes. In most cases the sentencing statute would leave judges with some discretion by specifying a range of sentences from which they must choose. Therefore, coupled with the provision of presumptive sentences reformers called for statutory *guidelines* that judges should consider when imposing criminal sentences. *Aggravating factors,* such as the use of weapon by the defendant, could be cited to justify added harshness in the choice of a sentence. *Mitigating factors,* such as the nature and length of a defendant's record of employment, could be used to justify a less severe sentence. Judges would weigh the aggravating and mitigating factors and impose a sentence within the presumptive sentencing range.

> Suppose a defendant were convicted of armed robbery for the second time. Were no special circumstances of aggravation or mitigation shown, he would receive the disposition which the guidelines specify as the presumptive sentence for a second armed robbery. Were there several participants in the robbery and his role in the crime a peripheral one, however, this could be a mitigating circumstance permitting

a limited reduction below the presumptive sentence (von Hirsch, 1976: 101).

For the most part, liberals hoped to accomplish two objectives in their push for sentencing reform. First, they sought to reduce judicial discretion and therefore the sentencing disparity and injustice which, they argued, flow from it. And second, they pressed for a system of determinate, or flat, sentences. Liberals argued that if inmates had predictable release dates, their sense of injustice would be reduced. Under the proposals put forth by the Committee for the Study of Incarceration,

penalties will be scaled down substantially. Incarceration will be restricted to offenses that are serious—and most prison sentences kept relatively short. . . . Severity would thus be substantially reduced, but we emphasize: these suggested punishments would not be so easily avoided (von Hirsch, 1976: 140).

Liberals were not alone in their attacks on official discretion. Conservatives too were fearful of it. Unlike the liberals, however, conservatives pointed to the unprecedented "carnage" wreaked by offenders, attacked the "folly of rehabilitation" as a correctional objective, and called for greater emphasis on deterrence and incapacitation (for example, Regnery, 1985, 1986). They called for a revised sentencing code and process that would ensure specified punishment for specified offenders. Conservatives were willing to ban judicial discretion altogether if this would get the criminals off of the streets. Consequently, conservatives generally supported the move to develop controls on judicial discretion. Together with liberals, they worked to enact so-called determinate sentencing legislation (Greenberg and Humphries, 1980).

There was, however, only a limited community of interest between liberals and conservatives:

It must be stressed that while the means shared by conservatives and liberals had common elements, their ends did not. Virtually all liberal treatises advocating determinacy specified that sentence lengths . . . should be reduced or remain the same, and that care should be taken to avoid gradual sentence inflation after implementation of reforms. This concern was not shared by conservatives who, if anything, advocated lengthier sentences. . . . Conservatives supported the increased use of law to sanction undesirable conduct and imprisonment as the preferred sanction . . . (Goodstein, 1984: 13).

The 1970s and 1980s saw a wave of sentencing reform sweep across the United States. This movement was played out in state legislatures across the country (Messinger and Johnson, 1978; Martin, 1983; Goodstein and Hepburn, 1985).

## Sentencing Reform American Style

In one of the most dramatic overhauls of correctional strategy in the past 50 years, between 1971 and 1981 nearly 40 states revised their sentencing codes (von Hirsch and Hanrahan, 1981; U.S. Department of Justice, 1983c; Shane-DuBow *et al.*, 1985: 280). Twenty-five states made major changes in their criminal codes and another 15 made piecemeal changes. Fifteen states adopted determinate sentencing. Thirty-three enacted or increased the penalties in their repeat- or habitual-offender laws. Forty-nine states enacted mandatory sentencing laws for selected offenses. Seven states experimented with sentencing guidelines. At the same time,

27 states tightened parole eligibility requirements, 14 states did not . . . , and eight states eliminated parole altogether. Four states loosened parole eligibility, but of those four, two loosened parole eligibility for some offenses

and tightened it for others. . . . Twelve states decreased good time, 11 increased it, and 28 did not change it (Shane-DuBow *et al.*, 1985: 280).

The move to revise was so intense that already "there have been modifications to initial modifications of sentencing statutes, alterations to the original underlying intent of new laws . . . and sometimes, misunderstandings as to what the reforms actually were and what they actually did" (Shane-DuBow *et al.*, 1985: 279).

The changes have modified the language of sentencing, giving us "presumptive sentences," and "aggravating" and "mitigating factors," "sentencing guidelines," "mandatory minimum sentences," and "class X" felony laws aimed at "career criminals." What is impressive about the wave of sentencing reform is that it reflects diverse intentions, plans, and notions of crime control. As one investigator notes, "The extent and diversity of sentencing reforms . . . represent a broad spectrum of theory and practice sometimes in conflict with each other" (Shane-DuBow *et al.*, 1985: 12). We can illustrate some of this diversity in the sentencing reforms enacted since 1971.

## Adjustments to Indeterminacy

Of the 36 states that retained indeterminate sentencing, a substantial majority modified some elements of the sentencing code. For example, Arkansas revamped its sentencing code in piecemeal fashion over several years. Although it retained a determinate sentencing scheme, Arkansas nevertheless raised the minimum sentence for all its felony classes (see Table 4.1). The Arkansas legislature also enacted more stringent penalties for repeat offenders. "A habitual offender is defined as someone convicted of a felony who has had more than two prior felony convictions or who has been found guilty

of more than two felony offenses" (Shane-DuBow *et al.*, 1985: 31). Permissible sentence ranges for habitual offenders are harsher than for other offenders. Habitual offenders are not eligible for probation. The Arkansas legislature also provided more stringent penalties for those who use a deadly weapon in the commission of a crime. For all offenders, both parole eligibility and good time were tightened. Arkansas judges retain a great deal of discretion in their sentencing decisions.

### Presumptive Sentences and Guidelines

Sentencing reform in Minnesota offers a marked contrast to the changes made in Arkansas (Goodstein and Hepburn, 1985; Shane-DuBow *et al.*, 1985). Minnesota enacted a system of presumptive sentence ranges and sentencing guidelines constructed by a sentencing commission. The guidelines include a ten-category scale for offense severity and a seven-point scale used to measure prior convictions. The two scales are merged into a 70-cell matrix.

Table 4.2 shows the dispositions and presumptive sentences available to Minnesota judges for each cell in the matrix. They suggest whether a defendant should be sent to prison and, if so, for how long. Acceptable aggravated and mitigating factors are spelled

TABLE 4.1   **Felony Sentences in Arkansas**

| Class | Prior to March, 1981 | Act 620 Changes Effective March, 1981 |
|---|---|---|
| Class Y | — | 10–40 years |
| Class A | 5–50 years | 6–30 years |
| Class B | 3–20 years | 5–20 years |
| Class C | 2–10 years | 4–10 years |
| Class D | Less than 5 years | Less than 6 years |

SOURCE: Shane-DuBow *et al.* (1985: 29)

out. Unacceptable factors, such as race, sex, and employment status are spelled out as well. A judge is permitted to use aggravating and mitigating factors to tailor decisions for specific defendants.

If the judge deviates from the presumptive sentence by ten percent or less for aggravating or mitigating factors, the sentence is considered as conforming to the guidelines. . . . The guidelines also provide presumptive rules for

TABLE 4.2 **Presumptive Sentencing Lengths (in Months), Minnesota**

Boldface numbers within the grid denote the range within which a judge may sentence without the sentence being deemed a departure.

| | | | | | Criminal History Score | | | |
|---|---|---|---|---|---|---|---|---|
| Severity Levels of Conviction Offense | | 0 | 1 | 2 | 3 | 4 | 5 | 6 or more |
| Unauthorized use of motor vehicle Possession of marijuana | I | 12* | 12* | 12* | 15 | 18 | 21 | 24 |
| Theft-related crimes ($150–$2,500) Sale of marijuana | II | 12* | 12* | 14 | 17 | 20 | 23 | 27 25–29 |
| Theft crimes ($150–$2,500) | III | 12* | 13 | 16 | 19 | 22 21–23 | 27 25–29 | 32 30–34 |
| Burglary–felony intent Receiving stolen goods ($150–$2,500) | IV | 12* | 15 | 18 | 21 | 25 24–26 | 32 30–34 | 41 37–45 |
| Simple robbery | V | 18 | 23 | 27 | 30 29–31 | 38 36–40 | 46 43–49 | 54 50–58 |
| Assault, 2nd degree | VI | 21 | 26 | 30 | 34 33–35 | 44 42–46 | 54 50–58 | 65 60–70 |
| Aggravated robbery | VII | 24 23–25 | 32 30–34 | 41 38–44 | 49 45–53 | 65 60–70 | 81 75–87 | 97 90–104 |
| Assault, 1st degree Criminal sexual conduct, 1st degree | VIII | 43 41–45 | 54 50–58 | 65 60–70 | 76 71–81 | 95 89–101 | 113 106–120 | 132 124–140 |
| Murder, 3rd degree | IX | 97 94–100 | 119 116–122 | 127 124–130 | 149 143–155 | 176 168–184 | 205 195–215 | 230 218–242 |
| Murder, 2nd degree | X | 116 111–121 | 140 133–147 | 162 153–171 | 203 192–214 | 243 231–255 | 284 270–298 | 324 309–339 |

1st degree murder is excluded from the guidelines by law and continues to have a mandatory life sentence.

*One year and one day
**The dark heavy line is the dispositional line; above the line indicates probationary sentences (OUT), under the line indicates sentences of incarceration (IN).

SOURCE: Shane-DuBow *et al.* (1985: 165)

the decision to award concurrent and consecutive sentences. Deviation from the guideline ranges is acceptable so long as judges provide written justifications for their decisions. . . . [The Minnesota law] abolished parole review, thus inmates are released at the expiration of their sentences minus earned good time. . . . Once released, the offender serves a period of "supervised release" equivalent to the total amount of good time earned (Goodstein, 1984: 22–24).

Minnesota's revised law represents perhaps the purest effort to devise a determinate sentencing scheme.

## Mandatory Sentences

Connecticut's 1981 sentencing code presents additional contrasts. It provides for determinate sentences, eliminates discretionary parole and parole supervision, redefines "persistent offenders," reduces good time

TABLE 4.3  **Mandatory Minimum Sentences, Connecticut**

| Offense | Mandatory Minimum Sentence |
|---|---|
| Assault I (B Felony) | 5 years |
| Assault I, victim 60 years or older (B Felony) | |
| Assault II, victim 60 years or older (D Felony) | 2 years |
| Assault III with a deadly weapon, victim 60 years or older (D Felony) | 3 years |
| Sexual assault I with a deadly weapon (B Felony) | 5 years |
| Burglary I (B Felony) | 5 years |
| Robbery I (B Felony) | 5 years |
| Manslaughter I | 5 years |
| Kidnapping II | 5 years |
| Manslaughter II | 3 years |

SOURCE: Shane-DuBow *et al.* (1985: 51)

for some sentences, and provides a system of mandatory minimum sentences. The mandatory sentence provisions stipulate that judges must sentence all offenders convicted of designated offenses (see Table 4.3). In other respects, however, the Connecticut law leaves judges with considerable discretion.

## Assessments of Sentencing Reform

What have been the consequences of the massive changes in sentencing codes that have occurred in recent years?

### The Death Penalty

The attack on the historical use of the death penalty was in the forefront of the movement to limit judicial sentencing discretion. Beginning in 1967, executions were successfully blocked, pending U.S. Supreme Court review of issues related to the use of the death penalty. After the *Furman* decision, the states moved quickly to rewrite their death penalty statutes so they would pass appellate muster. In Florida, a special session of the legislature was called to enact a new death penalty law immediately after the 1972 decision. Other states quickly followed suit.

The Florida death penalty statute employs the techniques and language of liberal reformers. Nine aggravating and seven mitigating factors are listed to guide judges and juries in their sentencing decisions (Radelet and Vandiver, 1986). In 1976, the U.S. Supreme Court upheld the constitutionality of Florida's new law. By 1985, 37 states had enacted new death penalty statutes (Legal Defense Fund, 1985). In 1976, the Court ruled that mandatory death penalty statutes were unconstitutional and approved the new "guided discretion" statutes. Available data show that the new statutes have done little to reduce racial discrimination in the use of the death penalty:

In the time between the 1976 Supreme Court decisions and September 1, 1985, 46 men and one woman were executed in the U.S. . . . Only four of the 47 executed defendants had black victims (one other had both white and black victims). . . . [All but three] of these post–*Furman* executions occurred in states of the former Confederacy. As of August 1985 there were 1,520 men and 20 women sentenced to death in the United States. Of these, 1,540 inmates, 783 (50.8%) were white, 640 (41.56%) were black, [and] 113 (7.34%) were other minorities. . . . Between 1930 and 1967, 50.09% of those executed for homicide were nonwhite, and in August 1985, 49.50% of those on death row were nonwhite—a difference of less than 2%. Despite all the emphasis on formal standards after *Furman*, it appears that the racial composition of the condemned population has changed very little (Radelet and Vandiver, 1986: 100).

The same authors conclude: "The idea that all of us are born with an equal chance of eventually dying in the electric chair remains a myth" (1986: 109).

## Prison Populations

As we noted earlier, the population of America's prisons began to rise in the early 1970s and continued into the late 1980s. The onset of this increase preceded the sentencing reform movement and "increases in prison population [occurred] in states that . . . adopted reforms and those that [did] not" (Blumstein *et al.*, 1983a: 33). This makes it difficult to determine to what extent the latter contributed to the former, and there is disagreement on the issue (Nagin, 1979; Blumstein *et al.*, 1983a; Shane-DuBow *et al.*, 1985; Carroll and Cornell, 1985).

As America's imprisoned population rose to unprecedented levels, it also became increasingly black. Here too there is disagreement whether new sentencing codes and practices have exacerbated this trend (Christianson, 1983; Hawkins, 1985; Langan, 1985).

## Other Consequences of Sentencing Reform

There are numerous case studies of the implementation and impact of sentencing reform in one or more of the states (Clear *et al.*, 1977; Nagin, 1979; Brewer *et al.*, 1981; Casper *et al.*, 1983; Hewitt and Clear, 1983; Covey and Mande, 1985; Davies, 1985; Goodstein and Hepburn, 1985; Kramer and Lubitz, 1985; Miethe and Moore, 1985). The bulk of this evaluation research falls into two categories. One group of investigators has examined changes in *perceptions* following sentencing reforms. A second group has examined objective changes in sentencing and correctional *practices*. Aside from the impacts we have discussed already, what does this body of research suggest about the impacts of sentencing reform? The findings are not summarized easily. Given the substantial diversity in sentencing code changes, this is hardly surprising.

The implementation of determinate sentencing procedures apparently improved inmate perceptions of release certainty and sentencing equity. However, one investigator concludes, "these perceptions apparently do little to influence the types of adjustments they make to prison life" (Goodstein, 1984: 60–61).

As regards the impact of sentencing reform on criminal justice practices and outcomes, the studies suggest that *formal* compliance with the requirements of reform legislation has been widespread. Informally, however, "when participants considered the new rules inappropriate, they routinely attempted to circumvent the procedural changes by filtering out those cases they believed should not be subject to [the new] rules" (Blumstein *et al.*, 1983a: 219). It appears that judges and lawyers modified case-processing procedures to achieve dis-positions of cases that were different from those specified in the new sentencing codes (Blumstein *et al.*, 1983a).

In some states, sentencing and parole guidelines backed by statutory or adminis-trative enforcement have reduced sentenc-ing disparity (Blumstein *et al.*, 1983a). Never-theless, this change has been modest. None of the various approaches to sentencing re-form have been shown to affect crime rates (Shane-DuBow *et al.*, 1985).

John R. Hepburn and Lynne Goodstein (1986) suggest that sentencing reform has centralized the power of correctional bu-reaucracies in some states. Before reform, the power of prison officials was limited by parole boards or similar administrative bod-ies that controlled inmate release. In states that have eliminated their parole boards, prison officials have consolidated their con-trol over release decisions.

Although there is substantial variation among the states, most observers agree that the overall impact of sentencing reform bears only modest resemblance to the hopes entertained by its liberal supporters. How-ever, there was substantial variation in the effects of sentencing reform; faithful com-pliance with the spirit and letter of the new laws was better in some states than in others. Blumstein *et al.* suggest that

> the extent of compliance with reforms . . . var-ied with: (a) the level of organizational or po-litical support for the reform; (b) the existence of statutory or administrative authority sup-porting the procedural requirement; and (c) the existence of credible monitoring and en-forcement mechanisms (1983a: 29).

Many of the original supporters of sen-tencing reform were dismayed and became cynical by the broad thrust of the reforms. Although the changes were meant to pro-mote equity and justice in sentencing, con-servative scholars and politicians coopted the movement for their own repressive purposes:

> The changes . . . bear only a superficial resem-blance to the principles of justice. While some of the changes may bring limited benefits to some defendants or prisoners, these benefits are likely to be compensated by other provi-sions which are detrimental to prisoner inter-ests. Primarily, these changes are designed to rationalize and thereby restore legitimacy to a system that has come under sharp criticism for its irrational and discriminatory practices (1977a: 20).

The variable results of sentencing reform suggest what can happen to well-intentioned proposals whose fate must be decided in a class society characterized by gross inequities in the distribution of property, privilege, and power (Greenberg and Humphries, 1980).

## A Look Ahead

The sentencing reform movement of re-cent years is not without historical precedent in the United States (Gatz and Vito, 1982; Albanese, 1984). On more than one occasion in the past 100 years, concern about lenient or harsh sentencing has prompted dramatic changes in dominant sentencing practices. It is interesting to ponder the eventual fate of the most recent sentencing reform move-ment in the light of Max Weber's distinction between two types of rationality in law: for-mal and substantive. Rationality here refers to the nature of the reasoning process by which legal decisions are reached. A formally rational decision is one that is reached in ac-cordance with formal, logical rules; it is logi-cally "correct." A substantively rational deci-sion is one reached on the basis of ethical or technical considerations; it is substantively "correct."

According to Weber, there is an inevitable

tension and conflict between these two types of rationality in law. Decisions that are formally rational often prove to be substantively irrational (that is, violating ethical or technical principles). Similarly, decisions that are substantively rational sometimes appear to be formally irrational. A son who intentionally killed his aged and terminally ill mother in order to spare her further suffering, though guilty of homicide, probably would not be sentenced to life in prison. To do so would be formally logical (that is, consistent with the logic of the criminal statutes), but it probably would be seen as a substantive injustice, as a violation of ethical principles.

Weber argued that an emphasis on one or the other of these two types of rationality is characteristic of legal systems. Further, over a period of time they tend to succeed each other in a cyclical fashion. Periods in which there is much emphasis on formal rationality give rise to criticism on substantive grounds.

This eventually produces a situation in which substantive rationality is ascendant.

Judicial decision making, which draws upon the supposedly arcane behavioral knowledge of treatment experts, may lead to sentencing practices that are abhorred on formal grounds. Lengthy periods of confinement for relatively minor infractions, even when this is justified as in offenders' "best interests" and intended to "meet their needs," strike many as legally indefensible. The rapid development of retributive sentencing practices presents the same potential for substantively irrational sentences. In fact, the entire sentencing reform movement may be a contemporary example of the process to which Weber pointed. It may confidently be predicted that in time these reforms, if they actually produce more rigidity and severity in the sentencing process, will be attacked for the substantive injustices they produce.

# 5

# Jails and
# Juvenile Detention
# Centers

A diverse set of agencies is clustered under the umbrella term *corrections*. Some have been the object of extensive theorizing and research, while others have received much less scrutiny. Paradoxically, jails, one of the oldest forms of correctional institutions, have been little studied. On the other hand, prisons and training schools have held a special fascination for investigators. In this chapter, and in the four that follow, we review what is known about a variety of correctional structures and strategies.

## Use of the Jail

### Historical Development

The jail has the longest history of any type of penal institution; it can be traced to the earliest forms of civilization and govern-

ment. Some of its predecessors were the unscalable pits, dungeons, suspended cages, and sturdy trees to which prisoners were chained pending trial on criminal charges (Mattick, 1974).

From the time of its adoption in America, the jail has remained a particularly local institution that reflects all the variation in financing, structure, and operation characteristic of local communities and governments (Flynn, 1983). The majority of American jails are located in rural areas, usually in the county seat. They were built from 50 to 80 years ago, hold small numbers of inmates, and are dirty and dilapidated. Although far fewer in number, a second major type of jail is located in large urban areas. Each of these jails holds as many as several thousand inmates and, collectively, they confine more than 50 percent of the nation's jail population. Of the total 3,338 jails in the United

States in 1983, 63 percent held fewer than 50 inmates, 30 percent held from 50 to 249 inmates, and 7 percent confined 250 or more inmates (U.S. Department of Justice, 1984). The typical local jail is under the control of the police, usually the county sheriff (American Correctional Association, 1978). The physical facilities, programs, and security of America's local jails vary greatly. Some are clean and well-run and secure, whereas others are both physically and operationally deplorable.

*The Jail's Inhabitants*

Historically, the jail has served multiple purposes and confined a diverse population. As one observer notes:

> The American jail is a curious hybrid between the 10th-century gaol with its principal function being to detain arrested offenders until they were tried, and the 15th- and 16th-century house of correction with their special function being punishment of minor offenders, debtors, vagrants, and beggars (Flynn, 1973: 49).

This population diversity continues today. Jails confine in one facility such disparate groups as persons awaiting trial, inmates serving misdemeanor sentences, suspected mental patients, alleged parole violators, felony prisoners in transit, and chronic drunkenness offenders in the process of "drying out." Moreover, some jails continue to serve as a place of pretrial detention for juveniles. In 1983, nearly 1 percent of the nationwide daily jail population were juveniles (U.S. Department of Justice, 1984: 4).

In 1983, the U.S. Bureau of the Census surveyed jail inmates in America. The data, although now several years old, provide the most complete and up-to-date picture of jail

inmates. Investigators conducted personal interviews with a sample of 5,785 jail inmates in July and August 1983. Inmates' age, marital status, educational attainment, work experience, confinement status, and income before incarceration were recorded. The investigations also examined inmates' length of sentence, most serious offense with which they were charged or sentenced, bail status, participation in rehabilitative programs, and past criminal record. Estimates for the total American jail population of approximately 207,783 persons are based on responses given by this sample of inmates. Table 5.1 is a summary of selected characteristics of jail inmates in the United States.

The reality of the assertion that the jail exists to deal with underclass conduct could

---

**PANEL 5.1**

*An Experience in a Suburban County Jail*

**M**y first night in jail, after sentencing, was one I shall never forget! After witnessing all the crying and carrying on of my family, relatives, and friends just hours before, I was in no mood to laugh and joke with the rest of the inmates on our tier in the county jail that night. As you might expect, since our county is less known for violence than most, those in our county were less violent. In fact, they were fairly decent fellows, as far as convicts go. All were not convicts, however; naturally we had our share of petty thieves, traffic violators, and drunks which made up over half of the population. My stay of ten days in the county jail was actually quite pleasant.

SOURCE: Dae H. Chang and Warren B. Armstrong, eds., *The Prison: Voices from the Inside* (Cambridge, Mass.: Schenkman, 1972), pp. 225–26.

not be any clearer than it is in Table 5.1. In no way could the profile of jail inmates be said to approximate that of the general population. Instead, jail inmates are disproportionately black, poor, and disadvantaged in other ways as well. Data such as these have led one critic of the jail to refer to it as "the ultimate ghetto of the criminal justice system" (Goldfarb, 1975).

An interesting revelation in the 1983 jail survey is the substantial variation between states in the number of jail inmates per 100,000 population. Ignoring Alaska's unusually low rate (8.0) and confining our attention to the 48 contiguous states, Table 5.2 shows that Iowa had a jail population in 1983 of 29 inmates per 100,000 population; the comparable rate for Georgia was 178. The reasons for this variation are not understood by social scientists.

TABLE 5.1   **Selected Social, Economic, and Legal Characteristics of Jail Inmates in the United States, 1983**

| | Percent | | Percent |
|---|---|---|---|
| *RACE | | CONFINEMENT STATUS | |
| White | 59% | Convicted | 59 |
| Black | 40 | Unconvicted | 40 |
| Other | 1 | BAIL STATUS OF | |
| *SEX | | UNCONVICTED JAIL INMATES | |
| Male | 93 | Not set | 13 |
| Female | 7 | Set, but not released | 82 |
| | | Released and returned | 5 |
| AGE | | | |
| Under 18 | 1 | LEGAL REPRESENTATION OF | |
| 18–24 | 40 | UNCONVICTED JAIL INMATES | |
| 25–34 | 39 | Without counsel | 25 |
| 35 or older | 19 | Court-appointed counsel | 60 |
| | | Hired own counsel | 15 |
| EDUCATION | | | |
| Less than 12 years | 59 | PRE-ARREST EMPLOYMENT | |
| 12 or more years | 41 | STATUS | |
| | | Employed | 53 |
| MARITAL STATUS | | Unemployed | 47 |
| Never married | 54 | | |
| Married | 21 | PRE-ARREST MEDIAN ANNUAL | |
| Other (separated, divorced, | | INCOME FOR THOSE FREE AT | |
| widowed) | 25 | LEAST ONE YEAR | $5,486 |
| CURRENT OFFENSE | | PRE-ARREST MEDIAN | |
| †Property | 49 | MONTHLY INCOME FOR | |
| Public order | 20 | THOSE FREE LESS THAN | |
| ‡Violent | 19 | ONE YEAR | $ 462 |
| Drug | 10 | | |

*These data are for 1984 (U.S. Department of Justice, 1986d).
†Includes primarily burglary, robbery, auto theft, larceny, stolen property, fraud, forgery, and embezzlement.
‡Includes primarily murder, attempted murder, manslaughter, rape, sexual assault, and assault.
SOURCE: U.S. Department of Justice (1985c).

**TABLE 5.2  Jails and Inmates by State and Ratio to General Population, 1983 \*\***

| | Jails | Average Daily Population | Number of Inmates Per 100,000 Population* |
|---|---|---|---|
| UNITED STATES | 3,338 | 227,541 | 98 |
| Alabama | 108 | 4,884 | 113 |
| Alaska | 5 | 34 | 8 |
| Arizona | 31 | 2,913 | 99 |
| Arkansas | 89 | 1,630 | 69 |
| California | 142 | 40,662 | 166 |
| Colorado | 60 | 2,523 | 88 |
| Florida | 103 | 14,950 | 137 |
| Georgia | 203 | 10,797 | 178 |
| Idaho | 36 | 661 | 61 |
| Illinois | 98 | 9,262 | 77 |
| Indiana | 93 | 3,838 | 66 |
| Iowa | 90 | 905 | 29 |
| Kansas | 86 | 1,313 | 55 |
| Kentucky | 96 | 3,833 | 100 |
| Louisiana | 94 | 8,207 | 192 |
| Maine | 14 | 557 | 49 |
| Maryland | 30 | 4,629 | 107 |
| Massachusetts | 17 | 3,516 | 57 |
| Michigan | 87 | 7,624 | 84 |
| Minnesota | 67 | 2,208 | 47 |
| Mississippi | 91 | 2,473 | 97 |
| Missouri | 129 | 3,937 | 76 |
| Montana | 50 | 416 | 50 |
| Nebraska | 67 | 951 | 53 |
| Nevada | 23 | 964 | 105 |
| New Hampshire | 11 | 492 | 50 |
| New Jersey | 32 | 6,297 | 80 |
| New Mexico | 35 | 1,308 | 96 |
| New York | 72 | 16,371 | 91 |
| North Carolina | 99 | 3,885 | 57 |
| Ohio | 121 | 7,578 | 66 |
| Oklahoma | 104 | 2,490 | 67 |
| Oregon | 39 | 2,342 | 87 |
| Pennsylvania | 77 | 10,265 | 85 |
| South Carolina | 58 | 2,840 | 82 |
| South Dakota | 31 | 337 | 45 |
| Tennessee | 108 | 6,269 | 128 |
| Texas | 273 | 15,366 | 97 |
| Utah | 24 | 944 | 56 |
| Virginia | 95 | 6,226 | 103 |
| Washington | 65 | 3,660 | 84 |
| West Virginia | 54 | 1,106 | 52 |
| Wisconsin | 72 | 3,118 | 64 |
| Wyoming | 26 | 383 | 88 |

*June 30, 1983
\*\*Data not reported for Connecticut, Delaware, Hawaii, North Dakota, Rhode Island, and
  Vermont.
SOURCE: U.S. Department of Justice (1984).

Beginning in the early 1970s, both the *number* of persons incarcerated in America's prisons and also the *rate* of imprisonment (number of persons incarcerated per 100,000 population) began to increase. By the end of the decade they stood at unprecedented levels, and their upward climb continued into the 1980s (Flanagan and McGarrell, 1986: 531). In some states, the combination of this development and judicial decrees capping prison populations generated a variety of operational problems for jail managers and employees. For example, some jail administrators increasingly are compelled to retain convicted and sentenced felons until space for them becomes available in prison. In 1983–84, the percentage of American jails that held inmates because of crowding elsewhere increased 41 percent, although those inmates still represented only 4 percent of all inmates in the 621 largest jails. Most of the increase was in the number of inmates held for state correctional authorities (U.S. Department of Justice, 1986d).

*Jail Conditions*

The general public becomes aware of jail conditions only through the misfortune of family members or acquaintances, or whenever a scandal or media exposé takes place. The latter occurs with predictable regularity, especially in larger cities. Filthy, dilapidated, unsafe facilities with inadequate food and medical care are characteristic of America's jails. Supervision is weak or absent, inmates are housed in large heterogeneous groups, and jails are run so as to ensure minimal problems and disruptions for custodial staff.

This leaves the inmates free to work out their own internal order. Under such conditions, individuals experienced in crime and accustomed to life in jails and penitentiaries assume positions of informal leadership and

control (see Panel 5.2). Daniel Glaser notes that "control over inmate behavior usually can be achieved by other inmates more immediately, directly, and completely in jails than in other types of confinement institutions, such as penitentiaries or state hospitals" (1971: 239). A glimpse of the extreme abuses that can result under such conditions is provided in a 1968 report of sexual assaults in the Philadelphia city prison system. The study found that such assaults were epidemic, and went on to state that "virtually every slightly built young man committed by the courts is sexually approached within a day or two after his admission to prison. Many of these young men are repeatedly raped by gangs of inmates" (Davis, 1968: 9). More recent research suggests that these extreme forms of predation may have decreased in frequency in American jails (Gibbs, 1982; Irwin, 1985). Nevertheless, they remain a source of great concern for many jail inmates.

Sociologist and ex-offender John Irwin's analysis of the jail is useful here. It is based on more than a year of observation of the San Francisco county jails, shorter periods of observation in several other jails, and his own experiences "in eight different city and county jails for periods up to 120 days" (1985: xii–xiii). During his period of observation in the San Francisco jails, Irwin also randomly selected 100 persons charged with felonies and 100 charged with misdemeanors from the jail's booking records. With a research assistant, he interviewed the felony arrestees and followed both samples of cases through the jail and court process until they were resolved. The general public, Irwin argues, assumes that

the jail holds a collection of dangerous criminals. But familiarity and close inspection reveal that the jail holds only a very few persons who fit the popular conception of a criminal—a predator who seriously threatens the lives and property of ordinary citizens (1985: 1).

Irwin argues instead that the American jail primarily holds persons who belong to a specific social category, the *rabble*. Members of

the rabble class share two characteristics, *detachment* and *disrepute:*

They are detached because they are not well integrated into conventional society, they are not members of conventional social organiza-

---

**PANEL 5.2**

## *The Cook County [Chicago] Jail*

When I entered the Cook County Jail I was assigned to cellblock H-4. This was intended for "young offenders," but it was a madhouse. There were over 140 inmates in a cellblock intended for 84. Inmates slept on every inch of floor space available, and fighting was an hourly occurrence. In the Cook County Jail only the strong survive as men—the weak are used for the sexual expression of the strong, the weak do the work.

Each cellblock was run by three inmates, the strongest, and no officer ever came inside the cellblock. During the time I was on H-4 (two months) no officer ever came inside. The officers allowed the count to be taken by the three strongest inmates, the food was distributed by these inmates, the cells assigned when they became available, etc.

The three inmates who run the cellblock or tier have titles as follows: the "Barn Boss," who is in charge of discipline among the inmates—the "Assistant Barn Boss" who, as his title implies, assists the "Barn Boss" in keeping discipline, and the "Tier Clerk," who keeps the count and assigns the cells, and handles the commissary orders (a very lucrative job).

While I was "Tier Clerk" on H-4 I also assisted the two "Barn Bosses" in keeping discipline because we were so very overcrowded, thus overworked. Usually, if someone got out of line on the tier it was neces-

sary to give them only a warning. However, if this warning was ignored, he didn't receive a second warning. He got his skull cracked. At night, after everyone was locked in their cells (the three men—the barn bosses and clerk's cells were never locked), the officer would open the offender's cell, and the three of us would go in on him. When we beat an inmate we used clubs, referred to as "shit-sticks," and the injuries were usually serious enough to require hospital treatment. After the inmate had been beaten he was dragged to the front of the tier, thrown into a bull-pen, and picked up by an officer. They never came back to that tier again, and they knew better than to act up on the new tier they were sent to after being released from the hospital. I beat one inmate before I became "Tier Clerk," and helped beat several others while "Tier Clerk."

I would also like to add that if a man wishes to survive in comfort in the Cook County Jail he must obtain a position of authority on his tier. These three positions are often fought for, the strongest holding them. I remember that Murphy, the "Tier Clerk," and the "Barn Boss" at the time, a fellow named Simms, used to practice boxing everyday. It was necessary and they became quite good.

SOURCE: Dae H. Chang and Warren B. Armstrong, eds., *The Prison: Voices from the Inside* (Cambridge, Mass.: Schenkman, 1972), pp. 49–50.

tions, they have few ties to conventional social networks, and they are carriers of unconventional values and beliefs. They are disreputable because they are perceived as irksome, offensive, threatening, capable of arousal, even pro-revolutionary (1985: 2).

### Daily Routine

As with all correctional structures, the day-to-day operations of the jail are designed to maximize the smooth, efficient processing of large numbers of inmates. This is accomplished primarily by routine work and operational procedures. Disruptions and conditions that are believed to threaten this routine, such as overcrowding and inmates with psychological problems, are among the principal concerns of jail administrators and employees. They are less concerned about the nearly total absence of constructive daily activities for inmates (Gibbs, 1983).

The personnel, size, physical facilities, and program offerings of local jails show considerable variation. But generally, the daily routine in American jails is one of unrelieved idleness. Card playing, conversations, meditation, and occasional television viewing are the only available recreational options. Only a small proportion of the total jail population has access to any social or rehabilitative services and programs. These programs are far more likely to be offered in large jails than in small ones. In 1972,

> approximately six out of every ten jails provided facilities for religious services, but no other single type of program was found in a majority of jails. Alcoholic treatment programs were available in only about one-third of the jails and drug addiction treatment programs in approximately one-fourth. Programs of inmate counseling, remedial education, vocational training, and job placements were found in slightly fewer than one-fifth of all jails. . . . In all, only about one-tenth of the inmate

population of the Nation's jails participated in federally and locally sponsored programs, religious services excepted (U.S. Department of Justice, n.d.: 9).

Only 8 percent of all sentenced jail inmates in the United States were participating in a work-release program in 1972.

> A related practice, namely, allowing selected sentenced inmates to serve their time on weekends, was permitted by nearly half the Nation's jails, including almost three out of every five of the large jails. Only about 900 inmates were serving their sentences on weekends, however (U.S. Dept. of Justice, n.d.: 10).

Along with other correctional structures, America's jails came under intensified judicial scrutiny during the 1970s and 1980s. In 1983, 24 percent of the 621 American jails that had an average daily inmate population of 100 or more were under court order to improve jail conditions. Of these jails, 47 percent were cited for deficient medical facilities and services, and 54 percent for inadequate recreational facilities or programs (U.S. Department of Justice, 1986d).

### Reform Proposals

The jail has been a disgrace to every generation since its inception. Each has called for its reform. The impetus to jail reform probably gained momentum in recent years because of inmates' efforts to improve their plight through court action. For example,

> in a case involving the Jefferson Parish Jail in Louisiana, the court was concerned about specific situations in the jail, particularly the many mentally disturbed people who are housed there and the physical conditions of the place which the court called "a combination medieval dungeon and zoo," used simply to "stow people" (Goldfarb, 1975: 436).

The fact that jails are locally controlled has long been seen as a fundamental impediment to reform. "Jails are left in a paradoxical situation: localities cling tenaciously to them but are unwilling or unable to meet even minimal standards. 'The problem of American jails, put most concisely, is the problem of local control'" (National Advisory Commission, 1973: 274).

There is no shortage of contemporary proposals for jail reform. Four specifically deal with local governments' refusal or fiscal inability to provide clean, safe, and adequately staffed jails with even minimal recreational and rehabilitative programs: (1) minimum standards for the construction and operation of jails; (2) state inspection or control of local jails; (3) the development of regional jails; (4) the development of diversified institutions for the jail's heterogeneous population; and (5) contracting with private corporations to operate jails.

At least two organizations, the Federal Bureau of Prisons and the American Correctional Association (1981), have developed and published minimum standards for the construction and operation of jails. Although proposals of this type will be discussed at greater length in Chapter 11, it will suffice now to point out that these efforts have met with limited success in mitigating the problems of jails in America.

In recent years some states have enacted legislation that transfers control of local jails to state government. Given the recency of this development, we do not know if it will succeed in ameliorating some of the traditional shortcomings of jails. However, if we can judge from the condition of America's prisons, which long have been under state control, we should not expect dramatic changes.

Many states have established procedures for state inspection of local jails, with the objective using state expertise and fiscal incentives to improve local jail conditions. The principal difficulty with such efforts is the absence of an effective means of enforcing jail standards. As of 1976, "there were 21 states without legislation which provides for enforcement and 34 states without legislation requiring any kind of jail inspection" (Matheny, 1976: 139).

Regional jails serve multiple cities or counties in one geographical area of a state, providing a way for fiscally poor counties that otherwise could not afford a modern jail to pool their resources. Data on the number of jails in the United States suggest that this movement has made some headway in recent years. While there were 4,037 jails in the U.S.

---

**PANEL 5.3**

*The Tombs (New York City)*

The cell—five by eight, with a seven-foot ceiling—was constructed of steel plate, with the usual bars on the front. I had a cot without a mattress, a toilet without seat, a diminutive wash basin with a single cold water spigot, a steel seat and a table, hinged to the wall. I was locked in the cell 19 hours a day. It was hot in the Tombs in August—and it smelled. No air moved near the ventilator opening in the wall. After breakfast I was permitted out of the cell for two hours, when I could walk up and down the aisle in front of the cell. After lunch I could promenade for three more hours. . . . Theoretically this was a jail, a facility for holding men for a short time prior to trial. Thus it had no yard, and no indoor recreational facilities. There were some old battered decks of cards around, and occasionally someone would produce a checker set out of nowhere. That was it. Somehow the men were supposed to pass the time doing absolutely nothing.

SOURCE: Morton Sobell, *On Doing Time* (New York: Charles Scribner's Sons, 1974), pp. 96, 100, 102.

in 1970, by 1983 this number had declined to 3,338, a decrease of 17 percent (U.S. Department of Justice, 1984).

A final proposal for overcoming some of the problems of the jail calls for creation of diversified facilities, each of which would confine one or more of the types of inmates now housed in the jail. The juvenile detention home represents an earlier effort to establish a more specialized facility. Later, detoxification centers were established in many American cities to provide an alternative for drunkenness offenders. More recently, a number of people have suggested that this movement toward diversified facilities be carried one step further by creating a special place of detention for those awaiting trial on criminal charges (for example, Goldfarb, 1975). They believe it is an injustice to confine those who have not been convicted of any crime with those who are serving penal sentences. Too often the former are subjected to intimidation and abuse from the latter, or receive the dubious benefit of their criminal experiences and perspectives.

## Detention Centers

Despite the movement in recent years to prohibit placing juveniles in America's jails, the practice persists today, albeit with considerable regional variation (Sarri, 1974; U.S. Department of Justice, 1984). Earlier we noted that nationwide in 1983, nearly 1 percent of America's daily jail population were juveniles. Although this proportion is small, it encompasses a substantial number of juveniles. Jail confinement can be especially difficult and disorienting for them (U.S. Department of Justice, 1980a).

For the most part, juveniles who are detained awaiting official action are lodged in a local *detention center*. These structures are the juvenile counterpart of the jail for adults.

They confine not only juveniles awaiting court action but also a variety of others who are placed there because local authorities and agencies believe there is no other place to put them (for example, youths considered dependent and neglected). Of juveniles confined in detention centers, 84 percent are placed there by the police; the remainder are referrals from a variety of agencies: Three percent are referred by parents or other relatives, 3 percent by school authorities, 4 percent by probation officers or other court

---

**PANEL 5.4**

*The Detention Home*

Oh, I can remember the first night I went [into detention]. I was in a room by myself. And they had a window in the door. And the next morning—this is when I was 12— they'd go walking by—the oldtimers—and they'd be lookin' in the window. They'd go "Umm, nice in there. How are you, baby?" The other inmates would always do this to new girls. But see, that's how they scare you. I was so scared after being searched and everything. You don't know what the fuck's going on, but these are older people telling you what to do, so you just get right in there and take off your clothes and whatever. So you sleep it through, and then you wake up and all's you see is these faces in the door, you know, yelling at you and telling you, "You better watch it, bitch." I was thinking, "They're going to kill me. What did I do? I don't know anybody—they're going to kill me." So when I came out of my room, I was high-stepping, hanging on the wall. How funny it is we become adjusted so fast . . . because two days later, I was looking in someone else's window, "Hey, bitch."

SOURCE: Kathryn Watterson Burkhart, *Women in Prison* (New York: Popular Library), 1976, p. 57.

personnel, and 5 percent from miscellaneous sources. Most referrals are for property offenses, but 20 percent are for status offenses, such as incorrigibility or running away from home, that would not be crimes if they were committed by an adult (U.S. Department of Justice, 1983b).

In 1985, there were 428 public short-term juvenile institutions in the United States (U.S. Department of Justice, 1986h). Presumably, most of these facilities are detention centers. Detention centers are a product of the juvenile reform movement of the last decade of the 19th century. One of the principal rationales for building them was to remove young people from local jails where, it was believed, they were exploited by adult inmates and exposed to criminalizing influences. Architecturally, however, detention centers often resemble jails. Many are located next door to a jail, and staff are used interchangeably in some jurisdictions (Pappenfort *et al.*, 1970).

The rate of juvenile detention, like the rate of jail use, varies greatly among the states. As with state variation in the size of the jail and prison populations, the reasons for this are not clear. On a typical day in 1982, America's detention centers held 15,203 juveniles, whose average age was 15.2 years. As Table 5.3 shows, the overwhelming majority of detention center inmates are males (82 percent). As compared with their representation in the general population—approximately 12 percent—minority youths are vastly overrepresented among detention center inmates (32 percent) (U.S. Department of Justice, 1983). In this respect, the detention center mirrors the American jail. The average length of stay in detention for those who subsequently are committed to another institution is approximately five times longer than for those who are released without commitment (68 days versus 13 days).

A mail survey of American juvenile deten-

tion facilities was conducted in 1980. The investigators were able to identify 400 such facilities and received completed questionnaires from 156, or about 39 percent (Hughes and Altschuler, 1982). The average daily number of inmates was 38.2 per detention home. Thirty-six percent of the respondents said that their detention home was a regional facility. Nearly 42 percent said that some juveniles are placed in jails or police lockups in their communities.

In contrast to local jail personnel, detention home administrators usually are not under police control. The majority of facilities that returned the questionnaire were under the control of the chief probation officer (24.3 percent), a director of court services (15.8 percent), or a judge (13.2 percent).

Generally, detention homes offer a few

TABLE 5.3 **Selected Demographic and Legal Characteristics of Short-Term Public Juvenile Facilities Inmates in the United States, 1982**

|  | Percent |
|---|---|
| SEX | |
| Male | 82% |
| Female | 18 |
| RACE | |
| White | 56 |
| Black | 32 |
| Other | 12 |
| REASON HELD | |
| Delinquency | 92 |
| Status offense | 8 |
| CUSTODIAL STATUS | |
| Detained | 81 |
| Committed | 18 |
| Voluntary admissions | 1 |
| AVERAGE LENGTH OF STAY | |
| Detained 13 days | |
| Committed 68 days | |

SOURCE: U.S. Department of Justice (1983).

## PANEL 5.5

### First Night in Detention

Juvenile Hall's front door was innocent in appearance but really impregnable to anything short of a bazooka. It could be opened only by an electric buzzer from inside a glass booth.

The detective handed his papers to a female receptionist. The reception area was roomy, with dark hard-backed benches along one pale-green wall, on which glass-framed prints of Norman Rockwell's visions of America were hung. The prints and the drapes covering the wire-mesh windows were the total decor. The half-glass control booth, with a periscope view of the outside, had a six-foot bulletin board, black, with removable white lettering and numbers giving the count by unit and then the total: 476 males, 53 females. Now the count would be increasing by four. A very pregnant black girl, her hair askew, sat weeping on a bench. . . .

Twenty minutes later . . . , he was dressed in faded, unpressed green khakis. The shirt-sleeves hung to his fingertips, and his pants were both rolled up at the bottom and folded at the waist beneath the web belt. . . .

The man behind the desk grunted; he was looking at the paper. "Attempted murder," he said, then "humphed" disparagingly. "Shit, they're never too young anymore." He made a sucking sound with his teeth while he opened a battered loose-leaf binder and inserted the paper in proper alphabetical order with fifty other identical papers. Each sheet was a log for an individual boy. The man opened the drawer and shoved a small brown-paper sack across the desk. It was stapled at the top. "Take it," he said to Alex. "It's a comb, toothbrush and—but you won't need the razor blades."

"You got him?" the escort said. "It's my lunch hour."

"You can go. I'll have him tucked in bed in a minute."

The gate clanged shut behind the escort, and the sound of his footsteps grew fainter as Alex waited. The man behind the desk swiveled his chair around and looked at a huge board that covered the wall. It had slots for tags, grouped according to dorms, and most of the slots were filled. The man wrote Alex's name on a tag and inserted it in an empty slot.

"Come on, Hammond," the man said, unwinding his legs from under the desk and startling the eleven-year-old with his six-foot-six height. He took a flashlight from a drawer and led Alex down a hallway. The dormitory door was a frame of heavy wire mesh. The man used the flashlight to judge the keyhole. "Third bed on the left," he said, locking the door behind Alex without waiting to see if the boy could find it.

Along each wall were ten beds, the blanket-covered mounds illuminated by a floodlight outside the windows. The glare was sliced into elongated rectangles by the bars on the windows.

Alex was surprised at the hospital bed, expecting a cot. He undressed quickly. A hospital stand was between each bed, but he didn't know which one went with his bed, so he dropped the ill-fitting clothes on the floor and got quickly under the sheets. He felt conspicuous and didn't want anyone to wake up and question him. The cool, clean sheets felt surprisingly good. . . . He stared at the lighted windows, at the bars, and he quaked in silence. He was rigid, holding back, but eventually the accumulated exhaustion of nearly two sleepless nights overcame everything else, and he fell into a troubled sleep, emitting moans that disturbed nobody.

SOURCE: Edward Bunker, *Little Boy Blue*. New York: Viking Press, 1981, pp. 37–42.

more program options to their inmates than do local jails. In most detention homes,

[programs] having to do with education and recreation are seen as essential. . . . [Eighty-three] percent of the sample cited school offerings, and 95.1 percent indicated a recreational program. In terms of the other types of programs, 51.6 percent indicated university involvement . . . In approximately 72 percent of the homes, the school program was part of the public school system (Hughes and Altschuler, 1982: 6).

Sixty-six detention homes responded to both the 1980 survey and a similar survey conducted in 1970. The investigators found very few changes during the 1970s (Reuterman and Hughes, 1984). There was no appreciable decrease in the use of adult jails to confine juveniles; the survey also showed that the 1970s did not bring the reduction in the use of detention that liberal reformers had projected in the 1960s. In sum, "procedures and programming within detention facilities changed little if at all during the 1970s" (1984: 332).

## The Jail and Detention Experience

Arguably, the jail and the juvenile detention center are the most important correctional institutions in America. First, each year the number of Americans who pass through the jail and detention home far exceeds the number who are admitted to and discharged from other types of correctional institutions. For example, the 250,000 admissions to America's 900 prisons in 1983 produced an average of 278 entries per facility (U.S. Department of Justice, 1984: 4); by contrast, there were more than 8 million admissions to America's 3,300 jails during the year ending June 30, 1983, or an average of more than 2,400 admissions per jail. When

the 7.9 million jail *releases* occurring during the same period are added to the admissions, the number of inmate transactions totals more than 16 million, or an average of 4,800 transactions per jail (U.S. Department of Justice, 1984: 4). Put differently, the jail is the part of the correctional apparatus that processes most citizens who become ensnared in the criminal process. Based on a 1980 survey, investigators estimated 694,000 yearly admissions to juvenile detention facilities in the United States. They note that this represents a considerable increase over the 488,800 yearly admissions estimated in a similar survey in 1970 (Hughes and Altschuler, 1982: 5).

Second, because the jail and detention home are points of entry to the criminal process, the experiences and perspectives that inmates acquire at this stage may color their appraisal of and responses to the process generally. If their initial experiences are embittering and negative, they may generalize these beyond the confines of the jail or detention home.

Although there have been few investigations of the day-to-day experiences of jail inmates, the findings persuasively support those who charge that jails are personally and socially destructive. Based on interviews with 182 inmates from a large urban jail, John J. Gibbs highlights the extreme stress that many inmates experience during their stay in jail. This begins with the shock of entry, during which inmates lose their autonomy as others make decisions that affect their fate without their advice or consent. The process often produces feelings of anxiety, confusion, and helplessness, and a "man's sense of control may be destroyed" (1982: 35). No longer able to manage their routine affairs in the outside world, inmates suddenly become dependent on family and friends in the community for assistance and support. For many jail inmates, this amounts to an abrupt role reversal and affects their sense of adequacy as competent adults.

The very nature of the jail environment adds to the stress that its inmates experience. The pervasive unpredictability of the jail and the criminal process "contribute to feelings of helplessness and confusion" and "during the seemingly eternal nights in jail" the inmate's anxiety is amplified (Gibbs, 1982: 38–39). Inmates have virtually no opportunity to engage in recreational or other activities that would help to reduce their anxiety. As a result, jail inmates are preoccupied with their problems, a process that may serve only to intensify them. For some,

> the difficulty is no longer simply one of solving, resolving, or in some way coping with a difficulty with the courts or family, for example, but develops into an issue of escaping from an unrelenting bombardment of painful thoughts and feelings (1982: 40).

Irwin's jail research led him to highlight four processes that all jail inmates experience, to varying degrees: *disorientation, disintegration, degradation,* and *preparation.* Like Gibbs, Irwin notes that the process of arrest, booking, and jail confinement is extremely disorienting. It "often produces a profound state of internal disorganization and demoralization" (1985: 53). Prisoners with previous jail or penitentiary experience may undergo the least discomfort and shock from this process, but those without previous experience suffer greatly.

Irwin argues that public officials, criminal justice employees, and the public "want prisoners to suffer and to be controlled" (1985: 46). But the nature and depth of their suffering exceed what most of these groups intend. One reason is that the jail experience is disintegrative for its inmates as they are torn away from social roles and relationships in the outside world. Jail inmates may lose whatever property they managed to accumulate and also the capacity to "take care of business."

Not only does this deprive the inmate of resources, sources of emotional support, and social assistance, but it also makes future participation and membership in society more difficult.

The disorientation and uncertainty experienced by many jail inmates may help explain why some commit suicide during jail confinement. In 1984, there were 278 deaths reported in the 621 American jails with the largest populations. About half the deaths were from natural causes, but 45 percent were suicides. Two percent resulted from injuries caused by other persons (U.S. Department of Justice, 1986d).

Along with disorientation and disintegration, inmates are degraded by the jail experience. At every turn, they are subjected to orders and commands from criminal justice personnel. Noncompliance meets with threats and whatever force officials believe is needed. Inmates also meet with contempt and hostility from criminal justice functionaries and judges, who tend to believe that the principal threat to public order is not crime itself but immorality. "And the major threat lies in the immorality of certain classes or types of people, most of them belonging to the rabble" (Irwin, 1985: 73).

Jail inmates often find it difficult to maintain personal cleanliness and their normal physical appearance, both of which are important to sustaining a favorable self-concept. Jail food may not be adequate to maintain health, and inmates are denied exercise. One result of this systematic degradation may be a rejection of conventional values, a loss of commitment to society, and migration "to deviant worlds and the rabble status" (1985: 84).

Irwin argues that the jail experience prepares inmates for the rabble existence. They gradually lose conventional sensibilities, acquire elements of the rabble mentality, acquire new or strengthened deviant perspectives and values, and develop ties to other

Jails and Juvenile Detention Centers

**PANEL 5.6**

*The Daily Routine in Detention Home*

The detention center was an old, four-story brick building that had seen better days and occupants other than delinquent children. In the rear was a small play area, bordered by a high, wire fence. A kitchen, dining room, waiting room, office, and recreational area filled the long, narrow first floor. The second floor had an apartment for the houseparents who supervised our daily activities. The third floor was comprised of two large rooms filled with chicken-wire cages containing a single cot and locker. It was in these cages that we slept. We were also put in them when there was nothing to do or as punishment. The cages were always locked when we were put inside. Above us on the fourth floor were the two small rooms used for the school.

I spent the first day padlocked inside one of the chicken-wire cages. The only time I was allowed to leave was when one of the houseparents came to take me to the toilet. Meals were brought by tray and slid under the door. Since there were no books, magazines, or toys for diversion, I could only walk the short length of the cage or lie on the cot and question my predicament. Was I really such a "bad" child? What would happen in juvenile court? . . .

After the first day of isolation I was allowed to mingle with the other kids. Less than a dozen of us made up the entire population. We all looked the same: sad, lost, confused, worried about what disaster tomorrow might bring. Family problems were often at the core of each life story we exchanged. Some stayed to themselves. Others constantly pushed, shoved, taunted, or fought whoever was available, transferring their pain to someone else. A few left for court, never to be seen by us again. New faces replaced them.

On weekdays we attended school. There was only one teacher to oversee our activities and assign lessons. But it was all just a joke. Magazines, comic books, and old torn texts that had been abandoned by public schools were used as the means of instruction. Using the *Adventures of Superman* seemed a strange way to teach English. Mostly, the teacher tried to keep us from tearing the place, and each other, apart. The moment his attention turned to the questions of one student, several others would get into a ruckus. Nobody could or would study under such conditions.

After school and on the weekend those of us who were not being punished for some indiscretion, and thus stuck in a cage, were sent to the recreation room, where there was little to do. Only a television and some reading materials were available in the sparsely furnished room and we were soon at each other's throats, acting out our discontent. Sometimes we were allowed to play in the fenced rear yard. But the games often turned into free-for-alls or arguments. The cages were where we spent most of the time, locked away like wild animals. We acted as we felt.

There were few interruptions from the boredom of the daily schedule of school, recreation, cage.

SOURCE: Waln K. Brown, *The Other Side of Delinquency* (New Brunswick, N.J.: Rutgers University Press, 1983), pp. 24–25.

members of the rabble class. Inasmuch as the official purpose of the jail is to control the behavior of those on the margins of American life, Irwin claims that there is a "cruel irony" in the fact that it is "the primary socializing institution of the rabble existence" (1985: 98).

Jails did not escape the inmate rebellions of the 1970s, and these, too, shed light on the nature of the jail experience. As Ronald Goldfarb notes,

> the protesting inmates' lists of grievances [were] remarkably alike. Fundamental to them all is a desire to be treated with some measure of personal dignity. The most damaging part of imprisonment, prisoners say, is the demeaning and dehumanizing stripping away of personal identity that begins when they enter the institution's receiving room. Such treatment is especially enraging when it is applied to pretrial detainees, who compose the majority of most jail populations, and who have been convicted of nothing (1975: 372).

Although we know comparatively little about the juvenile detention experience, much of what we have learned about the jail may apply here as well. Suffice it to say that Rosemary Sarri (1974: 14) speaks of the "overwhelmingly negative results of most juveniles' experiences with detention."

## Understanding the Jail

### Social Class, Criminalization, and Criminal Justice

Most types of individually and socially injurious conduct are distributed unevenly across the social class structure. This unevenness reflects the differential distribution of the volume and quality of resources available to persons at different positions in the class structure. An important consequence of this is that members of the economic elite are

able to perpetrate socially injurious acts that are not available to members of the underclasses. They can manipulate complex banking and credit transactions to generate illicit funds, pollute the environment, expose their employees to unsafe and unhealthy working conditions. Moreover, their positions in corporations and other large organizations permit them to manipulate and control the conditions under which midlevel managers and other employees must work. Consequently, the elite are able to use a variety of inducements and coercion to increase the likelihood that others will use criminal means to achieve organizational objectives.

Given all the resources controlled by members of the economic elite, it would be unlikely and indeed irrational for one of them to take another person's money by threat of bodily harm. The same cannot be said about members of the underclasses. Their power and resources are so limited that in most cases they confront their victims directly and employ guile, threats, or frontal assaults to carry out their criminal intentions. Also, they are less likely than members of the economic elite to constrain or in other ways influence others to commit crimes for them.

Not all types of socially or individually injurious conduct have an equal probability of being designated as criminal by the state. While sociologists have not been able to agree on the reasons for this, its validity is uncontested.

The injurious conduct of the underclasses has a much greater likelihood of being condemned by criminal law than that of elites. Demonstrably harmful elite behavior, if noticed at all by the state, is likely to be circumscribed by civil or administrative regulations, not the criminal law.

This differential state response to the injurious behaviors of members of different social classes continues even further, into the realm of official reactions to incidents of violation. We have one set of ideologies and institutions for dealing with the crimes of the underclasses, and a different set for dealing with the dangerous and harmful conduct of elites and those who do their dirty work. The jail belongs to the former class of crime control structures. As such, it requires a broad, macro-level interpretation.

## Interpreting the Jail

Few investigators have moved beyond technocratic reform proposals to offer an interpretation of the jail as a type of penal institution. John Irwin is an exception. He argues that the jail functions as a subsidiary to the welfare organizations that manage and regulate the poor in America. The rabble represent a permanent underclass in America, one that may "shrink or expand somewhat with changes in the economy" (1985: 104). But it is not economic forces alone that structure and maintain the rabble. Therefore, Irwin's interpretation of the rabble and the jail is a hybrid. It is not a "pure" radical interpretation because it incorporates "individualistic cultural values," "the continuing influx of nonwhite immigrants," "strong racial prejudices," the "'suspended' social status of American Youth," and "persistent . . . unemployment." In short, the rabble class "is a product of many of our basic social processes" (1985: 103–105).

Irwin candidly acknowledges that some members of the rabble class do commit crimes. But this does not explain the enduring, persistent campaign against the rabble by the police and other agencies of social control. In fact, after analyzing the offenses committed by his sample of 200 jail inmates, Irwin concluded that it is not the seriousness of their crimes that explains their arrest, detention, and sentencing, but the *offensiveness* of rabble behavior:

Offensiveness is a definition that conventional witnesses or their agents (the police) impose upon events; it is a summation of the meanings they attach to the acts, the context, and above all, the character of the actors. When a given act is performed by a disreputable—a person who is deemed worthless or of low character—it is not considered the same as when it is performed by an ordinary citizen. Thus, "horsing around" on a street corner is seen quite differently when it is done by "clean-cut" white teenagers or by "rowdy" black teenagers (1985: 23).

Another reason that the criminal justice apparatus focuses much of its resources on the rabble is its lack of success in its efforts to control more serious offenders. In other words, Irwin suggests that the campaign against the rabble is a "political diversion" (1985: 112). Moreover, the mass media and politicians support these efforts because they deflect attention from the more serious crimes committed by elites and by corporations. In other words, the campaign against the rabble contributes to a systematic delusion of the public about crime (1985: 114).

Irwin believes there are two potential reform strategies: "Either we . . . drastically reduce the size of the rabble class, a highly remote possibility, or . . . we abandon our self-serving fictions about crime and deviance" (1985: 115). He opts for the second strategy, but he also concedes that progress, "if it occurs at all, will necessarily be slow" because the jail as we know it developed over many years and "sluggish processes and static structures" change very slowly (1985: 118).

Steven Spitzer's analysis of processes of deviance production and control is more radical than Irwin's. Spitzer suggests that two categories of deviants are produced in monopoly capitalist societies: *social junk* and *social dynamite.* The former, "a costly yet relatively harmless burden to society," includes the mentally ill and chronic alcoholics (1975: 645). The latter, which includes many types of criminal offenders, represents a potential threat to established property relations and social order. Consequently, they are the objects of more intense legal controls. To a great extent, the local jail is our unspecialized catch basin for both types of deviants. It manages them to ensure that they do not disrupt existing social relations and the routine processes of everyday life. It accomplishes this mission today much as it has for the past 100 years, managing disreputable and potentially disruptive persons. While most are detained for a short period of time, others are dispatched to prisons or other structures for long-term confinement. We deal with these structures in the next three chapters.

# 6

# Men's Prisons

*A*t this writing, the assertion that the prison is a growth industry is not an overstatement. At the end of 1985, the total prison population in the United States stood at 503,601 (U.S. Department of Justice, 1986i), an all-time high. This figure is all the more remarkable when you consider that it does not include juveniles in confinement nor offenders housed in local jails or other custodial facilities.

## Who Goes to Prison?

As Table 6.1 shows, the number of prisoners at the close of 1985 represents a considerable increase over the average number of new prisoners added during the years 1978, 1979, and 1980 (Langan and Greenfeld, 1985; U.S. Department of Justice, 1986i). In

looking at Table 6.1, note also that while the largest rates of increase were during 1981 and 1982, the rate rose again in 1984, a trend that continued into 1985.

In 1985 the Bureau of Justice Statistics began to publish the percentage of the population imprisoned on any one given day as well as the percentage of the population that will ever serve a prison sentence during their lifetime. This new indicator makes possible some instructive assessments that complement the data presented in Table 6.1 and Table 6.6. These tables show both the number and the change in the rates of imprisonment.

Table 6.2 shows the prevalence of adults in prison at any one given day and gives the percentage of the nation's population that this number represents, categorized by race and sex. Thus during the period 1978–1982, the ratio of persons in prison to persons in the nation at large increased each year shown. In 1978, 0.175 percent of the adult population (or 1 in every 571 adults) were in prison; in 1982, 0.227 percent (or 1 in every 441 adults) were. These data show that the probability of being in prison varies more by sex than by race. Men, no matter which racial category, were about 17 times more likely to

be in prison than women of the same race, but black men have the greatest probability of being in prison at any one time. Between 1978 and 1982, black men were 8 times more likely than white men to be in prison. The 1982 figure indicates that on December 31 of that year, 2.044 percent of all black men in the population were in prison: 1 out of every 49 black men in the nation was in prison on that day (Langan and Greenfeld, 1985).

Table 6.3 gives estimates of the lifetime probability of ever being imprisoned. In 1979, the latest year used in the estimation, a person had a 2.7 percent chance of serving time in a state prison sometime in his or her life. This percentage, calculated from prison data and U.S. population data by sex and race, translates into a ratio of 1 in 37 chance. When these data are broken down by race, the likelihood of imprisonment becomes even more remarkable. If we calculate using the 1979 data in Table 6.3, a black man has an 18.7 percent chance, or a 1 in 5 probability, of spending some time in prison during the course of his life. The female ratios are better; however, here too a black woman is 8 times more likely to serve a prison sentence than her white counterpart. Looked at somewhat differently, black women and white men have similar chances of being imprisoned.

TABLE 6.1  **Change in the Total Prison Population, 1977–1985**

| Year | Number | Annual Percent Change |
|------|--------|------------------------|
| 1977 | 300,024 | — |
| 1978 | 307,276 | 2.4 |
| 1979 | 314,457 | 2.3 |
| 1980 | 329,821 | 4.9 |
| 1981 | 369,930 | 12.2 |
| 1982 | 413,806 | 11.9 |
| 1983 | 432,248 | 5.7 |
| 1984 | 463,866 | 6.1 |
| 1985 | 503,601 | 8.4 |

SOURCE: Adapted from U.S. Department of Justice (1984d, 1986f).

TABLE 6.2  **The Prevalence of State Imprisonment of Adults in the United States on December 31, 1978, 1980, and 1982**

|  | 1978 | 1980 | 1982 |
|--|------|------|------|
| **TOTAL** | .175% | .186% | .227% |
| *Male* | .353 | .373 | .455 |
| White | .204 | .218 | .266 |
| Black | 1.665 | 1.703 | 2.044 |
| Other | .192 | .189 | .229 |
| *Female* | .013 | .014 | .018 |
| White | .007 | .007 | .010 |
| Black | .062 | .062 | .082 |
| Other | .011 | .009 | .012 |

SOURCE: Adapted from U.S. Department of Justice (1985d).

TABLE 6.3  **Percentage of Population Expected to Serve a Prison Term in Their Lifetime Based on 1979 Data**

| Total | 2.7% |
|-------|------|
| *Male* | 5.1 |
| White | 3.3 |
| Black | 18.7 |
| *Female* | .4 |
| White | .2 |
| Black | 1.5 |

SOURCE: Adapted from U.S. Department of Justice (1985d).

## Education and Employment

While there tends to be variation (over time) in the use of imprisonment as a means of dealing with crime, reflecting different political strategies and ideologies of penal practice, there is considerable stability in who ends up in prison. Prison is reserved primarily for those who are convicted of street crimes. A brief look at the background characteristics of convicted prisoners does not indicate a profile reflective of success as usually understood and measured in American society.

The proportion of high school dropouts among prisoners is about three times that of those not imprisoned. About 6 percent of those who are in prison have had no formal schooling at all, and as one would suspect, very few ever went to college (U.S. Department of Justice, 1983b). Table 6.4 gives a more detailed picture of the educational background of prison inmates.

The employment histories of those who are confined is in accord with their educational background. As Table 6.5 shows, most in prison were unemployed before being arrested. A considerable proportion had never worked at all or were only sporadically employed prior to being confined. According to one study, of those prisoners who had been working before their arrests, close to half were in jobs they considered to be outside their usual employment. Many were underemployed (U.S. Department of Justice, 1983b).

## Trends in Imprisonment

Table 6.6 and Figure 6.1 illustrate the long-term trend in imprisonment from 1925 to 1985 and also show the rate of male and female prisoners in the nation. The rate of imprisonment is determined by finding the number of sentenced prisoners per 100,000 residents in the population. While we see a decline in the rate during the World War II years and from the late '60s into the early '70s, the rate has climbed steadily since 1973.

The year 1985 was a dubious banner year in the United States. For the first time in U.S. history, the rate of imprisonment surpassed 200 on a national level. While there are considerable regional differences (see Table 6.7), 13 of the 16 jurisdictions above the national rate are located in the South. Three above the national average are in the West, with Nevada scoring the highest incarceration rate in the nation (414 per 100,000). North Dakota has the lowest rate, with 52 per 100,000 (U.S. Department of Justice, 1986i).

TABLE 6.4  **Education of Prison Population**

| Years in School | Incarceration Rate (per 1000 inmates age 20–24) |
|---|---|
| 1–7 years | 259 |
| 8th grade | 83 |
| 9–11 years | 70 |
| 12th grade | 11 |
| 13–15 years | 6 |
| 16+ | 1 |

SOURCE: Adapted from U.S. Department of Justice (1983b).

TABLE 6.5  **Employment Status of Prison Population**

| Employment Status Prior to Confinement | Incarceration Rate (per 100,000 U.S. Population) |
|---|---|
| In labor force | 396 |
| Employed | 356 |
| Unemployed | 933 |
| Not in labor force | 442 |

SOURCE: Adapted from U.S. Department of Justice (1983b).

TABLE 6.6    Sentenced Prisoners in State and Federal Institutions: Number and Incarceration Rates, 1925–1985

| Year | Total | Rate | Males | Rate | Females | Rate |
|---|---|---|---|---|---|---|
| 1925 | 91,669 | 79 | 88,231 | 149 | 3,438 | 6 |
| 1926 | 97,991 | 83 | 94,287 | 157 | 3,704 | 6 |
| 1927 | 109,346 | 91 | 104,983 | 173 | 4,363 | 7 |
| 1928 | 116,390 | 96 | 111,836 | 182 | 4,554 | 8 |
| 1929 | 120,496 | 98 | 115,876 | 187 | 4,620 | 8 |
| 1930 | 129,453 | 104 | 124,785 | 200 | 4,668 | 8 |
| 1931 | 137,082 | 110 | 132,638 | 211 | 4,444 | 7 |
| 1932 | 137,997 | 110 | 133,573 | 211 | 4,424 | 7 |
| 1933 | 136,810 | 109 | 132,520 | 209 | 4,290 | 7 |
| 1934 | 138,316 | 109 | 133,769 | 209 | 4,547 | 7 |
| 1935 | 144,180 | 113 | 139,278 | 217 | 4,902 | 8 |
| 1936 | 145,038 | 113 | 139,990 | 217 | 5,048 | 8 |
| 1937 | 152,741 | 118 | 147,375 | 227 | 5,366 | 8 |
| 1938 | 160,285 | 123 | 154,826 | 236 | 5,459 | 8 |
| 1939 | 179,818 | 137 | 173,143 | 263 | 6,675 | 10 |
| 1940 | 173,706 | 131 | 167,345 | 252 | 6,361 | 10 |
| 1941 | 165,439 | 124 | 159,228 | 239 | 6,211 | 9 |
| 1942 | 150,384 | 112 | 144,167 | 217 | 6,217 | 9 |
| 1943 | 137,220 | 103 | 131,054 | 202 | 6,166 | 9 |
| 1944 | 132,456 | 100 | 126,350 | 200 | 6,106 | 9 |
| 1945 | 133,649 | 98 | 127,609 | 193 | 6,040 | 9 |
| 1946 | 140,079 | 99 | 134,075 | 191 | 6,004 | 8 |
| 1947 | 151,304 | 105 | 144,961 | 202 | 6,343 | 9 |
| 1948 | 155,977 | 106 | 149,739 | 205 | 6,238 | 8 |
| 1949 | 163,749 | 109 | 157,663 | 211 | 6,086 | 8 |
| 1950 | 166,165 | 109 | 160,309 | 211 | 5,814 | 8 |
| 1951 | 165,680 | 107 | 159,610 | 208 | 6,070 | 8 |
| 1952 | 168,233 | 107 | 161,994 | 208 | 6,239 | 8 |
| 1953 | 173,579 | 108 | 166,909 | 211 | 6,670 | 8 |
| 1954 | 182,901 | 112 | 175,907 | 218 | 6,994 | 8 |
| 1955 | 185,780 | 112 | 178,655 | 217 | 7,125 | 8 |
| 1956 | 189,565 | 112 | 182,190 | 218 | 7,375 | 9 |
| 1957 | 195,256 | 113 | 188,113 | 221 | 7,301 | 8 |
| 1958 | 205,643 | 117 | 198,208 | 229 | 7,435 | 8 |
| 1959 | 208,105 | 117 | 200,469 | 228 | 7,636 | 8 |
| 1960 | 212,953 | 117 | 205,265 | 230 | 7,688 | 8 |
| 1961 | 220,149 | 119 | 212,268 | 234 | 7,881 | 8 |
| 1962 | 218,830 | 117 | 210,823 | 229 | 8,007 | 8 |
| 1963 | 217,283 | 114 | 209,538 | 225 | 7,745 | 8 |
| 1964 | 214,336 | 111 | 206,632 | 219 | 7,704 | 8 |
| 1965 | 210,895 | 108 | 203,327 | 213 | 7,568 | 8 |
| 1966 | 199,654 | 102 | 192,703 | 201 | 6,951 | 7 |
| 1967 | 194,896 | 98 | 188,661 | 195 | 6,235 | 6 |
| 1968 | 187,274 | 94 | 182,102 | 187 | 5,812 | 6 |
| 1969 | 197,136 | 97 | 189,413 | 192 | 6,594 | 6 |
| 1970 | 196,441 | 96 | 190,794 | 191 | 5,635 | 5 |
| 1971 | 198,061 | 95 | 191,732 | 189 | 6,329 | 6 |
| 1972 | 196,092 | 93 | 189,823 | 185 | 6,269 | 6 |
| 1973 | 204,211 | 96 | 197,523 | 191 | 6,004 | 6 |
| 1974 | 218,466 | 102 | 211,077 | 202 | 7,389 | 7 |
| 1975 | 240,593 | 111 | 231,918 | 220 | 8,675 | 8 |
| 1976 | 262,833 | 120 | 252,794 | 238 | 10,039 | 9 |
| 1977 | 278,141 | 126 | 267,097 | 249 | 11,044 | 10 |
| 1977 | 285,456 | 129 | 274,244 | 255 | 11,212 | 10 |
| 1978 | 294,396 | 132 | 282,813 | 261 | 11,583 | 10 |
| 1979 | 301,470 | 133 | 289,465 | 264 | 12,005 | 10 |
| 1980 | 315,974 | 138 | 303,643 | 274 | 12,331 | 11 |
| 1981 | 353,673 | 153 | 339,375 | 303 | 14,298 | 12 |
| 1982 | 395,516 | 170 | 379,075 | 335 | 16,441 | 14 |
| 1983 | 419,346 | 178 | 401,870 | 352 | 17,476 | 14 |
| 1984 | 446,108 | 188 | 426,713 | 370 | 19,395 | 16 |
| 1985 | 481,616 | 201 | 460,210 | 394 | 21,406 | 17 |

SOURCE: U.S. Department of Justice (1986i).

Since 1980, the number of prisoners per 100,000 in the population has risen nearly 45 percent, from 139 to 201.

## The Social World of the Male Prison

Early prison scholarship assumed prisons to be *self-contained* entities and studied them as such. Stress was laid on what was assumed to be a *consensual* social structure within the prison. Hence emphasis was placed on identifying and describing a single overarching inmate code that regulated a single prisoner subculture based on a specific *status hierarchy*. While inmates and staff (particularly the guards or officers) were assumed to be in a

constant struggle over power and control of the prison and its resources, in fact, complex modes of *accommodation* were discovered that allowed the prison to function in spite of the preponderance of inmates over staff in an environment based on coercion. A review of some of these studies follows.

### Descriptive Prison Studies

When interest developed in analyzing the prison and its inhabitants, sociologists and criminologists took a lesson from anthropology and examined the prison as a separate entity, a "society of captives." What was available for study was the maximum-security fortresslike prison, the type that most closely resembled Hollywood's version of prisons in dozens of gangster films.

FIGURE 6.1  **Number of Sentenced State and Federal Prisoners, per 100,000 U.S. Population, Yearend 1925–85**

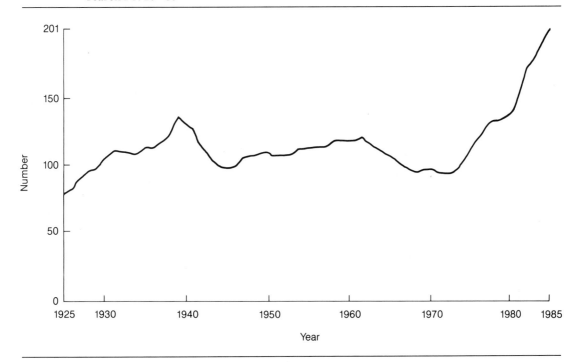

SOURCE: U.S. Department of Justice (1986i).

Chapter 6

TABLE 6.7 **Prisoners under the Jurisdiction of State and Federal Correctional Authorities, by Sex, Region, and State, Yearend 1984 and 1985**

| | Total | | | Sentenced to more than a year | | | Incarceration rates 1985 |
|---|---|---|---|---|---|---|---|
| | 1985 | 1984 | Percent change 1984–85 | 1985 | 1984 | Percent change 1984–85 | |
| U.S. TOTAL | 503,601 | 464,567 | 8.4% | 481,616 | 446,108 | 8.0% | 201 |
| Federal | 40,223 | 34,263 | 17.4 | 32,695 | 27,602 | 18.5 | 14 |
| State | 463,378 | 430,304 | 7.7 | 448,921 | 418,506 | 7.3 | 187 |
| Male | 480,510 | 443,717 | 8.3 | 460,210 | 426,713 | 7.9 | 394 |
| Female | 23,091 | 20,850 | 10.7 | 21,406 | 19,395 | 10.4 | 17 |
| NORTHEAST | 75,743 | 70,538 | 7.4% | 72,756 | 67,838 | 7.2% | 146 |
| Connecticut | 6,149 | 5,718 | 7.5 | 4,043 | 3,748 | 7.9 | 127 |
| Maine | 1,226 | 1,025 | 19.6 | 1,030 | 840 | 22.6 | 88 |
| Massachusetts | 5,447 | 4,890 | 11.4 | 5,447 | 4,890 | 11.4 | 93 |
| New Hampshire | 683 | 561 | 21.7 | 683 | 561 | 21.7 | 68 |
| New Jersey | 11,335 | 10,363 | 9.4 | 11,335 | 10,363 | 9.4 | 149 |
| New York | 34,718 | 33,155 | 4.7 | 34,718 | 33,155 | 4.7 | 195 |
| Pennsylvania | 14,227 | 13,090 | 8.7 | 14,119 | 12,998 | 8.6 | 119 |
| Rhode Island | 1,307 | 1,221 | 7.0 | 964 | 891 | 8.2 | 99 |
| Vermont | 651 | 515 | 26.4 | 417 | 392 | 6.4 | 78 |
| MIDWEST | 95,356 | 85,890 | 11.0% | 94,740 | 85,460 | 10.9% | 160 |
| Illinois | 18,634 | 17,187 | 8.4 | 18,634 | 17,187 | 8.4 | 161 |
| Indiana | 9,904 | 9,328 | 6.2 | 9,615 | 9,063 | 6.1 | 175 |
| Iowa | 2,607 | 2,836 | −8.1 | 2,607 | 2,836 | −8.1 | 90 |
| Kansas | 4,748 | 4,238 | 12.0 | 4,748 | 4,238 | 12.0 | 193 |
| Michigan | 17,799 | 14,604 | 21.9 | 17,799 | 14,604 | 21.9 | 196 |
| Minnesota | 2,343 | 2,167 | 8.1 | 2,343 | 2,167 | 8.1 | 56 |
| Missouri | 9,898 | 8,808 | 12.4 | 9,898 | 8,808 | 12.4 | 196 |
| Nebraska | 1,689 | 1,654 | 2.1 | 1,608 | 1,566 | 2.7 | 100 |
| North Dakota | 407 | 434 | −6.2 | 355 | 374 | −5.1 | 52 |
| Ohio | 20,864 | 18,694 | 11.6 | 20,864 | 18,694 | 11.6 | 194 |
| South Dakota | 1,047 | 917 | 14.2 | 1,006 | 900 | 11.8 | 142 |
| Wisconsin | 5,416 | 5,023 | 7.8 | 5,263 | 5,023 | 4.8 | 110 |
| SOUTH | 203,022 | 193,971 | 4.7% | 195,984 | 188,634 | 3.9% | 238 |
| Alabama | 11,015 | 10,482 | 5.1 | 10,749 | 10,246 | 4.9 | 267 |
| Arkansas | 4,640 | 4,454 | 4.2 | 4,605 | 4,427 | 4.0 | 195 |
| Delaware | 2,550 | 2,200 | 15.9 | 1,842 | 1,615 | 14.1 | 295 |
| District of Columbia | 6,404 | 4,834 | | 4,604 | 4,031 | 14.2 | 738 |
| Florida | 28,600 | 27,106 | 5.5 | 28,482 | 26,933 | 5.8 | 247 |
| Georgia | 16,118 | 15,731 | 2.5 | 15,208 | 14,944 | 1.8 | 252 |
| Kentucky | 5,766 | 5,502 | 4.8 | 5,766 | 5,502 | 4.8 | 155 |
| Louisiana | 13,900 | 13,919 | −.1 | 13,900 | 13,919 | −.1 | 308 |
| Maryland | 13,005 | 13,124 | −.9 | 12,303 | 12,442 | −1.1 | 279 |
| Mississippi | 6,392 | 6,115 | 4.5 | 6,208 | 5,974 | 3.9 | 237 |
| North Carolina | 17,344 | 16,371 | 5.9 | 16,007 | 15,219 | 5.2 | 254 |
| Oklahoma | 8,477 | 7,872 | 7.7 | 8,477 | 7,872 | 7.7 | 255 |
| South Carolina | 10,538 | 10,011 | 5.3 | 9,916 | 9,434 | 5.1 | 294 |
| Tennessee | 6,943 | 7,302 | −4.9 | 6,943 | 7,302 | −4.9 | 145 |

TABLE 6.7  **Continued**

| | Total | | | Sentenced to more than a year | | | Incarceration rates |
|---|---|---|---|---|---|---|---|
| | 1985 | 1984 | Percent change 1984–85 | 1985 | 1984 | Percent change 1984–85 | 1985 |
| Texas | 37,532 | 36,682 | 2.3 | 37,532 | 36,682 | 2.3 | 226 |
| Virginia | 12,073 | 10,667 | 13.2 | 11,717 | 10,493 | 11.7 | 204 |
| West Virginia | 1,725 | 1,599 | 7.9 | 1,725 | 1,599 | 7.9 | 89 |
| WEST | 89,257 | 79,905 | 11.7% | 85,441 | 76,574 | 11.6% | 177 |
| Alaska | 2,311 | 1,995 | 15.8 | 1,484 | 1,290 | 15.0 | 279 |
| Arizona | 8,518 | 7,845 | 8.6 | 8,264 | 7,638 | 8.2 | 256 |
| California | 50,111 | 43,314 | 15.7 | 48,280 | 41,780 | 15.6 | 181 |
| Colorado | 3,369 | 3,364 | .1 | 3,369 | 3,347 | .7 | 103 |
| Hawaii | 2,111 | 1,934 | 9.2 | 1,428 | 1,299 | 9.9 | 134 |
| Idaho | 1,381 | 1,282 | 7.7 | 1,381 | 1,282 | 7.7 | 137 |
| Montana | 1,163 | 1,005 | 15.7 | 1,163 | 1,005 | 15.7 | 140 |
| Nevada | 3,910 | 3,510 | 11.4 | 3,910 | 3,510 | 11.4 | 412 |
| New Mexico | 2,313 | 2,129 | 8.6 | 2,112 | 1,908 | 10.7 | 144 |
| Oregon | 4,833 | 4,563 | 5.9 | 4,833 | 4,563 | 5.9 | 179 |
| Utah | 1,570 | 1,419 | 10.6 | 1,550 | 1,407 | 10.2 | 93 |
| Washington | 6,909 | 6,821 | 1.3 | 6,909 | 6,821 | 1.3 | 156 |
| Wyoming | 758 | 724 | 4.7 | 758 | 724 | 4.7 | 148 |

SOURCE: U.S. Department of Justice (1986f).

Here researchers found a unique hierarchical social structure based on a complex network of *social types*. Colorful descriptions were given to these types, such as "punk," "wolf," "gorilla," "merchant" (Sykes, 1958), or "right guy," "square John," "politician," "outlaw" (Schrag, 1961). All of these types played definite roles in prison life; some were praised, others were scorned. For example, a merchant was an inmate whose job assignment gave him access to goods that he would steal and sell to others. But it was the interaction of these types that was perceived to form the inmate social structure and the peculiar culture of prison life. This depiction proved to be consistent in a number of different prisons studied; only the labels showed significant variation.

A complex stratification system for the allocation of prestige existed among inmates. The type of crime committed, previous criminal experience, the degree of one's commitment to antisocial values, ethnicity, and background all played some part in determining an inmate's place in the hierarchy. Those inmates who were looked up to by others were permitted more access to staff without the suspicion this would otherwise entail. Order was maintained by a tacit alliance between these elite inmates, whose high status gave them a vested interest in maintaining the status quo and preserving prison officialdom.

Other research concluded that prisoners did not have favorable attitudes toward the criminal justice system, the prison, its staff, or its programs. Indeed, inmates' beliefs and attitudes in these areas were preponderantly negative and often oppositional.

Social relationships among prisoners were found to be marked by an undercurrent of fear and suspicion. Inmates were expected by staff and peers alike to "do their own time"

## The Convict Code circa 1930

The code of the good hoodlum, while rigorous, is basically simple. Its cardinal tenet is the single commandment: Thou shalt not beef. Under no circumstances whatsoever must an adherent of the code turn to constituted authority. Beefing is the imparting to the authorities in any way whatsoever, directly or indirectly, of information detrimental to anyone. . . .

Finking [need not] be direct and straightforward. It may be done indirectly. For example, a fink may say to a fellow inmate within earshot of a screw, "Gee! Didn't Hank look funny coming out of the Bake Shop with those pies under his shirt?" Or, in casual conversation with a screw, he may let slip some remark conveying information about another prisoner. . . . The real hood, however, shuns these methods as completely as he does outright squawking. While he may be polite and courteous to screws, he doesn't spend too much time chatting with them; the con who talks a great deal with the screw, who "sits on the screw's lap," is suspect among his fellows. . . .

The good hood minds his own business. He may disapprove very much of what some other con is doing; but unless it directly affects him adversely, he merely shrugs and walks away.

The hoodlum code is stringent enough; the fellow who tries to live up both to it and the code of the gentleman has his work cut out for him! Unfortunately the hoodlum code, like the code of the gentleman, is often honored in the breach.

SOURCE: Nathan F. Leopold, Jr., *Life Plus 99 Years* (Garden City, N.Y.: Doubleday, 1958), p. 141.

and neither interfere nor act in concert with one another. Prison staff, it was found, promoted this philosophy as a means of keeping prisoners isolated from one another, thus preventing any collective response to their common condition. It was quite a successful strategy. Most inmates did their time while forming few friendships.

These studies also discovered the inmate belief system (the convict "code"), which prescribed how inmates should relate to one another and to the prison staff (see Panel 6.1). By one account (Sykes and Messinger, 1960), the chief tenets of the inmate code were:

**1. Don't exploit convicts.** Included in this maxim are several other directives, such as "don't break your word," "don't steal from other cons," and "pay your debts."

**2. Don't weaken.** The ideal inmate should "be tough, be a man." He should show courage, strength, and integrity in the face of privation and threats from others.

**3. Don't lose your head.** This places an emphasis on "playing it cool" and "doing your own time." Those doing time should curtail affect, minimize emotional frictions, and generally ignore the irritants of daily life.

**4. Don't interfere with convict interests.** The most inflexible directive in this category was "never rat on a con." Other directives included "don't be nosy," "don't have a loose lip," "don't put a guy on the spot," and "be loyal to your class—the cons."

**5. Don't be a sucker.** Prison officials should be treated with constant suspicion and distrust. In conflicts between inmates and prison employees, the latter were automatically to be considered in the wrong.

These were deemed the central norms of the inmate subculture as well as an expression of the values of the captive society. Inmates who subscribed to this code and accepted the values it represented were accorded a certain amount of esteem by their fellow captives and indeed were to an extent admired by officials as "good cons." Those who violated the maxims could expect to suffer the consequences, ranging from alienation to physical brutality to death at the hands of other inmates.

The code was not as inflexible as an accounting of it suggests, however. Often there were routine violations of the code with impunity. Therefore, it represented more of a Weberian ideal than a rigid reality. The most severely sanctioned maxim, "never rat on another," was most frequently violated. Although there may have been general adherence to the principle, each prison usually had an extensive network of informers, and those in charge of security often boasted about the number of "snitches" they had under their patronage.

Thus while overall the inmate subculture reflected a hostile stance toward the keepers, bridges of accommodation developed, were recognized, and were tacitly accepted.

The inmate social structure and its related belief system represented a means to thwart the staff and to provide certain amenities usually denied in prison as well as a network of accommodations in a wide variety of areas that resulted in a delicately balanced total milieu.

## Theoretical Explanations

Some of the most imaginative research on prisons has come from efforts to develop theoretical explanations for the distinctive nature of the inmate social structure and belief system.

There are two contrasting interpretations: *deprivation* and *importation*. In 1954, Lloyd McCorkle and Richard Korn suggested that inmate culture and social organization are functional responses by inmates to the deprivation and rejection they experience as they are processed through the criminal justice system.

> Observation suggests that the major problem with which the inmate social system attempts to cope centers about the theme of social rejection. In many ways, the inmate social system may be viewed as providing a way of life which enables the inmates to avoid the devastating psychological effects of internalizing and converting social rejection into self-rejection. In effect, it permits the *inmate to reject his rejector rather than himself* (1954: 89) (emphasis added).

A number of sociologists have presented explanations for inmate culture and social organization which, like the work of McCorkle and Korn, see them as functional adaptations to something inherent in the structure and experience of confinement. A peculiar set of structural arrangements characteristic of the prison is usually pointed to as the causative agent. Yet the structural argument has shown some variation from one observer to another, and few attempts have been made to systematically reconcile them.

Gresham Sykes (1958) and Sykes with Sheldon Messinger (1960) argue that the critical aspect of prison structure is that it imposes the *pains of imprisonment* on inmates. To the extent inmates endorse and abide by the dictates of the inmate code, and demonstrate a solidarity with one another, these pains are lessened; to the extent the code is ignored, and inmates prey upon one another, the pains experienced are more intense. But note these deprivations may also be eased by an accommodative stance with the staff, albeit with some risk.

Erving Goffman's interpretation (1961) stressed the causative significance of a different set of variables. He identified the prison—along with the military, convents, and mental hospitals—as one type of *total institution*. Presumably, any institution possessing the characteristics of "totalness" would generate similar responses on the part of its "inmates."

Goffman saw ordinary daily life separated into different components and spaces, noting that we tend to work, play, sleep in different places and have different associates in each of these places. Not so in the prison, where all these separate spheres of life are in one place, regulated and controlled by the same overall authority. This creates the "total institution" and a variety of adaptive styles on the part of its inmates.

Other research focused on how the culture of the prison was adopted; that is, how inmates were socialized into accepting the antagonistic norms and values that formed the content of the culture. To describe this process, Donald Clemmer (1958), in what became a classic study, coined the concept of *prisonization,* a process akin to assimilation, wherein prisoners adapt to prison customs. Though while this conceptualization implied that once prisonization took hold there would be no change, subsequent studies of socialization in the prison world consistently demonstrated that there was a U-shaped curve of expressed conformity with the convict code. As a rule, prisoners in the first six months and the last six months of their imprisonment tended to be more pro-staff in their expressed beliefs, while those in between tended to be more pro-prisoner in their beliefs. Despite all this research, one critic rightly noted that "it has yet to be established that antiprison attitudes and behaviors are predictive of postprison antisocial attitudes or behaviors" (Tittle, 1974: 390).

By contrast, other investigators suggest that no special explanation is required for the negativism and social organization of imprisoned individuals. According to the *importation* model, prisoners bring with them the beliefs, identities, and group allegiances that they held on the street, modifying them to fit prison conditions. The prison world thus becomes a microcosm of the demimonde existing outside (Irwin and Cressey, 1962; Irwin, 1970).

## Contemporary Sociological Views of the Prison

More recent sociological analyses of the prison have in large measure criticized these earlier studies as unrealistic and no longer applicable to today's prison conditions.

To begin with, critics have pointed out that the prison was studied in the past as though in a vacuum, isolated and unaffected by outside events. The walls were considered to not only keep the convicted in, but to hold the rest of the world at bay. While this view may have had some validity during the early decades of this century, subsequent events have made it virtually impossible to avoid taking into account the relationships between changes in the prison and sociopolitical currents in society at large.

Second, the assumption that the prison contained a *single* subculture to which all inmates belonged was challenged; such a finding would be a serious misreading of today's prison world. Third, early studies perceived the prison population as more homogeneous than it probably was; even if there was a semblance of homogeneity, this certainly is not the case today.

Racial and ethnic divisions have become a primary concern in prisons but have until relatively recently not been seriously studied. As James B. Jacobs (1979) points out, this was a significant omission, for prisons have had a long history of racism. In today's prison, blacks, Hispanics, Puerto Ricans, and other minority groups constitute the majority of prisoners (Jacobs, 1979). This fact alone would negate any conception of a uniform subculture in the prison of the '80s. As early as 1977, John Irwin recognized this condition when he stated:

Needless to say, there is no single "inmate culture" or "inmate social system." Nor is there an overarching inmate code. The variety of cultural and subcultural orientations (ethnic, class, and criminal), the variety of preprison experiences, and the intense, open hostility between segments of the prison population preclude this (1977: 32).

The reality of the contemporary prison is small friendship groups formed on racial or ethnic lines, with prisoners restricting most of their informal interactions to members of these groups (see Panel 6.2). Groups may also form on lines of mutual interest, such as groups of lifers, who share certain common problems of adjustment. In some instances, groups are formed for mutual protection from the predation of others, as well as to pursue crafts or academics. This newly recognized form of social organization has been labeled *ordered segmentation* (Irwin, 1977).

Sociopolitical events from the 1960s onward, coupled with ever-growing prison populations, have radically altered the prison's social contours. With the civil rights movement of the 1960s came the politicization of black prisoners, which aided in the formation of a collective identity that allowed them to perceive their plight in political terms. Hispanics went through a similar process, as to a lesser extent did Native Americans. These various race and ethnic groups formed significant power blocs in states where they were superior in numbers. White prisoners generally remained divided, although some formed white-supremacist groups based on neo-Nazi ideology.

In general, race relations in prison are a microcosm of the larger society's but are exacerbated in the coercive atmosphere and structure of the prison. Added to this is the fact that a good proportion of the younger inmates were members of street gangs and continue their gang loyalties and conflicts in prison, giving further credence to the importation model of prison subculture (Jacobs, 1974; Park, 1975; Irwin, 1980; Davidson, 1983). In some prisons, racial conflict and tensions reached dramatic proportions in the late '60s and '70s. This condition is still

---

**PANEL 6.2**

## Observations on Prison Friendships

It took, I was bemused to note, an astonishingly short time to become a reasonably seasoned jailbird. In no time at all I had learned the language, the prison terminology, the basic assumptions and the basic rules. . . .

Applying all this was a slightly more complex matter, of course, but the school was a rough one and rarely permitted mistakes, so the incentive was there to learn and learn fast. The first thing you needed was allies, and that as quickly as possible. The procedure tended to begin as soon as you were taken from court to the precinct jail, where they gathered the sentenced offenders and handcuffed them two by two for transport to maximum security. You sized up the guy you were handcuffed to and let your instincts do the rest; if he looked like a useful sort, you started up a conversation and established a rapport. You kept this procedure up until you knew enough people to generally cover the territory you were going to run in (e.g., your tier, the exercise yard, your place of work, the gym) and then you chose your friends and chose them carefully, keeping in mind that anything they were involved in would inescapably involve you too. Most of these maneuverings didn't happen as mechanically as this may sound, but the rationale behind them was unavoidably clear and few could afford to ignore the routine. A loner or loser in prison was a goner more often than not.

SOURCE: Andreas Schroeder, *Shaking It Rough* (Garden City, N.Y.: Doubleday, 1976), pp. 29–30.

unresolved and continues to simmer with the prison overcrowding of the '80s. Racial peace is in a precarious state in almost all prisons of the nation.

Indeed, these racial conditions have altered the whole system of norms, roles, and values governing the prison community.

> Racial conflict and stratification has not only changed prisoner values, but it has also changed traditional prisoner roles, many of which were developed around white prisoner domination of key prison jobs and hustles. While social segregation has always existed in our nation's prisons and jails, the degree to which race has become a basis for prisoner social organization . . . is unprecedented in corrections history (Fox, 1982: 85).

Much of what have become prison values, roles, and norms reflect outside tensions and outside practice. These racial tensions were brought into the prison and heightened by close confinement in what are now mostly overcrowded conditions, created by the heavy use of imprisonment coupled with longer sentences and restrictive parole release policies.

Another phenomenon that changed the workings of the contemporary prison was what became collectively known as the prisoners' rights movement, stimulated by the civil rights struggle. Impetus for the movement was given by Black Muslims in the late 1950s demanding certain religious freedoms denied them in prison. This opened the door to a host of subsequent legal challenges in almost every area of imprisonment where fundamental human rights had been reduced or completely denied (Jacobs, 1983).

But this was to change in the more liberal sociopolitical context of the '60s, with its sensitivity to issues of the poor, minorities, and systems of oppression. With links to outside groups, prisoners were able to crack the prison walls and expose the internal dynam-ics of prison life as never before. As we will show in Chapter 11, courts began to redefine their role and perceived prisoners as retaining certain constitutional rights even while confined. This in turn stimulated further challenges. Over the decade, courts dealt with a variety of issues under the constitutional umbrella of cruel and unusual punishment, religious freedom, and equal protection under the law.

But Jacobs' caution seems a realistic assessment reflecting the contemporary conservative political context:

> Prisoners' rights activists should not in the foreseeable future expect highly dramatic decisions that will mobilize social and political energies on behalf of prisoners. . . . Having liberated prisoners from being slaves of the state, this Court seems unwilling to establish them as citizens, behind bars (1983: 44).

While overall the prisoners' rights movement effected some important changes in such areas as medical treatment, living conditions, health standards, religious freedoms, and censorship, the prison as a social institution remains fundamentally unchanged.

## The Daily Experience

The daily experience of prison life is often lost in the conceptual abstraction that objective analysis demands. Everyday living in prison defies easy description and is an individual matter. There are, however, certain commonalities all inmates have to cope with and which in their entirety make up the daily prison experience.

### Routine

Even under the most favorable prison conditions, a routine pervades that produces for some a boredom that compels them to outrageous conduct for relief. Malcolm Braly's account is a good example of this fact (see Panel 6.3). This very predictability and sameness, however, makes it possible for others to find comfort in the dependency and routine. Some remove themselves from all but necessary interactions and "do their own time." One of the authors recalls the case of a California inmate, considered a model prisoner, who when moved from the single cell he had occupied for years into a situation requiring frequent interaction with others in preparation for release, experienced a psychotic episode, remaining in a catatonic state for several days. He had totally lost the ability to deal with others on any but a superficial level. His "model" adjustment to prison made him unfit for life outside, thus demonstrating one of the classic ironies of incarceration. While the routine of prison doesn't affect every prisoner in this extreme manner, the fact remains all must develop mechanisms to cope with the effects of a routinized existence.

### Suspiciousness

An air of distrust permeates all interaction in prison. This suspiciousness is of several varieties. One is the fear by staff that they will lose control of or be manipulated by inmates and then be held responsible for their laxness. Another is the fear by inmates that they will be accused of rule violations, mistreated, or in other ways coerced to suffer the consequences in punishment or longer time served.

Guards (as well as other staff) are constantly aware that they may be suspected of bringing contraband items into the institution or be accused of associating too closely with inmates. Again, a personal experience will serve as illustration. While an employee in a well-known prison, one of the authors gave a ride to an ex-inmate, who had permission to be on the prison grounds in his capac-

ity as a reporter. He was given a ride with other commuters and dropped off at his destination. The author was accused of "associating with ex-felons" by the associate warden of custody and had to defend this innocent action and prove he was not con-

---

**PANEL 6.3**

## On Serving Time

The hardest part of serving time is the predictability. Each day moves like every other day. You *know* nothing different can happen. You focus on tiny events, a movie scheduled weeks ahead, your reclass., your parole hearing, things far in the future, and slowly, smooth day by day, draw them to you. There will be no glad surprise, no spontaneous holiday, and a month from now, six months, a year, you will be just where you are, doing just what you're doing, except you'll be older.

This airless calm is produced by rigid routine. Custody doesn't encourage spontaneity. Walk slow, the Cynic says, and don't make any fast moves. Each morning you know where evening will find you. There is no way to avoid your cell. When everyone marched into the block you would be left alone in the empty yard. Each Monday describes every Friday. Holidays in prison are only another mark of passing time and for many they are the most difficult days. Most of the outrages that provide such lurid passages in the folklore of our prisons are inspired by boredom. Some grow so weary of this grinding sameness they will drink wood alcohol even though they are aware this potent toxin may blind or kill them. Others fight with knives to the death and the survivor will remark, "It was just something to do."

SOURCE: Malcolm Braly, *False Starts* (Boston: Little, Brown, 1976), pp. 181–82.

**A**fter the solid steel door, before the barred, locked gate into the visiting area proper, each visitor must pass through a metal-detecting machine. The reason for such a security measure is clear; the extreme sensitivity of the machine is less easily explained. Unless the point is inflicting humiliation on visitors. Especially women visitors whose underclothes contain metal stays and braces, women who wear intimate jewelry they never remove from their bodies. Grandmothers whose wedding rings are imbedded in the flesh of their fingers. When the machine bleeps, everything it discovers must go. You say it's a wire in your bra, lady. Well, I'm sorry about that, but you gotta take it off. Of course the women have a choice. They can strip off the offending garment or ornament, and don one of the dowdy smocks the state provides for such contingencies. Or they can go back home. . . .

The room's crowded now and noisier. I try to ignore other visitors, grant them the privacy I'm seeking with my brother when we sit down again on the little bit of turf we've claimed: two vinyl-cushioned seats with a low, eighteen-inch-square table between us. Some prisoners and their guests form huddles, some couples cling as long and hard as the rules allow, other groups sit three or four in a row, eyes front as if they're staring at a movie on the far wall. Their lips move but what they say is lost in the general din unless your face is a foot from theirs. In this coffin-shaped room filled with chairs and benches, there's no place to hide. People position themselves in various ways to steal a little privacy, but nothing shuts out the strangers crowded into this space we all must share.

SOURCE: John Edgar Wideman, *Brothers and Keepers* (New York: Penguin Books, 1984), pp. 185, 218.

sorting with criminals in violation of departmental rules. Custodial staff are suspicious of other prison staff and vice versa.

In terms of the inmates' daily prison experience, the most visible manifestation of mistrust is the constant counts and body searches, cell searches, and the total lack of control over personal possessions, which may at any time be confiscated or destroyed. Inmates also fear one another. Prisoner Jack Henry Abbott wrote:

> There is no "camaraderie" among prisoners as a whole any more; there is a system, a network of ties between all the tips (prison cliques) in the prisons, and it's this that resembles "comradeship" in general. Most prisoners fear almost *every* other prisoner around them (1982: 85).

This mistrust at all levels is a dynamic which drives daily prison life and sets limits to all activity.

### Noise and Lack of Privacy

No description of prison life would be complete without reference to the lack of privacy and the level of noise that infests all prisons. The popular description likening prisons to zoos is in this respect quite accurate. Most cells, like cages, are open to view, affording no privacy and allowing no respite from the ever-present surveillance that the 18th-century British jurist Jeremy Bentham considered the ultimate achievement of imprisonment and which is perhaps the ultimate manifestation of total domination over inmates.

The clang of the steel-barred doors, the coming and going of inmates and guards, the blaring of public address system, radios, and TV, the constant talk and shouting—all reverberate throughout the concrete and steel housing, creating a level of noise not unlike that of a monkey house. This unceasing din makes any task requiring a modicum of concentration virtually impossible. More than that, it is an intrusion that cannot be managed or controlled to individual sensory tolerances.

## Autonomy

Perhaps the most far-reaching facets of the prison experience are those that Gresham Sykes, as noted earlier, recognized as the "pains of imprisonment" in his study of a maximum-security prison (1958). Sykes identified the rejection by the community, the deprivation of heterosexual relationships, the deprivation of autonomy, material deprivation, and the forced association with others not of one's choosing as contributing conditions to the pain of being in prison.

Putting aside for the moment the rejection by the community, which is a condition extraneous to the prison, and the lack of heterosexual contact, which has varying impact and its own dynamic, we can concentrate on the last two deprivations, which are part of the everyday prison experience. Material deprivation, while significant, is at least partially offset by some of the material goods that are available in some prisons. On the other hand, since possessions are a symbol of status in capitalistic society and their illegal transfer the reason for being in prison for many, it is the main reason for the development of an underground economy, which creates its own problems of adjustment (Bowker, 1982).

Involuntary association often has serious consequences, threatening the inmates' sense of physical security. Recent increased accounts of prison sexual and physical violence indicate this to be a painful reality of daily prison experience (Davis, 1968; Park, 1975; Sylvester *et al.*, 1977; Bowker, 1980; Lockwood, 1980). The overcrowding prevalent in many of today's prisons exacerbates these conditions and adds its own component of stress (Toch, 1977). Idleness, which often is a result of overcrowding because of the reduced work opportunities, adds another measure to the daily coping problems of inmates (Lombardo, 1982).

## Security

The overriding concern in all prisons is security. Every activity in prison is measured against its potential threat of disorder or escape. Each inmate is given a custody designation that determines his ability to engage in activities and controls his freedom of movement. Those with high custody levels have the least amount of freedom, those with lower levels enjoy a greater ability to move about. The level of custody assigned to inmates is subject to change at any time, for any reason, without appeal. Some institutions are known for their overall higher security in terms of both their physical structure and their internal management. Depending on perceived conditions, custody levels may be increased in any institution when tighter security is considered necessary for greater control. The effect on inmates' daily lives varies. The comments of Lucien X. Lombardo are illustrative.

> Tight security is . . . capable of having positive and negative effects on different segments of heterogeneous inmate populations. For inmates who are concerned with safety and structure, tight security offers protection from physical assault by other inmates. It also provides certainty and predictability, reducing stress for inmates concerned with these issues. For others, however, tight security means loss of freedom and a lessened ability to control one's own life. Under such conditions, inmates are more likely to express concerns about the abuse of authority and officer harassment and to make more frequent demands for respect (1982: 80).

## The Changing Role of the Guard

The role of the prison guard must be understood in the light of what Everett C. Hughes (1971) called the *moral division of labor,* based on the respectability of the work that various groups or occupations perform. Those occupations that involve a great deal of *dirty work* tend to be seen as disreputable; the job of dealing with those convicted of crime is a type of societal dirty work that more respectable elements of the population delegate to correctional workers. Because they must deal on a daily basis with those whom society has cast aside, correctional workers, especially guards, are seen by some as suspect, and their occupation is accorded little prestige.

The guard, or correctional officer, has traditionally been perceived as the ultimate controller and enforcer of prison rules. While guards sometimes had to develop styles of accommodation, they were the ultimate authority in matters of discipline and security, often without review. As the conditions of imprisonment were increasingly challenged and modifications imposed, the guard's traditional role began to change also. Guards perceived the effect of these changes as a threat, feeling that the courts had undermined them. No longer could they do what they pleased to maintain discipline; their actions were now subject to legal challenge. These events stimulated a trend to organize begun earlier in less dramatic fashion, as correctional ideologies were turning away from the prison as merely a place to isolate and contain.

The low status and low pay of the guard job are features that ordinarily would make prison employees prime candidates for union organizing. However, as Norma Crotty (1983) noted, prisons are authoritarian institutions, run along paramilitary lines, with a tendency to view the top command (the warden, in particular) with respect. Until relatively recent times, prisons resembled medieval fiefdoms, with the warden the powerful lord of the manor who could squelch most union rumblings. But this was to change as bureaucratic correctional management supplanted the "monarch" warden with a system in which policies were set in remote bureaus. Wardens were made responsible to central offices in departments of correction that controlled the entire prison system. The era of independent, isolated prisons was over.

With the turn during the 1950s and '60s toward a rehabilitative ideology, the expectations for the guard role also changed. No longer were they mere guards, but correctional officers. What this new role definition was to encompass, however, was never made clear.

Reviewing this period, Crotty states:

> The guards no longer knew what was expected of them. There were no firm directives on how

---

### PANEL 6.5

### *On Officialdom*

The most frightening thing about prison, the most dangerous, senseless, wicked thing about it is that it is a place where people incapable of understanding or handling authority have it with impunity. They can throw it around, use it as a weapon, a threat, a crutch, a shield, or an entertainment. Such evil little people! I am safer with the inmates. The constant hazing, harassing and humiliating of inmates works to the detriment of each inmate. Many C.O.'s hate their jobs and seem to hate themselves for having the job, and their only outlet is to hurt people. We're certainly easy to hurt.

SOURCE: Jean Harris, *Stranger in Two Worlds* (New York: Macmillan, 1986), p. 311.

to function as counselors, and they were still required to carry out their traditional disciplinary role. This attempt to combine treatment and disciplinary tasks in the same role put the guards in a difficult position. They felt betrayed by the public and by college-educated administrators who seemed to favor the inmates (1983: 140).

Other changes during this period, such as the professionalization of certain aspects of prison work—classification, therapy, counseling, and vocational training—also did not sit well with segments of the guard force, who came to feel so threatened that unionization became increasingly attractive and the movement took hold.

It must also be remembered that the background characteristics of guards had always led them to clash with the more educated of the staff, and beginning in the '60s, with the urban-reared inmates as well. Guards were primarily white, from rural areas, relatively uneducated. Guard work was the only employment they could obtain that provided a steady (albeit low) income. John Irwin (1980) suggests that these characteristics are conducive to racial prejudice. As we noted in our discussion of the *principle of emergence* in Chapter 2, these background differences alone do not explain the adversarial nature of the prison world. Rather, the structural dynamics of prison bureaucracies are a major part of the explanation. It was this feature combined with a basic conservatism also stemming from these characteristics that contributed heavily to the conflicts and violence between politicized black urban prisoners and their white rural keepers during the last decade.

Beginning in the '70s, another transformation in correctional philosophy took place which, although an integral part of the larger canvas of change, may for analytical purposes be viewed separately. This was the disavowal of rehabilitation as a major correc-

tional ideology. Rehabilitation had been an accepted humanistic goal of imprisonment, resting on the belief that offenders were sent to prison *as* punishment, not *for* punishment. The time of incarceration was to be used to deal with what were assumed to be identifiable problems that led to the criminal acts. The aim of confinement, then, was to bring about sufficient behavioral change through a variety of programs to allow the prisoner, once released, to be reintegrated into the community. Unfortunately, this goal proved to be elusive for a host of reasons, not the least of which was the refusal of mostly everyone to see crime in other than personal terms. Moreover, rehabilitation often became a cynical excuse to keep offenders imprisoned for purely punitive purposes. When evidence mounted that prison programs did not lead to reformed offenders, rehabilitation as viable correctional objective was largely abandoned.

As rehabilitation was losing its credibility, a movement was already building for change in correctional goals. The end result was a swing of the penological pendulum to an earlier abandoned stance of retribution. Vengeance again emerged as an acceptable reason for punishing criminals. This reconstituted "just deserts" rationale is based on Immanuel Kant's assertion that the criminal is *entitled* to punishment because the law requires it and the criminal as a rational being has the right to expect it; to do otherwise would be unjust (von Hirsch, 1976, 1983; Honderich, 1982; Cavender, 1984). This has had a major impact on the internal dynamics of the prison: Sentences have been lengthened, filling prisons beyond capacity and exacerbating problems of management and control. Inevitably the role of the correctional officer will change again as the full effect of these ideological changes is realized.

We indicated earlier that correctional workers are stigmatized by the low status of their work. Recent years have seen efforts to change this perception and to create a new image of the correctional worker as a professional. Under the former Law Enforcement Assistance Administration, federal funds were made available to finance programs and studies for law enforcement and criminal justice careers. As a result, government agencies and universities began establishing programs and curricula for those wishing to pursue careers in criminal justice or upgrade their education. These programs are now part of the regular offerings of universities both on the undergraduate and graduate level and have gained academic respectability. Students also have shown considerable interest in pursuing academic degrees in criminology and criminal justice. Between 1971 and 1981, the number of bachelor's, master's, and doctoral degrees in

criminology, law enforcement, and corrections rose from 3,050 to 17,778, an increase of 483 percent (National Center for Educational Statistics, 1983–1984). But given organizational dynamics, this increase in education appears to have had little impact on the guard role (Jurik and Musheno, 1986).

With education, however, comes awareness. It should therefore not be surprising that the general academic upgrading coupled with unionization have resulted in an increased militancy among correctional officers. This has led to movements to gain public acceptance, sympathy, and support. Serious scholarship has also addressed the work of correctional officers (Lombardo, 1981), an indicator of renewed interest in their role in the scheme of corrections.

# 7

# Women's Prisons

Most of the research concerning prisons has focused on the male prison; women's prisons have received scant attention. One can only surmise that researchers considered women felons so much like males that no further study was necessary. Perhaps because the number of women confined in prison has always been small relative to male prisoners, the subject was not deemed worthy of comprehensive analysis in its own right. And sexism may have been a contributing factor in the lack of interest. Recent years have seen the number of studies concerned with female imprisonment increase considerably (for example, Ward and Kassebaum, 1965; Giallombardo, 1966; Arditi *et al.*, 1973; Burkhart, 1973; Chandler, 1973; Glick and Neto, 1977; Feinman, 1980; Freedman, 1981; Rafter, 1983, 1985; Baunach, 1985; Dobash *et al.*, 1986).

These studies showed the prevailing assumptions about the similarity between male and female prisoners to be false. While we can point to some similarities, as we shall see, the female prison experience is fundamentally different.

## Women Prisoners

In 1985, 503,601 persons were confined in the various prisons of the U.S. Of that number, 23,091, or more than 4.6 percent, were women (U.S. Department of Justice, 1986f). This percentage has been relatively stable over time. Note, however, the differences in rates for some states (see Table 7.1). Oklahoma, for example, has a high of 6.2, New York a low of 3.1.

Between 1930 and 1981, the number of women in prison rose more than 150 percent, while the increase for men was 78 percent. The net women's portion of the total number of persons confined, however, remained at 4 percent (U.S. Department of Justice, 1983b). Note, however, that in the decade between 1975 and 1985, the *rate* of imprisonment (number incarcerated per 100,000 residents in the population) for women doubled (see Table 7.2). As with men, the use of prison for convicted women has considerably increased. The proportional differences between men and women prisoners, however, has not changed significantly. What has occurred is simply that more men and women are sent to prison but at the same rate of difference.

Like their male counterparts, women who end up in prison generally have backgrounds not conducive to success in American society.

Several recent studies of women inmates lend support to this conclusion (Glick and Neto, 1977; Figueira-McDonough *et al.*, 1981; Goetting and Howsen, 1983).

Like male prisoners, a majority never completed high school, most worked in unskilled labor, the overwhelming number come from poor working-class backgrounds. What does seem to distinguish women is the nature of crimes they commit. A recent Bureau of Justice Statistics report relates:

Arrest, jail and prison data all suggest that women have stronger relative involvement than men in property crimes such as larceny, forgery, fraud, and embezzlement, and in drug offenses. Men are more likely to be involved in robbery or burglary (U.S. Department of Justice, 1983b: 35).

TABLE 7.1 **Women in State and Federal Institutions at Yearend, 1985**

| Jurisdiction | Number of women inmates | Percent of all inmates | Percent change in women inmate population, 1984–85 |
|---|---|---|---|
| UNITED STATES, TOTAL | 23,091 | 4.6% | 10.7% |
| Federal | 2,404 | 6.0 | 20.4 |
| State | 20,687 | 4.5 | 9.7 |
| STATES WITH AT LEAST 500 WOMEN INMATES: | | | |
| California | 2,906 | 5.8% | 25.8% |
| Texas | 1,599 | 4.3 | −5.4 |
| Florida | 1,304 | 4.6 | 11.0 |
| Ohio | 1,153 | 5.5 | 12.9 |
| New York | 1,061 | 3.1 | 4.9 |
| Georgia | 825 | 5.1 | 8.1 |
| Michigan | 816 | 4.6 | 19.5 |
| North Carolina | 747 | 4.3 | 6.4 |
| Illinois | 673 | 3.6 | 5.0 |
| Louisiana | 620 | 4.5 | 2.0 |
| Alabama | 562 | 5.1 | 7.9 |
| Oklahoma | 524 | 6.2 | 11.0 |
| South Carolina | 511 | 4.8 | 13.6 |
| Pennsylvania | 500 | 3.5 | 5.3 |

SOURCE: U.S. Department of Justice (1986f).

While the rate of women's involvement in crimes of violence is low in comparison to men's, a recent study profiling women in prison shows nearly half were serving time for violent offenses (Goetting and Howsen, 1983).

This does not contradict the fact that women tend to be less violent than men in relation to crimes known, but as with men, it shows that serious traditional crimes committed by women are treated with imprisonment. Moreover, since the sentences of those convicted of violent offenses are longer, their percentage of the prison population as a whole will be high.

Like black men, black women are over-represented as inmates in relation to their numbers in the population at large. According to surveys of several representative states, blacks constitute approximately 11 percent of the adult female population, but 50 percent of women prisoners are black. Hispanics, who are about 5 percent of the adult population of women, make up 9 percent of

incarcerated women. White women constitute 82 percent of the female population at large but make up only 36 percent of the women in prisons (U.S. Comptroller General, 1980; Glick and Neto, 1977).

Ethnic and racial minorities, male and female alike, find themselves disproportionately imprisoned. There are significant differences, however, in the social context of prison life among women in comparison to men.

## Historical Development

To fully appreciate the female prison experience, it is necessary to briefly review the evolution of female confinement in the United States (Rafter, 1983, 1985).

Prior to 1870, women were confined in the same prisons or lockups as males. Descriptions of these early places of confinement indicate that they resembled the "drunk tanks" of modern times. That is, everyone was locked up together in large rooms without regard to age, sex, offense, first offenders or repeaters. Eventually women were placed in a separate room or holding area.

With the advent of the penitentiary system and its emphasis on silence and strict separation of prisoners from one another in order to prevent criminal contagion, men were isolated in single cells. Women, on the other hand, continued to be housed together in a large room, usually in an out-of-the-way area of the prison. It was at this point, according to Nicole Hahn Rafter, that differences developed in how men and women prisoners were treated.

When New York's Auburn prison, the model institution of the congregate system (men worked and ate together in total silence but slept in separate cells), opened in 1821, female prisoners were still kept in an attic room.

TABLE 7.2 **Sentenced Women Prisoners in State and Federal Institutions: Number and Rates of Increase, 1974–1985**

| Year | Number | Rate of Increase |
|------|--------|------------------|
| 1974 | 7,389  | —  |
| 1975 | 8,675  | 8  |
| 1976 | 10,039 | 9  |
| 1977 | 11,212 | 10 |
| 1978 | 11,583 | 10 |
| 1979 | 12,005 | 10 |
| 1980 | 12,331 | 11 |
| 1981 | 14,298 | 12 |
| 1982 | 16,441 | 14 |
| 1983 | 17,476 | 14 |
| 1984 | 19,395 | 16 |
| 1985 | 21,406 | 17 |

SOURCE: Adapted from U.S. Department of Justice (1986i).

Food was sent up to them once a day, and once a day the slops were removed. No provision was made for privacy or exercise, and although the women were assigned some sewing work, for the most part they were left to their own devices . . . (Rafter, 1983: 135).

Not until the late 1830s were women placed in separate cells. But while they gained a modicum of privacy, discipline became stricter. As Rafter indicates, the quality of treatment women received still was inferior to that of men. One example of the general indifference toward women inmates was that in these early periods women tended to be supervised by men. As a result, sexual exploitation by male prisoners and guards was a frequent occurrence. The move to abandon the mass confinement of women prisoners in one room came partly because of continued abuse and sexual scandal. When women finally were supervised by other women, sexual exploitation by male guards was reduced but not eliminated.

Separate buildings for women were first instituted in 1837 in Columbus, Ohio, where a women's annex was built adjacent to the men's prison.

According to Rafter, the first separate penal institution for women opened in New York in 1839. Called the Mount Pleasant Female Prison, it was located behind Sing Sing.

As in other areas of correctional reform, managers of the prison establishment did not make changes based on humanitarian reasons. Insufficient space, inadequate food, and unsanitary conditions persisted until reports of prison inspections became public knowledge. Only then was change in the offing.

Stimulus for reform also came from across the seas. Elizabeth Fry, a Quaker reformer, attempted to bring about better treatment for women and children in London prisons in 1813. Fry was one of the first to recognize

that women prisoners' needs might be different from men's. She and her committee of women prison visitors saw to it that the women's section at Newgate prison became organized and disciplined with schooling, work, and religious services. She agitated for separate quarters for women, women matrons, and pay for prison work, and she was one of the first to recommend establishment of prison shops where prisoners could buy goods (Clear and Cole, 1986; Heidensohn, 1985). Her efforts became known in the U.S. and had considerable influence in Quaker reform circles. Quakers had established a tradition of prison visitation whereby middle-class women provided care and comfort to women prisoners. These volunteer efforts consisted of reading the Bible, teaching the inmates to read and write, and providing books and other materials (Rafter, 1983).

The United States also had its share of reformers. In what has become an increasingly rare occurrence in bureaucratized corrections, one of the women administrators at Mount Pleasant Female Prison, Eliza Farnham, attempted some progressive innovations between 1844 and 1847. She allowed books in cells, abolished the rule of silence, began an education program, allowed inmates to have flowers, hear music, and receive visitors. She also introduced a system of inmate classification. As a result of her work, conditions for women improved. But as history repeatedly has shown, innovators do not last in correctional circles. Conservatives attacked her for going counter to the established correctional ideology. She resisted, but eventually she gave up and resigned. Her now seemingly mild humane innovations were made in a harsh disciplinary context; thus they seemed that much more radical.

Conditions of imprisonment for women remained extremely harsh. Women who disobeyed prison rules were severely punished. Solitary confinement and bread-and-water diets were often supplemented by the strait-jacket and what was known as the "shower-bath," a brutal method of barraging inmates with water until they were close to drowning (Rafter, 1983).

Why such stringent methods? To understand them, one must be aware of the prevailing correctional ideology of the early 19th century concerning women convicted of crime.

Largely because few women committed crime and even fewer were placed in confinement, those who were confined were believed to be the most depraved of women, for whom there was no hope. As Rafter notes:

Because "true" women were considered the guardians of morality, when a woman transgressed she seemed to threaten the very foundations of society. . . . This early view of the female criminal as beyond redemption was related to the archetype of the Dark Lady, a woman of uncommon strength, seductive power, and evil inclination (1985: 49).

As a consequence, whatever befell these women was considered deserved since they were beyond redemption. This view of women was to change near the latter part of the century, as were their conditions of confinement.

### The Reformatory Movement

The year 1870 saw the beginning of the reformatory movement in America. While the notion had been percolating for some time, no actual steps were taken to implement the idea. It was during 1870 that the American Correctional Association declared its now famous principles which established the treatment concept, with rehabilitation

the ultimate goal of corrections. This became known as the treatment or medical model, which until the 1970s was the leading correctional ideology.

The Declaration of Principles as a whole set the tone of correctional practice to come. Its immediate impact was contained in Article XIX, which urged separate facilities for men and women.

Prisons, as well as prisoners, should be classified or graded so that there shall be prisons for the untried, for the incorrigible and for other degrees of depraved character, *as well as separate establishments for women* and for criminals of the younger class (Transactions of the National Congress on Penitentiary and Reformatory Discipline, 1871; emphasis added).

The development of men's and women's reformatories both shared the basic underlying new philosophy of treatment. Men's reformatories, however, tended to adhere to a prisonlike physical structure as well as a strict emphasis on discipline. Women's reformatories, on the other hand, were largely built on a cottage plan, to provide what was deemed a more "relaxed" atmosphere. Inmates were allowed their own rooms, which, with some restrictions, they could decorate to their individual tastes. Unlike the new male institution which housed felons, the reformatory for women housed only misdemeanants, such as prostitutes and petty thieves. Perhaps most significant of all, the new institution was now managed by a female staff, a considerable innovation. The institution emphasized reformation and the acquisition of domestic skills, to allow women to fit into conventional society as housewives or domestics.

Once again the influence of ideology may be seen in the creation of this new form of penal practice. The women's reformatory reflected a new conception of the female criminal. While the conception of the depraved

Chapter 7

woman was not completely abandoned, it no longer was the dominant view. Now women offenders were seen much like children to be cared for and socialized into their "correct" role in society. This paternalistic ideology led to the gender-specific programming of women's reformatories and the double standard of treatment between men and women prisoners.

Describing this new approach, Rafter writes:

[The reformatory's] greatest impact lay in the area of treatment: women's reformatories established and legitimated a tradition of deliberately providing for female prisoners treatment very different from that of males. This tradition of differential treatment persists and is the source of many of the problems which plague the women's prison system today (1983: 148).

The fact that reformers saw women as needing a different type of correctional experience led in some respects to a softening of the punitive process, but at the same time it cast women prisoners into a situation of dependency from which they still have not recovered. The reformatory meant that women were held to higher moral standards than men. They were confined for crimes men rarely were held accountable for (for example, prostitution) but were participating "victims" of. Once incarcerated, women were never offered programs equal to those (limited as they were) offered to men, in educational, vocational, or industrial training intended to encourage the development of marketable skills. For women there was little choice but to master skills that fitted their "womanly nature."

By the 1930s, women's reformatories began to hold a considerable number of convicted felons. Although some reformatories had contained a small number of felony pris-

oners since their inception, most women felons were still being housed in women's sections of male prisons. Once most of the female units of men's prisons were shut down and more felons were sent to the reformatories, misdemeanants once again went to jails, and the reformatory as a concept ceased to exist. Rafter notes a number of conditions that contributed to its demise: the Great Depression, needed space for male prisoners, the end of the Progressive era and the fading of the feminist movement that was spawned in the Progressive period.

There was considerable variation among regions of the country in the movement toward the reformatory and the women's prison. Much of this movement occurred in the Midwest and Northeast, with the South and West relatively slow in advancing toward separate facilities. Until the 1960s, the West had only one women's reformatory. Prior to that period, Western states kept women prisoners in men's institutions. According to Rafter (1985), the reasons for these regional variations lay in differences in wealth, population density, and rates of industrialization.

The reformatory increased the level of control over women. While some easing of the harshness of imprisonment may have been achieved by the reformatory concept, the categories of the female population to be controlled were expanded because of it. Minor offenders whose problems might have been resolved in the community were now also deemed to require confinement. Once the reformatory was established, it needed to be used. Another tool of control was at hand. We will see this process at work in other areas of the correctional spectrum.

From the foregoing it can be seen that there has been a lack of consistency in dealing with women offenders. There have been regional differences in programs and facilities. Both harshness and humane treatment have prevailed, the latter based on an ideology of gender that dominated a particular period. Both are ill conceived, and both are a legacy that continues to plague women's corrections.

## The Social World of Women's Prisons

The type of informal organization or subculture that develops in women's prisons results from the same features and conditions that give rise to the male prison subculture. However, its manifestation is qualitatively different. For both men and women, the social, psychological, and economic deprivations of prison life create problems to which the inmate subculture is a response. As we pointed out in the last chapter, there is disagreement as to whether the style of adaptation is the direct result of the deprivation of prison life or whether the style is imported into the prison from the outside. What is clear is that some form of informal social organization exists.

The major works on women's prisons (Giallombardo, 1966; Heffernan, 1972; Ward and Kassebaum, 1965; Burkhart, 1973) describe and characterize their informal social organization as different from that of men. Each found, unlike in male prisons, an extended kinship system based on pseudo-family relationships, with roles for "parents" and a variety of "relatives." These relationships tended to form loose networks of fictive families that varied in size and age composition.

These structures of relations functioned to ease the rigors of confinement in a much less exploitive fashion than among men prisoners. Of particular note is the area of sexual expression. While homosexual activity is found in all types of penal institutions, in men's prisons it is often based on displays of dominance and coercion and result in violence. Rarely are women's homosexual involvements the result of coercion. Rather, they are more often entered into voluntarily, with sexual involvement growing out of established relationships. Exploitation is present in some individual instances, but the overall pattern of sexual activity is based on sharing and emotional support.

---

**PANEL 7.1**

*On Homosexual Relations in Women's Prison*

---

The course of the homosexual love affair in the prison setting does not run smoothly despite the positive function it serves. However, since the same abstract statement has been made in regard to heterosexual affairs, we shall briefly compare some features of heterosexual and homosexual love affairs.

In some senses, prison homosexuality resembles normal heterosexuality both in its positive and negative aspects. Each relationship can be sought to assuage loneliness, give sexual satisfaction, provide meaning or purpose to daily life, and give status from the association with another person. It can also engender disenchantment and great unhappiness. Fears of desertion, lack of complementarity, jealousy, personality defects, sexual incompatibility, differing interests, and decreased intimacy over time can also characterize the homosexual affair.

A particularly relevant analogy is the adolescent love affair. In each of these types of affairs the emotional and sexual involvement is subject to a delay, if not a prohibition, against formal recognition of the relationship as a social unit. Both adolescent and prison lovers are subject to the control and scrutiny of others. Both are accused of being only infatuated and not being seriously in love.

SOURCE: David A. Ward and Gene Kassebaum, *Women's Prison: Sex and Social Structure* (Chicago: Aldine, 1965), pp. 194–95.

Interestingly, however, those women who assume the male role act in macho style, adapting various symbols of stereotyped maleness. As Rose Giallombardo relates:

For example, the crop their hair very short to resemble a masculine haircut . . . Their hair is worn straight, as curls are associated with femininity. Cosmetics are not worn . . . Inmates assuming the male role wear slacks styled like men's trousers . . . white blouses . . . are converted by the inmates into a cultural symbol of masculinity. The collars are heavily starched and when ironed are folded lengthwise in half in order to look like the starched collar of a man's shirt . . . Shoes worn by studs do not have heels . . . Studs wear their socks straight up (they do not wear nylon hose) to symbolize masculinity (1966: 137).

The general lack of exploitation also is evident in the area of economic exchange of scarce or contraband items, where the "family" system serves a mechanism for distribution. As in the male prison, there are "hustles" and illicit transfers of goods and services; however, the female prison underground economy is not as well developed as is the male's.

Lee H. Bowker (1981) points out that the reason for this difference lies in the fact that male prisons are larger than female prisons, and size is a chief determinant of the complexity of the underground economy. Moreover, since the underground economy is a response to the level of material deprivation, the greater the level of deprivation the more elaborate the underground economy. Because material deprivation tends to be less in women's prisons than in men's prisons, one would anticipate a less developed alternate economy. Evidence also suggests that women prisoners, more often than men, resort to simple thievery to acquire the commodities

they feel they need to offset the pains of imprisonment (Bowker, 1977: 91).

There are indications that certain adaptive role types develop in some women's prisons. Esther Heffernan (1972), for example, describes three general types she found in the prison she studied: "square," "cool," and "the life." The square does not have a criminal orientation; she's essentially conventional but has committed a serious crime that demanded imprisonment: for example, the woman who killed her lover under extreme circumstances. She doesn't follow a deviant lifestyle, doesn't develop a prison orientation, and identifies more with the administration and the outside than with other prisoners.

The cool adjusts to prison by manipulating the situation as best as she can to her own advantage. She knows how to make her circumstances as pleasurable as possible and still stay out of trouble.

The life has a confirmed criminal orientation. She has had previous prison experiences, identifies with other similarly experienced women inmates, violates prison rules, and in general carries on her life in prison not too differently than on the outside.

Women prisoners tend to be less committed than men to the convict code, and show little solidarity and collective opposition to prison staff. Some have claimed that solidarity seems undermined by women's tendency to see other women as rivals, and by their lower rate of involvement in criminal groups in the free community.

There are basic differences, then, in the adaptive patterns found in men's and women's prisons. Many of these differences may be related to societal gender role expectations that become severely distorted in the coercive pseudo-community that is a prison. Thus we find the traditional male role of provider, protector, competitor often turned into the conniver, aggressor, exploiter. When men are confined they involve themselves in the kinds of activities that gave meaning to their lives in the free world: activities that earn them a livelihood. In the prison this finds expression in the production and exchange of contraband (for example, sexually explicit pictures and books, loan sharking, or drugs). The traditional

---

### PANEL 7.2

## On Surviving in Women's Prison

When you're in prison, time stops. You come out with the same problems you go in with—and start all over again with their 12 extra rules of parole in addition. While you're there, you just learn to survive and manipulate any extra pleasure you can. A comparatively honest person who just committed a crime of passion would end up becoming a manipulator in prison. A girl who works in the kitchen takes extra slices of meat and gets cigarettes for them. Cigarettes are money in prison. There's nothing there to foster the qualities society wants. You become dishonest just to make it. All the qualities you're being sent there to get, they forget you won't have when you get back. You wind up doing all those little things just to make life more comfortable for yourself. Sixty percent of what you do is against some rule. If you have more than four slices of bread in your room, it's against the rules. An egg or rice—you get three days in punishment. I know a woman who got 19 days in punishment for refusing two slices of burnt toast. They'd have raids on your room. But they'd only look where you hide things. So I'd leave whatever I had that was contraband out in open view. I never got busted.

SOURCE: Kathryn Watterson Burkhart, *Women in Prison* (New York: Popular Library, 1976), p. 90.

---

male emphasis on aggressiveness and machismo inclines them to see every prison dispute as a character contest, with even lethal violence a justifiable response if the stakes are high enough.

Women's socialization experiences traditionally prepare them for dependent roles as marital partners rather than occupational roles in the labor force. Consequently, women derive much of their personal satisfaction from supportive involvements with others. They're less aggressive and less prone to violence, another reflection of their traditionally dependent status. Riots and other forms of collective challenges to prison staff and administration are considerably less common and less deadly in women's prisons as compared to men's (Heffernan, 1972). Indeed, even in their criminal involvements women act less independently, playing supporting roles to men.

All of these components of the traditional feminine role may be reflected in women's response to the pains of imprisonment. When women are confined they reportedly experience the loss of close supportive social relationships more acutely than men do. Therefore, to mitigate these deprivations, fictive family relations develop that mimic an extended-family system.

Much of the women's prison subculture researchers have described seems to support an importation model. As we have noted, a fair number of these patterns and structures may be attributed to gender role stereotypes imported from the outside. However, styles of behavior and gender role adaptation are not played out in a social vacuum. The often exaggerated and sometimes caricature adaptive styles are shaped in part by the formal administrative structure or organizational mandate of prison systems. A harsh disciplinary structure combined with severe deprivation of the usually accepted minimal necessities of ordinary life may shape more

## PANEL 7.3

### *On Petty Rules and Harassment*

A lieutenant pulled me aside tonight as I was on my way to medication and said in a very serious tone, "Mrs. Harris, we're having a good deal of trouble with several of your packages."

I said, "Why? What's the matter?"

He said, "Some of them have no address on the outside so they have to be returned to the sender without opening them."

"How do you do that?"

"Return them to the sender without opening them? Just stamp 'return to sender!' I'm just telling you, you better tell your friends to be sure to put an address on the outside, because, by law, we cannot open them if they don't have an address."

"But how will the mail know where to return them to if there isn't any address on the outside?"

"That's what I'm saying, Mrs. Harris. They just return it to the people who sent it."

"But if there isn't any address on it how do they know where to send it? You have to open the package to see if there's a name and address inside."

"I've just told you, Mrs. Harris, the law says you can't open a package that doesn't have an address on the outside."

Finally I said, "OK, just do whatever you have to do with it." God alone knows what was in the packages, or who sent them, or where they finally ended up.

The lieutenant must be a cousin of the C.O. who refuses to let me alphabetize the many names of my visiting list to make it easier for the C.O.s at the gate to find the names when people come to visit me.

"Mrs. Harris" he said, in the sort of tone one uses with a not very bright child after you've explained something simple to them at least five times. "It ain't gonna do no good to put 'em in alphabetical order. These people don't visit you in alphabetical order." . . .

I have, as I am allowed to have, a small lamp in my cell. You can have one as long it is not more than twenty inches high, and can't cost more than $20. Twenty seems to be the magic number. Mine is approved and I have a signed certificate proving it. Tonight I was reading in my cell when a C.O. came by, walked into my cell and turned on the overhead light, a terrible light that I never use. I said, "Don't turn it on, I have plenty of light with the lamp." She said, "You got to have it on. When the door is open you got to have the overhead light on. If you want dat lite out I got to lock your cell door first." Some new Mickey Mouse idiocy becomes a "rule" every day. It disturbs a C.O. almost to distraction to see me sitting quietly in my cell, minding my own business and not breaking any rules. There are some sick people in here in positions of authority. The idea that there might be such a thing as rehabilitation in here is simply false. After someone has been here for a few years, I think returning to a reasonably normal life will be six times harder than it was before.

SOURCE: Jean Harris, *Stranger in Two Worlds* (New York: Macmillan, 1986), pp. 300–10.

extreme patterns of adjustment. Conversely, a formal structure that allows more freedom and shares some decision-making power with inmates may result in a less exaggerated adaptive form and a more manageable prison.

The influence of the type of institution on inmate attitudes and behavior has been recognized in the literature on prisons but does not seem to have been taken seriously by decision makers (Akers *et al.*, 1977; Hartnagel and Gillan, 1980; Mahan, 1984). As gender roles change in society at large, one would expect these changes to filter into the prison society as well. But the criminal justice system as a whole is a conservative institution that lags behind contemporary trends. The correctional component of the system is the most resistant to innovation and change. Thus the women's movement's modest societal impact in changing gender role perceptions will only seep slowly into the women's prison.

Moreover, women who receive prison sentences tend to be traditional in their social–political outlook, and, given their powerless status, are hardly agents of change. When this is coupled with a conservative political environment little will change in the social organization, both informal and formal, of women's correctional institutions.

## Women Inmates and Children

A wrenching problem facing women in prison is the separation from their children. This is a major concern because between 50 percent and 70 percent of all women incarcerated have dependent children.

According to a study by Phyllis Jo Baunach (1985), a number of factors of child placement affect the impact of the women's separation from their children. If the mother was involved in placing her children with a caretaker, she seemed more satisfied with the placement. However, most of the women in the study had little, if any, involvement in making the decision. They felt inadequate, despondent, and had considerable feelings of guilt, since they saw themselves as ultimately responsible for their being separated from their children.

Most of the mothers wished to be honest with their children and tell them why they had to be separated and wanted to maintain ties in whatever ways possible. Most wished to reassume parental responsibilities upon release. But those whose children were placed outside the family context, such as with foster parents, feared they would not be able to regain custody.

Baunach points out that ongoing contact with children is of great importance and helps to alleviate the fear of separation these women experience. Unfortunately, many prisons are far removed from where children and family members live. As a result, visits are infrequent and often of short duration; this coupled with the strange surroundings of the prison often make visits tense.

A number of administrations have attempted to alleviate some of the difficulty by allowing extended visits and providing comfortable surroundings for visitation. A few jurisdictions provide accommodations where families may stay together for several days (Clear and Cole, 1986).

## Facilities and Programs

In general, male prisoners, depending on region, continue to be given more opportunities in vocational training, industrial experience, and certain services than women get. In recent years this disparity of treatment has been challenged in the courts on the basis of constitutional principles, with various decisions upholding the right of women to equal treatment. In line with gender-role socialization patterns of the past, women have not been as litigious as men in their attempt to improve prison conditions. On the other hand, the courts also have not taken as active a judicial role in rectifying wrongs in women's institutions as they have in men's. For a synopsis of the few major court decisions affecting women prisoners, see Table 11.1, Chapter 11.

Women's fight for equal opportunities in prison programs has been an uphill battle not only because of the usual inertia of the correctional bureaucracy but because of ingrained sexual stereotypes. This conclusion is drawn by a most unlikely source, the U.S. Comptroller General. The Comptroller General heads the General Accounting Office (GAO), an independent agency of the legislative branch. Among the varied duties assigned to the GAO are conducting studies, publishing reports, and making recommendations to provide congressional committees with information to enable them to carry out their functions. One such recent report indicates:

> The reasons for differences most frequently cited by penal officials were (1) the small numbers of women incarcerated did not justify the expense of duplicate facilities and programs, and (2) the women were not interested in the types of vocational training offered men. A less obvious reason may be the personal feelings of some penal officials on the appropriate roles for women or towards incarcerated women in general (1980: 20–21).

Administrators also argue that because there are fewer institutions housing women, there is less flexibility in programming open to them. One of the implications of this argument is that more women's prisons should be built. This ignores the more basic question of whether alternatives to prisons would not be better options to provide needed services and training for women (or men).

The existing conditions have a number of undesirable consequences. For example, women whose cases do not require high security are often kept in institutions with women whose cases are considered to require more secure levels of custody, only because there are no other facilities to which they might be transferred. Men nearing release are often placed in institutions close to their communities to facilitate release planning. This option is not now readily available to women, given the fact that many states have only one prison for women, located far from major population centers and community resources.

Thus women are at a disadvantage both within prisons, which offer unequal programs and services, and in planning their release.

## Common Facilities

One suggested solution to the problem of disparity in programs, services, and facilities suffered by incarcerated women ironically is a return to a sharing of facilities. The idea of a so-called coed prison has received increased attention in recent years (Ross *et al.*, 1978; Smykla, 1980). Unlike the 19th-century system, however, there would be an equal sharing of correctional resources. Some are already experimentally in operation in some states and at the federal level.

There are a number of advantages, according to one report: (1) a more normalized environment, with improvements in inmate language, dress, and grooming habits; (2) fewer fights and assaults, with a resulting safer environment for both staff and inmates; (3) a more extensive range of programs; (4) an improved community transition upon release; (5) more nontraditional training programs available to women; and (6) women can be located closer to their homes (U.S. Comptroller General, 1980: 27–28).

While this approach requires a good public relations effort and a less tradition-oriented staff attuned to the special circumstances of these arrangements, the normalization in prison conditions such efforts bring by itself makes this a worthy innovation. However, there must be a sensitivity to women's needs rather than an emphasis on mere administrative convenience in order for these measures to work. As Rafter warns:

> Most decisions to "go co-ed" have been made to solve bureaucratic needs (overcrowding at a men's institution and simultaneous underpopulation at a women's prison, for example) rather than out of concern to improve the lot of female prisoners. Decisions to maintain or terminate co-correctional programs are usually made by male administrators and tend to be dictated by concern for male prisoners, thus perpetuating the historical neglect of women's needs (1985: 187).

Rafter notes other drawbacks to co-corrections. For instance, women may be instrumentally used to keep men prisoners in line, by their presence reducing incidents of homosexual aggression. She points out that while women are better protected today against sexual attack in mixed prisons than they were when they were housed in men's prisons in the past, they still carry most of the responsibility for preventing sexual contact.

Nevertheless, if properly conceived and administered, cooperative ventures between men's and women's prisons hold considerable promise, as long as the special requirements of each group are taken into account.

Alternatives to confinement such as restitution to victims or community service work, combined with probation and support services, should not be overlooked and have much to offer to many women who present no danger to the community but are now needlessly incarcerated.

In the current conservative political atmosphere with heavy emphasis on punishment, it is doubtful that nonpunitive innovations will receive much support. Whatever progress there has been in correctional philosophy concerning women is not likely to advance in the immediate future; more likely is a toughening of attitudes toward women prisoners to equal those toward men.

Correctional change requires an enabling political atmosphere. When there is a heavy emphasis on punishment as part of the political rhetoric, it is doubtful whether nonpunitive innovations will receive much support. Further movement away from traditional responses will only occur when progressive politics allows it to happen.

# 8

# Juvenile
# Training Schools

Although residential institutions for juveniles first appeared in Europe more than three centuries ago, they were not adopted widely in the United States until the early 19th century. Called "houses of refuge," they were operated by private philanthropic societies in many of the largest cities of the Northeastern states (Rothman, 1971; Mennel, 1973; Krisberg and Austin, 1978). They accepted destitute and orphaned children as well as those convicted of crimes. Various types of restraint, corporal punishment, and a system of grades or classes based on individual behavior were used to maintain internal control. Reflecting the dominant correctional ideology of the era, refuge managers believed that inmates needed

an inflexible routine built around the workshop and the schoolroom, impressing them

with the importance of personal cleanliness, sobriety, frugality, and industry. Punishment would be the invariable result of rule violations. In this scheme, pious and orderly conduct by an individual child signified the success of reformatory methods; good behavior meant everything, noble thoughts little (Mennel, 1973: 26–27).

Refuge inmates labored in large workshops, making products for outside contractors who paid the refuges for the inmates' labor. When released from the refuge, inmates often were apprenticed to farmers in order to remove them from the city and its corrupting influences.

In the mid-1800s, local and state governments began to build and operate "reform schools" for delinquents. In many respects, these were indistinguishable from the houses of refuge. Like them, reform schools drew their inmates from a variety of sources and confined a diverse population. The institutional programs emphasized formal schooling, but the large workshops were retained and the reform schools continued the contract system of labor. Many were built in rural areas so their inmates could be trained in agricultural pursuits that were thought to be reformative. Architecturally, however, the reform schools were organized on a "cottage" or "family" plan.

Toward the end of the 19th century, reform schools introduced vocational education, military drill, and calisthenics into their institutional regimen. "These new routines were designed as much to reinforce the authoritarian type of control for which reform schools had been traditionally noted as they were to improve the physical condition of the inmates" (Mennel, 1973: 104). During this same era, some reform schools changed their name to "industrial school" or—later—"training school." For example, the Ohio Reform Farm School, opened in 1857, later became the Boy's Industrial School.

## Public Training Schools

Some of the nation's original training schools have survived to the present, albeit under new names. In 1982, there were 214 long-term public juvenile institutions in the United States that were designated either "strict" or "medium" custody (U.S. Department of Justice, 1983a). This number includes some of the original training schools as well as the smaller high-security institutions that some states have built in recent years, either to replace or to augment them. Again, Ohio serves as an example. In 1961 the state opened the Training Institution for Central Ohio (TICO), but it continues to operate the former Boy's Industrial School, since renamed the Fairfield School for Boys.

In 1985, there were 49,322 juveniles confined in public custody institutions in the United States, for a rate of 185 per 100,000 juveniles in the nation's population (U.S. Department of Justice, 1986b). This is a marked increase from the rate of 167 recorded in 1979 (U.S. Department of Justice, 1983a). As with jails and prisons, there is substantial state variation in the use of training schools and other juvenile confinement institutions. The confinement rate for Connecticut, West Virginia, and Massachusetts was less than 50 per 100,000 juveniles in the general population, while the corresponding rate for 14 states exceeded 200. California's rate of 384 led the nation (U.S. Department of Justice, 1986h). To some extent, this variation reflects state variation in the prevalence of juvenile crime. But the major reasons lie in structural, economic and cultural differences among the states.

Examination of the characteristics of inmates of public long-term juvenile institutions shows a pattern not unlike that of America's jails and prisons. They confine the disadvantaged and poor. As Table 8.1 shows, of the 33,498 juveniles confined in these institutions during 1982, the proportion of blacks and males far exceeds their proportion in the general population. Doubtless, some of this imbalance is because males and blacks tend to commit delinquencies that are more serious than those committed by females and whites. Also, blacks and males compile lengthier official records of delinquency than females and whites. Still, some part of this inequity is due to systematic discrimination. Table 8.1 also shows that the inmates' average age is nearly 16, which approximates the age of peak delinquency involvement.

Juveniles can be charged with and convicted of offenses for which adults cannot be charged or convicted. These *status offenses* include such behaviors as truancy, ungovernability, or being habitually wayward. Another significant statistic in Table 8.1 is that only 4.2 percent of the inmates were confined for status offenses. This represents a significant decrease from 1979, and continues a trend that began when Congress passed the Juvenile Justice and Delinquency Prevention Act of 1974. However, this decrease has been matched by a substantial increase in the numbers of status offenders confined in private institutions (Lerman, 1984). It is clear that the 1970s movement to deinstitutionalize status offenders, whatever else it may have accomplished, has shifted some of them from public to private cor-

rectional institutions (Schwartz *et al.,* 1984; Logan and Rausch, 1985).

As this suggests, public and private facilities differ significantly in the distribution of their inmates by detention status. In 1979, abused, dependent, and neglected children and voluntary admissions accounted for 2 percent of the juvenile population in public institutions, but 45 percent in private institutions (Lerman, 1984). The 1982 census counted about 33,000 juveniles housed in public facilities and about 30,000 in the more numerous, but typically smaller, private institutions.

TABLE 8.1  **Characteristics of Inmates of Public Long-Term Juvenile Institutions in the United States, 1982**

|  | Percent |
|---|---|
| RACE | |
| White | 58.2% |
| Black | 39.7 |
| Other | 2.1 |
| SEX | |
| Male | 88.8 |
| Female | 11.2 |
| REASON HELD | |
| Delinquency | 93.7 |
| Status offense | 4.2 |
| Other | 2.1 |
| ABJUDICATION STATUS | |
| Detained | 2.4 |
| Committed | 96.6 |
| Voluntary admission | 1.0 |
| AVERAGE AGE | 15.6 years |
| Males | 15.7 |
| Females | 15.3 |
| AVERAGE LENGTH OF STAY | 183 days |
| TOTAL NUMBER OF INMATES | 33,498 |

SOURCE: U.S. Department of Justice (1983a).

## Private Training Schools

America has witnessed at least two waves of privatization efforts in the area of juvenile corrections. The first occurred in the late 19th century, when training schools for juveniles were opened under private auspices. The Gibaut School in Terre Haute, Indiana, is an example. The second wave occurred in the 1970s and 1980s, as the drive to deinstitutionalize juvenile offenders gained momentum (Lerman, 1980, 1984; U.S. Department of Justice, 1986b). Private juvenile institutions have been a growth industry in the 1970s and 1980s.

Like the rate of use of public juvenile institutions, the rate of use of private juvenile institutions fluctuates over time. In 1982, the former stood at 175 per 100,000 population (age 10 to the upper limit of juvenile court authority) and the latter was 115. In 18 states the rate of use of private institutions exceeded the rate for public institutions (U.S. Department of Justice, 1986b: Table 3).

Whereas the earlier private institutions were products of philanthropic or religious impulse, the newer ones result from a more pecuniary, entrepreneurial drive. From the earliest days, private institutions attracted youths from more affluent backgrounds than those sent to public training schools. Many of America's newer private juvenile institutions have chosen to emphasize their mental health and drug treatment programs. In this way they are able to capitalize on young people from families who have medical insurance or who are able to pay the costs of their children's confinement and treatment (Schwartz *et al.,* 1984).

There were 1,877 privately operated juvenile detention and correctional facilities in 1983; about two of every three detention and correctional facilities operating in the United States in 1983 were privately operated (U.S. Department of Justice, 1986b).

Table 8.2 contains a summary description of the inmates of private long-term juvenile

institutions in the United States. (Data on the inmates of private group homes, ranches, and forestry camps are omitted from Table 8.2.) Note first that the number of youths confined in private training schools is only slightly less than the number in public ones. As compared with public training schools (see Table 8.1), private institutions confine more whites, more girls, significantly more status offenders and dependent and neglected youths, and a larger proportion of youths who were admitted "voluntarily." The inmates of private training schools also are somewhat younger than their public counterparts. More important, the average length of stay for inmates of private institutions is much longer than the average stay in public institutions (279 days versus 183).

There are several possible reasons for this disparity. First, the population of private institutions probably includes a larger proportion of dependent and neglected children who have few family resources. For these youths, the institution becomes a surrogate home placement, which may last for several years. Second, because confinement is a profit-making activity, many private institutions may be reluctant to discharge inmates so long as their families can pay the fare. Finally, private institutions are not forced to discharge inmates in order to make room for new admissions, as public institutions are.

Private institutions offer much greater diversity in programs and structures than public ones do. For instance, one of the private institutions included in a comparative study of six juvenile correctional institutions described its objectives thus:

> When a boy comes to us we are primarily interested, not in what he has done, but why he has done it. We are committed to demonstrate to our boys that the community is not hostile to the individual. We must symbolize to them the cooperative forces of our society which are interested, not in avenging aggressive acts, but in

TABLE 8.2 **Characteristics of Inmates of Private Long-Term Juvenile Institutions in the United States, 1982**

|  | Percent |
|---|---|
| **RACE** | |
| White | 71.7% |
| Black | 24.5 |
| Other | 2.9 |
| **SEX** | |
| Male | 72.1 |
| Female | 27.9 |
| **REASON HELD** | |
| Delinquency | 34.3 |
| Status offense | 20.3 |
| Other | 45.4 |
| **ADJUDICATION STATUS** | |
| Detained | 0.9 |
| Committed | 80.2 |
| Voluntary admission | 18.9 |
| **AVERAGE AGE** | 15.0 years |
| **AVERAGE LENGTH OF STAY** | 279 days |
| **TOTAL NUMBER OF INMATES** | 29,723 |

SOURCE: McGarrell and Flanagan (1985:636).

preventing them. We therefore inflict no punishment, either corporally or otherwise, in the handling of our boys. Treatment and education are the only tools we have. We are convinced that punishing teaches the child only how to punish; scolding teaches him how to scold. By showing him, by our own example, that we understand, he learns the meaning of understanding; by helping him, he learns the meaning of cooperation (Street *et al.*, 1966: 59).

Contrast this description with one in a brochure prepared by the staff of another private institution, located in the Southwest, which was sent to state departments of welfare, promoting the institution as possible placement for their youth.

Dear Friend:

After these years of operating the _____ Home for Girls, we are more convinced than ever that CHRIST meets every need. When a girl comes to our home, she must look at it as a real spiritual hospital and trust us and cooperate with us as much as she would her family doctor. We have some requirements . . . that have proven best for those who come for help. If for some reason you cannot or will not submit to these requirements, we cannot help you. And remember, those of us who lead you live under the same conditions. Be sure to bring a King James Version Bible. We receive you with open arms and open hearts and know that by faith that victory can be yours through the blessed Saviour.

### REQUIREMENTS

**1.** No coffee, tea, magazines, TV, radios, cigarettes, newspapers will be brought in the _____ Home.

**2.** No dresses or skirts above the knee. No pants or pant suits allowed.

**3.** No eye shadow of any kind.

**4.** Only two letters a week are written out, and those only to relatives or guardians.

**5.** All bags and boxes will be inspected on entering and leaving.

**6.** All money sent will be kept by the home and given as needed. No girl will be allowed to have money in her room.

**7.** If while at the home any girl should run away, her bags, clothes, etc. will not be sent home C.O.D. or express—they will be the property of the home.

**8.** If anyone brings pants, eye make-up or any of the items listed as not allowed, they will be taken up and destroyed.

**9.** No telephone calls will be made by the girls except in an emergency or of great importance.

**10.** Phone calls once a month from parents or guardians.

**11.** During the months of June, July, and August, all phone calls will be received only between 9:30 A.M. and 4:00 P.M. Monday through Friday.

**12.** Calls will be limited to five minutes unless an emergency.

**13.** No visiting in the girls' rooms—all visiting must be in reception rooms or one of the visiting rooms.

**14.** Any girl that leaves the dorm with parents must have permission from one of the staff when she leaves, and report in when returning.

**15.** The home will not be responsible for the girls' actions when they are with parents.

**16.** All medical, dental, and other personal bills made by your daughter will be mailed to you, the parent or guardian for payment.

We must not be misled by the diverse ideologies and strategies pursued one place or another in America's training schools. To a great extent, all generate an underlife that includes an informal social organization and an inmate code (Goffman, 1961).

## The Underlife of Training Schools

Those who have investigated the underlife of training schools have focused primarily on social structure and culture at the cottage level. There is substantial consensus in the research findings, although there are marked differences between institutions for boys and girls. The underlife of penal institutions is, to a great extent, a product of their formal structure. Consequently, research shows that private institutions also generate an underlife, one that differs only in degree from the underlife of public training schools.

As is true of other types of total institutions, training schools have an elaborate informal social organization and culture. The social organization includes a prestige hierarchy among inmates, and a variety of inmate social types or roles. The inmate culture includes a complex of norms that indicate how inmates should relate to one another, to staff members, and to the institutional regimen. Despite the fact that many of these norms are violated often, they receive strong verbal allegiance from inmates.

Researchers also agree that the informal social organization and culture perhaps exerts the strongest influence on inmates during their incarceration. The fact that staff members, in their day-to-day activities and interaction with inmates, take account of and thereby validate this sub rosa organization and culture also points to their importance. As one researcher noted, "the social system [in the cottage] appears not only to be the dominant force in the life of the boys living there but is potent enough to evoke a kind of

covert and unwitting support and collaboration from the institution itself" (Polsky, 1962: 7).

It would be a mistake to assume that the underlife of training schools is produced and maintained by those who happen to be inmates at any given time. Rather, it persists from year to year even though its inmates come and go. In short, it is an aspect of the institution itself. As Howard W. Polsky notes, "The removal of 'key' boys does not appear to affect the viability of the cultural patterns in the least. Other boys simply move into or are put into the vacated roles" (1962: 7). But as we shall see, this does not mean that the underlife of training school is a static, unchanging complex. Rather, it adapts to changes in the organization and regimen of the training school itself and the wider social context. But it does mean that the underlife cannot be altered to any degree simply by normal turnover in training school inmates.

### Boys

As in all penal institutions, inmates of boys' training schools develop and maintain an unofficial social order that influences their daily activities. Polsky's research in *Cottage Six* (1962) can serve as an example. Using techniques of participant observation, he found a system of roles and cliques in the cottage he studied. In Cottage Six, as in most training schools for boys, aggression and exploitation are pervasive qualities of daily life. Manipulation of these qualities is the chief means of gaining prestige in the cottage social system. New boys are subjected to testing and *ranking*—a process of invidious verbal comparisons—to determine their position in the cottage. Positions may be determined within a matter of hours after a new boy arrives:

If he is of middle-class origin, nonverbal, and effeminate, he may be subjected to prolonged testing and ranking. Depending upon his reaction to this ribbing, he may become further isolated from peers in circular fashion until he is overwhelmed by physical coercion, fear, or anxiety (1962: 83).

By virtue of their ability to dominate other boys through aggression or the threat of aggression, "toughs" occupy the top rung in the cottage hierarchy. "Con-artists" excel in ranking other boys. They boast of their ath-

---

### PANEL 8.1

## *The Unofficial Social Order in the Training School*

As there was an officially recognized structure on campus, there was also an officially recognized social order within the cottage. . . .

There was also an unofficial social order on campus and in each cottage. Referred to as the "wheels," the highest members of this group held the most direct influence over the everyday safety of the rest of the boys on campus. They were the bad asses, the fighters, the ones who lived by their strength and guts. Everybody quickly learned who they were, one way or another. Even the adults gave them special treatment. They were ranked by their fighting ability and shown the kind of respect that is born of fear and uncertainty.

Each cottage was a miniature version of the unofficial social order. Each had its wheels. They were easy to spot. They had their own meal table, which was always filled with food. They never worried about second or third helpings. The best lockers were theirs—the ones furthest from the showers, where a wall could be used as a backrest. The bedrooms at the end of the hallways, where only four slept, belonged to them. They always had plenty of cigarettes, candy, freshly pressed clothes, and other luxuries. They slept late, stayed up after lights out, seldom got reported for misdeeds, and never shined. Among the boys, their word was a commandment. Where a floorwalker would report a boy for breaking a rule, a wheel would break a head. Even the houseparents treated the wheels differently from the rest of us. They knew that if they kept the wheels happy,

their jobs would be easier. The wheels led a good life, as long as they stayed on top.

Then there were those boys who sought special privileges by brownnosing, "sucking ass" as we called it. "Suckies" were hated. They were the "rats," the "stoolies," the ones who kept the uncle informed about other people's activities. Sometimes they got a pat on the head or some small privilege for their reports. They also often ended up with a black eye.

The "flunkies" were the boys with little or no self-respect or confidence. In exchange for protection they did the bidding for the wheels and gave them cigarettes, candy, or whatever else they wanted. Usually the smaller, more frail boys, they followed every command and clung closely to their protectors.

On the lowest rung on the ladder were the "scurfs." They were the beggars, the ones who scrounged cigarette butts and ate food that had been on the floor, the ones who never changed their underwear or took showers, the objects used in sex play. Scurfs were treated like the plague.

Though there were some boys who never especially differentiated themselves with regard to any of the officially or unofficially recognized positions within the institutional social order, everyone knew of its existence and learned to operate within its boundaries. It directly affected each of us daily.

SOURCE: Waln K. Brown, *The Other Side of Delinquency* (New Brunswick, NJ: Rutgers University Press, 1983), pp. 122–24.

letic and sexual exploits and also take pride in conniving. Unlike the toughs and con-artists, "bush-boys" and their cliques occupy low status positions in the cottage social structure. They are characterized by "child-ish regressive behavior . . . [they] overreact to anyone's getting something 'on them' and [they rank] each other incessantly. . . . They [bicker] constantly and [display] blatant hos-tility among themselves." By contrast, "quiet types" are boys who "mind their p's and q's, and neither join up with tough guys nor ac-cept a bushboy status" (1962: 81–82). At the bottom of the cottage pecking order are the "scapegoats." They

are caught in the most vicious circle at [the training school]; as catchall targets, it is impos-sible for them to escape the constant pervasive exploitation of the overbearing toughs and manipulative "con-artists," and they are even prey to bushboys (1962: 84).

Some of the sociopolitical events of the 1960s produced results in training schools similar to those in penitentiaries. Perhaps the principal consequence was the intensifica-tion of racial conflicts and the solidification of the black inmate group. This fact, and its social effects in the daily routine in juvenile institutions, has been depicted in a study of the TICO, the Ohio youth institution men-tioned earlier. Clemens Bartollas *et al.* (1976) carefully describe the social roles and socio-metric and hierarchical relationships among the boys at TICO. They also describe the dynamics of interracial contacts—many of which consist of exploitation of whites by blacks. Boys' experiences within the institu-tion are largely determined by the repu-tation they acquire during their first three weeks.

Once boys were in the intake cottage, the other boys immediately subjected them to tests de-signed to ascertain whether they could be ex-

ploited for food, clothes, cigarettes, and sex. Sexual exploitation was found to be severe, with blacks pressuring whites in most of the encounters. If the new boy looked and acted tough, exploitation was minimized; if any weak-nesses were shown, he was immediately mis-

---

**PANEL 8.2**

*Daily Life*

The institutional setting, with its large number of aggressive boys confined in tight quarters, served to encourage fighting. Fights were a daily occurrence. Somebody was always upset about something. The rea-son did not matter, only the result. A wrong word, a wrong look, or being at the wrong place at the wrong time, could create a con-frontation. There was little to be done about it; either fight or be considered a "punk." Sometimes it was possible to find another way out, but not always. Usually it came down to a winner and a loser.

Fighting was more than a way to vent frustration. It was also a means of gaining status and self-respect. . . . To be consid-ered a "bad ass" was the highest compliment and afforded the greatest respect. A "rep" meant power, and power meant control over people and situations. The top-ranked boys on campus and in a cottage had the fewest hassles. Other boys usually left them alone, choosing boys of lower rank on whom to take out their frustrations. Nobody wanted to lose a fight; it was bad for reputation and rank. Nonetheless, the time inevitably came when a face-off with a boy of similar or higher rank could no longer be avoided. It was then that rankings often changed and the power that accompanied rank sometimes shifted.

SOURCE: Waln K. Brown, *The Other Side of Delinquency* (New Brunswick, NJ: Rutgers University Press), 1983, pp. 126–27.

used by the others. . . . As in many adult prisons, the whites were disorganized and the blacks stuck together. Boys were acquainted with the local version of the convict code shortly after arrival. This code had standards for all prisoners but also some that were specific to blacks or Caucasians. The general code items were "exploit whomever you can," "don't kiss ass," "don't rat on your peers," "don't give up your ass," "be cool," "don't get involved in another inmate's affairs," "don't steal squares" (cigarettes), and "don't buy the mind f--king." Additional norms for blacks were "exploit whites," "no forcing sex on blacks," "defend your brother," and "staff favor whites." For whites, the additional norms were "don't trust anyone" and "everybody for himself" (Bowker, 1977: 100).

As in all penal institutions, the boys had labels for the various social types (Fisher, 1961). Bartollas, Miller, and Dinitz found that staff members often used these same labels, plus some informal labels of their own, "including 'punk,' 'sickie,' and 'pussy.'" They often made open bets on a boy's future adjustment after release in front of him. Even worse, they sometimes used labels to pass on

---

**PANEL 8.3**

## On Keeping Order in the Training School

I came out of the reception center on a Friday afternoon. They put me in cottage C2. There were mostly Puerto Rican fellows in there, a few Negroes, and a sprinkling of white cats. The cottage parents were Puerto Rican. . . .

It was a pretty place. They had people walking around and looking like they were free, but you had to have a pass to go anywhere; and if you were gone too long, they had somebody out looking for you. They had what they called "area men," and the area men were like detectives up at Warwick. Anytime something happened—if something had been stolen or if someone had gotten stabbed—these were the cats who came around and investigated and found out who had done it. They were usually big cats, strong-arm boys. And they usually found out what it was they wanted to know.

The area men would come for you if you were gone from a place too long, and they would bring runners. Runners were like trustees. They would run after guys in the woods if they ran away, and they'd bring them back. The runners usually came from cottage A4 or one in the D group, where most of the big cats were. A4 was a crazy cottage. They had the nuts in there; they had the rapists, murderers, and perverts in there. These were the most brutal cats up there, and everybody knew it. A lot of times when people ran away, if they saw these cats behind them they would stop, because they knew they didn't have much chance of getting away. And if they gave the A4 guys a hard time, they'd catch hell when they were caught.

To someone passing by, Warwick looked just like a boy's camp. But everybody was under guard, all the time, and everybody had a job to do. You worked in the bakery or in an office or on the work gangs, and so on. . . .

Everybody had a place to fit into, so it seemed.

SOURCE: Claude Brown, *Manchild in the Promised Land* (New York: Macmillan, 1965), pp. 133–34.

a boy's sexually exploitable status to the other prisoners, "thereby inadvertently setting up a sexual attack" (Bowker, 1977: 101).

The picture this study presents does not differ significantly from the one presented in other studies of boys' training schools. An inmate code (probably honored primarily in the breach), collectively defined and recognized social roles, and exploitation and scapegoating among the boys seem to be near universal aspects of the training school. As noted, however, what does seem to be more recent is the phenomenon of black domination, at least in institutions where blacks form a substantial proportion of the inmate group (Feld, 1981; Bartollas and Sieverdes, 1981).

### The Staff

Bartollas, Miller, and Dinitz also present a revealing glimpse of the subculture of youth leaders in Ohio's end-of-the-line maximum security institution for boys. (Youth leaders are the lowest-level custodial personnel, roughly comparable to guards in the prison setting.) Unlike most American prisons, most of the youth leaders at TICO were black.

The authors suggest that youth leaders "go through a series of stages or 'plateaus' during their careers" and that their relations with inmates "vary with the plateaus reached and the promotions received."

The staff code . . . provides the guidelines for acceptable and unacceptable behavior. This code is divided into two sections, one of which is concerned with staff orientation to other staff, who will "make it" in the institution, what kinds of behavior to accept from others while on the job, and the acceptable attitudes toward various components of their work. The second part of the code concerns staff's approach to the youths, and consists of a series of tenets which are ranked from acceptable to unacceptable from the viewpoint of the staff (1976: 197–99).

The following are some of the significant components of section 1 of the staff code:

**1.** "Only Blacks 'Make It' Here": Staff believe that white youth leaders are resented by black inmates, are often socially impotent for that reason, and consequently do not last as long as youth offenders.

**2.** "Unless You Have Been There, You Don't Know What It's Like": Youth leaders must come from the same social background as the inmates if they are to work effectively with them.

**3.** "Be Secure": Youth leaders should maintain good security practices and be eternally vigilant about escapes.

**4.** "There Is a Certain Way to Inform on Staff": Informally established procedures should be followed when youth leaders criticize one of their own or register a formal complaint about a youth leader's performance.

**5.** "Don't Take No Shit": Staff members should not show hesitation in asserting their power in any confrontation with inmates.

**6.** "Be Suspicious": Youth leaders should always be suspicious because inmates will try to manipulate them at every opportunity.

**7.** "Be Loyal to the Team": Cottage employees should stick together, should assist one another, should not permit inmates to create dissension among them, and should try to settle all disputes internally, going to administrators only in cases of serious staff misconduct.

**8.** "Take Care of Yourself": Within certain limits it is permissible to exploit one's job and the institution itself for personal reasons.

**9.** "Stay Cool, Man": Do not lose your "cool" and overreact to emotional situations.

**10.** "The Administration Will Screw You": Administrators will try to exploit youth leaders in every possible way. Do not trust administrators.

**11.** "Don't Listen to Social Workers": Social

workers are believed to be naive, easily manipulated by inmates, inclined to make poor decisions about inmates, and using their present position as a stepping-stone to a better job. Consequently, they should be pressured and co-opted to youth leaders' values so they do not interfere with the cottage functioning.

**12.** "Don't Do More Than You Get Paid For": Youth leaders should not do work unless it is stated in the job description (1976: 200–206).

The second part of the staff code focuses on negligence in their work, exchange relations with inmates, and exploitation of inmates. Youth leaders should not be overly negligent in their duties because this may lead to serious incidents that bring "flak"

---

**PANEL 8.4**

*Consequences of Punishment*

[A]fter the escape] I was assigned to A Company. A Company was . . . a disciplinary unit, reserved for hardheads and stone fuck-ups. We were not affected during the day on our jobs or school assignments, but company life itself was designed to be stern. . . .

I liked A Company. I liked knowing it was as bad as it could get and nothing was being held back to be awarded if you were quiet and cooperative. Sucking the Man's ass bought you nothing. We were denied the hope of small mitigations and I discovered I didn't care. I realize something of what I gained by managing to stand firm with the hard asses, and this was dear to the rum, the suspect punk, but I also learned there were things more important than the hope of comfort.

SOURCE: Malcolm Braly, *False Starts* (Boston: Little, Brown, 1976), pp. 59–60.

---

from supervisors. It is permissible for youth leaders to use threats of bad reports and unsanctioned privileges to do their work and maintain a smoothly run cottage. Finally, while youth leaders are permitted to employ deception as a means of controlling inmates, other practices are impermissible: (1) encouraging victimization of one inmate by another; (2) physical brutality; (3) aiding escapes; and (4) exploiting inmates for sexual purposes (1976: 206–15).

The picture presented in studies of training schools for boys seems similar to what is known about men's prisons, with two exceptions. First, there may be less solidarity among male juveniles than among male penitentiary convicts. For instance, collective disturbances and rebellions are much less common in boys' training schools. And second, although fights are common in boys' training schools, lethal violence is not as common as it is in penitentiaries.

### Girls

Historically, training schools for boys and girls emerged at about the same time and developed along parallel lines. The first state-operated institution, the Massachusetts State Industrial School for Girls, opened its doors in 1856 (Brenzel, 1983). Other states quickly followed suit.

As in the case of women's prisons, the regimen of girls' training schools has reflected prevailing notions of appropriate gender roles. While the earliest training schools prepared boys for farm or industrial employment, girls were trained and placed as domestic workers. As late as 1969, the former superintendent of Connecticut's Long Lane School wrote that the institution's program emphasized:

pre-vocational training with special emphasis on homemaking since the girls will eventually be homemakers, religious training, extracurricular activities through Girl Scouts, Tri-Hi-Y, Garden Club, 4-H Club, Acrobatics Club, etc., all [of which] give youngsters an opportunity to taste success and raise their usually low self-esteem (Rogers, 1972: 224).

In some respects, the social organization and culture of girls' training schools appears to have more in common with that of women's prisons than with that of institutions for male juveniles. Investigations in many girls' training schools have found that inmates tend to establish fictive marital and family structures, which become the major axes of social organization.

Rose Giallombardo (1974) studied three training schools for girls, one each in an Eastern, Midwestern, and far Western state. The institutions differed considerably in the emphasis they placed on treatment as compared with custody and security. Notwithstanding this difference, Giallombardo found a strikingly similar structure of kinship ties in the three institutions.

The girls in the training schools recognized the roles of "parents" and "children," as well as more distant relationships with "aunts," "uncles," and others. The "mother" and "father" in the family group usually had a homosexual relationship. This interlocking system of kinship and sexual relationships was known by different names—as "the racket," "the sillies" and "chick business"—in the three institutions.

Homosexual relationships were common in the three institutions, and were based on romantic love. Unlike institutions for males, they were not coercive. Homosexual attacks were infrequent and usually were directed at inmates who were unwilling to engage in homosexuality but zealously ridiculed inmates who do so. Physical aggression does occur, but "most differences [among girls] tend to be settled verbally."

Besides the kinship system, Giallombardo found a complex of role types in all three institutions, many of them revolving around homosexual relationships. For example, in the Western training school, "fems" were girls who assume a female role, "butches" the male role in homosexual relationships. "Finks" or "snitchers" were inmates who vol-

---

**PANEL 8.5**

### *Consequences of Training School Confinement*

The most serious and persistent charge leveled against institutions like Preston is that they function as crime schools where young naive boys are tutored in criminal techniques by the more experienced. . . .

The "crime school" charge . . . bears some examination. It isn't, I think, information one gets here. I heard many accounts of how to hotwire cars to bypass the ignition so they could be stolen without the key, but this technique never became clear to me, and I've never used it. And today anyone with the price of a movie ticket or access to a television can see the most elaborate criminal techniques worked out in accurate detail and presented as entertainment.

What one learns to want in a "crime school" is the respect of one's peers. This is the danger. The naive will be drawn into competing for status in a system of values that honors and glorifies antisocial behavior. We're none of us total strangers to the desire to simplify the restraints under which we live, and the yearning for freedom is never entirely unmixed with the yearning to set aside for oneself those finical considerations that bind the lives of others. This unraveling process goes swiftly in an atmosphere like Preston, where the ideal of criminal freedom was the common ambition.

SOURCE: Malcolm Braly, *False Starts* (Boston: Little, Brown, 1976), pp. 51–52.

untarily divulged information to staff about other inmates and their activities. "Cops" or "junior staff" referred to inmates who tried to assume the functions of the staff in their relationships with other inmates. Those inmates who were oriented to noncriminal values and identified with staff were known as "squares" and "straights." "Sissies" were inmates who established close, stable friendships with other inmates that were outside of the kinship system.

Giallombardo argues that the extended kinship groupings in training schools for girls persist because they fulfill important needs for inmates, specifically, "emotional reciprocity and emotional security, mutual aid, and protection against other inmates when necessary." Inasmuch as "parents" and other members of families expect one another to avoid flagrant violations of institutional rules, kinship structures also contribute to institutional order and routine.

### Why the Differences?

How can we account for differences in the underlife of boys' and girls' training schools? All training schools, whether for males or females, are total institutions as Erving Goffman (1961) used that concept. All impose a high degree of segregation from the free world; all are socially, materially, and psychically depriving places of involuntary confinement. Despite this similarity, there are some major differences in the social organization and culture of their inmates. Recall that female prisoners tend to be less violent, possibly less cohesive, less committed to the inmate code, and more likely to create fictive marital and family structures. As with explanations for the differences between men's and women's prisons, the reasons for these differences in training schools highlight the interplay of deprivation and importation variables.

Most researchers seem agreed that the explanation lies in (1) differences in the pre-confinement criminal experiences of boys and girls, and (2) traditional sex-role differences. The latter function as latent roles and identities that prisoners bring to training school with them. As a result, boys, both individually and collectively, respond to the pains of imprisonment in typically masculine ways while girls respond to them in typically feminine ways.

Some have argued that when girls are confined they experience the loss of close supportive social relationships more acutely than do boys. Homosexual liaisons and pretend-family groups represent attempts to mitigate these deprivations. The traditionally non-violent behavior of girls and their socialization to be nonaggressive—except perhaps on a verbal level—finds characteristic expression in the relative absence of violence in training schools for girls. By contrast, many of the common interpersonal and social dynamics of training schools for boys are an attempt by adolescent males to prove their mettle and establish their independence.

## Inmate Perspectives on the Training School and its Programs

Regardless of the specific ideology that animates them, training school supporters and their staff generally argue that many youths benefit from the training school experience. Doubtless some do (see Brown, 1983). However, many do not. The nature of the inmate subculture is one reason for this.

While they are confined, inmates are immersed in a culture that interprets the institution, its staff, and many of its programs in negative, oppositional terms. This perspective diminishes the likelihood that inmates will define the training school experience as a beneficial one. In this respect, the training school is similar to the prison. In both, we emphasize, inmates acquire a fundamental perspective on the institution and its staff that conflicts with the official story. Based on her comparative research in three training schools, Giallombardo offers this summary description:

> In the main, the girls saw the institutions as places of punishment. Contrary to what one might be led to expect, this assessment is not based altogether on the fact that room confinement and group punishment were widely used as forms of social control, although, to be sure, the inmates defined them both as punishment. Rather, the inmates questioned whether a solution to their problems could be provided in the institution where they found themselves, as they insisted that their problems were external to it—*outside* with their parents, drugs, and school teachers, for example. . . . It was the consensus of the inmates that they had only been "sent away" (1974: 265, emphasis in the original).

These observations probably apply generally to training school inmates throughout the United States. Even those institutions that have exemplary treatment-oriented regimens are able to make only limited inroads against this inmate perspective (Street *et al.*, 1966; Feld, 1981).

# 9

# Probation and Parole

*robation* is the release of convicted offenders to supervision instead of incarceration. *Parole* is the release of convicted offenders to supervision following a period of incarceration. Although parole historically is used primarily for felons, probation is used both for felons and misdemeanants. In 1984, about 51 percent of adults on probation in the United States had been convicted of misdemeanors (U.S. Department of Justice, 1986g). Offenders are placed on probation by a sentencing judge; they are placed on parole by an executive agency, usually called a *parole board*. Offenders who violate the terms of probation can be returned to court and ordered to prison, but only by a judge. Offenders who violate the terms of parole can be removed from parole and returned to prison, but only by the parole board or its representatives.

Notwithstanding these formal differences between probation and parole, they are quite similar as day-to-day social and bureaucratic processes. In fact, where federal offenders are concerned, both probation and parole supervision is provided by one group of federal employees, called U.S. Probation Officers. Some states also have merged these two mandates and processes into a single agency. For these reasons, we discuss probation and parole together.

## Patterns of Use

Historical forerunners of probation and parole can be found in a number of places in Europe and other parts of the world. They appeared in the United States in the late 19th century. Although the impetus to and the process of development varied somewhat from state to state (Messinger *et al.*, 1985), by the early 20th century probation and parole had taken firm root in American corrections. Today they are standard parts of the correctional strategies and structures of nearly all the states.

In some areas of corrections and in some states, parole and other types of conditional release are known by different names. For example, juvenile parole in many states is known as *aftercare*. Eight states have formally abolished parole (Shane-DuBow *et al.*, 1985: Table 34). Nevertheless, in most of the eight, offenders released from prison are under some form of official supervision (Reiber, 1985). Of all adults under correctional supervision in the United States in 1983, 65 percent were on probation and 11 percent were on parole (U.S. Department of Justice, 1986c).

During 1979–84, America's adult imprisoned population grew by 47.7 percent. During the same period, the adult probation and parole populations also grew—by 57.5 percent and 22.7 percent, respectively (U.S. Department of Justice, 1986g). For the nation as a whole, the *rate* of parole use for adults increased from 138 per 100,000 adult residents in 1979 to 155 in 1984 (Flanagan and McGarrell, 1986: 551; U.S. Department of Justice, 1986g). These changes reinforce the picture of an expansive crime control apparatus in the America of the late 1980s.

It is worth noting that probationers and parolees increasingly are required to pay for their offenses with more than just curtailment of their freedom. In many states they now must pay a monthly fee to the state while they are under supervision. In 1984, at least 18 states permitted or required these fees (Flanagan and McGarrell, 1986: Table 1.44). Most states justify these fees by using them to offset the costs of probation and parole supervision. Others use them to help pay for drug testing for those under supervision, or to supplement the state's victim-compensation fund.

We have seen in earlier chapters that the rate of confinement in jails and prisons varies greatly among the 50 states. The same is true of the use of probation and parole. Table 9.1 shows state variation in total numbers and rates for these correctional strategies. By regions, the rate for both probation and parole is highest in the South and lowest in the Midwest. Although we have only the sketchiest understanding theoretically of the reasons for this variation, it appears to be only weakly related to variation in the rate of serious crime.

### Juvenile Probation and Parole

When compared with what is known about adult probation and parole, we know little about the use and process of juvenile probation and parole. The most recent nationwide survey of state programs was conducted in 1975 and 1976. At that time, there were 328,854 juveniles on probation and 53,347 on parole in the United States. About 24 percent of the juvenile probationers and 21 percent of the juvenile parolees were girls (U.S. Department of Justice, 1978). Between 1976 and 1984, the number of adults on probation and parole in the United States increased by 85 percent and 72 percent, respectively (U.S. Department of Justice, 1978; 1986g). If we assume that the number of juveniles on probation and parole increased at a similar rate, the combined juvenile probation and parole populations in 1984 numbered about 700,000.

## Probation–Parole Outcome

A substantial amount of research has been done on the outcome of probation and parole supervision. As is true of correctional evaluation research generally, *recidivism* is perhaps the most widely used measure of the

TABLE 9.1    **Adults on Probation and Parole in the United States, 1984**

| State | *Number on Probation | †Probationers per 100,000 Population | *Number on Parole | †Parolees per 100,000 Population |
|---|---|---|---|---|
| UNITED STATES | 1,711,190 | 986 | 268,515 | 155 |
| Alabama | 16,338 | 567 | 2,194 | 76 |
| Alaska | 2,064 | 611 | 147 | 43 |
| Arizona | 16,687 | 760 | 1,660 | 76 |
| Arkansas | 6,800 | 401 | 3,463 | 204 |
| California | 197,413 | 1,041 | 30,843 | 163 |
| Colorado | 16,693 | 719 | 1,709 | 74 |
| Connecticut | 46,681 | 1,939 | 868 | 36 |
| Delaware | 6,373 | 1,391 | 830 | 181 |
| Florida | 108,833 | 1,286 | 5,661 | 67 |
| Georgia | 100,821 | 2,398 | 7,246 | 172 |
| Hawaii | 6,686 | 889 | 526 | 70 |
| Idaho | 3,151 | 464 | 581 | 86 |
| Illinois | 63,477 | 754 | 11,383 | 135 |
| Indiana | 36,004 | 903 | 2,900 | 73 |
| Iowa | 11,924 | 561 | 1,662 | 78 |
| Kansas | 12,487 | 699 | 1,997 | 112 |
| Kentucky | 14,930 | 555 | 3,617 | 134 |
| Louisiana | 26,733 | 860 | 3,087 | 99 |
| Maine | 4,368 | 514 | 122 | 14 |
| Maryland | 64,827 | 1,986 | 7,046 | 216 |
| Massachusetts | 23,141 | 522 | 5,967 | 135 |
| Michigan | 55,674 | 845 | 9,409 | 143 |
| Minnesota | 31,440 | 1,035 | 1,418 | 47 |
| Mississippi | 6,570 | 365 | 3,108 | 173 |
| Missouri | 25,900 | 701 | 4,563 | 124 |
| Montana | 2,712 | 461 | 694 | 118 |
| Nebraska | 10,763 | 925 | 361 | 31 |
| Nevada | 5,226 | 772 | 1,187 | 175 |
| New Hampshire | 23,782 | 384 | 455 | 63 |
| New Jersey | 47,053 | 831 | 12,206 | 216 |
| New Mexico | 4,155 | 421 | 1,149 | 116 |
| New York | 90,361 | 677 | 24,212 | 181 |
| North Carolina | 52,600 | 1,152 | 3,892 | 85 |
| North Dakota | 1,517 | 311 | 159 | 33 |
| Ohio | 37,055 | 471 | 9,065 | 115 |
| Oklahoma | 18,107 | 762 | 1,894 | 80 |
| Oregon | 21,659 | 1,102 | 1,787 | 91 |
| Pennsylvania | 64,310 | 715 | 11,371 | 126 |
| Rhode Island | 7,147 | 971 | 397 | 54 |
| South Carolina | 16,762 | 706 | 3,372 | 142 |
| South Dakota | 1,514 | 303 | 438 | 88 |
| Tennessee | 23,598 | 680 | 6,524 | 188 |
| Texas | 235,568 | 2,090 | 40,783 | 362 |
| Utah | 6,550 | 638 | 1,220 | 119 |
| Virginia | 16,598 | 394 | 6,986 | 142 |
| Washington | 43,089 | 1,351 | 5,253 | 165 |
| West Virginia | 3,473 | 244 | 724 | 51 |
| Wisconsin | 23,240 | 666 | 3,666 | 105 |
| Wyoming | 1,698 | 484 | 350 | 100 |

*December 31, 1984
†Ages 18 and older
SOURCE: U.S. Department of Justice (1986g).

effectiveness of probation and parole (Maltz, 1984). "Recidivism may appropriately be defined as the proportion of a specified group (e.g., released prisoners) who sustain an outcome defined as negative (e.g., new arrest; new conviction) within a given period of time (e.g., three years from date of release)" (Hoffman and Stone-Meierhoefer, 1980: 54). As these comments suggest,

> recidivism has no universally accepted meaning among criminal justice researchers. Different studies have defined it variously as a new arrest, a new conviction, or a new sentence of imprisonment, depending on the kinds of data they had available and their project goals. As a result, it is exceedingly difficult and complex to make comparisons among their results (Petersilia et al., 1985b: 20).

Studies of the outcome of probation and parole using multiple definitions of recidivism indeed show that the percentage of those who "succeed" depends on the definition (for example, Hoffman and Stone-Meierhoefer, 1980; Gottfredson et al., 1982; Petersilia et al., 1985b). Also, the percentage who succeed varies substantially from one study to another. An early study by Ralph W. England (1955) of 490 federal felony offenders revealed that only 17.7 percent had new convictions after being placed on probation. A more recent study of 1,672 felony probationers in two California counties produced markedly different results: 65 percent of the entire probation sample were *arrested* during the 40-month follow-up period, and 51 percent were formally charged and *convicted* (Petersilia et al., 1985b: 20). Most studies show, however, that a majority of offenders who are placed on probation or parole complete it successfully. In fact, of the more than one-half million adults who were discharged from probation in the United States during

1984, 80.9 percent had completed their terms successfully (U.S. Department of Justice, 1986g).

What is true of probation is also true of parole: A majority of those placed in the program complete it successfully. Of all adults who exited parole in the United States during 1984, 63.7 percent successfully completed their parole term (U.S. Department of Justice, 1986g).

Probation and parole success rates do vary somewhat according to the background characteristics of offenders. For the adult probationers in their sample, Joan Petersilia et al. found considerable variation by conviction offense in the percentage of those who had new criminal charges *filed* against them during the 40 months after placement on probation. The highest proportion of failure—29 percent—was for offenders originally convicted of theft, forgery, or auto theft. The proportion of failures for other offenders: burglary, 22 percent; possession and sale of drugs, 14 percent; and robbery, 9 percent. The lowest proportion of failures—3 percent—was for homicide and rape offenders (1985b: 24).

The picture is similar for adult parolees. In 1972, 20,576 felons (19,500 men and 1,036 women) were paroled by states that subsequently provided three-year follow-up data for the Uniform Parole Reports (National Probation and Parole Institutes, 1976). At the end of three years, 74 percent of the men and 82 percent of the women still were on parole or had completed their terms successfully. Parolees who failed had absconded from supervision (4 percent of the men and 5 percent of the women) or had been returned to prison for violating parole rules (15 percent and 10 percent, respectively). In other words, the largest percentage of failure cases were returned to prison for technical violations of parole rules, such as changing place of residence without notifying the parole agent, buying a car without permission, or frequenting bars or taverns. These and other violations of parole rules, such as purchasing a car without permission or associating with other ex-offenders, are not criminal offenses. However, many times offenders are returned to prison for technical violations as an alternative to prosecution for new offenses they may have committed while on parole. A subsequent three-year follow-up of 1975 adult parolees produced findings similar to those from the study of 1972 parolees (U.S. Department of Justice, 1980b). Table 9.2 shows variation in the success rate for offenders convicted of different crimes. Homicide offenders had the highest success rate, forgers the lowest.

There are no comparable state-level data for juveniles. We do know, however, that the younger the parolees or probationers, the higher the violation rate. Patrick G. Jackson's study of nearly 4,000 offenders randomly placed on parole by the California Youth Authority in 1975 confirms this generalization. Overall, 52 percent completed parole suc-

TABLE 9.2 **Three-Year Follow-up of 1972 Adult Parolees, United States**

| Offense | Percent Successful on Parole | |
| --- | --- | --- |
| | Men | Women |
| Homicide | 82 | 88 |
| Aggravated assault | 76 | 90 |
| Rape | 75 | * |
| Armed robbery | 68 | 77 |
| Auto theft | 67 | * |
| Larceny/theft | 74 | 70 |
| Forgery | 64 | 68 |

*Not enough cases for reliable statistical analysis
SOURCE: National Probation and Parole Institutes, *1972 Parolees, Three-Year Follow-up and Trend Analysis.* (Davis, Calif.: National Council on Crime and Delinquency, December 1976).

cessfully, which is substantially lower than the success rate for adult parolees. Success rates were lowest for property offenders (burglary, theft, robbery) and highest for violent ones (rape, homicide, assault) (1983: Table A2-1).

## Comparative Outcome Research

A number of investigators have examined the comparative effectiveness of probation or parole and other correctional dispositions for comparable offenders. In a recent study, Petersilia *et al.* (1986) compared matched samples of convicted felons sentenced in two California counties. One group of 511 were sentenced to prison and the other 511 were placed on probation. In the two years after sentencing, 31 percent of the probationers were sent to jail or prison. By contrast, in the two years after release from prison, 47 percent of the former prisoners returned to jail or prison after conviction for new crimes.

Whereas Petersilia *et al.* compared the performance of probationers and prisoners, Howard R. Sacks and Charles H. Logan (1979) compared the performance of minor offenders discharged early from confinement and similar offenders released to parole supervision. They found that 37 percent of the parolees were convicted of new crimes during the first year after their release, whereas 63 percent of the early-discharge, non-parole offenders failed. Similarly, Lerner examined the postrelease arrest records of 195 misdemeanants who were released either to parole or when their sentence expired. The parolees performed better than the releasees, which led Lerner to conclude that "parole supervision reduces criminal behavior of persons released from local correctional institutions" (1977: 220). Research on felony offenders likewise shows that the percentage of parolees who succeed is higher than for other types of prison releases. The differential in performance does vary, however, from one study to another (Waller, 1974; Hoffman and Stone-Meierhoefer, 1980; Gottfredson *et al.,* 1982).

Although the findings from this type of research generally are consistent, research by Charles A. Murray and Louis A. Cox, Jr. (1979) produced different results. They compared several groups of serious youthful offenders who received various forms of correctional intervention to determine the crime *suppression effect* of the different correctional dispositions. Some youths were sentenced to the state training school, others were placed on regular probation, and still others were placed in experimental community programs. Based on the number of times that members of the various treatment groups were arrested during the follow-up period, the study suggests that the suppression effect of training school was greater than probation. Moreover, the suppression effect of probation exceeded the rate for other, even less restrictive, community programs.

There is no way to resolve these discrepant findings. The available research literature doesn't help us much. To begin with, most investigations of the impact of correctional treatments have used research designs that are flawed in one way or another. All the studies mentioned above, for example, used comparison groups that cannot be considered equivalent. The results from studies that compare nonequivalent groups of offenders can be interpreted in several ways. Inevitably, this casts doubt on any particular interpretation of the findings. Also, some have suggested that the apparent success of probation and parole over harsher strategies may have little to do with the programs at all. Perhaps success rates appear good because judges and parole boards are good at guessing who will be successful.

**PANEL 9.1**

*On Returning to the Free World*

One of the great games we played in the joint was to imagine what we would do our first night out. I'm going to get a good room, take a big healthy shit and a long hot shower, catch a shave and go out to the best restaurant I can find and order the biggest steak on the menu. This is possible if you want to spend all your gate money the first night, but soon fantasy slips in, and the waitress is a fine chick, and you come on to her and discover she's really a jazz singer, weathering a dry spell between gigs, and you arrange to pick her up when she gets off, and the two of you hit the after-hours spots, dig the sounds until dawn, when you walk arm-in-arm up Telegraph Hill to the very top where her pad overlooks both bridges and most of the bay, and there on the coffee table are *The Prophet* by Kahlil Gibran and Walter Benton's *This Is My Beloved.* She pours wine, rolls a joint and puts Bird on the record player. You kiss and she sighs and says, You must of really been lonely, baby. And when you make it, you don't come immediately as you will for weeks, but ride on and on, Oh, Lord, as her apartment windows slowly turn bright with the sun.

Nothing like this happens. I was too shy to speak to anyone. I wandered down into North Beach and went to a jazz club where I sat at the bar and stared at myself in the mirror. A male Cinderella, already a little too old for the part.

SOURCE: Malcolm Braly, *False Starts* (Boston: Little, Brown, 1976), pp. 264–65.

# Parole under Attack

Although parole developed at different times and along different lines in the 50 states, by the middle of the 20th century supporters of the medical model claimed it as an important correctional strategy. They argued that behavioral experts could make informed, accurate release decisions, determining who needs additional confinement and who is ready for release. Release on parole, then, would occur at the point when the offender had received the maximum benefit from confinement and no longer posed a significant threat to the community. However, since it is impossible to specify in advance how much time will be required to cure offenders, discretion and flexibility would be needed so they could be treated as long as necessary.

In the 1960s and early 1970s, prisoners and parolees mounted numerous legal attacks disputing the fairness of traditional correctional strategies, including parole. Together with liberal critics of correctional policies, they paid particular attention to the broad and largely unchecked discretionary powers of parole authorities. The secrecy and apparent arbitrariness of parole procedures were decried as well. Critics charged that these procedures were abused, thus fueling the sense of injustice widely shared by prisoners (Irwin, 1970). Traditional parole practices also came under critical scrutiny in the context of challenges to the indeterminate sentence. Inmates and critics alike argued that, coupled with the use of these sentences, parole board policies functioned to coerce prisoners to take part in rehabilitative programs of dubious value.

Responding to these criticisms, a former member of the U.S. Board of Parole charged that many of the inequities of the parole process originate in sentencing. Indeed, "the fairness of the parole process depends al-most directly on the fairness of the sentencing process" (Sigler, 1975: 48).

Parole, however, was not without defenders who saw advantages in the way it operates. They argued that historically parole boards have functioned to bring a measure of equity to the implementation of indeterminate sentence laws:

> A parole system allows us to advertise heavy criminal sanctions loudly at the time of sentencing and later reduce sentences quietly. . . . In a system that seems addicted to barking louder than it really wants to bite, parole (and "good time" as well) can help protect us from harsh sentences while allowing the legislature and judiciary the posture of law and order. . . . One function of parole may be to even out disparities in sentencing behavior among different localities (Zimring, 1977: 7–8).

In short, parole boards historically have functioned to mitigate the harshness and disparity of criminal sentences.

## Parole Board Decision Making

Judging from what is known about parole practices, there seems to be ample justification for these attacks on parole. Research indicates, for example, that parole board mem-

TABLE 9.3 **Average Number of Parole Hearings per Day: 51 Jurisdictions, 1972\***

| Average # of Cases Heard per Day | Number of Parole Boards |
|---|---|
| 1–19 | 11 |
| 20–29 | 15 |
| 30–39 | 14 |
| 40 and over | 11 |

\*Excludes Georgia, Hawaii, and Texas
SOURCE: O'Leary and Nuffield (1972)

bers spend only a few minutes on inmate release hearings. Table 9.3 shows that most parole boards hear a rather large number of cases on a typical day. Another study shows that they spend an average of 15 minutes interviewing each inmate, with an approximate range of from 4 to 30 minutes (Stanley, 1976: 38–39). Many question whether this is sufficient time to make a thorough appraisal of an inmate's strengths, weaknesses, and readiness for parole. Parole boards respond that they spend a great deal more time studying the convicts' records.

Vincent O'Leary and Joan Nuffield (1972) surveyed 51 parole boards in the United States and found that 40 did not record the reasons for their decisions to release or not release on parole. Both Robert O. Dawson (1966) and a team of Yale Law School researchers (Genego *et al.*, 1975) found that a host of variables extraneous to both the inmate's "condition" and the likelihood of recidivism affect the parole board's release decisions. Reasons that parole boards often deny parole include: (1) poor institutional adjustment—which serves to reinforce prison disciplinary practices; (2) a perceived obligation to protect the public from those who have shown themselves capable of violent behavior; (3) the belief that a prisoner may have served too little time for the institution to "get to know him" and his case; (4) to give inmates time to benefit from prison programs; (5) the belief that an inmate has not served enough time for the type of crime committed; and (6) to avoid criticism of the parole system should a released prisoner commit a new crime—especially one that is widely publicized (Schmidt, 1977: 123).

Joseph E. Scott (1974) examined the relationship of various factors considered by the parole board to the number of months inmates actually were imprisoned in one Midwestern state. He found that the seriousness of the crime was the best predictor of the severity of punishment. Janet Schmidt (1977) conducted similar research on a sample of 7,286 federal prisoners who appeared for a parole hearing between November 1970 and June 1972. The population from which the sample was chosen was all cases considered for parole during that period. The data consisted of information on the background characteristics and past and present performance of the potential parolees. Schmidt wanted to determine if parole decisions were made on the basis of the factors that the U.S. Board of Parole said were the basis for its decisions. Her analysis pointed to a discrepancy between the board's professed decision-making guides and those it actually employed. Three variables, in combination, had the greatest overall effect on the parole decision: (1) the amount of time the inmate had served; (2) the length of the sentence; and (3) the inmate's prison custody classification (minimum, medium, or maximum).

Critics point to evidence such as this to support their claim that parole boards devote their energies to retrying inmates for

---

**PANEL 9.2**

*Inmate Perceptions of the Parole Board*

We had our body of wisdom and our intuitions as to how they must function, but they also had learned something about us. They had been subjected to the most artful and elaborate cons until now they took nothing on faith. They knew we would say anything to get out. Every man who came before them sat there with a single purpose—to somehow leave that room with his freedom restored. Few cared how.

SOURCE: Malcolm Braly, *False Starts* (Boston: Little, Brown, 1976), p. 253.

their past crimes. Parole boards, they argue, use their discretionary power to ensure that inmates who have committed serious crimes are punished sufficiently, and to maintain order in the prison. Along these lines, J. S. Carroll *et al.* (1982) used posthearing questionnaires and case files from 1,035 actual parole decisions to examine the decision making of the Pennsylvania Parole Board. Their results generally are consistent with earlier studies. The investigators found that inmates' institutional behavior and predictions of risk to the community explain most of the variation in release decisions.

But others suggest that parole boards are not so unpredictable or punitive as critics allege. Vincent O'Leary and Daniel Glaser sent questionnaires to all state parole board members in the United States; about half of them, or 139, responded. They were asked to estimate how often in the preceding year they considered various items in their decisions to grant or to deny parole. The results reveal that "no matter how one designates or tabulates it, the leading preoccupation of most parole board members, in their decisions to grant or to deny parole, is their judgment of whether or not the prisoner is likely to commit a serious crime if paroled" (1972: 138).

In either case, the research literature raises questions about the alleged expertise of probation–parole decision makers, the purpose of the discretionary parole decision, and the fairness of the entire parole process.

*Probation–Parole Decision Making*

Correctional strategies such as probation and parole that look to the medical model for justification can work effectively only if it is possible to make accurate diagnoses of offenders and reliable predictions about their future behavior. Abundant research casts doubt on our ability to do so. Michael Hakeem (1961) asked ten parole officers and ten lay persons to read ten actual standardized cor-

rectional case summaries and to predict whether the subjects of the reports would violate the terms of their parole. He found no appreciable difference between the two groups in the accuracy of their predictions.

Paul Takagi and James O. Robison (1969) asked 316 parole agency employees to read ten actual case histories involving suspected parole violations and to decide whether the alleged violators should be continued on parole or returned to prison.

> Judgments of the 316 agency staff members varied wildly. Among them were five who recommended ten returns to prison, and one who recommended no returns. About half the staff members would have returned either six or seven of the parolees—however, even those who would have returned the same number of cases were not in agreement about which cases they would return. Agents who came from a background of prison work would have returned many more alleged violators to prison than those who came from some outside social work position (Mitford, 1973: 221).

Other research casts doubt on the claims of rehabilitation functionaries because of what it reveals about their diagnostic decision-making process. Consider research that examines expert decision making in a "pure" fashion—without bureaucratic intrusion. Robert M. Carter and Leslie T. Wilkins conducted a simulation study of decision making by probation officers. Using a methodology employed earlier by Wilkins (1965), they asked 14 U.S. probation officers to read a series of pieces of information about five different defendants and to recommend for or against probation. The information was presented so that subjects could view only one piece at a time; the investigators noted the order in which the subjects examined the pieces.

Carter and Wilkins observed only minimal similarity in the probation officers' decision-making processes.

A brief examination of the "decision-making" of the probation officers indicates that each officer develops his own style. . . . None of the officers selected information at random; instead they followed a common basic pattern that was still somehow unique to the individual (1967: 209).

Just as important, they found that probation officers make decisions regarding presentence report recommendations with relatively small amounts of information—an average of 4.7 items of information.

The research procedure also permitted Carter and Wilkins to determine whether subjects changed their minds about their decisions and, if so, the type of information that prompted the changes. Receiving additional information after the recommendation seemed to have little effect in most cases, except to serve as confirmation of a decision already reached. Subsequent investigations show similar results (Gottfredson, Wilkins, and Hoffman, 1978). Given this individuality in probation officers' decision making, and the fact that they rarely change their decisions even after receiving additional information, critics may suggest that their status as trained "experts" is dubious.

Seymour Z. Gross asked 70 Minnesota juvenile probation officers to rank the various sections of the presentence report according to their usefulness in determining recommendation of disposition. "The probation officers ranked as most important (1) the child's attitude toward the offense, (2) family data, and (3) previous delinquency problems" (1967: 214). What is interesting about these rankings is the relative unimportance of the kinds of information which probation officers would be expected to rank highly on the basis of the medical model (for example, psychological test data, psychiatric examination results). The kinds of data the subjects found useful suggest they are less oriented toward the psychodynamics of offenders than they are toward rather straightforward, commonsensical notions, such as whether defendants are repentant.

## Parole Prediction Research

Social scientists have been conducting parole prediction research for nearly 60 years. In recent years the same type of research has been extended to probation. Using official records as data, and multivariate statistical procedures, investigators sort offenders into groups with known risks of committing new crimes (for example, Bonham *et al.*, 1984). The objective is to develop experience tables that can be used by parole boards and other decision makers.

This research has uncovered a variety of factors which, taken singly and in combination, are correlated with probation–parole success (O'Leary and Glaser, 1972). As we have noted, parole violation rates tend to be lower for homicide and rape offenders. Unlike property offenses, these are crimes that least often serve as a vocation for offenders. Parole success rates (1) increase with the age of prison releasees and (2) decrease as the length of offenders' previous record increases.

These actuarial prediction methods generally have proved their technical merit. Paul E. Meehl (1954) reviewed previous studies that compared the accuracy of behavioral predictions made by clinicians (psychiatrists, psychologists) with those made on the basis of statistical methods. The latter proved overwhelmingly to be more accurate. Findings such as these are typical (Glaser, 1985).

Parole boards and judges have been urged to employ prediction tables as an aid in decision making. Nevertheless, questions remain as to the value of these procedures.

The trouble with prediction is simply that it will not work—that is, it will not work for individuals, only for groups. A parole board may know that of 100 offenders with a certain set of characteristics, 80 will probably succeed and 20 will fail on parole. But the board members do not know whether the man who is before them belongs with the 80 or the 20 (Stanley, 1976: 56).

Despite these and other criticisms, probation–parole prediction research not only continues but has gained new popularity in recent years. In the process it has taken on a new appellation: *risk assessment.*

## Probation–Parole Agents and Their Work

From their inception, probation and parole have had dual functions. Probation–parole personnel are combination social workers and police officers, simultaneously providing assistance to offenders to increase their chances of finding a conventional niche in the community, and controlling and monitoring them to prevent new crimes. From time to time over the past 100 years, a preoccupation with one or the other of these two functions has dominated public debate over the efficacy of probation and parole. At least until recent years, the liberal-inspired assistance mandate carried the day.

### Types of Agents

Probation–parole officers are permitted considerable discretion in the way they perform their work and in the kinds of information they report to their superiors. The manner in which they exercise this discretion and reconcile their often conflicting job demands varies substantially from officer to officer. It has been the focus of considerable speculation and some research.

Several investigators have distinguished variation in the personal style and orientation of parole officers as they carry out their tasks. For instance, Lloyd E. Ohlin *et al.* distinguished three styles of officer performance and related these to three concepts of parole work:

**1.** The "punitive officer" is the guardian of the middle-class community morality; he attempts to coerce the offender into conforming by means of threats and punishment and his emphasis is on control, protecting the community against the offender, and systematic suspicion of those under supervision.

**2.** The "protective agent" . . . vacillates between protecting the offender and protecting the community. His tools are direct assistance, lecturing, and praise and blame. He is recognized by his ambivalent emotional involvement with the offender and others in the community as he shifts back and forth in taking sides with one against the other.

**3.** The "welfare worker" . . . [has as his] ultimate goal the improved welfare of the client, a condition achieved by helping him in his individual adjustment within limits imposed by the client's capacity. He feels that the only genuine guarantee of community protection lies in the client's personal adjustment since external conformity will be only temporary and in the long run may make a successful adjustment more difficult. Emotional neutrality permeated his relationships. The diagnostic categories and treatment skills which he employs stem from an objective and theoretically based assessment of the client's situation, needs, and capacities (1956; quoted in Glaser, 1964: 430).

George Pownall (1963) and Daniel Glaser (1964) adopted and modified this scheme by adding a fourth type—"passive agents" who see "their jobs as sinecures, requiring only a minimum effort"—and changing the label and description of the protective agent to the "paternal officer." Their resulting fourfold typology is derived by cross-classifying two variables: emphasis on control and emphasis on assistance, as shown in Table 9.4.

Paul Takagi devised another scheme of parole officer types:

**1.** The "rebels," who dissipate most of their energies fighting the agency. These workers find themselves in conflict with the agency rules and their supervisors. Such agents believe that the organizational rules and procedures are silly and hamper their best efforts, and they criticize the supervisors for lack of knowledge and competence.

**2.** The "accommodator" also experiences severe frustrations and conflicts, but primarily in the area of providing services to the client. This type agent is committed to his profession and to the ideology of treatment which he believes can be implemented in an administrative structure. . . . He attempts to work within the framework of organizational policies and administrative relationships.

**3.** The "noncommitted," whom parole agency administrators refer to as "bodies filling positions in the organization." His work style is guided by task objectives and ignores the goals of the organization. He is neither oriented toward the needs of the client nor the needs of the supervisor. He is thoroughly familiar with the routines of the job; and he can be de-

pended upon to do the minimum; that is, eight hours of work for eight hours of pay.

**4.** Finally, the "conformist," who does not find himself in conflict with agency rules and procedures. He works within the framework of the administrative structure to achieve tasks objectives as well as the officially stated goals of the organization (1967; quoted in Irwin, 1970: 129–41).

Others have turned the research spotlight on variation in the day-to-day work behavior of different types of parole officers. Using questionnaires, Glaser found some differences among parole officer responses to hypothetical parolee-problem situations. For example,

over 90 percent of the passive and welfare officers reported that they practically never request a violation warrant when a parolee changes jobs without permission, whereas over 40 percent of the paternal and punitive officers reported that they request a warrant occasionally or more often in such cases (1964: 437).

Robert O. Dembo developed a twofold typology of parole officers and examined variations in the behavior of the two types. Ninety-four New York State parole officers were interviewed, and agency files were examined to determine variations in their actual case-handling procedures. He found a relationship between parole officers' orientation and their recommendations to return parolees to prison for technical violations.

The results . . . show the existence of two parole officer groups, originally uncovered by Reed and King (1966) in their study of North Carolina probation officers: (1) an urban-liberal, probationer-oriented group favoring unofficial actions short of revocation and (2) a rural-conservative group, with a preference

TABLE 9.4  **Types of Parole Officers**

| Emphasis on Assistance | Emphasis on Control | |
|---|---|---|
| | **High** | **Low** |
| High | Protective agent | Welfare worker |
| Low | Punitive agent | Passive agent |

SOURCE: Glaser (1964:431)

for officer-oriented, or social-order rationalizations favoring revocation.

Pursuing this line of thought, Dembo further suggests that

> apparently, the experience of living in the cosmopolitan, urban culture sensitized officer awareness and fosters reintegrative concern for the antisocial products of indigenous slums. And, conversely, prolonged life experience in the predominantly white, Protestant, rural culture does not stimulate concern and involvement in antisocial persons, making it conducive to punishment orientation (1972: 209).

Elaine A. Anderson and Graham B. Spanier (1980) used questionnaires to explore the relationship between probation officers' conceptions of self and work and their decisions about juvenile probationers. Their data, gathered from 255 Pennsylvania probation officers, show that service-oriented officers are less likely than law-oriented officers to label juvenile acts as delinquent.

There seems to be little doubt that different types of parole and probation officers can be identified via empirical research. We also have a limited understanding of how these types respond differently to evidence of violations by parolees, especially technical violations. However, bureaucratic forces probably work to minimize these differences in official response. This is an issue we will examine later in this chapter.

But it is questionable whether this type of research will aid us in understanding differences in the behavior of *parolees*.

> This is because these types are constructed from variables which (1) result in differences in parole-agent behavior which are not visible to the parolee and (2) are related to differences in agent behavior which though visible to the parolee are not important to him. For instance, in

their actual performance in regard to the parolee it has been pointed out that persons with a "social-worker" orientation are in effect more "punitive" than "cop-oriented" parole agents. . . . An officer who is concerned primarily with the welfare of the parolee and has a treatment orientation to parole work can still be very intolerant of deviant behavior. Persons trained in social welfare usually have middle-class orientations and have often had much less contact with deviant subcultures than, say, an ex-policeman. Furthermore, other writers have suggested that authority can be a "treatment" tool. . . . Consequently, the treatment–punishment dichotomy does not make a meaningful division in parole-agent behavior relative to the parolee (Irwin, 1970: 165–66).

*Probation–Parole As Social Process*

William Arnold has noted an unusual paradox in the American approach to probation and parole. Given the importance of these correctional strategies, "it would seem that the parolee–parole officer relationship [would] be the focus of considerable attention by authorities on correction. In point of fact, however, very little has been written about its nature" (1970: 65). Many probation–parole officers are left to work out their own supervision practices and work routines. What do we know about the day-to-day realities of the supervision process? What is it like? To begin with, according to Irwin,

> the parole social system has brought into close contact, in an agent–client relationship, two people who represent different social worlds— one, the parole agency, which is unduly influenced at the formal level by conservative segments of society; and the other, a deviant sub-society (1970: 157).

Second, parole managers and agents operate with a conception of the *successful* parolee that is limited and agency-derived. Success for them means parolees who do not commit additional crimes. But it is important to understand that some parolees may operate on the basis of a different conception:

> From the standpoint of the felon a successful post-prison life is more than merely staying out of prison. . . . From [their] perspective it must be dignified. This is not generally understood by correctional people whose ideas on success are dominated by narrow and unrealistic conceptions of non-recidivism and reformation (Irwin, 1970: 204).

Third, precisely because parole agents are empowered to confine parolees when there is evidence of rule violation or new crimes, parolees are guarded in their contacts with parole agents. A New York study concludes that parolees tend to feel that the conditions and terms of parole make "honest interaction with an officer impossible" (Citizens' Inquiry, 1975: 123).

But there is little evidence of animosity in these relationships. Eliot Studt's study of parole supervision in California concludes that

> parolees are, in general, not actively hostile toward the agents as persons, tending instead to blame "the system." . . . They often find agents more decent as persons than they expected . . . And personal antipathy is not the ubiquitous block to [this] helping relationship that it has sometimes been described as being.

Nonetheless, Studt also noted that most agent–parolee relationships are "bland and diffuse," with a tendency to avoid "confronting tough issues until a problem situation becomes openly critical" (1973: 109).

Arnold's research on juvenile parole supervision led him to conclude that "the contacts [between agents and parolees] are rather perfunctory" (1970: 73). The findings from

---

**PANEL 9.3**

*Some Interactional Dynamics of Parole*

I began to have a series of curious collisions with my current parole officer. When I had first transferred to the Hollywood office I had been assigned to the caseload of the sort of officer I was familiar with—you didn't give him trouble, he was willing to leave you alone. If you seemed to be going along reasonably well, he was willing to put you on "hold" in his mind and concentrate on those who were obviously failing. If you sent your reports in on time, lived quietly, didn't collect a wreath of traffic tickets, beat the shit out of your old lady or get picked up for D and D, you could wear out your parole with a minimum of interference.

But you were also, not infrequently, transferred from one caseload to another without notice, and this is what happened to me. For months the parole office had shown no interest in me, no one had even taken the trouble to come by to confirm I actually lived at the place where I reported my address. Then twice, ten days apart, I found the card of a new P.O. under my door. He had called, found me not home, and left his spoor. I called the parole office, asked for him, but he wasn't in. I left a message, but he didn't call back. I thought of going by to see him. It was a small ploy some of us used. Invent or exaggerate a problem, ask for advice, let him imagine he's helped you, and, meanwhile, he's reassured and isn't likely to drop by your home unannounced.

SOURCE: Malcolm Braly, *False Starts* (Boston: Little, Brown, 1976), pp. 342–43.

a British study are similar. P. Morris and F. Beverly interviewed 69 parolees three times in the six months after release from prison. They conclude:

> There is little doubt that for the most part [parole] officers were seen by the parolees as reliable people who treated them as adults, even in some cases as friends. . . . Nevertheless, the most overwhelming impression to emerge from the interviews with parolees were of the irrelevance and superficiality of supervision. Most parolees thought that the understanding officers had of them as people, and of their life-style, was very limited, and such views persisted throughout the six months follow-up period (1975: 137).

### Organizational Constraints

One shortcoming of some research on parole officers and their decision making is that it neglects the influence of bureaucratic structures and processes. Parole agents, like police officers, do not have unlimited discretion. Their power is constrained by "the complex limits set by operations manuals, by district officer supervision, and by career concerns" (Martinson *et al.,* 1964: 36). In this respect, the process of producing parole violation rates is similar to the process of producing crime rates; it necessitates an understanding of bureaucratic processes and their impact on official decision-making (Minor and Courlander, 1979). As a result, studies of the parole-violation-rate process must overcome the traditional tendency to regard parole outcome "as simply the function of parolee behavior to the neglect of the parole agent as decision maker" (1964: 37). If we want to understand parole supervision and parole violation, we must examine some of the forces that influence probation–parole officer decision making (Kitsuse and Cicourel, 1963). Organizational forces play an important part in this process.

Richard McCleary's research (1978) in a large district parole office in Illinois highlights the operation of a bureaucratic dynamic in parole supervision. According to McCleary, district parole administrators and agents want to maintain autonomy from the central office. Much of their day-to-day work can be understood only in light of this objective. Parole agents generally maintain only superficial contacts with most of their parolees—called *paper men*. Agents consider these men predictable and controllable, therefore unlikely to bring heat on the district office and operations. On the other hand, *dangerous men* are considered unpredictable, hence uncontrollable. Unlike paper men, they are supervised closely.

Robert C. Prus and John R. Stratton used questionnaires, interviews, and observation to collect data from all 45 parole agents in a Midwestern state. In the questionnaire, agents were presented with four cases in the form of vignettes describing incidents of parole violation. For each violation, agents were asked whether they *personally* thought parole should be revoked, and what their *official response* would be.

The investigators found:

> While the personal orientations of parole agents are important in determining their private definitions of parolees as warranting revocation, [it is clear] that agents endeavor to create official parolee definitions consistent with those they consider most desired by the organizational network to which they find themselves accountable.

Specifically,

> agents felt that those who counted in the organization . . . tended to evaluate [agents] on the basis of their revocation rates. There was the feeling among the agents that those agents who revoked over 10 percent of their cases were . . . not performing their jobs adequately" (1976: 53).

## *Stress and Burnout*

Earlier we noted that probation–parole officers are expected to perform both a service and a surveillance role. Given these conflicting expectations, perhaps it is not surprising that they experience a good deal of role conflict. Research has shown that this fosters a high level of stress and job burnout (Whitehead, 1985; Whitehead and Lindquist, 1985).

## Trends in Probation and Parole

The survival and growth of probation and parole over a century or more suggest that these strategies can and have been refashioned from time to time, and rejustified accordingly, to serve a variety of ideological masters. This pattern, arguably, is apparent in some recent developments in probation and parole.

In the 1960s and 1970s, appellate courts imposed stricter due-process standards on correctional bureaucracies and the exercise of discretion by correctional decision makers (Cohen, 1983). Correctional administrators responded by developing *risk assessment instruments* and *parole guidelines.*

The movement to structure and limit discretion reached full bloom in a broader context of increasing severity in parole eligibility requirements and parole practices. As of early 1983, 33 states had modified their sentencing codes to make these procedures more restrictive. Of the 36 states that retained elements of indeterminate sentencing, 19, or 52.8 percent, adopted more severe parole policies. Of the 15 states that adopted determinate sentencing codes, 14, or 93.3 percent, now have more severe parole policies (Shane-DuBow *et al.,* 1985: 311). Eight states eliminated parole entirely (Shane-DuBow *et al.,* 1985: Table 34). However, most still provide for some form of discretionary conditional release and community supervision of released offenders.

## *Parole Guidelines*

The principal reform has been the development and use of decision-making guidelines (Gottfredson, 1983; Hoffman, 1983). These are intended to remove some of the uncertainty and disparities that have characterized parole board decision making in the past. They also deflect judicial criticism of the arbitrary and capricious conduct of parole boards. In October 1973, the United States Board of Parole put into operation a general reorganization and regionalization plan. Case decision-making authority has now been delegated to panels of hearing examiners, using explicit policy guidelines established by the Parole Commission, as the former U.S. Board of Parole is now called. The new structure also provides a two-level administrative appeal process for prisoners who choose to contest the decision. Another part of the plan provides for prisoners who are denied parole to be given a written statement of the reasons (Hoffman and De-Gostin, 1974).

The new policy guidelines created a three-step process (Sigler, 1975). When reviewing a prisoner's case, the examiner panel first gives the case a *salient factor score,* ranging from zero to 11; the higher the score, the better the prospects for successful completion of parole. Table 9.5 contains the salient factor scores used today. The case is then given an *offense severity rating* on a scale of 1–8. This rating does not depend only on the subjective rating of the examiners. Instead, they are given a chart that lists offense categories under each severity rating.

Then, with the salient factor score and the offense severity rating, the examiners refer to another chart, which indicates the amount of time an offender should serve, assuming relatively good prison performance. Table 9.6 shows how an individual's salient factor score and offense severity rating are cross-classified to arrive at averages for the amount of time to be served before release on parole.

These guidelines are intended to improve fairness in the parole selection process, by ensuring that prisoners with similar back-grounds and offenses serve about the same amount of time. In cases in which the clinical judgments of the examiners suggest the pris-oners have a much better chance of success on parole than their scores and ratings indi-cate, the examiners can shorten the amount of time to be served specified by the guide-lines. Alternatively, in cases where the pros-

TABLE 9.5   **Salient Factor Scores Used by the U.S. Parole Commission**

**Item A: PRIOR CONVICTIONS/ADJUDICATIONS (ADULT OR JUVENILE)** ........................ ☐

None ............ = 3
One ............. = 2
Two or three ..... = 1
Four or more ..... = 0

**Item B: PRIOR COMMITMENT(S) OF MORE THAN THIRTY DAYS** ............................. ☐
**(ADULT OR JUVENILE)**

None ............ = 2
One or two ....... = 1
Three or more ... = 0

**Item C: AGE AT CURRENT OFFENSE/PRIOR COMMITMENTS** ................................. ☐

Age at commencement of current
offense
   26 years of age or more ..... = 2
   20–25 years of age ........ = 1
   19 years of age or less ...... = 0

   ***Exception: If five or more prior commitments of more than thirty days (adult
   or juvenile), place an "X" here _____ and score this item .......... = 0

**Item D: RECENT COMMITMENT FREE PERIOD (THREE YEARS)** ............................. ☐

   No prior commitment of more than thirty days (adult or juvenile) or released to
   the community from last such commitment at least three years prior to the
   commencement of the current offense ................................. = 1
   Otherwise ................................................... = 0

**Item E: PROBATION/PAROLE/CONFINEMENT/ESCAPE STATUS VIOLATOR THIS TIME** ........... ☐

   Neither on probation, parole, confinement, or escape status at the time of the
   current offense; nor committed as a probation, parole, confinement, or escape
   status violator this time .................................... = 1
   Otherwise ................................................... = 0

**Item F: HEROIN/OPIATE DEPENDENCE** .................................................. ☐

   No history of heroin/opiate dependence ...... = 1
   Otherwise ............................... = 0

**TOTAL SCORE** ..................................................................... ☐

SOURCE: U.S. Parole Commission (1985:45)

pects for success on parole are judged to be worse than the score and rating indicate, the examiners can extend the amount of time to be served beyond that specified in the guidelines. As Table 9.7 shows, many states have followed the federal lead and established guidelines and an increasingly formalized decision-making process (Gottfredson, Cosgrove *et al.* 1978; Hoffman, 1983).

### *Intensive Parole–Probation*

As American prison populations increased in the 1970s and 1980s, many states found their prisons filled beyond capacity. Federal courts have ordered many states to limit or reduce their prison populations. Some states are compelled to release inmates early in order to meet court-ordered prison population levels (Austin, 1986). Thus many states began to search for alternative strategies for offenders, ideally something that conservative legislators would support, judges would use in lieu of prison, and that would cost less to establish and operate than prison. Intensive probation and parole are among the programs that some jurisdictions have created to meet these problems (Erwin, 1984; Petersilia, 1985; Conrad, 1985; Pearson, 1985). They reassure conservative politicians by promising intensive control for some offenders, satisfy federal judges that official discretion is being used properly, and obviate the need to commit new funds for prison construction.

In one sense, there is little that is new in

TABLE 9.6 **Guidelines for Decision Making, U.S. Parole Commission**

| **Offense Characteristics:** | **Offender Characteristics: Parole Prognosis (Salient Factor Score 1981)** | | | |
|---|---|---|---|---|
| **Severity of Offense Behavior** | **Very Good (10–8)** | **Good (7–6)** | **Fair (5–4)** | **Poor (3–0)** |
| | | **Guideline Range** | | |
| Category One (for example, possession of small amount of marijuana, communicating threats to kill) | <=4 months | <=8 months | 8–12 months | 12–16 months |
| Category Two (for example, obtaining drugs for personal use by fraudulent means, unlawfully entering the U.S.) | <=6 months | <=10 months | 12–16 months | 16–22 months |
| Category Three (for example, perjury, escape) | <=10 months | 12–16 months | 18–24 months | 24–32 months |
| Category Four (for example, involuntary manslaughter, communicating threats to kill) | 12–18 months | 20–26 months | 26–34 months | 34–44 months |
| Category Five (for example, robbery, extortion, safecracking) | 24–36 months | 36–48 months | 48–60 months | 60–72 months |
| Category Six (for example, illegal disposal of hazardous waste, assault with bodily injury) | 40–52 months | 52–64 months | 64–78 months | 78–100 months |
| Category Seven (for example, voluntary manslaughter, rape, arson) | 52–80 months | 64–92 months | 78–110 months | 100–148 months |
| Category Eight (for example, murder, treason, espionage) | 100+ months | 120+ months | 150+ months | 180+ months |

SOURCE: U.S. Parole Commission (1985 : 12)

these programs. Probation and parole managers and officers for years have sorted offenders into categories requiring greater or lesser supervision. For the most part, these have been ad hoc efforts grounded in the day-to-day bureaucratic and interactional experiences of probation and parole workers (McCleary, 1978). In some states, the correctional system formalized these procedures as a "case management" tool. What does distinguish these "old" forms of intensive supervision from the "new" ones is the support the latter have received from correctional scholars. The new intensive supervision has been the recipient of considerable publicity and the kinds of ideological work that must accompany credible efforts to reform correctional strategies.

An obvious advantage of the new intensive supervision programs is that they seem to offer something for everyone. As much as they would prefer to abolish or curtail the use of probation and parole, conservatives are aware that the prospects for doing so are extremely remote (Wilson, 1983). Consequently, if we must have probation and parole, conservatives naturally opt for the intensive brand. For liberals, support for in-

TABLE 9.7  **Provisions for Parole Guidelines, January 1983**

| Jurisdiction | Guidelines for paroling decisions are written into statutes | Guidelines for paroling decisions are system-wide policy but are not written into statutes | Guidelines for paroling decisions are selectively applied |
|---|---|---|---|
| Federal system | □ | | |
| District of Columbia | | □ | |
| Alaska | | □ | |
| California | | □* | □** |
| Florida | □ | | |
| Georgia | | □ | |
| Maryland | | □ | |
| Massachusetts | | | |
| Minnesota | | | □ |
| Missouri | | □ | |
| New Jersey | | □ | |
| New York | □ | | |
| Oklahoma | | □ | |
| Oregon | | □ | |
| Pennsylvania | | □ | |
| Rhode Island | | | |
| Utah | | □ | |
| Vermont | | | |
| Washington | | □ | |
| Wisconsin | | | |

*The California Department of the Youth Authority. The Department of the Youth
  Authority has a parole board separate from the Department of Corrections. In addition to
  its juvenile commitments the Department of the Youth Authority can accept at its discretion
  adult court commitments for those up to age 21; it may hold offenders up to age 25.
**The California Department of Corrections.
SOURCE: Flanagan and McGarrell (1986:114)

tensive supervision seems to hold some potential for stemming the tide of conservative crime control ideologies and strategies of the recent past. Petersilia argues that

[t]he U.S. criminal justice system has never developed a spectrum of sanctions to match the spectrum of criminality. This, we believe, is the challenge now facing criminal justice. We argue that the system must develop intermediate forms of punishment, more restrictive than routine probation but not as severe as prison (1985: 344).

As the name suggests, offenders placed in an intensive supervision program are moni-

---

**PANEL 9.4**

*Parole Risk Assessment Instrument (Tennessee, 1986)*

| Risk Factor | Category | Score | |
|---|---|---|---|
| Number of previous paroles on this sentence | None | 0 | |
| | One or more | 5 | _____ |
| Maximum sentence length at time of release | 5 years or less | 0 | |
| | 6–9 years | 2 | |
| | 10 years or more | 5 | _____ |
| Age at first juvenile adjudication | No juvenile record | 0 | |
| | 13 or younger | 1 | |
| | 14 or over | 3 | _____ |
| Number of previous felony incarcerations | None | 0 | |
| | 1 or more | 4 | _____ |
| Instant offense was burglary, forgery, or fraud | No | 0 | |
| | Yes | 3 | _____ |
| Living arrangement with spouse or parents | Yes | 0 | |
| | No | 3 | _____ |
| Age at incarceration on current offense | 32 or older | 0 | |
| | 22–31 | 1 | |
| | 21 or younger | 3 | _____ |
| Employment status at first parole contact | Employed | 0 | |
| | Unemployed | 2 | _____ |
| Parole officer assessment of attitude | Positive | 0 | |
| | Generally positive | 2 | |
| | Generally negative | 5 | |
| | Negative | 7 | _____ |
| Parole officer assessment of risk | Minimum | 0 | |
| | Medium | 1 | |
| | Maximum | 2 | _____ |
| | | Total Score: | _____ |

*Score Ranges:* 0–10 minimum, 11–17 medium, 18–24 maximum, 25+ Intensive Supervision

tored by their probation or parole agents more closely than their garden-variety criminal peers. Offenders are selected for intensive supervision by the use of classification and risk–needs assessment instruments (Warren, 1971; Lerner *et al.*, 1986; Alexander, 1986). In fact, in the rush to display their classification and prediction devices, correctional managers in many states have adopted those developed elsewhere or at any earlier time with little regard for their transituational validity (Clear and Gallagher, 1985).

In Tennessee, a risk-assessment instrument is used to divide parolees into risk categories. Those who score highest are eligible for intensive supervision. Parolees in this program must maintain personal contact with their agents. Agents also are expected to initiate frequent checks on and contacts with the parolees. Intensive-supervision parolees also may be subject to more restrictions on their activities and movements than other parolees. Intensive parole may be combined with other strategies, such as home incarceration or electronic monitoring. In all

respects, the objective is to monitor more closely the movements and, therefore, the criminal opportunities of certain offenders.

John P. Conrad argues that programs of intensive supervision "offer realistic prospects for a wide-ranging renovation of American penology" (1985: 411). Already researchers are touting the effectiveness of these new programs (Pearson, 1985; Erwin, 1984).

While some liberals attack the intrusiveness of some of these new controls, conservatives scoff at the critics. They argue not only that offenders *deserve* such treatment as retribution for their crimes, but also that they should be required to forfeit some of their civil liberties. A radical critic counters, "The practice has not changed but, rather, is now openly declared. . . . The mechanisms of social control are tightening up, illustrative of the way in which intensification of punishment is a response to deteriorating social and economic conditions" (Schmidt, 1977: 141).

# 10

# Historical
# Correctional Change

We have previously stated that the structures, strategies, and ideologies of correctional practice do not exist in a social vacuum but are molded or at least limited by the political–economic context. Thus at any one time these macro-social forces create a dynamic that constrains the type and scope of correctional development. On the other hand, this same dynamic enables certain correctional strategies to develop because they are consonant with an ideology that is part of the current political–economic climate.

Historically, we can point to particular periods when correctional structures, ideologies, or strategies underwent fundamental transformation. For example, the early 19th century witnessed the institutionalization of the penitentiary system in America. During the Reconstruction period that followed the Civil War, Southern states established peni-

tentiaries where formerly there had been none. Likewise, in the late 19th and early 20th centuries, America was swept by the reformatory movement, during which numerous states constructed a new type of prison (Currie, 1973). At about the same time, 1880–1920, parole and probation became accepted parts of the correctional policies of many states. The treatment of women prisoners changed with the establishment of separate institutions. Later, as the medical model gained ascendancy as a rationale for various correctional programs, psychiatrists and social workers were hired to work in correctional agencies and to establish classification programs for newly admitted offenders. Expansion of corrections into community programs was another step that may also be seen as an example of correctional change. Let us now look at how changes in corrections are perceived and interpreted.

# Three Perspectives on Correctional Change

Discussions and interpretations of correctional change are dominated by three ideologies of the state: conservatism, liberalism, and radicalism. These perspectives differ in their conceptions of the causes of correctional change, and their assessments of the relative weight that should be assigned to these causes. More important, they differ in their conceptions of the social and political processes that give rise to correctional changes. We need to probe these differences if we are to understand correctional change and reform.

There are key reasons for including consideration of political ideologies in any discussion of correctional change. First, as we pointed out earlier, the punishment of offenders is an inherently political act that is provided for, carried out by, and justified by the state and its representatives. Therefore, any treatment of correctional issues is a treatment of political processes and beliefs as well. Any decision to change correctional methods requires action by political actors, whether they be administrative, legislative, or judicial. Whatever political perspective is dominant in any one historical period affects the correctional ideology that will prevail.

## Conservatism

Conservatives generally seek to preserve existing social arrangements and institutions and favor gradual rather than abrupt change. They believe that tampering with social institutions is an inherently risky undertaking which can easily create more problems than it solves. Consequently, conservatives do not have much faith in government's ability to solve problems through social planning and welfare programs. Nevertheless, social institutions and practices do change, and conservatives are well aware of this. However, unlike liberals and radicals, conservatives seem to lack a unifying, recurrent, or consistent interpretation for these changes. Unlike liberals, conservatives make no assumptions about unidirectional progress or improvement in history. Rather, they are inclined to be skeptical about historical change and to assume that change can be regressive just as easily as progressive.

Conservatives see punishment as a ritual and symbolic means of retribution because of the moral value people invest in rule conformity (Ignatieff, 1981: 184). Hence punishment follows the dictates of the community. The conservative perspective sees change in dealing with offenders as an outcome of a consensus on generally held values. Thus change toward a more punitive correctional stance is the result of a re-emphasis on traditional values that support such a change. Conservatives tend to see correctional change in terms of manipulating various aspects of control, such as increasing lengths of sentences, incarcerating more criminals, and making the correctional apparatus more efficient, thus increasing the cost of crime.

## Liberalism

Liberals view the political process as an arena in which private citizens and organized groups compete to influence government to their advantage or to urge change in a direction consistent with their beliefs. One group of citizens might urge a zoning variance to permit operation of a halfway house for offenders in an urban neighborhood, while another group, perhaps of residents in the area, insists that the variance not be issued. These groups naturally conflict with one another and mobilize resources to support their interpretations of the likely consequences should the government not accede to their wishes. Likewise, they may seek to marshal public opinion in support of their respective positions.

However, the conflict is usually orderly. Underlying it is a high degree of consensus on the "rules of the game." Those parties in conflict that refuse to compromise their objectives are derided as extremist, and criticized for placing parochial interest ahead of the public good.

From the liberal perspective, the political process is equally open to all. Similarly, the process is not rigged in favor of any particular group or stratum of the population. Instead, victory goes to the side whose position is best supported by the "objective facts" (the group that has "truth" on its side) or that is better organized and thus more effective in pressing its claim.

Liberals adhere to a gradual, piecemeal approach to political and correctional change. Specific, limited reforms are sought, usually on the assumption that reform itself is an incremental or evolutionary process and that each of these finite reforms will ultimately help perfect the correctional system. Although there may be occasional short-term regressions, the overall trend in the treatment of offenders is one of progress, improvement, and increasing rationality.

Liberals assign a critical role in the process of correctional change to charismatic or innovative individuals. Thus liberal interpretations of correctional change often amount to a celebration of the individual actors involved.

Unfortunately, liberals as well as conservatives are silent when it comes to explaining the specific sociohistorical appearance of various combinations of interest groups. Both ideologies tend to ignore the social—historical context out of which these groups emerge, or at least they pay little attention to the correspondence between the characteristics of social settings and the characteristics and motives of interest groups. Thus liberals

often offer ad hoc retrospective explanations for specific historical changes, assigning causal importance either to the spontaneous appearance of specific interest groups or to the workings of such free-floating forces as *humanitarianism* or *social progress.*

David Rothman's liberal interpretation of fundamental correctional change that occurred during the Progressive period in America sees it as a result of "conscience" and "convenience."

> We begin first with conscience, for the Progressive programs were the invention of benevolent and philanthropic-minded men and women and their ideological formulations were essential to promoting change. Coming from the world of the college, the settlement house, and the medical school, the Progressive reformers shared optimistic theories that at once clarified the origins of deviant behavior and shaped their efforts to control it. They marched under a very appealing banner, asking citizens not to do less for fear of harm, but to do more, confident of favorable results. . . . Progressives aimed to understand and to cure crime, delinquency, and insanity through a case-by-case approach. . . . To Progressives, knowledge about and policies toward the deviant had to follow a far more particular bent. The task was to understand the life history of each offender or patient and then to devise a remedy that was specific to the individual (1980: 5).

Describing penal changes during the first quarter of the 20th century, such as the indeterminate sentence, probation, and parole, Rothman comments:

> The rapidity with which these transformations occurred, the fact that criminal justice assumed a new character within twenty years, reflected the broad nature of the *supporting coalition.* State after state passed probation and parole legislation with little debate and no contro-

versy. Concerned citizens, settlement house workers, criminologists, social workers, psychologists, and psychiatrists stood together with directors of charitable societies, judges, district attorneys, wardens, and superintendents. To find a common goal uniting such a diverse group is itself surprising (1980: 44–45, emphasis added).

Another example of a liberal analysis of more recent correctional change is John Irwin's interpretation of the emergence of the "correctional institution."

The correctional institution's emergence was related to broad changes in our society. Briefly, the postwar United States—prosperous, urbanized, and mobile—confronted a new set of pressing social problems. Hard times, natural disasters (floods, droughts, and tornadoes), epidemics, illiteracy, and the "dangerous classes" had been updated to or replaced by poverty, mental health, family disorganization, race relations, juvenile delinquency, and urban crime. Americans faced these with a fundamentally altered posture. The Great Depression and World War II had moved them from their isolationist and individualist position, and they accepted, even demanded, government intervention into conditions that they believed should and could be changed (1980: 37–38).

Another focus in liberal interpretation of change is a faith in "scientific" explanation. According to Irwin, the social-scientist approach became appealing in correctional circles for it focused on discovering the causes of human behavior.

The [social scientists] searched in various realms or levels—the psychological, biological and sociological—and amassed a large body of social scientific theories that purported to explain or identify the causes of human behavior. The innovative penologist kept abreast of the developments in the new social sciences and

began constructing a philosophy of penology based on the concept that criminal behavior was caused by identifiable and changeable forces. This led them to the conclusion that the primary purpose of imprisonment should be "rehabilitation," a new form of reformation based on scientific methods (1980: 39).

Thus to liberals, change in correctional practice is perceived to be primarily the result, singly or in combination, of group compromises, individual reformers, progressive trends, innovation, and scientific progress.

Akin to the liberal perspective, most correctional employees subscribe to what might be called a "popular sovereignty" theory of correctional change. This theory maintains that scientific knowledge and changing public opinion stimulate or slow correctional reforms. Thus changing correctional ideologies can produce comparable modifications in corrections only if scientific knowledge and public opinion are supportive. According to this position, a misinformed and unsupportive public is largely responsible for the persistence of archaic correctional practices. Hence, failure to "educate the public" about desirable changes is likely to doom those changes.

However, public opinion and changes in the correctional knowledge base may be largely secondary in efforts to understand historical transformations of correctional structures and practices. Instead, changes in public opinion and scientific knowledge are "discovered" whenever necessary; that is, when changes in some fundamental structure, such as the economy, mandate a modified correctional structure.

## Radicalism

The radical perspective on correctional development and change has as its point of departure a more complex set of propositions than either the liberal or the conservative perspective. Radicalism implies getting to the roots of things. Although there are different emphases within the perspective, radicals insist that prevailing correctional ideologies, strategies, and structures can only be understood in terms of their sociohistorical context. Moreover, the type of economic relations that predominate in a particular period shapes the type of social relations that exist as well as the prevailing stance that is taken toward those considered criminal.

While liberals assume that the political process affords all groups an opportunity to share in the exercise of power on equal terms and that no single group has consistent control, radicals think otherwise. As we saw previously, radicals maintain that the social class that owns the means of production represents a ruling elite able to control the major social institutions to serve its own needs and pacify other classes.

Recent radical interpretations of historical correctional changes have taken the assumed deficiencies of liberal explanations as their starting point. In Elliott Currie's work on the American reformatory movement, he notes that

> strong supporters of the treatment ethic in modern penology are generally laudatory and uncritical in their praise of the movement and its leaders. According to this interpretation, the Reformatory movement was a humanitarian and progressive effort, far ahead of its time, that held the key to the problem of crime and punishment, but whose great promise has never been fulfilled—largely because of a lack of public support and understanding. Its leading figures are described as farsighted humanitarians animated by a generous concern for the downtrodden (1973: 3).

But he suggests that

> a close analysis of the theory and practice of the Reformatory movement leads to a very dif-

ferent interpretation of its social origins, its character and its historical role. From the beginning . . . it was an authoritarian and conservative movement, created by upper-class reformers and propelled by the central aim of instilling industrial discipline in the "idle and vicious" masses of the post–Civil War industrial cities (1973: 4–5).

Radicals point to what they see as the underlying process in correctional change, not what may be emphasized for ideological purposes or what may appear to be adequate explanation on the surface. By focusing on the larger political economic framework, they explain correctional innovation as part of larger sociopolitical patterns at a specific time. Thus what happens to corrections is intimately connected to the dominant political ethos, and cannot be attributed to an isolated individualistic stance or theory of reform.

Radicals part company with conservatives and liberals over the relative importance they assign to public opinion as an originator of correctional transformations. Radicals view justificatory references to public opinion as attempts to ratify decisions already made on the basis of other considerations, or as support for the failure to make reforms. More important, theoretical and research interest have focused on processes by which elites employ the mass media and public information campaigns for purposes of maintaining ideological dominance. Such work generally builds on the premise that public opinion, while playing some part in the political process, is so manipulated by elites that it is usually supportive of policies they favor.

## Alternative Explanations

By necessity these comments on the contrast between conservatism, liberalism, and radicalism have been brief. To further illustrate explanations of correctional change, we will comment on some of the differences in emphasis of a few representative studies that challenge accepted views.

In his work on the child-saving movement of the late 19th and early 20th centuries, Anthony M. Platt maintains, for example:

> The child-saving movement was not a humanistic enterprise on behalf of the working class against the established order. On the contrary, its impetus came primarily from the middle and upper classes who were instrumental in devising the *new forms of social control to protect their power and privilege.* The child-saving movement was not an isolated phenomenon but rather *reflected massive changes in the mode of production* from laissez-faire to monopoly capitalism, and in strategies of social control from inefficient repression to welfare state benevolence (1977: xx; emphasis added).

Paul Takagi suggests an alternative interpretation for the creation of the Walnut Street Jail in 1773 in Philadelphia—widely viewed as the forerunner of the penitentiary in America. He notes that "most of us have been led to believe that the 'gentle and humane' Quakers founded the prison as an alternative to the sanguinary English laws then in effect, and that the idea of a prison was based upon the prevailing theory of human reason. There are problems with these interpretations" (1975: 18–19). He argues that establishment of the jail was intended to centralize the powers of the state.

Others who write in the radical tradition but do not emphasize class and economic relations still see correctional change in sociohistorical context. Michel Foucault perhaps best reflects this attempt to chronicle change that has come about in the philosophical or ideological underpinnings of punishment and correctional efforts. He describes how punishment shifted from its expression on the body of the offender to a different realm—that of the soul or, in less metaphysical terms, the mind. Speaking of the early use of torture, Foucault points out the function it served: "It made it possible to reproduce the crime on the visible body of the criminal; in the same horror, the crime had to be manifested and annulled. It also made the body of the condemned man the place where the vengeance of the sovereign was applied the anchoring point for a manifestation of power, an opportunity of affirming the dissymmetry of forces" (1979: 55).

Punishment also demonstrated the awesome power of the sovereign, later the state, that would be marshalled against an offender. This "dissymmetry of forces," this unequal power in the potential use of all the control resources of the state, remains but is manifested in much different forms up to contemporary times. We move from torture, public execution, physical mutilation, and corporal punishment to confinement, where the power shifts to methods of control, discipline, and manipulation of the mind of the offender through the imposition of either religious dogma or psychological doctrines of correction.

Less philosophical is Georg Rusche and Otto Kirchheimer's work, originally published in 1939 but still a refreshing and pioneering attempt to provide an alternative interpretation of changes in penal methods. Writing from a Marxist point of view, they note that changing methods of punishment can't be explained merely by pointing to certain ideas on progress or the changing requirements of ways of dealing with crime. For while some of these may contribute to an explanation, they are by themselves insufficient to account for penal practices.

> Punishment must be understood as a social phenomenon freed from both its juristic concept and its social ends. . . . Every system of production tends to discover punishments which correspond to its productive relation-

ships. It is thus necessary to investigate the origin and fate of penal systems, the use or avoidance of specific punishments, and the intensity of penal practices as they are determined by social forces, above all by economic and then fiscal forces.

The nature of a society's system of production strongly influences the "selection" of certain penal methods.

The disappearance of a given system of production makes its corresponding punishment inapplicable. Only a specific development of the productive forces permits the introduction or rejection of corresponding penalties. But before these potential methods can be introduced, society must be in a position to incorporate them as integrated parts of the whole social and economic system (1939: 6).

Rusche and Kirchheimer analyze the major transformations in penal methods that have occurred since the Middle Ages. While their analysis focuses on the relationship between the political economy and various styles in punishment, it avoids the reductionism of earlier attempts to relate the economy to crime and punishment (for example, Bonger, 1916).

On the contrary, Rusche and Kirchheimer's analysis is informed by the recognition of more complex patterns and forces. As one commentator notes, they "analyze changing economic conditions, shifts in the nature of political and legal rule, evolving patterns of criminal activity and the religious, philosophical, and fiscal resources available to authorities in charge of administering punishments" (Adamson, 1984: 436).

While radical scholars generally praise Rusche and Kirchheimer's pioneering effort, it is not without its critics and those who have continued to expand and refine their argument. Joan Smith and William Fried, for example, object to Rusche and Kirchheimer's assumption that penal methods change as a direct result of economic changes. They charge that "this unilateral model of social change is deceptive since it treats the state, law, and doctrine as mere ideological trappings" (1974: 12–f.n.).

Other contemporary writers have given alternative explanations of correctional change that are generally consistent with earlier Marxian analyses but go beyond them in certain ways. For example, Dario Melossi and Massimo Pavarini argue that the prison as it developed in the 19th century served several related functions. Thus they see the prison as fulfilling a class control function as well as serving as a mechanism for instilling the necessary discipline to prepare prisoners, part of the "surplus population," for the factory.

The concept of the penitentiary as a focus of economic activity has never been useful and ... it would be incorrect to talk of prison as a manufactory or as a factory (of commodities). It would be more correct to say that the first historic instances of prisons were modeled ... on the factory. ... The object was thus not so much the production of commodities as the production of men. From this point we can see the real dimensions of the "penitentiary invention": a "prison as a machine" capable of transforming, after close observation of the deviant phenomenon ... the violent, troublesome and impulsive criminal ... into an inmate ... into a disciplined, into a mechanical subject. In the end, this is not just an ideological aim but an economic one ... the production of subjects for an industrial society ... the production of proletarians by the enforced training of prisoners in factory discipline" (1981: 143–44).

Michael Ignatieff sees the development of the prison during the 19th century in somewhat different terms. While he too focuses on the harsh disciplinary measures of the penitentiary in his analysis, he interprets this disciplinary emphasis as an element in a larger strategy to prevent social chaos, the great fear of the propertied and powerful. The concept of the prison gained acceptance because it was portrayed by reformers not only as a way of dealing with crime but as response "to the whole social crisis of a period, and as part of a larger strategy of political, social, and legal reforms designed to reestablish order . . ." (1978: 210). Prisons had to replace the brutality of earlier punishments because terror produced only half-hearted compliance and increased the possibility of disorder by the masses.

> In a period of tumultuous economic and social change, coerced compliance was no longer enough. Social order . . . had to be guaranteed by something stronger than a frayed and increasingly hollow paternalism, backed by hangings. Social stability had to be founded on popular consent, maintained by guilt at the thought of wrongdoing, rather than by deference and fear (1978: 211).

Prison, therefore, again is seen as serving a class control function, part of an overall strategy of maintaining order and stability from the point of view of the privileged in a class society. Somewhat later, Ignatieff (1981) points to the need for more empirical examination of social theories on a grand scale that purport to explain social relations in terms of power and subordination.

More recently, Christopher Adamson points out that while Rusche and Kirchheimer and others recognized the class and crime control function of the prison as well as the fact that it served at times as an industrial and financial organization, they did not consistently differentiate between these various functions of punishment. According to Adamson, Rusche and Kirchheimer do not make clear whether a particular form of punishment—for example, hard labor or solitary confinement—was the result of class/

crime control or for reasons of fiscal/industrial development. Adamson then argues that the "labor supply and the business cycle influence how populations are processed through the criminal justice system: whether they are treated as threats to the capitalist mode of production and/or as economic resources to exploit" (1984: 437).

He attempts to answer such questions as why at one time was prison labor eliminated as being too lenient a form of punishment whereas another time it was considered too severe a form of punishment? Or why prisoners were sometimes allowed to work while at other times forced to remain idle? What caused prison labor to be both brutal and profitable at one period and lenient and profitable at another? Depending on business cycles and labor supply conditions, Adamson maintains, prison populations are treated either as a threat or as a resource to be exploited.

During the postrevolutionary period in the U.S., "there was a growing demand for, and a persistent scarcity of, labor. . . . The shortage of skilled labor, coupled with the view that industriousness, especially in household manufacturing, would prevent social decay, explains why reformers thought it desirable to establish trades within prison" (1984: 440).

Following the War of 1812, the country underwent a serious recession, with high levels of unemployment and stiff trade competition following normalization of trade, which brought business failure to many who could not compete. Skilled workers lost their jobs and an underclass of vagrants and beggars emerged. During this period, prison conditions became harsh; indeed, prisoners were seen as having it too easy, receiving free food and shelter while others were suffering. The result:

> Penologists developed two ways of increasing the effectiveness of crime control. The first was

to make prison labor extraordinarily harsh by introducing the treadmill. . . . The second was to deprive inmates of labor altogether and to introduce a system of total solitary confinement (Adamson, 1984: 442).

Adamson analyzes other historical periods with similar results. In another study, Christopher T. Link and Neal Shover examined the determinants of sentencing reform in the United States. Using a set of variables derived from a liberal perspective and a set of variables derived from the radical perspective, they used multiple regression analysis to determine which set of variables had more explanatory power. "The functionalist perspective suggests that sentencing reforms develop in contexts characterized by an increase in violent crime, a rising tide of political conservatism, and a well-educated citizenry" (1986: 333). On the other hand, "the materialist perspective suggests that new sentencing policies . . . developed in contexts characterized by deteriorating economic conditions, the state's worsening fiscal difficulties, and the need to control a potentially disruptive problem population" (1986: 332). Their findings suggest that declining economic conditions and increased fiscal strains had the greatest influence on sentencing reform. They conclude: "States which experienced the most severe economic decline enacted the most extensive reforms" (1986: 338). Although the statistical relationships were modest, the variables that reflected a radical approach had superior explanatory power.

# Contemporary Correctional Changes

Let us now briefly examine the direction of contemporary changes in corrections, in particular the movement toward private involvement as well as the new uses of house arrest.

## Privatization

The private sector's involvement in the correctional enterprise is not entirely new. During the era of expanding industrial capitalism in the 19th century, prison labor was used by private industry in several ways. Under the *contract labor* system, prisoners' labor was used to manufacture goods for a private contractor who furnished all tools and materials and supervised the work in prison. The *piece-price system* involved a contractor furnishing raw materials, with prisoners being paid for the completed goods on a per-piece basis. The *lease system* involved the leasing of prisoners to contractors to work in farming, construction, mining, plantations, or other hard labor, with the contractor having complete control over the prisoner (Inciardi, 1984).

These were extremely exploitive systems; the latter was the equivalent of slavery. Some Southern states actually did replace slaves with prisoners (Adamson, 1983). The private use of prison labor was eventually abandoned because of opposition from competitors, who considered it unfair to their business, and the emergence of organized labor, which objected to the practice.

In juvenile corrections, privately run programs and facilities have been in existence for some time, but on a relatively small scale and in selected areas.

Current conceptions of private enterprise in corrections are much greater in scope. In general, the private sector has become involved in three areas: (1) participation in prison work programs; (2) financing of prison or jail construction; (3) managing and operating prisons or other correctional facilities (Mullen, 1985). In early 1985, there were 26 projects that involved private business in various arrangements with prison industries (Sexton *et al.*, 1985).

The second area is perhaps more novel and involves the use of large brokerage firms

TABLE 10.1  Facility Management Contracting Activity in Early 1984[1]

| Federal Contracts | State Corrections Contracts | Local Jail Contracts |
|---|---|---|
| IMMIGRATION & NATURALIZATION SERVICE<br>• 4 facility contracts for aliens awaiting deportation were operating (in San Diego, Los Angeles, Houston, Denver), providing a total capacity of 625 beds.<br>• 3 facility contracts were nearing award (in Las Vegas, Phoenix, San Francisco), providing another 225 beds.<br>• 2 additional facility contracts offering a total of 270 beds were planned in the near term (Laredo and El Paso, Texas).<br><br>U.S. MARSHALS SERVICE<br>• 2 small (30-bed) facilities operated under contract in California.<br>• Plans to open a larger (100- to 150-bed) contracted facility in Los Angeles for alien material witnesses.<br><br>FEDERAL BUREAU OF PRISONS<br>• Plans to operate a 400- to 600-bed contracted facility for sentenced aliens in Southwest region. (Project delayed due to siting difficulties.)<br>• A 60-bed facility in La Honda, California, operated under contract for offenders under the Federal Youth Corrections Act. | SECONDARY ADULT FACILITIES<br>• 28 states reported the use of privately operated prerelease, work-release, or halfway house facilities. Largest private facility networks found in California, Massachusetts, Michigan, New York, Ohio, Texas, and Washington.<br><br>PRIMARY ADULT FACILITIES<br>• No contracts reported for the confinement of mainstream adult populations; most private proposals still focused on community corrections facilities.<br>• Two interstate facilities for protective-custody prisoners planned by private contractor.<br><br>JUVENILE FACILITIES<br>• A 1982–83 survey of private juvenile facilities found 1,877 privately operated residential programs holding a total of 31,390 juveniles, 10,712 of whom were held for delinquency. Only 47 institutions were classified as strict security and 426 as medium security.[2]<br>• Departing from the small, less secure settings characteristic of contracted juvenile facilities, a private contractor operates the Okeechobee (Florida) Training School for 400 to 500 serious juvenile offenders. | LOCAL JAIL CONTRACTS<br>• Legislation enabling private jail operations was pending in Colorado and had passed in New Mexico and Texas. While the National Sheriffs' Association registered formal opposition to privately operated jail facilities, corporate providers reported significant interest and a number of pending proposals for jail operations in the Southern and Western regions.<br>• In Hamilton County, Tennessee, a private contract took over the operations of a local workhouse holding 300 males and females awaiting trial or serving sentences up to 6 years in length.<br><br>SHARED FACILITIES<br>• One private organization in Texas is planning to construct and operate a facility that would serve local detention needs as well as the needs of Federal agencies responsible for confining illegal aliens.<br>• Other proposals have called for the development of regional jail facilities that would serve multicounty detention needs. |

1. Reported in phone contacts made in January/February 1984 with additional followup later in 1984.
2. Unpublished tables from *Children in Custody: Advance Report on the 1982/83 Census of Private Facilities,* U.S. Department of Justice, Office of Juvenile Justice and Delinquency Prevention, Washington, D.C.
SOURCE: Mullen, 1985.

such as E. F. Hutton and Merrill Lynch in arranging the financing and construction of correctional facilities. The third area is the most comprehensive of all. Here a private corporation manages and operates a correctional facility under a lease arrangement with the federal, state, or local government. A number of private corporations already manage and operate detention centers used by the Immigration and Naturalization Service in Texas, Colorado, California, and Nevada. Others operate county jails in Minnesota and Florida. This area of corporate correctional activity is already well developed (see Table 10.1).

The most ambitious project to date is a proposal by the Corrections Corporation of America (CCA) to take over the Tennessee correctional system and run it as a private corporation. This scheme involves Merrill Lynch Capital Markets and the Massey Burch Investment Group, a venture capital firm, which "will design, market and manage the acquisition of resources for capital improvements to the system" (CCA, 1985: 3).

CCA proposes to build new facilities, renovate existing structures, place all corrections employees under its management, and develop inmate programs. The financial arrangements are complex but include inflation adjustments and a guaranteed fixed per diem rate with a guaranteed 80 percent minimum occupancy for the two new institutions the corporation proposes to build. The latter condition points to one of the significant problems with the profit prison: In order for the corporation to be successful, it requires prisoners, potentially leading to a policy of warehousing people to satisfy corporate profits, not correctional needs. ·

Making corrections a private enterprise, of course, raises other important legal, financial, and moral questions which have not been fully addressed. Privatization is touted as being efficient and economical. This has yet to be demonstrated. One evaluation

study of a privately operated youth facility showed no significant reduction in operational cost (Jericho, 1985). Others have argued that private-enterprise prisons are filling a void in the "criminal justice market" created by an undersupply of facilities as well as excessive costs of correction (Logan and Rausch, 1985).

Privatization is a development that highlights points raised previously concerning conceptual tools that may be employed to gain a better understanding of the process of change in corrections. Privatization reflects a *strategy* of corrections that arose in a specific political–economic context that *enabled* it to develop. Part of the reason for its persistence is that it is in accord with a political *ideology* that uses the idiom of the marketplace as the key to addressing social issues. For example, it would have been highly unlikely for a strategy of private entrepreneurship to arise in the '60s, simply because the *enabling* context was not present. The political ideology favored government responses to social issues.

Privatization also illustrates the point made by radical scholars of the close connection between the socioeconomic–political context, the interests of a ruling elite, and the strategies of punishment.

*Home Incarceration*

One of the approaches to correctional change has been to suggest alternatives to the formal correctional apparatus. The emphasis is either to intervene during an early stage of the criminal justice process to divert the offender from the system, or to find alternatives to the formal sanctioning process. While alternatives were first proposed primarily for juvenile offenders, it was soon recognized that adults who committed minor offenses or those with special problems, such as alcoholics, might also profitably be given dispositions other than jail terms. This, it was reasoned, would save precious court time, reduce overcrowding in jails, lessen the negative impact of criminal justice processing, and lower costs. A recent expression of this idea has been confinement at home.

*House arrest* is not a new concept. Used in the past, and in some countries still, as a means to control political dissidents, it is being resurrected here and viewed in a new light. No longer seen as a negative measure, home confinement is advocated as a humane strategy that is cost effective and a protection to the public (Corbett and Fersch, 1985).

Others have indicated that home incarceration has both theoretical and practical advantages. It allows the offender to be reconciled with the community, and at the same time "official confinement to the home for a specified period would appear to provide, at least for certain offenses, a clear statement of retribution, a utilitarian form of incapacitation, and the possibility of reformation within a more 'normal' environment" (Ball and Lilly, 1987). These researchers also point to practical features of this strategy: Home incarceration may be tailored to a variety of situations. These include confinement during specific times, used in combination with regular jail confinement, used at different stages of criminal proceedings, and employed in the case of severe illnesses or other special problems more easily dealt with in the offender's home than in formal confinement. On the surface, therefore, home incarceration offers a flexibility not available in other types of criminal dispositions.

Envisaged for the relatively minor offenders who might ordinarily be confined for periods up to a year in the county jail, home incarceration was advocated as a cost-effective alternative to the traditional jail term. Counties, it was felt, would not only be spared the expense of maintaining the prisoner, the offender would be able to hold a job and pay either a fine, restitution, or both, depending on the case.

Monitoring could be effected through phone calls and unannounced visitation, with responsibility given to probation departments, who in turn could use probation volunteers to accomplish the task. The use of volunteers would offer several advantages. They would be "unofficial" persons dealing with offenders, a rare opportunity for direct public involvement in the criminal justice process. Volunteers would have the additional advantage of separating the counseling and surveillance functions of the probation officer's responsibility, thereby avoiding the role conflict these often clashing elements create.

Not surprisingly, the trend toward home incarceration caught on. By early 1986, about 60 percent of the states had jurisdictions where home incarceration was an option (Petersilia, n.d.; Ball and Lilly, 1987). What was probably not anticipated for this correctional change was the introduction of electronic monitoring devices, which fundamentally transformed the entire idea.

Part of the ever-increasing arsenal of surveillance technology, telemetric, or monitoring, devices are being manufactured and sold to correctional agencies. The device is an electronic transmitter worn on the wrist or ankle that emits a signal received by another device connected to the telephone in the subject's house. The signal is then relayed to a central computer in the probation department or other designated office. If the subject moves beyond a specified distance from the phone or tampers with the device, the interruption of the signal is recorded by the computer and an alert is sounded. Adjustments may be made for different times of day—for example, to allow a person to go to work but to be at home at a specified time. Other devices can monitor a subject's whereabouts and pinpoint his or her location on a grid. Only the imagination limits the technological control that can be imposed. As

Gary Marx (1985) notes, technology has created the "nonhuman informer," a development that is radically changing the contours of corrections.

Let us for the moment postpone considering the wider social implications of this technological control and focus on its more immediate impact. Among the reasons for home incarceration as an alternative strategy were its reduction in cost, as well as its potential for reintegrating the offender into the community and involving the community with the offender through the use of volunteers. As Richard A. Ball and J. Robert Lilly (1987) write:

> [with the use of volunteers], the offender would be involved with representatives of his or her community rather than only with official functionaries representing some governmental bureaucracy. At the same time, the use of volunteers would contribute to the further involvement of the public in the system of juvenile and criminal justice, helping to allow for community penetration into these rather closed systems.

The use of surveillance technology takes away this opportunity, thus eliminating a possible advantage home incarceration might have had, leading Ball and Lilly to conclude: "the rapid development of electronic monitoring now suggests that the system . . . may be more interested in maintaining bureaucratic control . . . than involving the community in the monitoring of compliance."

The introduction of surveillance technology with house arrest has also raised a host of new issues. These include: its legality, its efficacy, the impact on the privacy of the individual, and theoretical implications for correctional policy. A number of studies are addressing these issues (Ball and Lilly, 1985; Berry, 1985; Ball, Huff, and Lilly, 1987; Huff, Ball, and Lilly, 1987). The outcome of these analyses is still unclear, but the effort directed at this correctional change points to the importance of the issue.

## Interpretation of Correctional Change

We have presented two major developments in contemporary correctional change, privatization and home incarceration. How might these changes be explained by the three perspectives we outline earlier?

### Conservatives

Representatives of the conservative perspective might explain these recent changes as a return to traditional values held by the majority of Americans which require criminals to be punished or incapacitated as a deterrent to others. Moreover, government has proved to be inefficient and costly in this regard; the operation of prisons by the private sector or other private solutions of correctional problems is an inevitable and welcome development. The use of house arrest is made possible by the return to the belief that the swift and efficient control of criminals is the best means to deal with crime. If private ingenuity helps in this process by the development of efficient, technological devices, this is to the good.

### Liberals

A liberal interpretation might emphasize a number of events that in combination have brought about the current approaches. There has been a shift in public opinion concerning the issue of crime and the treatment of criminals as a result of the minimal impact of earlier programs of the '60s and '70s which focused on improving social conditions. The public believes welfare programs are a costly failure. Research also has shown that rehabilitative efforts do not work; hence the public is concerned with more efficient means to control crime. Private innovations are welcome by the public. House arrest is appealing because it is humane and efficient. Given certain safeguards, it might be better than long-term confinement.

## Radicals

While there are differing radical emphases, one radical explanation might focus on the state of the political economy as generating present conditions. Corrections is in a period of both a rising crime rate and a fiscal crisis of the state (Michalowski, 1983). This has resulted in limited public funds for cor-

rections at the same time the need to *control* problem populations has increased. Prisons are overcrowded, and other resources of control, the major strategy to deal with crime in a conservative era, are limited. The ideology of capitalism supports private solutions. In a conservative political context that stresses a laissez-faire market ideology and perceives all government bureaucracy in domestic areas as wasteful and inefficient, prisons for profit become a distinct possibility.

We close this chapter with these brief, admittedly oversimplified views of how current correctional changes may be interpreted. We will have more to say about the wider implications of these directions of correctional change in Chapter 14.

# 11

# Humaneness
# and the Rule
# of Law

Despite the deficiencies of psyche, character, or intellect they are believed to suffer, prisoners, probationers, parolees, and any others caught up in the correctional process are human beings. Therefore, we would expect consensus with the assertion that correctional programs must be consistent with fundamental standards of humane treatment. Yet treatment that violates these standards can still be found in contemporary corrections.

## Organizational Dynamics and Technocratic Thought

Bureaucracies are organized on the basis of a division of labor, a hierarchy of authority, formal channels of communication, and the use of both indoctrination and ma-nipulation of sanctions to secure compliant, predictable behavior from employees. However, the process of breaking down large-scale tasks into smaller ones creates conditions conducive to the kinds of illegal or deviant behavior that individuals perhaps would not commit outside of the work sphere. Stanley Milgram, who conducted pioneering research on the willingness of individuals to defer moral judgments to higher authorities, has pointed to this tendency, stating that within bureaucracies there is

a fragmentation of the total human act; no one man [decides] to carry out the evil act and is confronted with its consequences. The person who assumes full responsibility for the act has evaporated. Perhaps this is the most common characteristic of socially organized evil in modern society (1974: 9).

As a result, the salience and personally perceived relevance of moral and ethical considerations decrease for individual employees.

Milgram demonstrated with his experiments that people from all walks of life rarely question what they perceive to be legitimate authority. They tend to follow orders even if these orders require tasks that harm others. In the experimental setting, Milgram told his naive volunteer subjects that they were part of a learning experiment. They were "teachers" and were to ask questions of the "learners." When the "learners" did not answer a question correctly, the "teachers" were to administer an electric shock. The intensity of the shock was to be increased for each wrong answer.

Although no actual shocks were being given, the subjects believed they were administering them to people who eventually screamed with pain, and pleaded that the procedure stop; in one variant of the experiment, a confederate feigned a heart attack. In each instance the "experimenter" ordered the subjects to continue giving shocks because "the experiment required it." A surprisingly large percentage of the subjects continued giving shocks even though they believed the "learners" to be suffering and in pain. What is most distressing is that none of these volunteer subjects were prevented from stopping and, indeed, could have simply walked out of the experiment. At the end of the experiment, when they were debriefed and asked why they did not stop, they placed the responsibility on the "experimenter."

This unquestioning obedience saw its ultimate extreme in the extermination camps of Nazi Germany and in the massacres in Laos, Cambodia, and Vietnam. Named after the official in charge of the Nazi extermination policy, the extreme manifestation of this tendency has become known as the *Eichmann defense*. "I was only following orders," the almost universal excuse of those held responsible for atrocities carried out in the name of an authoritarian or bureaucratic structure, exemplifies this process.

Bureaucracies divide large-scale tasks into smaller ones under the dominance of organizational ideologies. This is true of correctional bureaucracies, where punishment and rehabilitative ideologies suggest that offenders are different from "normal" people. Thus it is even easier for correctional employees—indeed, for all of us—to overlook the essential humanness of offenders and to regard them as inanimate material, to be manipulated and processed for the greater good of reducing crime rates or recidivism.

In correctional bureaucracies, as in other types of organizations, employees can become so fixated on ultimate objectives, such as punishment or rehabilitation, that short-term ends and means are evaluated only with regard to their relationship to and efficiency at achieving these long-range goals. In short, correctional organizations may foster *technocratic* thought. We defined this earlier as a preoccupation with means (or techniques) for achieving goals to the exclusion of consideration of the goals themselves and whether they are desirable or appropriate. Richard Korn's poignant reflections on his own correctional employment highlight the nature and consequences of technocratic thought:

> In 1952, at the age of 29, I was appointed to the post of Director of Education and Treatment at the New Jersey State Prison. . . . In our efforts to wrest control of the prison from the inmates, we developed a number of innovations which later became widely emulated. One of these involved building a more secure "prison within the prison" for "persistently recalcitrant or dangerous inmates." I spent considerable time in this prototype of the modern "adjustment center" and, later, after I left the prison, considerable time thinking about it.
>
> The result of this thought was the produc-

tion of a Manual for the Treatment of Adaptive Offenders, by which term I meant the treatment of offenders inaccessible to the treatment strategies I originally had at hand. . . .

At the time I practiced and wrote about these measures, it never occurred to me to question whether I was doing anything that was wrong. I had tacitly accepted a technique for breaking the resistance of my clients as an acceptable means for achieving the goals of eventual release into the community. If anyone had told me that I was collaborating in a process of torture which used isolation and frustration as its weapons, I would have been startled. But I probably would not have agreed. I had accepted my final goal as valid, and the only question I asked of my means was whether they were efficient (1971: 31–32).

### What Is Humane Treatment?

If correctional practices are to be judged by how closely they conform to principles of humane care and treatment, a question immediately arises: What *is* humane treatment? How is it to be defined? This is a difficult problem because, presumably, what would be inhumane treatment from the perspective of one individual or group might be considered quite acceptable by others. However, there is a way out of this apparent impasse. In the United States, many of the challenges about the humaneness of correctional practices allege violations of the Eighth Amendment to the Constitution, which prohibits cruel and unusual punishment. We can learn something about correctional inhumanity by examining litigation and by using the criteria that the courts have established and applied in cases alleging cruel and unusual punishment.

## Correctional Inhumaneness: Illustrations and Challenges

We will briefly review inhumane conditions and treatment that came to light in appellate reviews of cases. No attempt will be made to present an exhaustive coverage of the issues and cases that have been litigated. A few typical cases will suffice. Note, however, that only some of the most shocking practices have come under the scrutiny of the courts.

In *Jones* v. *Wittenberg* [323 F. Supp.93 (N.D. Ohio 1971)], inmates of the Lucas County (Toledo, Ohio) jail challenged in federal district court the conditions under which they were confined. In granting the plaintiffs' request, the court stated that

> when the total picture of confinement in the Lucas County Jail is examined, what appears is confinement in cramped and overcrowded quarters, lightless, airless, damp and filthy with leaking water and human wastes, slow starvation, deprivation of most human contacts, except with others in the same sub-human state, no exercise or recreation, little if any medical attention, no attempt at rehabilitation, and for those who in despair or frustration lash out at their surroundings, confinement, stripped of clothing and every last vestige of humanity, in a sort of oubliette. . . . If the constitutional provision against cruel and unusual punishment has any meaning, the evidence in this case shows that it has been violated. The cruelty is a refined sort, much more comparable to the Chinese water torture than to such cruelties as breaking on the wheel (p. 99).

Several cases originating with prisoners confined in Arkansas prison have shed light on inhumane practices and conditions. *Jackson* v. *Bishop* [404 F.2d.571 (8th Cir. 1968)] exposed the use of harsh modes of punishment for alleged infractions of prison rules.

Later, in *Holt* v. *Sarver* [309 F. Supp. 362 (E.D. Ark. 1970)], inmates brought a class-action suit alleging that the conditions of confinement in Arkansas prisons constituted cruel and unusual punishment. The court found a complex pattern of inhumane conditions in Arkansas, including inadequate supervision of living quarters, which resulted in murders and homosexual assaults; a "trusty" system, which permitted favored inmates to dominate and abuse other inmates; filthy, rodent-infested solitary confinement cells; and an absence of recreational or training programs, which resulted in idleness and violence. Eventually the court ruled in favor of the plaintiffs and ordered the state to make extensive improvements in the conditions of its prisons.

*Ruiz* v. *Estelle,* a suit begun in 1972, eventually culminated in a wide-ranging decree against the Texas Department of Corrections that ordered sweeping changes in their operation: a termination to triple and quadruple celling, reduction and restriction in the use of force by personnel, upgrading of health practices, ending arbitrary disciplinary practices, improving fire and safety standards, and allowing inmate access to courts, attorneys, and public officials (Marquart and Crouch, 1985).

The conditions under which prisoners are forced to live during solitary confinement have been the basis for a number of challenges. In *Hancock* v. *Avery* [301 F.Supp. 786 (M.D. Tenn. 1969)], the court enjoined officials of the Tennessee State Prison at Nashville from using punishment cells that were found to be dirty and unlighted, in which naked inmates were forced to sleep on a bare concrete floor.

In a later case, *Hatto* v. *Finney* [437 U.S. 678 (1978)], the Supreme Court held that it was cruel and unusual punishment for an Arkansas prisoner to be confined for more than 30 days in an isolation cell. Limits were

also placed on the number of persons that could be confined to a single isolation cell.

Although we have seen a plethora of challenges to correctional programs on Eighth Amendment grounds, it has been primarily the *physical* conditions of confinement that have received most of the attention; *psychological* consequences of correctional processing have not been systematically litigated. But prisoners may be denied visits, library privileges, radio listening, or television viewing, all activities that affect the psychological state of inmates (*Gibson* v. *Lynch,* 652 F.2d 348 [3rd Cir. 1981]) (Palmer, 1985).

### Reasonable Force and Corporal Punishment

There has never been a question about the use of reasonable force against prison inmates. Questions arise, however, about the situations in which force may be used against prisoners, and what is considered reasonable.

In general, courts have held that prison officials may use reasonable force for self-defense, in the defense of a third party, in the enforcement of prison rules and regulations, to prevent escape, and to prevent the commission of a crime. Force to be considered reasonable must be necessary under the facts and circumstances of each case (Palmer, 1985). Any use of force that does not meet this test may be considered unreasonable and cruel under the Eighth Amendment.

The determination of whether the use of force by prison employees on inmates is justified is usually a lengthy process, provided the issue is raised and brought to the court's attention.

According to John Palmer (1985), until the late 1960s corporal punishment was upheld by courts. He cites a 1963 Delaware case, *State* v. *Cannon* [55 Del. 587, 190 A.2d 514], wherein the court upheld whipping as a valid form of punishment. The court reasoned that because the state had permitted whipping since the 18th century, but had barred other punishment formerly used, whipping was not considered cruel and unusual punishment by the people of Delaware.

Not until 1968, in *Jackson* v. *Bishop* (cited previously), was whipping as a means of enforcing prison discipline held unconstitutional. The U.S. Court of Appeals for the Eighth Circuit reasoned as follows:

(1) We are not convinced that any rule or regulation as to the use of the strap, however seriously or sincerely conceived and drawn, will successfully prevent abuse . . . (2) Rules in this area often seem to go unobserved . . . (3) Regulations are easily circumvented . . . (4) Corporal punishment is easily subject to abuse in the hands of the sadistic and the unscrupulous. (5) Where power to punish is granted to persons in lower levels of administrative authority, there is an inherent and natural difficulty in enforcing the limitations of that power. (6) There can be no argument that excessive whipping or an inappropriate manner of whipping or too great frequency of whipping or the use of studded or overlong straps all constitute cruel and unusual punishment. But if whipping were to be authorized, how does one, or any court, ascertain the point which would distinguish the permissible from that which is cruel and unusual? (7) Corporal punishment generates hate toward the keepers who punish and toward the system which permits it. It is degrading to the punisher and to the punished alike. It frustrates correctional and rehabilitative goals . . . (8) Whipping creates other penological problems and makes adjustment to society more difficult. (9) Public opinion is obviously adverse. Counsel concede that only two states still permit the use of the strap (Palmer, 1985: 23).

Since 1968, courts have generally held that while inmates can be segregated from the general prison population on the grounds of maintaining security, these inmates must be treated humanely. "Reasons of security may justify confinement, but that is not to say that such needs may be determined arbitrarily . . . 'Security' or 'rehabilitation' are not shibboleths to justify any treatment" [*Landman* v. *Royster*, 333 F. Supp. 621, 645 (E.D. Va. 1971)].

Court challenges regarding extreme conditions in prisons have been few in number. The traditional tendency of the courts has been to ignore inmates' complaints about their treatment and to defer to correctional administrators on any problems that occur within their jurisdiction. This pattern of judicial conservatism became crystallized in the "hands off" doctrine and was to change in the '70s.

## The "Hands-Off" Doctrine

An extreme version of the hands-off doctrine is found in an 1871 case [*Ruffin* v. *Commonwealth*, 62 Va. (21 Gratt.) 790 (1871)]. The Virginia Supreme Court declared that an inmate has, "as a consequence of his crime, not only forfeited his liberty but also his personal rights, except those which the law in its humanity affords him." The court went on to assert that "he is, for the time being, the slave of the state." A more typical case, however, was *Stroud* v. *Swope* [187 F.2d 850 (9th Cir. 1951)], in which a federal circuit judge declared: "We think it well settled that it is not the function of the courts to superintend the treatment and discipline of persons in penitentiaries, but only to deliver from imprisonment those who are illegally confined" (quoted in Rothman, 1973: 12). This reflected the dominant judicial belief that only disruption and mischief could result from the courts' intervention in prison matters.

The earlier period of judicial reluctance

to interfere in correctional affairs was based on a number of rationales: the theory of separation of powers; an assumed lack of judicial expertise in correctional issues, and the corollary assumption of expertise by correctional personnel. There was also the fear that intervention by the courts would subvert discipline (Goldfarb and Singer, 1970).

Judicial abstention extended also to probation and parole. The courts' refusal to interfere was generally based on an interpretation of probation or parole as a "privilege" rather than a "right" that need not, therefore, be circumscribed by due-process rights or other safeguards. Other legal doctrines were similarly fashioned or adapted so as to preclude judicial intervention. For example, the "constructive custody" doctrine was employed to argue that even while on probation or parole, offenders actually remained in the custody of prison or jail officials and, therefore, could be removed to those premises should their behavior warrant it (Fisher, 1974).

While courts were reluctant to interfere, issues of humane treatment were not totally disregarded. A number of standards and rules of conduct for the humane treatment of prisoners were formulated over the years, by a number of different sources.

## Fashioning Standards

One source of such standards was those U.S. Supreme Court decisions that did deal with the issues of humaneness. A second source was the United Nations Standard Minimum Rules for the Treatment of Prisoners, a broad prohibition of "all cruel, inhuman or degrading punishments" which details guidelines for the treatment of prisoners.

A third source was the Model Act issued by the National Council on Crime and Delinquency in 1972. This Model Act, to provide for minimum standards for the protection of rights of prisoners, contained a number of provisions designed to explicitly prohibit "inhumane treatment." They are as follows:

**1.** Striking, whipping, or otherwise imposing physical pain upon a prisoner as a measure of punishment.

**2.** Any use of physical force by an employee except that which may be necessary for self-defense, to prevent or stop assault by one prisoner upon another person, or for prevention of riot or escape.

**3.** Sexual or other assaults by personnel or inmates.

**4.** Any punitive or restrictive measure taken by the management or personnel in retaliation for assertion of rights.

**5.** Any measure intended to degrade the prisoner, including insults and verbal abuse.

**6.** Any discriminatory treatment based on the prisoner's race, religion, nationality, or political beliefs (National Council, 1972).

In 1973, the National Advisory Commission on Criminal Justice Standards and Goals also adopted a set of model standards for the protection of offenders' rights.

The preceding would indicate that efforts were made to develop minimum standards of humane treatment of offenders, at least in the abstract. Their actual implementation in specific circumstances is another matter. Given the varying contexts of state and federal jurisdictions and the administrative machinery of their enforcement, minimum standards are variously interpreted and their actual impact is difficult to assess.

# Renewed Concern with Justice and Legality

Perhaps the greatest impact in the area of humaneness and the use of law in recent years came from the correctional clientele themselves. Stimulated by the political events of the '60s and '70s, which created a sensitivity and increased awareness of injustices in the criminal justice system in general and corrections in particular, prisoners took their grievances to the courts.

This came at a time when research began to cast doubt on the ability of corrections to truly correct, and academicians also rediscovered corrections and developed a renewed interest in the issue of correctional justice.

All this was a long time in coming, for as we have seen, abuses and violations of prisoners' rights were known to exist but were never acted upon by the courts in any consistent manner.

## The Reversal of "Hands-Off"

In its 1971–72 term, the U.S. Supreme Court decided eight cases directly affecting convicted offenders and at least two others with implications for the operation of corrections. In all eight cases directly involving corrections, the offender's contention prevailed. As much as anything, this demonstrated how fundamental the change in the courts' stance toward corrections was.

Although it is difficult to say with confidence just why the courts began to reverse their traditional policy of abstention toward corrections litigation, this change was part of an emerging critical stance toward criminal justice agencies during the 1960s. In the context of the civil rights and antiwar movements, a Supreme Court with an already established liberal record on social issues began

enunciating a stricter set of standards for criminal justice agencies. Perhaps the rapidly accumulating research literature, suggesting the inability of corrections to correct offenders, made it even more difficult for the courts to continue to ignore correctional injustice (Rothman, 1973). In any case, once the courthouse doors were ajar, they were quickly opened all the way. The courts themselves facilitated this opening by broadening their interpretations of the federal civil rights acts, the writ of habeas corpus, and other doctrines providing for federal court intervention. This resulted in an outpouring of litigation, primarily from the prisons. Leonard Orland's appraisal of the impact of this is hyperbolic but reasonably accurate:

> The collective result of this litigation has been nothing less than the achievement of a legal revolution within a decade. . . . To a large extent, the Bastille has been stormed in the quiet of the courtroom. . . . What has emerged is a grass-roots political entity—a people's movement. Significant change has been wrought by prisoners themselves. Such a development is unprecedented in the annals of Anglo-American penal history (1975: 11).

### The Substance of Challenges to Corrections

Although prison inmates were in the forefront of the legal challenge to corrections, jail inmates and those involved in community programs also shared in the struggle. For the most part, the federal courts were the arena for these legal battles.

The rights that inmates sought to establish fell into four categories (Goldfarb and Singer, 1970). The first category involved the right to be free from cruel and unusual punishment, and the right to the minimal conditions necessary to sustain life. The second category—the first one recognized by the courts—protected prisoners' access to the courts and to others outside of correctional channels. The third category included rights usually termed "civil rights" when applied to persons outside the correctional apparatus: freedom of religion, freedom of expression, the right to vote, and freedom from racial discrimination. Finally, the courts recognized offenders' rights, giving the benefit of reasonable standards and procedural protections when decisions were made that had a significant impact on them. Such decisions usually involved transfers, the denial of parole, and the revocation of "good time" for violations of prison rules. The First, Eighth, and Fourteenth Amendments to the Constitution were the principal avenues by which these claims were pressed. A brief review of several important cases demonstrates not only the substance of these challenges but also shows several significant developments in correctional law.

Black prisoners, especially Black Muslims, were the vanguard of challenges to the actions of prison administrators (King, 1969). *Jackson* v. *Godwin* [400 F.2d 529 (5th Cir. 1968)] illustrates the increasing refusal of black prisoners during the 1960s to tolerate racially discriminatory treatment. Herman Jackson, a 24-year-old black inmate under a death sentence in Florida State Prison, charged that his constitutional rights had been violated when prison officials refused to permit him to subscribe to black publications. He argued that since white prisoners were permitted to subscribe to white publications, this restriction on black prisoners amounted to denial of equal protection under the law, prohibited by the Fourteenth Amendment. In ruling in Jackson's favor, the appeals court said that as a rule there must be "some substantial and controlling interest which requires the subordination or limitation of these important

constitutional rights, and which justified their infringement." In applying that test, the court concluded that Florida prison officials had been arbitrary in their policy on publications. Accordingly, the court held, the "necessary effect and result of such regulations, even if not arbitrary and though even-handedly enforced, is racial discrimination in violation of . . . Fourteenth Amendment rights."

In other instances, prison officials had long maintained restrictions on the right of prisoners to assist one another in preparing legal petitions or papers. These restrictions, aimed at so-called jailhouse lawyers, were justified on a number of grounds. Officials maintained that such assistance raised unrealistic hopes in other prisoners, that inmates used their services to gain sexual favors from other prisoners, exploit the legal naivete of their peers, and simply clog the courts with frivolous and poorly prepared legal petitions.

In February 1965, a man named Johnson, serving a life sentence in the Tennessee State Prison, was transferred to the maximum security building in the prison for assisting other prisoners in preparing writs. The Supreme Court held that since the state of Tennessee didn't provide a reasonable alternative to assist illiterate or poorly educated inmates in preparing petitions, the state could not validly enforce a regulation that absolutely bars prisoners from furnishing such assistance to other prisoners. To do so, declared the Court, is to deprive "those unable themselves, with reasonable adequacy, to prepare their petitions, of access to the constitutionally and statutorily protected availability of the writ of habeas corpus" [*Johnson* v. *Avery* 393 U.S. 483 (1969)].

In *Bounds* v. *Smith* (1977), the Supreme Court held that prisoners must have meaningful access to the courts by being provided with adequately staffed libraries to allow legal assistance, particularly to those who are illiterate. The cases described, plus others which affected the parole process (*Morrissey* v. *Brewer* 408 U.S. 471 1972) and the probation revocation process (*Gagnon* v. *Scarpelli* 411 U.S. 788 1973) represented an era of judicial activism which lasted about a decade, between 1965 and 1975, and had wide impact on the correctional spectrum. However, the court's activism was not to last.

While all cases decided in the courts are applicable to both male and female prisoners, most concern issues raised in prisons for men. The '70s, however, also produced a few important cases that were applicable specifically to conditions in women's prisons. A number of these cases dealt with inequities suffered by women prisoners as well as issues concerning matters of health and privacy. These cases are summarized in Table 11.1.

## The End of Judicial Activism

The signs of a retreat by federal courts from their interventionist stance became apparent in 1974 in *Wolff* v. *McDonnell,* a case which challenged prison disciplinary practices. The primary issue in *Wolff* was the extent to which due process was applicable to

TABLE 11.1   **Some Major Judicial Decisions Concerning Women Prisoner Issues with Reference to Constitutional Principles**

**14th Amendment Suits**

*Glover* v. *Johnson,* No. 77-1229 (E.D. Mich. October 16, 1979).
The court found that women inmates had fewer and inferior educational and vocational programs than did male inmates throughout the state.

*Barefield* v. *Leach,* No. 10282 (D.N.M. 1974).
The court found the state had failed to provide parity in vocational programming, assignment to wage-paying work within the institution, and adequate facilities for vocational projects.

*Grosso* v. *Lally,* No. 4-74-447 (D. Md. 1977).
The parties entered a consent decree in which the Division of Corrections agreed that programs, conditions, and opportunities for women would be "no less favorable, either quantitatively or qualitatively" than for men.

*Molar* v. *Gates,* 159 Cal. Rptr. 239 (4th Dist. 1979).
The court held that the county jail system could not provide special programs and facilities for men only.

**Eighth Amendment Suits**

*Estelle* v. *Gamble,* 429 U.S. 97, 104 (1976).
The court held that deliberate indifference to serious medical needs of prisoners violated the Eighth Amendment.

*Todaro* v. *Ward,* 431 F. Supp. 1129 (S.D.N.Y. 1977).
A women's correctional facility's medical system was found to be unconstitutionally defective and was ordered improved.

**Fourth Amendment Suits**

*Forts* v. *Ward,* 471 F. Supp. 1095 (S.D.N.Y. 1978).
The district court ruled the employment of male guards in contact positions at a female facility violated the females' rights to privacy.

SOURCE: Adapted from U.S. Comptroller General, 1980: 8–10.

disciplinary hearings where prisoners face punitive confinement or loss of "good time." Although the U.S. Supreme Court pointed out that "there is no iron curtain drawn between the Constitution and the prisoners of this country" in deciding the case, it refused to extend the full panoply of due-process rights to prisoners who faced disciplinary hearings, stating that due-process demands must be balanced against institutional needs so that prison officials can maintain discipline and institutional security. Stating that due process is a flexible concept, the Court declared that it is applicable to a disciplinary hearing only to the extent that a prisoner (1) must be given written notice of the charges at least 24 hours before the hearing and (2) is entitled to a written statement of the evidence relied on by the prison officials in reaching their decision, and of their reasons for taking disciplinary action. The Court denied inmates the right to submit documentary evidence, to call witnesses in their own behalf, and prohibited the right to confront and cross-examine adverse witnesses. The Court proclaimed that confrontation and cross-examination are not "rights universally applicable to all hearings."

Another important decision signaling retreat was rendered by the U.S. Supreme Court in the case of *Jones* v. *North Carolina Prisoners' Labor Union, Inc.* [97 S. Ct. 2532 (1977)]. In this case, the Court let stand regulations of the North Carolina Department of Corrections that effectively prohibit establishment or operation of a prisoners' union. In *Meachum* v. *Fano* [96 S. Ct. 2532 (1976)], an action was brought to the U.S. Supreme Court by Massachusetts prisoners who alleged that their transfers to less favorable institutions without adequate fact-finding hearings deprived them of liberty without due process of law. The Court held that the due-process clause of the Fourteenth Amendment does not entitle state prisoners to such a hearing.

*Meachum* represented a turning point in that it signaled once again a subordinating of prisoners' rights to the authority of correctional officials and a return to a hands-off policy. Even though constitutionally protected rights were at stake, the courts revived the position that they had no jurisdiction nor authority to resolve cases of conflict between prisoners and their keepers (Schwartz, 1984).

Subsequent cases have followed a similar line, particularly those that involve the transfer of prisoners from one prison to another. It is generally recognized that transfer could have considerable adverse consequences for an inmate and therefore necessitate due-process protection. For example, transfer may interrupt family visits or terminate programs and activities important to the inmate and his future. This issue was addressed by the Supreme Court in *Wakenikona* v. *Olim* (1983), a case that involved the involuntary transfer of an inmate from a Hawaii prison to one in California. The inmate challenged the transfer on due-process grounds. The Court upheld it, indicating that institutional officials had "unfettered discretion" to make the disciplinary transfer (Schwartz, 1984). This return to the earlier "hands-off" policy is evident in other areas of prison management and control as well.

### The Totality-of-Conditions Concept

Overcrowding is one of the persistent problems of imprisonment. But while prisons historically have been filled beyond capacity soon after their construction, it is only in recent years that courts have taken notice and in some instances declared entire prison systems unconstitutional. This was the case of the Texas prison system, the largest in the nation (*Ruiz* v. *Estelle,* mentioned earlier).

In general, the federal courts have looked to the Eighth and Fourteenth Amendments as the source of their rulings. The courts generally have used three criteria to deter-

mine whether there are constitutional violations in specific instances: (1) Is the punishment shocking to civilized society? (2) Is the
punishment cruel and unusual? (3) Does the
punishment go beyond the legitimate domains of correctional authority?

In recent cases dealing with overcrowding
in the nation's prisons and jails, courts have
abandoned these criteria in favor of a highly
restrictive new concept known as the *totality-
of-conditions concept.*

This concept implies that a certain condition (for example, overcrowding) by itself
does not violate Eighth Amendment requirements, but intolerable conditions taken in
their entirety would. Thus an inhumane condition which in previous instances triggered
constitutional remedies must in overcrowding cases be shown to exist in combination
with others before it violates the Constitution.

For example, in a 1978 case, *Hutto* v. *Finney,* the Supreme Court held that confinement in a segregation unit under poor conditions for brief periods did not violate the
Eighth Amendment; however, if the confinement was for an indeterminate period in
combination with other intolerable conditions, taken as a whole this would be a violation of the prohibition against cruel and unusual punishment.

A case that directly challenged overcrowding, *Rhodes* v. *Chapman* (1982), involved
double celling in the Southern Ohio Correctional Facility. The Supreme Court asserted
that double celling *by itself* does not violate
constitutional requirements if it does not result in "unnecessary or wanton pain." It must
be shown that overcrowding causes "deprivation of basic human needs," which are those
that if not met result in "wanton pain."
Courts must determine whether crowded
conditions affect medical services, violence,
the quality of food, sanitary conditions, and
recreational opportunities or whether deficiencies in these areas are the result of poor
administration, indifference, or lack of fund-

ing (Angelos and Jacobs, 1985). If the latter,
there is no judicial remedy.

An earlier related case, *Bell* v. *Wolfish*
(1979), involved among other concerns rights
of pretrial detainees, persons who presumably had not yet lost or placed in jeopardy
their personal rights because they had not
been tried and found guilty. A specific issue
was double celling. The Supreme Court,
however, reasoned, as Claudia Angelos and
James B. Jacobs point out, "loss of freedom is
inherent in pretrial detention and that if the
custodian has a legitimate management reason for imposing a restriction or condition
. . . a reason apart from a specific desire to
punish . . . it is not punishment and is lawful
under the due process clause unless it is an
arbitrary or excessive restriction" (1985: 104).
Double celling by itself, therefore, was not
considered punishment, since daytime facilities away from the cell were available and the
average length of stay in detainment was not
considered excessive.

Despite evidence of a return to judicial
conservatism, prior litigation and the attendant publicity have cast the spotlight on how
far traditional correctional practices had operated at variance with legal guarantees and
safeguards. A similar effect was achieved by
the numerous prison rebellions of the 1960s
and early 1970s, when inmates dramatically
and poignantly portrayed the web of injustice in which they were caught. In the aftermath of both these movements, much
time and effort was expended in attempts to
rectify some of the more glaring injustices.

## Institutional Consequences

### Bureaucratic Resistance

How did correctional officialdom respond
to the challenges brought against their collective domains? First, as long as administrative discretion was unfettered and inmates
confronted a policy of judicial abstention,

correctional administrators made few efforts to assure that inmates were treated consistently with due-process and equal-protection guarantees. Only when the courts began to return decisions critical of them and to intervene in the operations of their agencies did they adopt a strategy that some might see as typical of bureaucracies when faced with a source of environmental uncertainty: They developed programs to routinize and control legal challenges.

When called to defend prison conditions, officials typically cite the need to maintain security. They also claim that budgetary limitations make improvements impossible. Rarely, however, do they challenge inmate presentations of the facts about conditions.

In many respects, corrections officials' reaction to court decisions that challenged their perception of the correctional role and mission was similar to the police response to court decisions they considered threatening to their interests and to "good police work" (Pepinsky, 1970). Charges that the courts were meddling in administrative matters, that they had no understanding of correctional issues, that they were threatening the stability of corrections, that correctional administrators lacked the funds to make sweeping changes, and that the courts seriously eroded staff morale were all reminiscent of police reactions to such decisions as *Mapp, Miranda,* and *Escobedo.* There are two important reasons for this similar response. One relates to the similarity of organizational structure of correctional and police bureaucracies. The second has more to do with the tension between occupational expertise and legal processes.

Dennis C. Sullivan and Larry L. Tifft (1975) suggest a relationship between the way an organization's employees are managed and the way they, in turn, manage their clients. They further suggest that the adoption of court-ordered due-process mandates by correctional bureaucracies is directly re-

lated to the presence of managerial due process for their own employees. Organizations that are unresponsive to employee due-process rights are unlikely to be receptive to judicial directives that they respect the rights of their clients. Correctional and police organizations traditionally are quasi-military structures, epitomizing the type of organization that resists court orders.

Correctional resistance to court orders can also be viewed as an example of the more generic conflict between occupational "experts" and what they often claim to be untrained, unknowledgeable outsiders. Correctional employees consider themselves experts in handling offenders. While they frequently acknowledge the deficiencies of their programs, they attribute these to conditions beyond their control. They believe that they are best qualified to formulate and implement remedial actions to correct these deficiencies. They feel that neither the courts nor anyone else fully understands the operations of correctional agencies, and that the courts have made "unrealistic" or "dangerous" demands on their agencies. Consequently, the response of correctional personnel to court directives is likely to be cool at best, hostile or indifferent at worst. With such an attitude, it is not surprising that correctional administrators have sometimes defied court orders. Often, however, the courts' findings are used to gain more resources for corrections, such as more personnel and the building of more prisons.

## Model Standards

Earlier we mentioned various sets of model standards developed by groups interested in the correctional process. Virtually all of these sets of standards contain provisions for establishing and protecting offenders' rights and their access to the courts.

Similar to model standards as a response to the legal shortcomings of corrections is the issuance of policy statements or model legislation by correctional interest groups. We referred to the Model Act for the protection of rights of prisoners developed by the National Council on Crime and Delinquency (1972). In addition, the NCCD board of directors issued a policy statement on the peaceful settlement of prison conflict (1974) that proposed a seven-point program for "reducing causes of conflict and for preventing and resolving crises in correctional institutions." NCCD proposed that each state:

**1.** Establish by legislation or administrative order minimum standards for the protection of rights of prisoners that prohibit inhumane treatment.

**2.** Establish in each of its institutions formal procedures for handling individual and collective grievances.

**3.** Enact legislation authorizing prisoners to engage in negotiations as a means of providing peaceful democratic alternatives to violence.

**4.** Provide a means whereby, if an impasse is reached in negotiations, "professionally trained third-party neutrals" could be asked to participate in the negotiations.

**5.** Authorize in each of its institutions a prisoner organization for the purpose of credibly representing prisoners.

**6.** Provide a means whereby, at times of prison crisis, a team of specially trained and selected personnel could be brought together for settling the crisis without violence.

**7.** Establish training for both prison personnel and prisoners in techniques of conflict resolution.

*Changes in Legislation and Administrative Codes*

Until recently, statutes regulating the provision of correctional services and the power of correctors were rare. Whatever legislative standards did exist were vague. For example, laws in some states directed that prison food and clothing be "wholesome," "coarse," "cheap," "plain," or "sufficient to sustain health." Seldom were correctional facilities required to be anything more than "clean and healthful" (Goldfarb and Singer, 1970). Much of this has changed.

## Grievance Mechanisms

Many states have modified their statutes or administrative codes to provide more detailed regulations. In some states these changes have included explicit recognition of offender rights and procedures for dealing with grievances. One motivation for making these changes was the belief that judicial intervention was an unwieldy or inherently unworkable means for producing correctional reforms (Rubin, 1971). It is possible, too, that such changes were motivated in many places by the simple desire to curtail the flood of prisoner litigation made possible under the provision of the Civil Rights Act (42 U.S.C.sec.1983). This strategy was seized upon as one way of making changes while still retaining control within the correctional agency.

*Mediation and Ombudsmen*

The passage by Congress of the Civil Rights of Institutionalized Persons Act of 1980 directed the attorney general to develop standards and procedures to create alternative administrative mechanisms for institutions to address the issues raised by grievances of inmates in litigation. If correctional systems established such mechanisms and were certified in meeting the attorney general's standards and procedures, federal courts could require that these administrative measures be exhausted before accepting cases for review.

Methods of dispute resolution common in other sectors of society have been adopted by some correctional systems, with varying rates of success. One such method is *mediation,* a process whereby parties to a dispute—unable to resolve it through negotiation—agree to call in a third disinterested party (the mediator) to help them reach accommodation. Both parties also agree ahead of time to abide by the outcome. Mediation has a number of advantages, according to G. F. Cole *et al.* (1982), which should make it conducive to the correctional setting.

**1.** Its informal process should facilitate solutions better than the complex, adversarial proceedings in courts.

**2.** It is best used to settle practical problems arising out of administrative procedures that may be addressed by administrative solution.

**3.** Mediation is faster and more economical than litigation.

One attempt to initiate mediation programs, at the Danbury Federal Correctional Institution between 1980 and 1981, showed little success, however. This negative outcome was the result of a number of conditions primarily related to institutional rigidities. Many of the complaints did not lend themselves to mediation (for example, habeas corpus action), and all parties would not or could not agree to discuss all issues, particularly matters of policy. Also problematic were such matters as loss of face by staff if certain stipulations were agreed upon. The project demonstrated that the prison setting is one

that makes problem solution by means useful in normal settings difficult. Mediation requires flexibility and respect for each side of a dispute. Given the imbalance of power inherent in prison, there are severe obstacles to reaching satisfactory solutions.

The use of the *ombudsman* is another alternative. The ombudsman is a public official who investigates complaints by citizens about the action of government officials and recommends remedies. Correctional use of the ombudsman position was first established by Minnesota in 1972, and other states followed suit. Typically the ombudsman deals with cases of complaints in the following categories:

PAROLE—concerning any matter under the jurisdiction of the releasing authority (work release, temporary parole, special review, etc.).

MEDICAL—concerning availability of treatment or accessibility of a staff physician or other medical professional.

LEGAL—involving legal assistance or problems with getting a response from the public defender or other legal counsel.

PLACEMENT—concerning the facility, area, or physical unit to which an inmate is assigned.

PROPERTY—dealing with loss, destruction, or theft of personal property.

PROGRAM—relating to a training, treatment program, or work assignment.

DISCRIMINATION—concerning unequal treatment based on race, color, creed, religion, national origin, or sex.

RECORDS—concerning data in inmate or staff files.

RULES—regarding administrative policies establishing regulations which an inmate, staff member, or other person affected by the operation of a facility or program is expected to follow (visits, disciplinary hearings, dress, etc.).

THREATS/ABUSE—concerning threats of bodily harm, actual physical abuse or harassment to an inmate or staff.

OTHER—concerning issues not covered in previous categories (food, mail, etc.) (State of Minnesota, 1985).

Ombudsmen are empowered to investigate complaints, to dismiss those that are frivolous, to report their findings and to make recommendations to administration or public officials. Their power lies in their ability to make conditions public and in their impartial and independent status. Their findings and recommendations are only advisory. Nevertheless, the ombudsman serves a useful function in airing grievances in an impartial and nonlitigious context.

In some states these procedures have been attacked by correctional personnel who believe that they undermine correctional authority and ability to control inmate populations. Once more we see the development of resistance. Even minimal modification of the absolute power of control over inmates threatens their role as correctional workers. In Michigan, as in most other prison systems, disciplinary charges against inmates traditionally were heard by a committee of custodial personnel. The operation of these "rubber stamp" committees fueled inmate dissatisfaction and feelings of injustice and unrest. When infractions were reviewed by hearing officers, corrections personnel complained that erosion of discipline would result.

### Court Decisions' Limitations

The hope some had held for the power of court decisions to radically alter correctional structures has not been realized. Certainly some court decisions have had impact in the extreme case and in the short run. The long-term effects of changes brought about through court action are only now being investigated.

President Andrew Jackson reportedly responded to a decision by the U.S. Supreme Court with which he disagreed, "Mr. Marshall [Chief Justice] has made his decision. Now let him enforce it." This points up one of the most serious deficiencies of efforts to employ court decisions to reform correctional operations: the absence of a ready, responsive, and reliable enforcement apparatus. Courts possess very limited powers or abilities to coerce compliance with their decisions in the face of adamant resistance or even procrastination. The essential ineffectiveness of *Brown* v. *Board of Education* in integrating public schools attests to the validity of this assertion.

The fact that courts proceed on a case-by-case basis also detracts from their effective impact. Having made a decision in one case, the court's seeming intention for similar cases can be ignored by others unless their own case is explicitly litigated. Often, corrections officials simply ignore the implications of a court decision for their own agency if it is in their interest to do so. Other aggrieved parties must begin the difficult and time-consuming process of litigation if they hope to see the earlier decision applied to their situation.

Indeed, the extreme length of time—and the special expertise—required to litigate are among the most serious deficiencies of the courts as a vehicle for reform. Many complaints of correctional clients will either become moot or will go unrectified because of the complications presented by these two considerations.

Another problem with relying on the courts to reform corrections arises from the judicial reluctance to engage in confrontations with executive agencies. As a result, it is precisely in cases of administrative defiance that judges are most likely to become timid and fearful of the charge of attempting to usurp the powers and prerogatives of a coequal branch of government. This may be one reason for the return by the courts to the hands-off policy of the past. Some have suggested that the impact of litigation be viewed as an ongoing process, rather than an end in itself implying a dialectical relationship. On balance, court decisions, while not having made prisons more tolerable, have made them at least less intolerable (Hardesty and Thomas, 1986).

*Impacts and Consequences*

An in-depth case study of a Texas prison by James W. Marquart and Ben M. Crouch that evaluated the impact of a federal court's sweeping order for reform in *Ruiz* v. *Estelle* found mixed results. As high levels of discretion in prison operation became more consistent with constitutional requirements of due process and fairness, the prison became less orderly, with lessened control and an increased risk to inmates' safety.

As the researchers state: "While prisoners in many institutions [in the Texas system] now have enhanced civil rights and are protected by many of the same constitutional safeguards as people in a free society, they live in a lawless society at the mercy of aggressive inmates and cliques" (1985: 584).

The study points to the dilemmas inherent in prison reform. Whether these problems are long-term or short-term effects remains to be seen. The study certainly does *not* suggest that efforts to bring about humaneness are wrong or doomed to failure; it may imply, as Marquart and Couch suggest, that reform measures should be "(1) phased in gradually rather than established by rigid time tables; (2) implemented with a fundamental appreciation of the entire network of relationships and behaviors involved; and (3) undertaken with a healthy sensitivity to unanticipated negative consequences . . ." (585).

Further follow-up studies of this kind may well find over time that as reform measures bring about fundamental changes in structural interactions, new ways of perceiving and resolving these dilemmas will emerge. This, of course, would mean a radical change in the nature of imprisonment. Whether this is possible in American society as it is currently structured is another question that cannot readily be answered.

# 12

# Correctional
# Evaluation Research

*A* trend toward increasing rationalization is characteristic of crime control strategies in modern industrialized states (Spitzer, 1979). This is evident in the preoccupation with corrections as technique. Increasingly, public debate over correctional ideologies, strategies, and structures is dominated by technocratic issues of effectiveness and efficiency. *Effectiveness* means the extent to which a strategy or program actually achieves its intended objective. *Efficiency* refers to the fiscal cost of a correctional strategy. Here the question is whether the resources expended to achieve results can be justified when they are compared with the costs of alternative programs. *Evaluation research* is the process of collecting and analyzing information on the operational consequences of correctional programs (Campbell, 1971; Cook and Campbell, 1979; Hagan, 1982; Casper and Brereton, 1984).

Evaluation research is a growth industry in the America of the late 20th century, touted by groups across the political spectrum as the process with the greatest potential for providing definitive answers to the question "What works?" in dealing with street crime. Consequently, if we are to understand the nature and outcome of correctional debate in contemporary America, we must understand the technical rudiments of evaluation research. In the next chapter we shall comment critically on the process and the assumed promise of evaluation research.

## Concepts and Definitions

Our explication of evaluation research begins with a discussion of four components: the treatment, or independent variable;

comparison units; criterion measures, or dependent variables; and the follow-up period.

## The Treatment (Independent Variable)

Following convention, we designate the correctional technique or program that is evaluated as the *treatment,* or independent variable. Examples include reduced caseloads of probationers or parolees for correctional workers; group counseling for prisoners; special, lengthy sentences for repetitive offenders; methadone maintenance programs for heroin addicts.

Independent variables (that is, the correctional treatments being evaluated) should possess certain qualities. First, an independent variable must be defined operationally, so the components of the treatment can be clearly identified. As Charles H. Logan notes, "It is not enough to know that a particular program ended in success or failure if we cannot determine *what it is* that succeeded or failed" (1972: 378). This problem can be especially thorny if the treatment is so broad that it includes a whole range of different activities. Second, the treatment should be capable of routinization in diverse settings and times. Its impact should not depend too heavily on any unique personal characteristics of either offenders or correctors, or on unusual historical or social circumstances. For example, a treatment program that is successful with offenders from minority religious groups in a setting where that group resides might prove to be either ineffective or difficult to employ with religiously mixed offenders in a different locale. Finally, care must be taken to ensure that the treatment does not change while the program is being evaluated. In fact, this has proven to be difficult, as Paul Lerman (1975) discovered in his reanalysis of the treatment given to experimental subjects as part of the California Community Treatment Project.

## Comparison Units

Any evaluation of a correctional treatment program's effectiveness must present a comparison of performance in at least two groups or settings: one in which a special program or reform was introduced and a second, similar group or setting from which the program was withheld. A raw success or failure rate indicates nothing significant about the effectiveness of a treatment or program. Suppose we are told that a program's "success" or "effectiveness" is indicated by the fact that only 25 percent of those subjected to it were rearrested. What can we make of this claim? Nothing, because the recidivism rate for a comparable group of offenders who did not receive the treatment is not reported.

Statements about the comparative effectiveness of a treatment are valid only when the comparison units are alike. When they differ, especially on some attribute related to outcome, claims for the treatment's effectiveness are extremely difficult to interpret with confidence.

## Criterion Measures

The measure of outcome used to evaluate a program customarily is designated the *criterion,* or the dependent variable. Although a wide variety of criterion measures have been used in correctional evaluation research, recidivism is one of the most frequently used (Maltz, 1984). As we saw in Chapter 9, recidivism has no universally accepted meaning among criminal justice researchers. Other measures include changes in attitudes, career aspirations, or work habits; personality characteristics; disciplinary record within an institution; abstinence from alcohol or drug use; and earnings after release from imprisonment. An important challenge in evaluation research is selecting and employing the most useful criteria for different programs and circumstances.

On the basis of past evaluation research, investigators have identified a number of characteristics of "good" criteria. Daniel Glaser (1973: Chapter 3) suggests that criterion measures should be: (1) "hard" or objective, rather than "soft" or subjective; (2) numerically continuous rather than categorical; (3) relevant to attainable goals; and (4) useful in determining appropriate levels of funding for a program. Let's discuss each of these briefly.

Too often, claims for the effectiveness or ineffectiveness of a correctional treatment are based solely on subjective evaluations, usually by those who support or administer a program. Examples of subjective criteria are: staff impressions of the degree of behavioral or attitude change by the participants in a special program, testimonials by selected offenders who have taken part, and citations of the alleged improvements shown by one or more participants. The use of subjective evaluations is common whenever those "evaluating" a program have a political, personal, intellectual, or career investment in its outcome. The tendency to employ subjective evaluations in such circumstances is one reason some have suggested that the responsibility for evaluating correctional programs be given to personnel independent of the correctional establishment (Ward, 1973).

Examples of objective criteria include scores on a standardized personality test, the size of parolees' earnings from legitimate employment, and numbers of new arrests. These criteria are externally observable, based on actual behavior. Since one of the professed goals of corrections is to change the behavior of offenders, the latter quality is especially desirable. It is on this point that the use of recidivism as a criterion measure has been faulted.

Not all new crimes or technical violations are discovered, so the official recidivism rate presumably underestimates return to crime. Another difficulty: any measure of recidivism is a measure of how one or more decision-makers (police officers, parole agents, parole board members) respond to information about people's behavior. While this response presumably depends in some way on people's behavior, the relationship need not be simple, invariant from one penal system to another, or constant over time (Greenberg, 1972: 4–5).

A good criterion measure for evaluating correctional programs also should be capable of continuous rather than discrete or categorical measurement. The latter type (for example, committed new crimes or did not commit new crimes) does not allow the same degree of sensitivity to program impact as does the former type (for example, total *number* of crimes committed). Moreover, a discrete criterion does not permit us to make more exact statements on the *degree of impact* or improvement shown by those receiving treatment as does a continuous criterion.

No criterion variable is perfect. Each measure is subject to various types of measurement biases (Campbell, 1971). Moreover, experimental programs nearly always produce a variety of potential benefits and unwanted side effects. Thus it usually is desirable to employ *multiple criteria* in evaluation studies of correctional treatments. By doing so we increase the likelihood of understanding a range of impacts possibly stemming from experimental treatments. The use of multiple criteria also is helpful when there is a high possibility that any one of them will become the object of political conflict. In such a case, alternative measures of treatment impact can be cited.

When choosing a criterion measure, we must consider the short-range goals of a program, rather than goals that are remote and difficult to measure—if not attain. Glaser refers to short-range goals as the "most attainable" ones (1973: 19). He suggests that researchers should avoid using criteria which past experience suggests either are far removed from any reasonable expectation of program impact or overly global in nature. In such circumstances a wide variety of confounding variables could make it impossible to confidently untangle the impact of the correctional treatment alone.

A good criterion measure also should be useful when research results are provided to help administrators or legislators make budgetary decisions. Partly because of this quality, cost–benfit analysis of correctional programs has gained popularity in recent years.

### Follow-up Period

Reliable information on the effectiveness and social costs of alternative correctional programs requires that comparison units be monitored for some period of time after one of them is exposed to the treatment. For example, when groups of offenders are the comparison units, "the key principle of evaluation is to follow up those persons whom an agency tried to change to see if they do change, and to follow up a control or comparison group to see whether they also change, even if nothing is done to them or if an alternative kind of treatment is given them" (Glaser, 1973: 840). During this follow-up period, the investigator collects data on the criterion measures.

When conducting evaluation research, decisions must be made about when the follow-up period begins and ends. It is difficult to specify in an ad hoc fashion just how long a follow-up period should be. It should not extend past the "consequential period" for the treatment being evaluated, the time of significant change in the criterion behavior.

Similarly, the follow-up period should be long enough to permit changes to occur in the criterion behavior. Decisions on the length of the follow-up period must be made in part on the basis of the hoped-for nature of behavioral change and the type of offenders with which the program deals.

Despite the temptation to delay the start of the follow-up period until after the completion of treatment, the follow-up period should begin as soon as comparison units are constructed. The logic of doing so is easiest to grasp when cost–benefit analysis is used, because a complete accounting of the costs and benefits of a treatment program must include all the costs (especially those associated with the administration of the program itself). But the same logic applies equally well in cases where recidivism or the commission of new crimes is used as the criterion. To wait until after offenders have been released to the community is to ignore the crimes they may commit while imprisoned. We can ignore these crimes only if we define prison inmates as nonpersons.

Despite the best-laid plans and hopes of correctors and researchers, after the experimental and control groups are constructed there will be some dropouts from each group. When examining the criterion behavior of subjects, we should include all offenders who were original members of the comparison groups:

> In comparing an experimental and a control group, evaluators have sometimes compared only those who completed the experimental program, on the grounds that the inclusion of others who did not complete the program would be unfair to the program. Yet, if those who are least motivated or least amenable to the program are those who do not complete it, the assumption that the program would have been successful with them had they remained

in it may well be in error, and their omission from the comparison a possible source of distortion. When the dropouts considerably outnumber those who complete a program, as is sometimes the case in addiction treatment programs, quoted success rates for survivors can be highly misleading (Greenberg, 1974: 2–3).

To omit dropouts from the analysis arbitrarily biases an evaluation in favor of the "success" of the experimental treatment. Just how misleading the results of this practice may be is apparent when we consider two different ways of arriving at a success rate for the Highfields study.

Highfields was a special residential treatment program for delinquent boys operated by the state of New Jersey. Participants were 16- or 17-year-old males with juvenile court convictions who agreed to join in the program. They were screened by the Highfields staff. Those who were accepted took part in a program of "guided group interaction," a type of group counseling (Weeks, 1958). To evaluate the postrelease behavior of Highfields's boys, a matched comparison group was constructed of boys admitted to the state reformatory at Annandale. Not all boys who were originally accepted into the Highfields program completed it: Some were removed from Highfields and sent to Annandale. Using recidivism as the criterion, when these dropouts are not counted as members of the treatment group, the Highfields success rate is 66 percent. However, when these "internal failure" cases are included, the success rate drops to 48 percent—as compared to a rate of 48 percent for boys in the control group (Lerman, 1968).

The Highfields study also highlights the problem of selecting or constructing comparison units. Given the need to base estimates of the effectiveness and efficiency of correctional programs on the results attained with comparable groups of offenders or in comparable settings, a variety of research designs have been employed to construct such units.

## The Classic Experimental Design

In the classic experimental design, *experimental* and *control groups*—usually groups of individuals—are randomly selected from a population. The population's elements may be individuals, geographic settings, or time periods. For the most part, we will limit our discussion to examples of the first type, usually a population of offenders.

Subject to the laws of chance, comparison units selected or constructed at random are assumed to be equivalent. The treatment is administered to the experimental group but withheld from the control group. The investigator tries to ensure that the two groups are treated exactly alike in every other way. The occurrence of the independent variable is the only thing that differentiates the two groups; therefore, any subsequently observed difference on the criterion can be attributed only to the treatment variable. Figure 12.1 is a schematic representation of the structure of the true experimental research design.

The Transitional Aid Research Project (TARP) is an example of a true experimental design (Berk *et al.*, 1980; Rossi *et al.*, 1980). TARP was built on the assumption that economic problems are among the most important reasons that ex-felons commit new crimes when released from prison. The program was designed to determine whether providing released offenders with unemployment benefits would affect reinvolvement in crime. Some 2,000 persons who were released from the state prisons of Georgia and Texas during a six-month period in 1976

were assigned randomly to one of four experimental groups or to one of two control
groups. One experimental group received
only job placement assistance; the other
three received unemployment benefits under
varying conditions: the maximum number
of weeks for which benefits could be provided and the tax on earnings from legitimate employment. Ex-prisoners could receive up to either 13 or 26 weeks of benefits,
and weekly payments could be reduced either dollar for dollar (100 percent tax) or
25¢ on the dollar (25 percent tax). Table 12.1
is a summary description of the six groups.

P. H. Rossi *et al.* used unemployment
agency files, personal interviews, and criminal justice records for data on multiple criterion measures in the study. The measures
included: (1) arrests for property crimes; (2)
arrests for nonproperty crimes; (3) number
of weeks employed; and (4) amount of time
spent in jail or prison. The investigators used
a 12-month follow-up period. Although the
results of the study are not germane here, we
briefly summarize them:

> There were no significant overall differences
> in either state between experimental and con-
> trol groups in average numbers of arrests on
> property-related charges during the post-
> release year . . . There were no overall differ-
> ences in other types of arrests. . . . The work-
> disincentive effects of TARP payments groups

were considerable . . . , with persons in payment groups working considerably fewer
weeks . . . And there were no very strong differences in the total annual earnings of experimental as compared to control groups
(1980: 16).

A true experimental research design also
was employed by California researchers who

TABLE 12.1 **Description of Groups Used in the TARP Experiment**

| TARP Group | Number of Georgia Parolees | Number of Texas Parolees |
|---|---|---|
| Group 1: 26 weeks of payments, 100% | 176 | 175 |
| Group 2: 13 weeks of payments, 100% | 199 | 200 |
| Group 3: 13 weeks of payments, 25% | 201 | 200 |
| Group 4: job placement only | 201 | 200 |
| Group 5: interviewed controls | 201 | 200 |
| TOTAL | 976 | 975 |
| Group 6: noninterviewed controls | | |

SOURCE: Berk *et al.* (1980).

FIGURE 12.1 **The Structure of the Classic Experimental Research Design**

→ Time →

| Groups constructed by random assignment (therefore, assumed equivalent) | Groups receive identical processing (except for the treatment variable) | Both groups measured on the criterion variable(s) (any differences attributed to the treatment) |
|---|---|---|
| EXPERIMENTAL GROUP | Receives the Treatment | |
| CONTROL GROUP | Treatment Withheld | |

examined the effectiveness of group counseling both on the in-prison and postrelease behavior of inmates (Kassebaum *et al.*, 1971). The medium-security institution in which the study was conducted is divided architecturally into quadrants. Inmates were assigned randomly to one of the quadrants for their term of imprisonment. In two of the quadrants, inmates received varying types and degrees of group counseling; inmates in the other quadrants, the control group, received the regular prison program but without group counseling. The investigators found that the claimed benefits of group counseling could not be substantiated.

The logic of the classic experimental design is straightforward and simple. However, this design and others have not found a great deal of use in correctional evaluation research, despite the fact they can provide persuasive evidence on the impact of correctional strategies (Farrington, 1983). The difficulty is that "more often than not, political or administrative constraints make an experimental design with any type of randomization absolutely impossible" (Glaser, 1973: 64). Why is this so? The reasons include:

**1.** Sometimes a decision on the effectiveness, level of funding, or continued support for a program must be made quickly. This time constraint may not allow the conduct of a true experimental evaluation.

**2.** Administrators may simply delay plans for evaluation. Often the decision to evaluate is made after subjects already have been selected for the program. At other times the treatment program may no longer be in existence, so there is no opportunity randomly to assign subjects to it.

**3.** Occasionally politicians or correctional administrators may object to assigning some subjects to the treatment program if the treatment to be tested is perceived by officials as more lenient than traditional practice.

**4.** Administrators may resist randomly assigning subjects to a control group because they see this as unethical or unprofessional.

**5.** Random assignment may conflict with governmental goals other than changing offenders—for example, with the presumed goal of deterring others from committing crimes (Glaser, 1973: 64–68; Adams, 1975: 60–61).

**6.** Administrators may fear an objective evaluation because negative results may have serious repercussions for the continued operation of a program.

As a result, we have seen the use of alternative strategies for choosing or constructing comparison units.

## Quasi-Experimental Designs

Quasi-experimental research designs are employed in evaluation research when comparison units are constructed but equivalence cannot be assumed because random selection is not used (Cook and Campbell, 1979). Hence the comparison groups are not called experimental and control groups, as in the classic experiment. Instead, they are called *treatment* and *comparison groups*, respectively. The most commonly employed method for constructing such groups is *matching*.

### Matching

There are three ways to match treatment and comparison groups: by profile analysis, by individuals, or by base expectancy scores.

In the first, the researcher tries to ensure, for example, that the percentage of blacks in each group is comparable, that the average age of the two groups is equivalent, or that the percentage of those in each group with previous criminal convictions is alike. In matching by individuals, the researcher identifies pairs of offenders who are alike in their personal attributes, and then randomly assigns one member to the treatment group and the other to the comparison group.

Unfortunately, whether groups are matched by individuals or by profile analysis, they still may differ on attributes for which they were not matched. And these may be related to the outcome of correctional treatment. Because it is difficult to determine whether this is the case, matching is much less reliable than random assignment in the construction of comparison groups.

A matching procedure was employed in a study designed to evaluate the effectiveness of Southfields, a Kentucky residential treatment program modeled after Highfields, to which boys were assigned by juvenile judges (Miller, 1970). The evaluation research examined the recidivism of the first 191 boys to complete the program. Two comparison groups were constructed by matching. One group consisted of similar boys placed on probation, and the other consisted of boys sent to Kentucky Village, a regular correctional institution. The investigator found that both probation and Southfields were about equally effective in reducing recidivism. Both proved to be somewhat superior to regular correctional confinement.

Base expectancy scores are a means of sorting offenders into groups with substantially different probabilities of recidivism (i.e., risk groups). The scores are calculated using information about offenders available at the time of their admission to a correctional system. Glaser (1973: 142–43) pro-

vides examples of base expectancy score groups (B.E. Categories) for California Youth Authority wards released in 1964:

> B.E. Category 1, scores over 545 . . . . 22% recidivists
>
> B.E. Category 2, scores 419 to 545 . . . 35% recidivists
>
> B.E. Category 3, scores 337 to 418 . . . 41% recidivists
>
> B.E. Category 4, scores 290 to 336 . . . 47% recidivists
>
> B.E. Category 5, scores 195 to 289 . . . 56% recidivists
>
> B.E. Category 6, scores below 195 . . . 68% recidivists

We also quote at length from Glaser's description of how these score groups are constructed and used in California to evaluate prison programs:

> The term "base expectancy rate," applied to a group of offenders, refers to their expected violation rate when they are first admitted. For this reason, all items of information used to calculate [base expectancy rates] for them is restricted to what is known at the time of their admission; deliberately omitted is the additional information available such as their assignments, performance, escapes, and family communications while confined. If those in a given base expectancy category actually have a lower recidivism rate after parole from a particular institution or program than the predicted rate for their category from all institutions and programs in California, then the particular institution or program they were in would be credited with reducing recidivism rates. Thus some programs from which releasees had high recidivism rates might be regarded as favorable because their expected

recidivism rates, according to the B.E. categories of the inmates they received, were even higher than their actual rates.

An analogy may be helpful here. Suppose that individuals at birth are placed in life expectancy groups ("L.E. Categories") purely on the basis of information known about them and their families. Presumably, individuals with certain characteristics and family backgrounds will have more favorable L.E. scores than those with other characteristics and family backgrounds. Suppose we are interested in examining the impact of various life experiences on longevity—for example, the effect of diet or smoking. We could do this by examining the actual longevity of subgroups of individuals within particular L.E. categories who experienced different dietary and smoking habits. If those who abstain from smoking live longer than would have been expected from their L.E. scores, we would have some confidence in attributing part of this increased longevity to abstinence from smoking.

*Time-Series Analysis*

Interrupted time-series analysis is another form of quasi-experimental research (McCleary and Hay, 1980). Whereas matching designs are used to compare the performance of groups of *individuals,* time-series analysis generally is used to examine the impact of correctional reforms on the operations and results of the criminal justice system over time or in different locales. Time-series analysis lends itself well to studies of the impact of criminal justice reforms in specific states, counties, or cities.

An investigator uses data obtained from observations of a phenomenon over time, both before introduction of a treatment or reform and for some time after its imple-

mentation. Thus the investigator compares performance on a criterion measure *after* treatment with performance *prior to* treatment. The logic of time-series analysis is simple and straightforward. First, one begins by plotting graphically observations of the criterion variable. If the introduction of a treatment has a significant impact on the criterion measure, this should affect the *level* or the *slope* of the time-series.

A hypothetical example may be helpful here. Let's assume that the Massachusetts state legislature has enacted a statute requiring employment counseling and assistance for all felons released from its penitentiaries. The statute was passed in hopes of reducing unemployment and, therefore, crime among ex-prisoners. The effective date of the new law was January 1, 1987. Figure 12.2 depicts the average number of days of employment for all prison releasees. If the law achieved its intended effect, we should see a significant change in the time-series beginning in January 1987. We have drawn Figure 12.2 to show changes in both the level and the slope of the time-series after introduction of the treatment.

Note that the time-series shows considerable fluctuation over time. This represents both cyclical, seasonal changes as well as random shifts, or "noise." The problem statistically is to determine whether any changes observed in the level or the slope of the time-series after the treatment intervention exceeds these normal fluctuations. The use of standard statistical techniques allows the investigator to determine if any posttreatment shifts are sufficiently large that they probably did not occur because of chance alone.

Jonathan D. Casper *et al.* (1983) used interrupted time-series analysis to examine the impact of California's Uniform Determinate Sentencing Law (DSL), which took effect in July 1977. The investigators selected three counties that differed in a variety of respects. They used multiple criterion measures, including the prison commitment rate. The time-series for this criterion is presented in Figure 12.3. Unfortunately, because the time-series contains too few observations or data points, the investigators were unable to use rigorous statistical procedures to analyze the effects of the DSL.

Note that the monthly prison commitment rate for all three counties increased after the effective date of the DSL. However, the investigators point out:

> In all three [counties], the rate of imprisonment appears to begin to rise in 1976 or earlier, too soon to be attributed to the effects of the DSL . . . and, moreover, they have not continued to rise consistently in the years since implementation (1983: 417).

Casper *et al.* concluded, therefore, that "the evidence does not permit a clear inference,

for these counties at least, that the [DSL]" has produced an increase in prison commitment rates (1983: 420).

Colin Loftin *et al.* (1983) used multiple interrupted time-series analysis to examine the impacts in Detroit of Michigan's felony firearms statute (gun law). Effective January 1, 1977, the new law imposed a two-year mandatory add-on sentence for defendants convicted of possessing a firearm while committing a felony. The gun law was publicized widely and extensively, and it was enforced vigorously by the county prosecutor's office. The law's proponents were confident that it would decrease the rate of crime in which a gun is used.

Loftin *et al.* examined time-series for eight crimes: gun homicides, nongun homicides, armed robberies, unarmed robberies, gun assaults, nongun assaults, stranger homicides, affinal homicides, and the proportion of (1) gun homicides to total homicides; (2) armed robberies to total robberies; (3) gun

FIGURE 12.2   **Hypothetical Interrupted Time-Series Showing the Impact of Mandatory Employment Counseling and Assistance on Average Days' Employment by Adult Male Prison Releasees, Massachusetts**

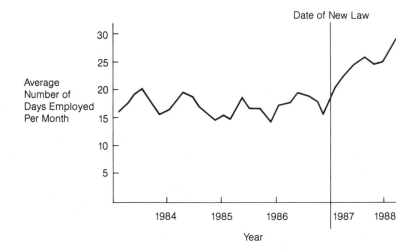

assaults to total assaults. Monthly official crime report data were used to operationalize these criterion variables. However, the number of pretreatment and posttreatment months was different for the various time-series. The results of the statistical analysis were mixed. This led the investigators to conclude, "When all of the evidence is considered, it appears the Gun Law did not have a discernible effect on the level or the pattern of violent crime in Detroit" (1983: 309).

A quasi experiment is the best that can be employed in many research situations. But it is important to understand why we cannot have as much confidence in the findings from quasi-experimental studies as we can have in those from true experiments. This

necessitates a discussion of the concept of *validity threats,* and some of the more common types of them. As we shall see, nonexperimental evaluation research is much more vulnerable to these than is quasi-experimental research.

## Validity Threats

In conducting evaluation research, we want to attribute any differences between comparison units on criterion measures to the treatment. We seek to rule out the possibility of *plausible rival explanations* for the observed differences. When we depart from the classic experiment, there may be a variety

FIGURE 12.3    **Prison Commitment Rates for All Superior Court Convictions, 1974–1980 (San Bernardino, San Francisco, and Santa Clara Counties, California)**

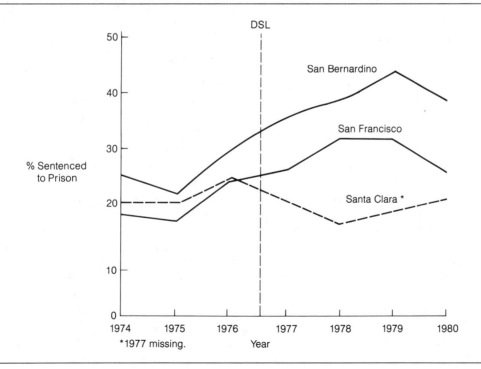

SOURCE: Casper *et al.* (1983:416).

of plausible rival explanations for differences on criterion measures that logically cannot be ruled out. These rival explanations are *validity threats* (Campbell and Stanley, 1966; Campbell, 1971; Cook and Campbell, 1979). We shall discuss several that have proved especially troublesome in correctional evaluation research. As we do so, it should be apparent that even the classic experiment, as typically conducted in the real world of corrections, is not free from some of these problems.

### Selection and Mortality Biases

Whenever units to be compared are formed by a process other than random selection, we cannot assume that they are equivalent. Even when matching and base-expectancy scores are employed, comparison units may differ on other attributes or on other treatment besides the experimental treatment. For example, if a treatment group is constructed from inmate volunteers and a comparison group is constructed by matching from among the general prison population, we cannot confidently rule out *selection biases* as an explantion for subsequent differences on the criterion. Although comparison groups of offenders may be similar "with respect to easily documented variables like age or prior arrest record, [they may be] dissimilar in aspirations or strength of motivation to avoid future criminal involvement, attributes which may have a strong bearing on outcome" (Greenberg, 1974: 2).

Comparison groups that are thought to be equivalent at the beginning of a follow-up period may become progressively dissimilar during the period of the study because of *differential mortality* (dropouts) from the two groups. Researchers who believe in the treatment being evaluated may be tempted to eliminate from the evaluation those cases that did not complete it. This has occurred in several well-known instances (for example, the Highfields study). Such a temptation must be resisted. As noted earlier, "a program to change people should be evaluated on the basis of all those whom it undertook to change. Therefore, those who do not remain in the program must be considered with those who remain; together they comprise the totality that was to be changed" (Glaser, 1973: 71).

### Reactive Arrangements

Whenever offenders are assigned to a special program or treatment, we must recognize that they may for that very reason perform differently on a criterion than would have been the case had they not been part of a special program. This tendency for research subjects to behave differently when they participate in "something special" is known as *reactive arrangements*. It is possible for experimental subjects to perform better or worse than expected, depending on how they define their special status. The lesson for correctional evaluation research is clear: Whenever participants in a treatment program are aware of their special status, this becomes a plausible rival explanation for the research findings.

Moreover, something similar may occur in the behavior of correctional *employees* involved in a special program. Generally it is neither possible to hide from them the fact that a special program is being evaluated nor the identities of those receiving the treatment. As a result, employees sometimes act in a fashion that ensures the program will be "successful." This does not always mean that they intentionally bias the results of the study. They simply may try harder with experimental subjects than with members of the control group.

The problems this can create in evaluation research can be illustrated with data from the California Youth Authority's Community Treatment Project (CTP). Eligible youths randomly were assigned to either a control group confined in an institution and then given regular parole, or to an experimental group released immediately to probation. Follow-up study showed that the experimental subjects had a higher success rate than the control group. However, as we noted earlier, "within certain boundaries the recidivism rate can be influenced by the decision-making authorities" (Robison and Smith, 1971: 70). This happened in the CTP. In reanalyzing the data, Lerman found that while on parole "the experimentals [actually] had more known delinquent offenses per boy than the controls (2.81 to 1.61)" (1968: 57). His analysis suggests that the parole-violation behaviors of experimentals and controls were treated differently by parole authorities. Generally, the experimental subjects received more lenient treatment (1975: 60).

Presumably, one solution to the problem of reactive arrangements is to obtain measures of the behavior of offenders that are "pure" and uncontaminated by the effects of official discretion. Unfortunately, we have not yet developed such measures. An alternative solution is to *blind* the special treatment so that employees don't know which offenders are receiving it. The investigator may go one step further by using a *double blind*, whereby *neither* officials nor subjects are aware of which offenders are receiving the treatment.

## Maturation

Maturation refers to naturally occurring changes within offenders that alone or in combination with the treatment may affect performance on criterion variables. Random selection of comparison groups presumably avoids the possible biases of maturation differences between comparison groups. In the absence of random assignment, the members of the experimental group may, for example, show a greater spontaneous growth in self-awareness during the period of the evaluation. This, not the occurrence of the independent variable, may account for whatever changes in their behavior are subsequently observed. Or perhaps the members of the control group naturally develop a greater fear of imprisonment during the course of their correctional careers and, as a result, perform better on a criterion than the treatment group. In this case, differential maturation effects would make it appear that the treatment was ineffective, when it might have been effective if truly equivalent groups had been compared.

## History

History refers to occurrences external to comparison units after they are constructed that affect performance on a criterion variable. In later discussion we will see that historical differences are a special problem in cohort analysis. But they can similarly contaminate the results of even true experiments if the follow-up period for the experimental and control groups, though the same length for both, begins and ends at different points in time. In such a case, the possibility that one group experienced greater difficulty finding employment because of changes in the economy could account for their poorer performance, irrespective of the treatment they received.

History is the most serious threat to the validity of time-series analyses. As applied to this design, history means events occurring at about the time of the treatment that may produce effects mistakenly attributed to the treatment. There are no cookbook procedures for examining the possible effects of history in time-series analysis. Instead, investigators must deal with the problem creatively in the confines of specific analyses (for example, Loftin *et al.*, 1983).

### *Inability to Generalize*

All the validity threats we have discussed thus far are *internal* threats—threats to our ability to confidently attribute any criterion differences solely to manipulation of the experimental treatment. It is not enough, however, for a study to be internally valid; we also strive for *external* validity (Campbell and Stanley, 1966). Because nearly all research is conducted on samples of offenders, we are always interested in generalizing our research findings to extant groups or populations not involved in the research. Unfortunately, the nature of the population from which our comparison units are drawn affects our ability to generalize the conclusions we draw from our experiments. If this population is atypical, the applicability of the experiment's conclusions for other populations is questionable.

For instance, in the Community Treatment Project a true experimental design was used, but only after 25 percent of the original population was screened out. Thus it would be dubious to generalize the study's results to all offenders (Levin, 1971). Similarly, the Provo experiment in delinquency treatment was conducted in an area heavily populated by members of the Mormon church (Empey and Rabow, 1961). Presumably, Mormon youths represented a significant proportion of the experimental group. If true, this makes it very difficult to generalize the study's results to other parts of the United States, and to offenders of other religious backgrounds.

## Nonexperimental Research Designs

The foregoing are some of the more commonly encountered threats to validity in correctional evaluation research. We suggested that the classic experiment and the quasi experiment are less vulnerable to them than are some of the other types of evaluation research employed in corrections. In view of the frequent use of other designs, it is important to understand them and the various ways they are vulnerable to validity threats.

### *Nonequivalent Comparison Group Designs*

Research by Howard R. Sacks and Charles H. Logan (1979) on the impact of parole supervision for less serious felony offenders exemplifies the nonequivalent comparison group design. The opportunity to conduct the study was provided by a 1974 Connecticut Supreme Court decision that said the state legislature had violated the state constitution when it authorized sentences in excess of one year for Class D felons. (Class D felonies include burglary, unarmed robbery, and assault.) Following the decision, 167 state prison inmates were discharged because they had received sentences longer than one year and already had served the court-mandated maximum sentence. After excluding some cases, Sacks and Logan were left with 115 discharges in their experimental group. They constructed a comparison group of 57 adult male Class D felons released on parole some six months before the court decision. The principal objective of the research was to determine if parole supervision improved postrelease behavior or, as the title of their research report puts it: *Does Parole Make a Difference?*

The investigators collected data on arrests

and convictions, new sentences, and civil commitments for drug abuse. They used a one-year follow-up period and multiple criteria: (1) success/failure—conviction for any offense other than minor traffic offenses; (2) the gravity of failure—the seriousness of new criminal offenses committed by members of the treatment and comparison groups; (3) time in the community—the percentage of the follow-up year that each offender spent in the community; and (4) time to first failure—the percentage of the follow-up year from the date of release to the date of failure (1979: 9–16).

### Before–After Designs

The investigator who employs a before–after research design compares a group's performance before treatment with its subsequent performance. In other words, the "comparison group" is the treatment group's pretreatment performance. An example of such a study is giving offenders a standard personality test before placing them in a special treatment program and retesting them after completion of the program. Any changes on the personality test are attributed to the treatment program. For obvious reasons, this type of design is inappropriate for examining the effects of treatment on the recidivism rate of a group. However, it is used in examining the impact of a treatment on a host of other criteria (for example, academic functioning).

As should be apparent, the potential validity problems with the before–after design are numerous. Since there is no comparison group, the investigator usually assumes either that no change would have occurred in the group or setting in the absence of treatment or that the change would not have been as great as was subsequently observed. History, maturation, selection/mortality biases,

and reactive arrangements, either singly or in combination, are rival explanations for any changes in the treatment group between the pretest and posttest observations.

Earlier we discussed multiple time-series research on Michigan's felony firearms statute (gun law). Milton Heumann and Colin Loftin examined implementation of the gun law in Wayne County (Detroit). They were interested primarily in the law's effects on the processing and court disposition of felony cases. They collected data on the courts' handling of 1976 cases of felonious assault, other assaults, and armed robbery before the gun law went into effect, and for the first six months of 1977, after the effective date of the law. In other words, they employed a before–after research design. Recall that the gun law required a two-year mandatory add-on sentence for defendants convicted of possessing a firearm while committing a felony. The investigators' comparison of data for the two time periods reveals "only a slight upward shift in the average sentence [in firearms cases]. Clearly there [was] no massive increase in the number of cases that receive[d] a sentence of two years or more" (1979: 416).

## Efficiency and Cost–Benefit Analysis

When we evaluate correctional treatments, we generally want to know not only how effective they are but also how efficient they are. Since effectiveness must be weighed by the costs expended, we want to know something of the efficiency of alternative types of correctional treatment.

Some of the more obvious advantages of translating the comparative costs and benefits of programs into monetary terms are that it facilitates communications with administrators and legislators, and it makes arriving at truly comparative assessments of the payoff from alternative correctional programs much easier (since each has a monetary figure attached to it). It is the use of a monetary criterion measure that makes possible *cost–benefit analysis*.

> In its simplest form, the monetary criterion focuses on differences in the costs of processing control and experimental subjects. If post–release behavior is similar, advantage lies with the program in which the processing costs are lower.
>
> In more elaborate forms, the monetary criterion examines benefits as well as costs. The corrected offender not only reduces his future correctional costs, he also takes his family off welfare, earns wages or salary in regular employment, is a productive worker, and otherwise augments the economic and social condition of the community (Adams, 1974: 1026).

Cost–benefit analysis (also referred to as social cost analysis) uses criterion measures that allow us to assess a program's efficiency (Weimer and Friedman, 1979). Some observers have argued that it is the "wave of the future" in correctional evaluation research (Martinson, 1976).

## Evaluation Research Using Statistical Controls

To this point, we have discussed evaluation research that makes use of experimental controls to rule out alternative explanations of results. There is another genre of evaluation research, however, that uses statistical controls to accomplish the same objective (for example, Murray and Cox, 1979). Multiple regression, a statistical analysis technique that permits the simultaneous statistical control of a number of different

independent variables, is commonly used. Unfortunately, this type of research yields findings that can be very difficult to interpret, and we cannot place as much confidence in them as we can in the findings of experimental research (Levin, 1971).

## Qualitative Analysis

While stressing the need to employ equivalent comparison units in evaluation research, we have noted that the principal objective of this research is to determine how the manipulation of correctional treatments affects one or more criterion measures. Most evaluation researchers pursue this objective with research techniques that yield data suitable for statistical analysis. Largely because the objective of most evaluation studies is to produce precise knowledge on the impacts of rational reforms, these investigators emphasize the use of quantitative data and rigorous statistical analyses.

Despite the gradual accumulation of research that employs sound design and procedures, oftentimes evaluation studies produce inconsistent or even contradictory findings. The results of other studies may be ambiguous and subject, therefore, to a variety of interpretations. Thus the results of many of these studies have been unsatisfying. Research often suggests that reform strategies and programs either failed to achieve the effects projected by their supporters or, worse, the impacts of reform are impossible to untangle or create new, unanticipated problems.

It is not surprising that reviews of the findings from existing correctional evaluation research conclude that we have a great deal yet to learn of the impacts of most correctional strategies. Some social scientists believe that greater use of *qualitative* evaluation research may aid in the development of valid, generalizable knowledge on the impact of various types of correctional treatments. Qualitative research techniques include systematic observation, participant observation, and nonstructured but focused interviews. Use of these techniques, either alone or combined with quantitative procedures, enables us to *interpret* statistical findings in terms of the organizational and interorganizational routines and processes that comprise what we refer to globally as criminal justice.

Earlier we reviewed research on the impact of the California Determinate Sentencing Law (Casper *et al.*, 1983). The investigators combined their time-series analyses with qualitative data and analysis of pretrial and sentencing practices. The qualitative data consisted of interviews with courtroom participants and direct observation of pretrial conferences and plea-bargaining sessions in the three sample counties. The focus of the qualitative research was the process by which the DSL was implemented at the local level.

Recall that the investigators were unable to conclude with confidence that the DSL affected prison commitment rates. The qualitative analysis confirmed what others (Davies, 1985) found as well, that the DSL shifted much of the control over sentencing and sentence length to courtroom participants, particularly the judge and prosecutor. For the most part, they used their new discretionary powers to maintain the "going rate" of punishments for various types of offenders and offenses, despite the provisions of the new law. The investigators concluded that the effects of reform

> are mediated by settled patterns within court systems, by the need to dispose of cases by negotiation and the consequent inclination to treat [reforms] as not only policies but resources, and by the relationship between the legislative policy and participants' developed

norms about what types of outcomes are appropriate (Casper *et al.*, 1983: 431).

Qualitative evaluation research on the fate of juvenile diversion programs is another example. The originators of diversion programs believed they would benefit youthful offenders by presenting less formal, less stigmatizing procedures for handling their cases. The impact of diversion programs has been the object of empirical studies in many communities in the United States. Although a degree of controversy surrounds the results of these studies (Lemert, 1981; Binder and Geis, 1984; Polk, 1984), the preponderance of evidence suggests that diversion has produced results very different from those intended by its supporters. As implemented, diversion programs have extended the official control net in many communities (Austin and Krisberg, 1981).

Research by Charles E. Frazier and John K. Cochran interprets this phenomenon. In their study of the implementation of juvenile diversion programs in eight Florida counties, they found that youth diverted out of the juvenile justice system were in other ways treated much the same as those who were not diverted. In this respect, the intended objectives of the diversion program generally were not realized. Frazier and Cochran suggest two reasons this was so. First, they note "Justice agencies and agents have a well-known ability to resist change or to subvert change initiatives, making them serve long-standing practices." This was the case with the criminal justice system's response to the diversion program. "Interruption of the standard practices of processing was guarded against carefully. . . . Justice officials were oriented to a set of ideas and practices that they could not or would not easily abandon" (1986: 169–70). A second reason for the program's failure was that "supervisory and . . . caseworker staff held to ideas of professional practice that were not compatible with the idea of limiting intervention" (1986: 171).

John R. Hepburn and Lynne Goodstein (1986) also used a variety of research procedures to examine the implementation of determinate sentencing reform in Minnesota, Illinois, and Connecticut. Like the other investigators discussed here, they found that one of the keys to understanding the impact of reforms is to examine how they are filtered through and shaped by the organizational imperatives of correctional bureaucracies.

## Obstacles to the Routinization of Evaluation Research

Many social scientists have urged correctional administrators to conduct evaluation research to rationally restructure the correctional apparatus. Glaser (1965), for example, refers to situations where evaluation research is conducted routinely and used to modify correctional practice as an "elusive paradise." Like Glaser, most social scientists and correctional managers apparently believe that evaluation research is an appropriate vehicle for improving correctional effectiveness. Consequently, they have focused on some common impediments to the use of evaluation research. We briefly review some of these.

### Conflicting Ideological Stances

Because of their training and experiences, correctional administrators and employees tend to have faith in the efficacy of correctional ideologies and strategies. Researchers tend, on the other hand, to be skeptics and to insist that correctional claims be subjected to empirical test. Moreover, correctional personnel have an immediate practical concern, which makes them impatient with those who seem intent on developing long-range knowledge or who seem unable to answer practical

questions without designing and conducting a lengthy study. These conflicting ideological predispositions naturally produce a certain wariness and misunderstanding between correctors and researchers. While this may not prevent limited cooperation on occasional research projects, it militates against the successful institutionalization of evaluation research.

### Organizational Programs

Historically, there are two patterns of organizational arrangements for conducting correctional evaluation research. The first involves individuals or organizations external to correctional agencies. For example, the Ford Foundation funded a study of the federal prison and parole systems, which was conducted by Daniel Glaser (1964). In recent years, however, private research organizations have become more prominent in research of this type. These organizations conduct research for a fee, on a contractual basis. The second organizational model is research units within correctional agencies or departments (Ohlin, 1974). Although these alternative research arrangements present somewhat different problems for the routinization of evaluation research, they also share some problems.

Experience suggests that research units and the conduct of research projects should be closely integrated in the day-to-day operations of correctional agencies—though not so integrated that they become completely dominated by administrators. A high degree of integration increases the likelihood that correctional personnel will be involved in all phases of research projects, from conception and planning to data collection and analysis. Such cooperation and communication decrease the chances that the research unit or project will be seen as alien, disruptive, or threatening. An excellent example of this process of close communication with correctors is found in the study by G. Kassebaum *et al.* (1971) which evaluated the effectiveness of group counseling in a California prison. This study utilized criterion measures that were developed with correctional staff. They were encouraged to list what they thought were the benefits of group counseling, and these assumed benefits were among the multiple criterion measures used by the investigators.

When there is little routine communication and coordination between correctional personnel and research staff outside specific research projects, researchers are more likely to pursue idiosyncratic or esoteric projects that have little relevance for the host correctional agency. Glaser (1965) points to this as one reason that the early attempt to establish and routinize evaluation research in the Illinois prison system failed. The absence of close communication and supervision by superiors permitted researchers to pursue projects related to their own interests and goals rather than those of the correctional agency.

## Administrative Stance

Organizational problems such as these can be minimized if there is sufficient administrative understanding of and support for evaluation research. Unfortunately, administrators often seem unable to maintain such a stance. After all, implicit in the very notion of evaluation research is the possibility that some program which has been touted as effective in changing offenders will be shown to be ineffective. This potential for negative results can be threatening to correctional administrators and employees, producing feelings of vulnerability and a resistance to permitting or conducting research. Within correctional agencies and agency departments, the possibility of negative findings may disrupt the balance of power and privilege, thus creating problems for admin-

istrators. Various occupational groups may, then, have a vested interest in discouraging research. When administrators are differentially sensitive to or dependent on these groups, they may proceed with extreme caution in the area of research.

## Environmental Supports

Administrators may resist research if they have developed beneficial relationships with outside groups or organizations that presume the effectiveness of correctional treatment. In such a situation, negative research findings may prove disruptive of these sources of support. Although the legislature is the best example of this, there are, in addition, various professional and private correctional groups and organizations. Not all of these groups may understand or support evaluation research, and in such a situation the administrator may either veto the research altogether or else move to isolate its potentially disruptive effects and thereby minimize its impact.

At a more general level, the routinization of correctional evaluation research depends on some minimal prior degree of support for and understanding of it by key groups in the environment. It is difficult, for example, to imagine the routine conduct of evaluation research by a correctional agency whose relations with environmental groups are essentially feudal in nature. In commenting on these environmental prerequisites for research, Glaser (1965) suggests there must be a certain type of "cultural base." This is an apt way of calling attention to the critical dimension of environmental conditions and relationships.

## Divergent Interests of Researchers

For their part, the personnel of research units may contribute to their own lack of significant impact on correctional structures and practices. When left to their own devices, they may pursue research that is calculated to advance their careers in other spheres (for example, the university). Moreover, they may engage in esoteric or idiosyncratic research projects of little demonstrable relevance to agency concerns or problems. This is the basis for the claim by correctional personnel that researchers are too concerned with "impractical" problems or trivial theoretical issues.

The appearance of the research-for-fee system has brought a new potential problem: Researchers may become *too* sensitive to the expressed problems and "needs" of correctors, in the hope of doing more business in the future. Under such circumstances, researchers may focus too much attention on insignificant problems, thus failing to as-

sume the role of impartial challenger and innovator.

To summarize, the likelihood that evaluation research will become routinized in a correctional agency is enhanced when there is a supportive and understanding environment, when administrators understand and are committed to the use of research, when the agency is relatively free of internal conflicts that could be exacerbated by research, and when researchers, in consultation with agency personnel, explore questions of relevance to agency problems.

Now that we have reviewed the principles of evaluation research and some obstacles to conducting it, in Chapter 13 we move to a critical discussion of the promise and use of evaluation research.

# 13

# Evaluation Research As a Social and Political Process

Most social scientists who call for greater use of evaluation research to restructure corrections share a common, *objectivist* perspective on the nature of the social world, the research process, and the implementation of research findings. They believe that the social world, like the physical one, is an objective realm of factual realities. The nature of this world, especially the cause–effect relationships within it, can be discovered or laid bare by scientific research methods. Social research, like research in physics, biology, or chemistry, is believed to be primarily a *technical* process. It consists of applying well-defined principles and methods to empirical problems. "Good" research is distinguished from "bad" research by how closely it conforms to these widely accepted principles of research design.

Objectivists draw a sharp distinction between "scientific" and other criteria for evaluating the consequences of correctional strategies and programs. They see themselves as analytically rigorous, objective experts unaffected by "emotional" concerns:

> Research which confirms the popular is often popular; that which does not is frequently discredited on emotional grounds. For example, let us assume that research has discovered that whipping men for their misbehavior has a beneficial effect upon the recidivism rate. This conclusion would probably be accepted or rejected upon the basis of whether or not one did or did not believe in whipping, on grounds quite unrelated to its effectiveness as a correctional treatment (Schnur, 1958: 773).

Undaunted by what others may do, these tough-minded realists are determined to employ scientific methods to confront "the hard policy choices" of corrections (Wilson, 1983: 160). Evaluation research is sketched as an unbiased and objective means of developing factual knowledge to guide the policymaking process.

In short, objectivists celebrate the potential benefits of "correctional science" (Fosen and Campbell, 1966). They acknowledge that political or administrative problems occasionally may hinder the process of evaluation research, but these obstacles are not insurmountable. In fact, problems of this nature also can be researched. Once we have identified the recurrent obstacles to research, we can devise informed strategies to overcome them and implement correctional reforms. Just as there is good and bad research, so there are good and bad strategies for implementing evaluation research findings.

Despite the growing rationalization of crime control in America and the technocratic fixation of politicians and correctional managers, not all social scientists accept uncritically the objectivist position. To begin with, many believe that "technical efficiency cannot be the sole criterion upon which to base a policy that involves the reality of coercion" (Lerman, 1975: 88). They believe that questions about the fundamental humaneness and legality of correctional programs are of primary importance. Accordingly, they are less inclined than some of their peers to brush aside the moral, ethical, and legal issues of the research process (Baunach, 1980). Beyond these fundamental concerns about evaluation research, critics contend that every aspect of research is shaped and negotiated politically. The process of interpreting research findings illustrates these political processes in evaluation research.

## Interpreting Research Findings

In Chapter 12 we saw that true experimental research designs are touted as the preferred way to develop reliable, objective knowledge about the impact of correctional strategies. Because of a variety of impediments, however, these designs have not found wide use in correctional evaluation research. One observer notes that no more than 10 percent of evaluation studies have employed randomized designs (Adams, 1974: 10). Charles H. Logan (1972: 380) reviewed 100 studies and concluded that "there is not yet one single study of correctional or preventive effectiveness that will satisfy the most minimal standards of scientific design."

In addition to the infrequent use of true experimental designs, other problems plague existing correctional research. For example, often it is difficult to identify the treatment employed in a study because it is imprecise or overly broad—for example, "probation." "It is not enough to know that a particular program ended in success or failure if we cannot determine what it was that succeeded or failed" (Logan, 1972: 379). Although it is useful to know that probation is at least as successful as imprisonment in reducing recidivism, we would like to know precisely what it is about probation that accounts for this success.

But it is arguable that the current state of correctional knowledge and practice would be appreciably different if randomized experiments were used widely in correctional research. The reasons for this are two. First, investigation of social phenomena is qualitatively different from investigations of physical or chemical processes. The subject matter of research in the physical sciences is neither volitional nor self-aware in the research process. We saw in Chapter 12 that the subjects of true experimental research designs in most instances are aware that they are participating in "something special." Rarely, if ever, do the individuals and organizations that are part of an experiment respond passively to the special circumstances created by the experimental design. Instead, they respond creatively and use the altered circumstances to manage their work problems or to ensure the success of the program. In other words, reactive arrangements usually are a plausible rival explanation for results obtained in social research, even in randomized experiments. Thus the distinctive nature of the social world and social research may limit both the internal and external validity of research findings.

The principal goal of true experiments is to create a situation in which the investigator can control extraneous variables. This enables the investigator to observe the consequences on a criterion measure of manipulating one or a series of independent variables. This brings us to a second problem with experimental research designs. Experimental research requires rigorous controls which, in most cases, cannot be obtained with human subjects or social processes in the day-to-day world. However, this high degree of control can be attained easily in *laboratory* settings. Small-group studies epitomize this process. In return for a high degree of experimental control, investigators must pay the price of creating an artificial social world. Since individuals do not live their daily lives in laboratories, the external validity of the laboratory findings is limited. Correctional researchers are, then, in a paradoxical situation. Data collected in randomized experiments may provide the best evidence of correctional effectiveness, but even the results of these studies are subject to serious validity threats.

From an objectivist perspective, science is the great arbiter of correctional issues. It provides definitive answers—at least over a long enough period of time and research—on the basis of which correctional structures and practices can and should be refashioned. Using the principles of research as a guide, persons of diverse backgrounds, organizational allegiances, and political persuasions presumably can evaluate research studies and agree that it is "good" or "bad" research. But there is reason to question whether this accurately describes how research findings are judged in the real world.

What does this debate mean for the process of correctional evaluation research? It means, simply, that the results of research rarely speak clearly. We are mistaken to believe that we will find one or even a series of critical studies that will give us an unambiguous answer to important questions about corrections. Since nearly all social research suffers from one or more validity threats, we necessarily ask not *whether* we can have confidence in it but *how much* confidence it merits. This is not a *technical* issue, because it cannot be answered simply by formula or by citing objective research principles. It can only be answered on the basis of a negotiated, political process.

The case of research on the effects of marijuana is instructive in this regard. Erich Goode (1969) asks how it could be that after conducting so much research, scientists seem unable to agree whether smoking marijuana is harmful, and if so, to what degree and in what ways. After analyzing the debate, Goode concludes:

> The marijuana controversy is primarily a political rather than a scientific debate. It is a struggle to establish moral hegemony. Stances toward marijuana use and legalization are largely a manifestation of prior basic underlying ideological commitments. Scientific truth or falsity seem to have little or no impact on the positions taken—although both sides will invoke scientific findings and in fact will actually believe them—and have been preselected to verify a position already taken (1969: 83).

Goode contends that the "objective facts" about marijuana smoking are largely irrelevant to the debate over its effects. He suggests that it is extremely difficult, perhaps even impossible, for those who have prior ideological commitments to different positions on the issue to lay aside these differences and come to one "correct" interpretation of the research literature.

Consider another example. Statistical research over more than 20 years points to the harmful health consequences of cigarette and cigar smoking. As in the realm of correctional research, much of the research on the harmful effects of smoking are based on statistical comparisons, of rates of disease among smokers and nonsmokers. Not surprisingly, scientists employed by the tobacco industry take exception with these findings. Repeatedly they point out that research has not shown a *causal* relationship between smoking and disease. This debate suggests it is unlikely that scientists, more than other groups of individuals who differ in their backgrounds and organizational allegiances, can somehow put aside these differences and agree on one "correct" interpretation of a body of theory and research. Consequently, it should come as no surprise to learn that diverse groups of social scientists disagree about the effects of a variety of correctional strategies.

Conflicting interpretations of correctional evaluation research demonstrate clearly how social forces shape this interpretational process. In the past two decades, many investigators have offered summary assessments of the results of evaluation research on rehabilitative strategies. Walter C. Bailey examined a sample of 100 studies of the effectiveness of these strategies and concluded that "evidence supporting the efficacy of correctional treatment is slight, inconsistent, and of questionable reliability" (1966: 159). Based on a review of several well-known research projects conducted in California, James O. Robison and Gerald Smith concluded: "There is no evidence to support any program's claim of superior rehabilitative efficacy" (1971: 80). David F. Greenberg claimed that

many correctional dispositions are failing to reduce recidivism. . . . Much of what is now done in the name of "corrections" may serve other functions, but the prevention of return to crime is not one of them. Here and there a few favorable results alleviate the monotony, but most of these results are modest and are obtained through evaluations seriously lacking in rigor (1974: 140–41).

D. Lipton *et al.* (1975) reviewed 231 studies and concluded that while "some treatment programs have had modest successes, it still must be concluded that the field of corrections has not as yet found satisfactory ways to reduce recidivism by significant amounts." Finally, a Panel of the National Academy of Sciences concluded:

The entire body of correctional evaluation research appears to justify only the conclusion that we do not now know of any program or method of rehabilitation that could be guaranteed to reduce the criminal activity of released offenders. Although a generous reviewer of the literature might discern some glimmers of hope, those glimmers are so few, so scattered, and so inconsistent that they do not serve as a basis for any recommendation other than continued research (Sechrest *et al.,* 1979: 3).

By no means are these generally discouraging research results limited to rehabilitative strategies. Research on the effectiveness of deterrence strategies offers little cause for optimism either. In 1975, the National Academy of Science established a Panel on Research on Deterrent and Incapacitative Effects in order "to provide an objective technical assessment of the studies of the deterrent and incapacitative effects of sanctions on crime rates" (Blumstein *et al.,* 1978: 16). The panel concludes that while existing research does "offer some credible evidence of the existence of a deterrent effect . . . we cannot yet assert that the evidence warrants an affirmative conclusion regarding such an effect." Many observers are less optimistic than the panel, noting that deterrence research is plagued by many shortcomings that limit our ability to generalize from it (for example, Piliavin *et al.*, 1986). In fact, even conservatives seem doubtful about the likely payoff from deterrence strategies. For example, James Q. Wilson acknowledges:

> Deterrence works only if people take into account the costs and benefits of alternative courses of action and choose that which confers the largest net benefit (or the smallest net cost). Though people almost surely do take such matters into account, it is difficult to be certain . . . what change, if any, in crime rates will result from a given, feasible change in . . . the costs of crime . . . (1983: 145).

In recent years, conservatives increasingly have embraced incapacitative strategies for reducing the rate of street crimes. Stated simply, "as long as there is a reasonable presumption that offenders who are imprisoned would have continued to commit crimes if they had remained free, there is unquestionably a direct incapacitative effect [of imprisonment]" (Blumstein *et al.*, 1978: 9). Studies of the effects of incapacitative policies necessarily make assumptions about critical parameters that characterize individual criminal careers. Thus "to determine the amount of crime that is prevented by incarcerating a given number of offenders for a given length of time, the key estimate we must make is the number of offenses a criminal commits per year free on the street" ["lambda"] (Wilson, 1983: 147). Using both self-reports and analyses of arrest records, the search for the value of lambda has consumed considerable research time and federal funds in recent years (for example,

Blumstein and Cohen, 1979; Peterson and Braiker, 1980).

Although researchers disagree about the magnitude of lambda, there is little disagreement over the likely effects of collective incapacitation strategies both on crime rates and prison populations. For one thing, when pursued in more than one jurisdiction, a strategy of incapacitation might work differently in each. As the National Academy of Sciences Panel noted:

> The expected incapacitative effect of any change in imprisonment policy is quite sensitive to the current value of the individual crime rate and to the current value of imprisonment policy variables. When the current rate of imprisonment per crime and the individual crime rates are low, the percentage increase in prison population needed in order to achieve a given percentage reduction in crime is large. Since the high-crime-rate jurisdictions that are most likely to be looking to incapacitation to relieve their crime problems also tend to have relatively lower rates of time served per crime, they can expect to have the largest percentage increased in prison populations to achieve a given percentage reduction in crime (Blumstein *et al.*, 1978: 10).

More important, statistical estimates show that a policy of incapacitation could achieve significant reductions in crime only at the cost of astronomical increases in the size of the prison population (Avi-Itzhak and Shinnar, 1973; Clarke, 1974; Greenberg, 1975a; Shinnar and Shinnar, 1975; Van Dine *et al.*, 1977; Boland, 1978; Palmer and Salimbene, 1978; Petersilia and Greenwood, 1978; Cohen, 1983a, 1983b). Even conservatives find these results "sobering" (Wilson, 1983: 152).

Despite the accumulation of research that points to minimal crime reduction effects of rehabilitative and incapacitative strategies, heated controversy over these matters continues. Surveying the same body of correctional research literature, some feel reason for optimism, while others conclude that correctional treatment seems largely ineffective. Drawing from the assessment of rehabilitative effectiveness by Lipton *et al.*, Robert Martinson (1974) cautiously suggested that correctional treatment has not yet proved to be very effective.

The tentative and restrained tenor of his remarks, along with the conclusions presented in other summary reviews of evaluation research, contrast with interpretations that others have drawn. For example, Ted Palmer (1975) leveled a sweeping and detailed attack on the analytic methods and conclusions of Martinson's paper. Both Palmer and Stuart Adams (1974: 1021) believe there is reason for optimism.

There is little reason for surprise over this clash of opinion. In fact, given the high stakes that so many have invested in the presumed efficacy of correctional treatment, it is precisely what we would expect (see Martinson, 1976). The debate calls to mind Donald R. Cressey's discussion (1958) of how correctional personnel develop and use a *vocabulary of adjustment* to discount or attack the results of research that show their favorite programs to be ineffective. As Cressey noted, research of this type presents correctional personnel with a serious dilemma. On one hand, they profess a commitment to the use of evaluation research. On the other hand, many have substantial personal and organizational commitments to specific correctional strategies and programs. "Fortunately, there is a solution to the dilemma. Stated simply, it is to insure that any research results can be interpreted as 'conclusive' if they favor continued utilization of the technique and as 'inconclusive' if they do not" (1958: 759).

Promoters and supporters of correctional strategies, whether these be rehabilitative or punitive, are not content simply to level broad attacks. They pursue other lines of contention as well.

## Differential Treatment

Promoters of a variety of correctional ideologies and strategies generally acknowledge only that no single correctional treatment works well with all types of offenders or in all settings. They argue, therefore, that we must move to determine which *types of treatment* work best with which *types of offenders*. For example, Marguerite Q. Warren candidly acknowledges that "studies of the impact of treatment on client populations have been generally discouraging." She suggests two possible reasons for this. Perhaps, she says, "treaters simply don't know how to bring about changes in individuals via a treatment process." Alternatively, she suggests that evaluation research results are plagued by *masking:*

> By lumping together all subjects, the beneficial effects of a treatment program on some subjects, together with the detrimental effects of the same treatment program on other subjects, may each mask and cancel out the other.
>
> It is very likely that, in many treatment studies, this masking effect has occurred, either because the data have not been viewed in sufficiently complex fashion, or because the crucial dimension, the classification of subjects in a treatment-relevant way, was missing (1971: 245–46).

In other words, while the overall success rate for a strategy or treatment may be low, some offenders' positive response to the treatment may be canceled out or masked by the unfavorable response of other offenders. The belief that masking occurs frequently in correctional evaluation research has reached the point of near dogma in contemporary correctional literature (for example, Palmer, 1975).

The solution, many argue, is to examine *differential treatment* effects—the effects of a treatment on different types of offenders. An illustration of the alleged promise of differential treatment is the results of the Pilot Intensive Counseling Organization (PICO). This project, which began in 1955, was designed to study the effects of individual therapy on older delinquents. Treated youths were to be compared with control youths on personality and behavioral changes, both while confined in a medium-security correctional institution and after release on parole. Before admission to Deuel Vocational Institution, California Youth Authority wards were screened for possible inclusion in the PICO program. Those with any of the following characteristics were rejected: a sentence of less than six months, probable out-of-state parole, psychosis, gross mental deficiency, non-English-speaking, or serious reading difficulty. After screening, subjects were randomly assigned either to the experimental group or to a control group.

However, one additional determination was made about each subject—his degree of amenability to treatment. This was ascertained through pooled clinical judgments by a team that studied the subjects at their admission to the reception–diagnostic center. Use of judgments about each subject's amenability, along with assignment to either an experimental or control group, resulted in four groups: (1) treated amenables, (2) treated nonamenables, (3) control amenables, and (4) control nonamenables.

For the experimental subjects, treatment consisted of once- or twice-weekly individual counseling sessions. These sessions continued for an average of about nine months for both the treated amenables and the treated nonamenables. During the nontreatment hours, the experimental subjects pursued the same program as the control subjects— a full schedule of academic and vocational training.

A variety of criterion variables were used to assess the effectiveness of the treatment. The results generally were consistent for all criteria. Treated amenables performed better than the other groups, followed by the control amenables, the control nonamenables, and lastly, by the treated nonamenables. In other words, those subjects judged to be nonamenable to treatment actually performed worse than if they had received no treatment at all.

The TARP project, which we discussed in Chapter 12, offers another example of differential treatment effects. The investigators examined the effects of unemployment payments on the postprison behavior of parolees in Georgia and Texas. Overall they found that extending unemployment benefits to parolees immediately upon release from prison had little effect on their criminal behavior. However, the investigators reasoned that masking or "counterbalancing" occurred. Consequently, they employed statistical techniques to analyze their data and concluded that, in fact, unemployment benefits do have a beneficial impact on the behavior of some ex-prisoners. Nonetheless, unlike the PICO investigators, they were unable to identify a subgroup of the study samples for which this was true (Zeisel, 1982a, 1982b; Rossi *et al.*, 1982). Thus demonstration of their counterbalancing model rests on statistical procedures alone.

Some argue that projects such as PICO and TARP indicate the need for offender typologies to facilitate differential treatment. Warren (1971) reviewed 16 such typologies and suggested that six offender subtypes are common to all of them: (1) asocial, (2) conformist, (3) antisocial–manipulator, (4) neurotic, (5) subcultural identifier, and (6) situational offender. She believes the recurrence of these six types is cause for optimism; perhaps correctional researchers and personnel are gradually developing some consensus on fundamental types of offenders. In R. G. Hood's words, "The key to progress in treatment research is the development of typologies, both of offenders and treatments. . . . What kinds of people would respond best to discipline, counseling, therapy, fining, intensive case-work, limited supervision?" (1971: 178).

## Selective Incapacitation

Although much of our discussion here has focused on the debate over rehabilitative strategies, the same processes and criticisms apply to research on punitive correctional strategies. For example, after investigators raised serious doubts about the effectiveness of collective incapacitation, conservatives moved to an alternative strategy, one that is grounded in assumptions about high-rate offenders, or "career criminals":

> If a community experiences one thousand robberies a year, it obviously makes a great deal of difference whether these robberies are the work of ten robbers, each of whom commits one hundred robberies per year, or the work of one thousand robbers, each of whom commits only one robbery per year (Wilson, 1983: 147).

Conservatives contend that, in fact, a small group of offenders is responsible for a high proportion of street crimes (see Chaiken and Chaiken, 1982; Forst *et al.*, 1982). Armed with this premise, conservatives argue that incapacitative strategies could be implemented selectively. This is differential treatment, conservative style. Wilson asserts that

> all the evidence we have implies that, for crime-reduction purposes, the most rational way to use the incapacitive powers of our prisons

would be to do so selectively. Instead of longer sentences for everyone, or for persons who have prior records, or for persons whose present crime is especially grave, longer sentences would be given primarily to those who, when free, commit the most crimes (1983: 153–54).

Assuming that an offender is in custody, how will we know if she or he is among the "hard core" who likely will commit further crime? By what external signs will we recognize the "career criminal" (Forst *et al.*, 1982)? Peter W. Greenwood suggests that they have these characteristics:

**1.** A prior conviction for the crime type that is being predicted.

**2.** A juvenile conviction prior to age 16.

**3.** A history of heroin or barbiturate use in the two-year period preceding the current arrest.

**4.** A past commitment to a state or federal juvenile facility.

**5.** Employed less than half of the two-year period preceding the current arrest.

**6.** Incarcerated more than half of the two-year period preceding the current arrest.

Offering an example of the crime control benefits that might result from a sentencing strategy based on his research, Greenwood claims that

> among California robbers, . . . a selective incapacitation strategy that reduced terms for [some robbers] while increasing [them] for high-rate robbers could achieve a 15 percent reduction in the robbery rate with only 95 percent of the current incarcerated population level for robbery (1982: xix).

As we noted in Chapter 3, these proposals for selective incapacitation have been criticized on moral and legal grounds (Currie, 1985). As we shall see, the research that underpins proposals for selective incapacitation has been attacked on empirical grounds as well (Gottfredson and Hirschi, 1986).

## Choosing and Framing Research Problems

Earlier we noted that regardless of how closely it conforms to methodological formulas, research cannot be, and is not, judged entirely on technical grounds. Instead, the process of judging and interpreting research is a negotiational one. In the remainder of this chapter we suggest other reasons for maintaining a skeptical stance toward the promised benefits of evaluation research.

We have questioned whether "objective" research findings can win the support of groups who have accumulated political, intellectual, and career investments in the presumed validity of any particular correctional ideology. We maintain that judgments about "good" research, "reliable" research findings, or "reasonable" inferences from research vary with the evaluators' backgrounds, social contexts, and organizational affiliations. Let's consider the process of choosing research problems.

Although there is an infinite array of potentially researchable problems in the world of corrections, only some of these are chosen to receive research attention. But the problems selected are not distributed randomly. The selection is socially and politically determined. How does this occur?

Some time ago, Herbert Blumer recognized the inherent biases of research conducted or sponsored by state bureaucracies, particularly people-processing organizations. He charged that "agency-determined research" characteristically "ignores the in-

terests, rights, and claims of the people who are the objects of inquiry" (1967: 165). This remains an accurate description of most correctional research. It builds on a *hierarchy of credibility* (Becker, 1967), meaning that the problems and perspectives of superiors are more readily adopted than those of subordinates because they are thought to have more credibility.

This is manifested in the tendency of researchers to employ variables defined or produced by correctional bureaucracies. Moreover, the use of official records reduces investigators' ability to transcend the official reality and to generate or appreciate alternative perspectives on correctional structures and problems. One reason for this may be expedience. Data gleaned from official records can be quantified easily and lend themselves to multivariate, computer analysis.

Another misconception about the process of choosing and framing research problems is the notion that research experts are disinterested, that they have "no moral or financial axes to grind" (Young, 1975: 65). The error of this notion is shown by the expanding largess of federal funding agencies, which shapes the research problems and agendas of investigators.

Generally, research problems are defined in terms sympathetic or experientially relevant to only certain groups or organizational strata. Correlatively, the problems and perspectives of other groups or strata may never be solicited or given serious consideration. Given these facts, it becomes important to explore the political and ideological biases that inevitably are embedded in official definitions of problems. Although there are some important exceptions, most correctional research ignores the problems and perspectives of inmates and lower-level correctional employees.

Several implications of the constriction of research problems are noteworthy. First, evaluation research seems incapable of generating proposals or programs that represent truly fundamental or radical alternatives to existing correctional arrangements. In other words, most evaluation researchers examine or propose programs that are only incrementally different from existing ones and that do not fundamentally challenge them. Second, there is limited interest in or understanding of correctional issues from the vantage point of subordinate groups or strata.

### An Alternative Look at Selective Incapacitation

Let's turn now to a critical analysis of correctional research, one that employs the insights we have presented here. Specifically, we review a critical discussion of the movement to develop selective incapacitation. Although some investigators have questioned claims for the potential merits of selective incapacitation on narrow, technical grounds, it remained for Michael Gottfredson and Travis Hirschi (1986) to level a broad attack.

Two concepts figure prominently in the armament of deterrence and incapacitation investigators: "career criminal" and "criminal career." Gottfredson and Hirschi take dead aim at both. While the notion of the career criminal dates to the turn of the century, they note that the concept achieved a renewed impetus because of research by Marvin E. Wolfgang *et al.* (1972). They argue, however, that definitions of this pivotal concept are neither precise nor uniform. Nevertheless, the existence of career criminals has become a matter of faith in federal funding agencies. Consequently, research grant proposals that ignore the career criminal do not receive funding priority. Much of this funded research appears to be highly sophisticated and is carried out by large private research corporations under contract with federal and criminal justice agencies. Many of these studies are narrowly con-

ceived and focus on devising more efficient ways to identify and control deviant populations.

Gottfredson and Hirschi argue that belief in the existence and importance of career criminals is not limited to federal funding agencies. Academic scholars also have accepted it.

> Being derived from policy concerns, career criminal terminology sounds immediately policy-relevant to those in charge of the nation's research agencies, and the circle is closed. Academics supply the terms that justify the funds provided them (1986: 244).

Strategies of selective incapacitation are based on faulty premises, say Gottfredson and Hirschi. They note research shows conclusively that criminal involvement peaks in the middle to late teenage years and then declines with age. To be effective, therefore, incapacitative crime control strategies would necessitate locking up children for long periods of time. Supporters of selective incapacitation counter that high-rate offenders begin their criminal careers early in life and persist at crime longer than other offenders. Gottfredson and Hirschi show that these mistaken assumptions are based on statistical artifacts. They conclude that while the twin notions of criminal careers and career criminals have little merit, they have influenced the allocation of criminological research funds and spawned ill-conceived policies.

## Lessons

The purpose of this chapter is not to argue that evaluation research lacks merit or that it is incapable of helping us understand or resolve questions about the consequences of alternative crime control strategies. To the contrary, we believe that the results of evaluation studies can be extremely useful. Nevertheless, we also tried to suggest that there are reasons to maintain a critical, analytic stance toward the evaluation research process. For one thing, we have argued that much of what is learned via evaluation research is skewed, because it is filtered through official prisms. Presumably, correctional programs can succeed in changing offenders only if officials take account of the perspectives of the former's perspectives. Consequently, the paucity of research from the vantage point of underlings probably hinders our ability to change offenders. Moreover, it suggests a need to democratize the process by which research problems are identified, conceptualized, and investigated.

At the same time, we have tried to suggest that we cannot permit fixation on research *techniques* to obscure the fundamental political nature of corrections and correctional debate. We believe it is important not to accept an overly naive view of the promise of evaluation research, one that obscures the process of its application to the realm of socially and politically negotiated realities.

We must understand that the most significant forces that constrain and transform corrections simply are not amenable to experimental control. Correctional change occurs when there are changes in its social and political–economic context. Evaluation research can only marginally aid us to modify these and thereby promote alternative correctional strategies and structures.

# 14

# The Changing Face
# of Corrections

Throughout this text we have argued that in order to understand corrections, one must have an awareness of the political, social, and historical context in which it is embedded, the dynamics of organizational structures of which it is a part, and the interorganizational processes and constraints which give it shape. We have indicated in passing that corrections is a component of an interdependent but uncoordinated system of justice. To add further complexity, corrections also must be understood in relation to the wider structures of social control in American society. It is in the interplay between formal and informal structures of social control that perhaps the most significant developments have occurred affecting the direction of corrections.

## Foucault's Vision

In order to have a better understanding of the extent and complexity of these structures of social control, we must have an appreciation of their development. One compelling multilevel explanation of control ideologies, strategies, and structures was that of the French philosopher Michel Foucault, who traces the history of punishment (1979). For our purpose we are interested in his elaboration of the concept of the prison of the 19th century. The feature of the prison which attracted Foucault was the method developed to control not only the freedom of movement of those confined but their minds as well. Foucault focused on an idea articulated by Jeremy Bentham, the utilitarianist philosopher, that prisoners be confined in a structure arranged so that a guard could be in the center of the building and see into each cell without himself being seen. A prisoner thus would have the impression that he was always being watched by an omnipresent representative of the state. Bentham called the prison he envisioned and the principle it encompassed the Panopticon.

What the concept of the Panopticon meant to Foucault was the potential ability to have total power over selected populations. As he writes:

Hence the major effect of the Panopticon: to induce in the inmate a state of conscious and permanent visibility that assures the automatic functioning of power. So to arrange things that the surveillance is permanent in its effects, even if it is discontinuous in its action; that the perfection of power should tend to render its actual exercise unnecessary; that this architectural apparatus should be a machine for creating and sustaining a power relation independent of the person who exercises it; in short, that the inmates should be caught up in a power situation of which they are themselves the bearers (1979: 201).

Foucault also saw the prison of the 19th century as a system of power and domination transferable beyond the prison to other areas of the social spectrum. It is this method of control that he terms *discipline*. He saw this method of discipline (means of coercion and training) and what he calls technologies of power diffused to schools, asylums, hospitals and then spreading to areas other than institutional structures.

The idea of the Panopticon and total surveillance was also a means to obtain knowledge of those confined and thus a further means of control. Foucault reasoned that if one is under the impression of always being under surveillance, an automatic functioning of power is assured. Eventually there is

no need for the physical presence of an actual enforcer; the individual incorporates the power to control himself. As Foucault states it:

He who is subjected to a field of visibility, and who knows it, assumes responsibility for the constraints of power; he makes them play spontaneously upon himself; he inscribes in himself the power relation in which he simultaneously plays both roles; he becomes the principle of his own subjection. By this very fact, the external power may throw off its physical weight; it tends to the non-corporal; and, the more it approaches this limit, the more constant, profound and permanent are its effects: it is a perpetual victory that avoids any physical confrontation and which is always decided in advance (202–03).

It is precisely this feature which has diffused into ever-widening facets of social space. The dispersal of discipline into "hundreds of tiny theatres of punishment" has become the new mode of control. Increasingly, we are watched by omnipresent video cameras, and all types of personal information is known about us through research and data banks. Formerly private domains are invaded to gather personal data for uses unknown to us. The computer has become a new power in its ability to manipulate knowledge of individuals. As Mark Poster, commenting on Foucault's work, writes:

The techniques of discipline no longer need rely on methods of regulating bodies in space . . . In the electronic age, spatial limitations are bypassed as restraints on the controlling hierarchies. All that is needed are traces of behavior: credit card activity, traffic tickets, telephone bills, loan applications, welfare files, fingerprints, income transactions, library records and so forth. On the basis of these traces, a computer can gather information that yields a surprisingly full picture of an individual's life. As a consequence, Panopticon monitoring extends not simply to massed groups but to the isolated individual . . . in his or her home, at play, in all mundane activities of everyday life (1984: 103).

If we fit modern corrections into this larger context of social control, we have a better grasp of the direction correctional strategies are taking. In Foucault's analysis, the wider structure of control is an outgrowth of mechanisms and concepts used to manage confined deviant populations. It is ironic that these mechanisms thought to have been diffused into society from the prison in turn now influence penal practice and correctional ideology. Regardless whether Foucault's analysis as to the origins of broader control mechanisms is correct, the increased prevalence of them cannot be denied.

## Ironies of Correctional Reform

This expansion of control has been recognized among criminologists and correctional reformers. However, the means used to remedy the problem have had unanticipated consequences. Much has been done, for example, in attempting to soften the negative effects of harsh control measures such as imprisonment. Beginning in the 1960s, "decarceration," "deinstitutionalization," "diversion," and "community corrections" became familiar rhetoric of movements to provide alternatives to the prison. The idea was simple enough. If offenders could be controlled with methods other than imprisonment, the stigma of imprisonment would be resolved. Offenders could be managed in the community and reintegration problems associated with confinement, often leading to repeat offenses, could be avoided. Labeling

theory had taught that societal reaction to behavior labeled delinquent or criminal was the source of the greatest difficulty. Moreover, it was the communities' responsibility to deal with their own offenders.

Diversion took the matter one step further. If the correctional system was stigma producing and contributed to secondary deviation (Lemert, 1951), then why not avoid the system altogether through alternative means? Provide alternative services that are not part of the formal correctional system. Treatment of offenders or delinquents would then be more individualized and geared to offenders' needs, thus assuring greater rates of success. Diversion caught both the professional and popular imagination. With calls for radical nonintervention (Schur, 1973), diversion programs proliferated (Lemert, 1981). Part of the responsiveness to diversionary efforts came from the fact that deinstitutionalization of the mentally ill, elderly, and retarded also was taking place (Warren, 1981); diversion of criminal offenders was a facet of a larger movement in mental health that already had taken hold.

An amazing range of programs and agencies were created, all with the purpose of providing "alternatives" to institutions and other formal correctional measures. But as critics began to point out, there was a big gap between the rhetoric of diversion and what was actually happening. Indeed, it became clear that instead of a weakening of state control, the correctional structures became stronger (Cohen, 1985), the nets of control became wider (Austin and Krisberg, 1981), and confinement was not reduced (Scull, 1984).

The persons selected for diversion to community programs were often minor offenders who under normal conditions either would have been dismissed or otherwise treated leniently with a fine or other simple disposition. These populations were now added to the correctional network, thus expanding the numbers in the population under some form of correctional control. At the same time, however, the numbers sentenced to prisons were not reduced but, as we have seen, considerably increased. Moreover, in some areas criminal justice organizations set up their own "diversion" process that totally defeated the principle envisioned. Nowhere was this more apparent than in the juvenile justice field. An early proponent of diversion, Edwin Lemert, writes:

> A salient unintended consequence of the diversion movement has been its substantial preemption by police and probation departments. In many areas they have set up in-house programs, hired their own personnel, and programmed cases in terms of their special ends and circumstances. . . . The effect has been little more than an expansion in the intake and discretionary powers of police and a shuffling of such powers from part of their organization to another (1981: 40).

This produced ever larger numbers of juvenile offenders because police, who usually release about one-half the youth with whom they have contact, under pressure to justify program funding "presumably have done what comes naturally or perhaps most easily, by dipping into this reservoir of youths who otherwise would have gone free in order to make desired referrals" (41).

It was not only among juvenile offenders that alternatives had the opposite effect. For example, halfway houses did not serve as replacements for prisons. Instead, offenders were exposed to both (Greenberg, 1975). Additional examples of various critical evaluations of alternatives to corrections abound (Cohen, 1985; Austin and Krisberg, 1981, 1982; Hylton, 1981, 1982; Lerman, 1980; Rutherford and Bengur, 1976; Klein, 1979).

This ironic expansion of the reach of officialdom in attempts to reduce or change it can be seen in other areas of crime control as well. The movement toward community participation in policing, ostensibly to bring about more neighborhood involvement in the formulation of crime control policy, has largely been coopted by the police, with citizens' efforts becoming mere adjuncts to and supports of established police practices (Einstadter, 1984). Seemingly, efforts to move from traditional correctional and law enforcement structures and radically change correctional practice consistently have had the opposite effect. By adding to the correctional apparatus, we have substantially increased the control over increased numbers of the population.

Another case in point is home incarceration. It represents a well-intended strategy of melioration gone awry in the context of a technological revolution. What was thought to be a strategy of reintegration has been transformed into a strategy of intrusion and control under the guise of allowing an offender the privilege of remaining in the community. Home incarceration cannot be seen apart from the development of a new surveillance industry that needs to find markets for its technology. Thus we see indications of corrections increasingly becoming the target of "social-control entrepreneurs" (Warren, 1981; Ball and Lilly, 1987) whose presence promises to further influence the direction of correctional change in line with their commercial interests. With home incarceration we see a unique transformation of a correctional strategy arising from a liberal ideology of melioration into one fitting a conservative ideology of efficiency and control through technological innovation. The control features of home incarceration were of course implicit at the outset; what has changed is the difference in emphasis and the rationale of its implementation.

## The True Face of Corrections?

Recall that the direction private correctional entrepreneurs are taking is not limited to program development but extends to the management of entire prisons and prison systems. Akin to Andrew T. Scull's (1981) description of aftercare treatment of mental patients under private auspices as a new "trade in lunacy," we can speak of the development of a new "trade in criminality." Since ultimately "investors" in corrections must meet costs and make profits, they have a stake in the continual flow of "raw material," to be processed at the lowest cost possible. Thus there is a strong tendency not only to have sufficient numbers of prisoners, since current programs run on a per capita contract basis, but to keep services at a minimum. Consequently, one would expect more persons imprisoned, under poorer conditions.

Whether this scenario will play out is conjecture. Yet the indicators (the heightened use of prison, the increasing number of persons under correctional supervision, an ideology favoring control as a crime policy, and an ideology of the marketplace that favors private over public solutions) are such that this is a realistic possibility. However, how long management of prisons and other correctional practices can last under private auspices without "eroding the rational–legal legitimations upon which the broader structure of . . . control is built" (Spitzer, 1979: 202) is open to question.

The direction corrections is taking, then, is generally one of expansion in mechanisms of control. Whether the expansion is in structures or in the use of technological devices, the emphasis remains the same. Of interest in terms of our previous references to conservative, liberal, and radical categories is the fact that alternative or diversionary measures described above were essentially the result of a liberal ideology of making system adjustments to improve correctional conditions. The strategy floundered because it failed to appreciate bureaucratic dynamics and proceeded on certain assumptions about the nature of the local community which did not match reality.

It was also a strategy that played into the hands of conservatives, who saw it as means to expand control over deviant populations, demonstrating once more the principle of emergence (see Chapter 2). This process of increased and often unrecognized measures of social control is compatible with the conservative turn of American politics which has emphasized control as its most prominent strategy of managing deviant populations. We have seen this realized in the general hardening of criminal justice policy, with the correctional system receiving increased numbers of prisoners for longer periods of time, the tightening of probation, and the abandonment or at least severe restrictions of parole. The treatment ideology was abandoned and the "justice model" was substituted.

## Beyond Corrections

### Inclusion and Exclusion

In a recent work on social control, Stanley Cohen (1985) argues that one can see the history of social control (including corrections) as cycling between periods where exclusionary measures predominate and those eras where inclusionary methods are uppermost in dealing with crime and deviance.

By exclusion he means such measures as "banishment and expulsion, segregation and isolation, designation, signification and classification, stigmatization." Inclusion refers to measures that employ "integration, assimilation, accommodation, normalization, toleration, absorption, engulfment, incorporation."

Cohen points to the 19th century as exclusionary in its approach to crime. Exclusionary correctional methods led to a reliance on brick, mortar, and steel, aversive "therapies," long-term confinement, and policies which resulted in restriction of civil rights of the accused. We would add that the 1980s have primarily emphasized an exclusionary mode.

By contrast, the 1960s were chiefly an inclusionary period. Inclusionary correctional methods involve a "softer" approach, with a greater reliance on less intrusive methods of control; prison is held as a last resort. More emphasis is placed on alternatives or community containment as a first step.

It is true that the movement toward diversion led to incredible paradoxes; however, as Cohen notes: "The inclusionary impulse . . . sensed what was wrong with the old (and now stronger) exclusionary systems . . . It still makes some sense to look for more humane, just and effective alternatives to such exclusionary institutions as prisons . . ." (1985: 267).

This conclusion does not deny the seriousness of some crimes, and the suffering such crimes cause their victims. The prison will always remain, not because imprisonment is a successful social practice, but because the prison symbolizes the anger generated by crime. How much exclusionary methods versus inclusionary methods are to be employed is a most complex question that cannot be answered here. But there are limits to the infliction of pain (Christie, 1981). The almost total reliance on control and exclusionary methods we are currently witnessing is a policy that history has shown to be inhumane. Moreover, in a society that professes democratic principles, an overreliance on control and exclusion raises questions of jus-

tice and creates conditions of resistance which may ultimately prove counterproductive.

Although subordinate to other agencies in the criminal justice network, corrections is the ultimate social control mechanism which defines societies' moral boundaries. The correctional system, however, cannot be relied on as the ultimate crime preventer; that task lies elsewhere. The task is to attempt to eliminate those features and conditions of society that have been shown to generate violent crime, the type people fear most and whose perpetrators end in the correctional system. What are these conditions and how could such a society be described?

If we wished to depict such a society, a society that contains a high amount of violence, it would, Elliott Currie cogently notes,

separate large numbers of people, especially the young, from the kind of work that could include them securely in community life. It would encourage policies of economic development and income distribution that sharply increased inequalities between sectors of the population. It would rapidly shift vast amounts of capital from place to place without regard for the impact on local communities, causing massive movements of population away from family and neighborhood supports in search of livelihood. It would avoid providing new mechanisms of care and support for those uprooted, perhaps in the name of preserving incentives to work and paring government spending. It would promote a culture of intense interpersonal competition and spur its citizens to a level of material consumption many could not lawfully sustain (1985: 278).

Does this society seem familiar? Perceived in these terms, it is perhaps easier to comprehend that the crime this society generates cannot be abated by ever harsher measures of control or by an ideology of corrections

**Chapter 14**

that produces strategies of exclusion. Indeed, precisely those conditions which prevent persons from becoming productive, socially conscious members of society, conditions which exclude and cast them out, are the conditions which create the dangerous crime potential we wish to prevent.

The current direction corrections is taking is exclusionary. Whether the cycle will change in the near future remains an open question, but our ultimate well-being as a democratic society depends on the answer.

# Bibliography

Abbott, Jack H.
1982  *In the belly of the beast.* New York: Vintage.

Adams, Stuart
1970  The PICO project. In *Sociology of punishment and correction,* ed. N. Johnston, L. Savitz, and M. E. Wolfgang, 2d ed., pp. 548–61. New York: Wiley.
1974  Measurement of effectiveness and efficiency in corrections. In *Handbook of criminology,* ed. D. Glaser, pp. 1021–49. Chicago: Rand-McNally.
1975  *Evaluation research in corrections.* Washington: U.S. Department of Justice, Law Enforcement Assistance Administration.

Adamson, Christopher
1983  Punishment after slavery: Southern state penal systems, 1865–1890. *Social Problems* 30: 555–69.
1984  Toward a Marxian penology: captive criminal populations as economic threats and resources. *Social Problems* 31: 435–58.

Akers, R. L., N. B. Hayner, and W. Gruninger
1977  Prisonization in five countries. *Criminology* 14: 527–54.

Albanese, Jay S.
1984  Concern about variation in criminal sentences: a cyclical history of reform. *Journal of Criminal Law and Criminology* 75: 260–71.

Alexander, Jack
1986  Classification objectives and practices. *Crime and Delinquency* 32: 323–38.

American Correctional Association
1978  *National jail and adult detention directory.* College Park, Md.: American Correctional Association.
1981  *Standards for adult local detention facilities.* College Park, Md.: American Correctional Association.

## Bibliography

American Friends Service Committee
1971 *Struggle for justice*. New York: Hill and Wang.

Anderson, Elaine A., and Graham B. Spanier
1980 Treatment of delinquent youth: the influence of the juvenile probation officer's perceptions of self and work. *Criminology* 17: 505–14.

Angelos, Claudia, and James B. Jacobs
1985 Prison overcrowding and the law. *Annals of the American Academy of Political and Social Science* 478: 100–12.

Arditi, R. R., F. Goldberg, Jr., M. M. Hartle, J. H. Peters, and W. R. Phelps
1973 The sexual segregation of American prisons. *Yale Law Journal* 82: 1269–71.

Arnold, William R.
1970 *Juveniles on parole*. New York: Random House.

Austin, James
1986 Using early release to relieve prison crowding. *Crime and Delinquency* 32: 404–502.

Austin, James, and Barry Krisberg
1981 Wider, stronger, and different nets: the dialectics of criminal justice reform. *Journal of Research in Crime and Delinquency* 18: 165–96.
1982 The unmet promise of alternatives to incarceration. *Crime and Delinquency* 28: 374–409.

Avi-Itzhak, Benjamin, and Reuel Shinnar
1973 Quantitative models in crime control. *Journal of Criminal Justice* 1: 185–217.

Bailey, Walter C.
1966 Correctional outcome: an evaluation of 100 reports. *Journal of Criminal Law, Criminology and Police Science* 57: 153–60.

Bailey, William C., and Ruth D. Peterson
1981 Legal versus extra-legal determinants of juvenile court dispositions. *Juvenile and Family Court Journal* 32: 41–59.

Balbus, Isaac D.
1973 *The dialectics of legal repression*. New York: Russell Sage.

Ball, Richard A., and J. Robert Lilly
1985 Home incarceration: an international alternative to institutional incarceration. *International Journal of Comparative and Applied Criminal Justice* 9: 85–97.
1986a The potential use of home incarceration for drunken drivers. *Crime and Delinquency* 32: 224–47.
1986b A theoretical examination of home incarceration. *Federal Probation* 50: 17–24.
1987 The phenomenology of privacy and the power of the state: home incarceration with electronic monitoring. In *Critical issues in criminology and criminal justice*, ed. J. E. Scott and T. Hirschi. Beverly Hills, Calif.: Sage.

Ball, R. A., R. C. Huff, and J. R. Lilly
1987 Introduction. In *House arrest and correctional policy*, ed. J. Inciardi. Newbery Park, Calif.: Sage.

Bartollas, C., S. J. Miller, and S. Dinitz
1976 *Juvenile victimization: the organizational paradox*. Beverly Hills, Calif.: Sage.

Bartollas, Clemens, and Christopher M. Sieverdes
1981 The victimized white in a juvenile correctional system. *Crime and Delinquency* 27: 534–43.

Baunach, Phyllis Jo
1980 Random assignment in criminal justice research: some ethical and legal issues. *Criminology* 17: 435–45.
1985 *Mothers in prison*. New Brunswick, N.J.: Transaction Books.

Bayer, Ronald
1981 Crime, punishment, and the decline of liberal optimism. *Crime and Delinquency* 27: 169–90.

Becker, Howard S.
1963 *Outsiders*. New York: Free Press.
1967 Whose side are we on? *Social Problems* 14: 239–47.

Beirne, Piers, and Richard Quinney, eds.
1982 *Marxism and law*. New York: Wiley.

Berger, Peter L., and Thomas Luckmann
1966 *Social construction of reality*. Garden City, N.Y.: Anchor.

Berk, R. A., K. J. Lenihan, and P. H. Rossi
  1980  Crime and poverty: some experimental evidence from ex-offenders. *American Sociological Review* 45: 239–47.

Berk, R. A., S. L. Messinger, D. Rauma, and J. E. Berecochea
  1983  Prisons as self-regulating systems: a comparison of historical patterns in California for male and female offenders. *Law & Society Review* 17: 547–86.

Berk, R. A., D. Rauma, S. L. Messinger, and T. F. Cooley
  1981  A test of the stability of punishment hypothesis: the case of California, 1851–1970. *American Sociological Review* 46: 805–20.

Berry, Bonnie
  1985  Electronic jails: a new criminal justice concern. *Justice Quarterly* 2: 1–22.

Binder, Arnold, and Gilbert Geis
  1984  *Ad populum* argumentation in criminology: juvenile diversion as rheoric. *Crime and Delinquency* 30: 624–47.

Blau, Peter, and W. Richard Scott
  1962  *Formal organizations.* San Francisco: Chandler.

Blumberg, Abraham S.
  1967  *Criminal justice.* New York: Franklin Watts.

Blumer, Herbert
  1967  Threats from agency-determined research: the case of Camelot. In *Rise and fall of Project Camelot,* ed. I. L. Horowitz, pp. 153–76. Cambridge, Mass.: M.I.T. Press.

Blumstein, Alfred, and Jacqueline Cohen
  1979  Estimation of individual crime rates from arrest records. *Journal of Criminal Law and Criminology* 70: 561–85.

Blumstein, A., J. Cohen, and P. Hsieh
  1982  *The duration of adult criminal careers: Final report to the National Institute of Justice.* Pittsburgh: Carnegie-Mellon University.

Blumstein, A., J. Cohen, S. E. Martin, and M. H. Tonry, eds.
  1983a  *Research on sentencing: the search for reform* (vol. 1). Washington: National Academy Press.
  1983b  *Research on sentencing: the search for reform* (vol. 2). Washington: National Academy Press.

Blumstein, A., J. Cohen, and D. Nagin, eds.
  1978  *Deterrence and incapacitation.* Washington: National Academy of Sciences.

Bohm, Robert M.
  1982  Radical criminology: an explication. *Criminology* 19: 565–89.
  1984  Beyond employment: toward a radical solution to the crime problem. *Crime and Social Justice* 21–22: 213–22.

Boland, Barbara
  1978  Incapacitation of the dangerous offender: The arithmetic is not so simple. *Journal of Research in Crime and Delinquency* 15: 126–29.

Boland, Barbara, with Ronald Sones
  1986  *The prosecution of felony arrests, 1981.* Washington: U.S. Department of Justice, Bureau of Justice Statistics.

Bonger, Willem A.
  1969  *Criminality and economic conditions* (original English language translation published in 1916). Bloomington: Indiana Univ. Press.

Bonham, G., Jr., G. Janeksela, J. Bardo, and R. Iacovetta
  1984  Predicting parole outcome via discriminant analysis. *Justice Quarterly* 1: 329–41.

Bortner, M. A.
  1982  *Inside a juvenile court.* New York: University Press of America.
  1986  Traditional rhetoric, organizational realities: remand of juveniles to adult court. *Crime and Delinquency* 32: 53–74.

Bowers, William J., with G. L. Pierce and J. F. McDevitt
  1984  *Legal homicide: death as punishment in America, 1864–1982.* Boston: Northeastern University Press.

Bowker, Lee H.
  1977  *Prisoner subcultures.* Lexington, Mass.: D.C. Heath.

1980 *Prison victimization.* New York: Elsevier.

1981 Gender differences in prisoner sub-cultures. In *Women and Crime,* ed. L. Bowker, pp. 409–19. New York: Macmillan.

1982 Victimizers and victims in American correctional institutions. In *The pains of imprisonment,* ed. R. Johnson and H. Toch, pp. 63–76. Beverly Hills, Calif.: Sage.

Box, Steven, and Chris Hale

1982 Economic crisis and the rising prisoner population in England and Wales. *Crime and Social Justice* 17: 20–35.

1985 Unemployment, imprisonment and prison overcrowding. *Contemporary Crises* 9: 209–28.

Braly, Malcolm

1976 *False starts.* Boston: Little, Brown.

Brenzel, Barbara M.

1983 *Daughters of the state.* Cambridge, Mass.: M.I.T. Press.

Brewer, D., G. E. Beckett, and N. Holt

1981 Determinate sentencing in California. *Journal of Research in Crime and Delinquency* 18: 200–31.

Brim, Orville G., Jr., and Stanton Wheeler

1966 *Socialization after childhood.* New York: Wiley.

Broach, G. T., P. D. Jackson, and V. H. Ascolillo

1978 State political culture and sentence severity in federal district courts. *Criminology* 16: 373–82.

Brown, Claude

1965 *Manchild in the promised land.* New York: Macmillan.

Brown, Waln K.

1983 *The other side of delinquency.* New Brunswick, N.J.: Rutgers Univ. Press.

Bunker, Edward

1981 *Little boy blue.* New York: Viking.

Burkhart, Kathryn W.

1973 *Women in prison.* Garden City, N.Y.: Doubleday.

Burns, Tom, and George M. Stalker

1961 *Management of innovation.* London: Tavistock.

Campbell, Donald T.

1971 Reforms as experiments. In *Readings in evaluation research,* ed. F. G. Caro, pp. 233–61. New York: Russell Sage.

Campbell, Donald T., and H. Laurence Ross

1968 The Connecticut crackdown on speeding: time-series data in quasi-experimental design. *Law & Society Review* 3: 33–53.

Campbell, Donald T., and Julian C. Stanley

1966 *Experimental and quasi-experimental designs for research.* Chicago: Rand McNally.

Carlen, P.

1983 *Women's imprisonment: a study in social control.* London: Routledge and Keagan Paul.

Carlson, Rick J.

1976 *Dilemmas of corrections.* Lexington, Mass.: D.C. Heath.

Carroll, J. S., R. L. Wiener, D. Coates, J. Galegher, and J. J. Alibrio

1982 Evaluation, diagnosis, and prediction in parole decision making. *Law & Society Review* 17: 199–228.

Carroll, Leo, and C. P. Cornell

1985 Racial composition, sentencing reforms, and rates of incarceration, 1970–1980. *Justice Quarterly* 2: 473–90.

Carter, Robert M., and Leslie T. Wilkins

1967 Some factors in sentencing policy. *Journal of Criminal Law, Criminology and Police Science* 58: 503–14.

Carter, Timothy J.

1979 Juvenile court dispositions. *Criminology* 17: 341–59.

Carter, Timothy J., and Donald Clelland

1979 A neo-Marxian critique, formulation and test of juvenile dispositions as a function of social class. *Social Problems* 27: 96–108.

Cartwright, Dorwin

1951 Achieving change in people; some applications of group dynamics theory. *Human Relations* 4: 381–92.

Casper, Jonathan D.

1978a *Criminal courts: the defendant's perspective.* Washington: U.S. Department of

Justice, National Institute of Law Enforcement and Criminal Justice.

1978b Having their day in court: defendant evaluations of the fairness of their treatment. *Law & Society Review* 12: 237–51.

Casper, Jonathan D., and David Brereton

1984 Evaluating criminal justice reforms. *Law & Society Review* 18: 121–44.

Casper, J., D. Brereton, and D. Neal

1983 The California determinate sentence law. *Criminal Law Bulletin* 19: 405–33.

Cavender, Gray

1984 Justice, sanctioning and the justice model. *Criminology* 22: 203–13.

Chaiken, Jan M., and Marcia R. Chaiken

1982 *Varieties of criminal behavior.* Santa Monica, Calif.: Rand Corporation.

Chandler, Edna W.

1973 *Women in prison.* Indianapolis: Bobbs-Merrill.

Christianson, Scott

1981 Our black prisons. *Crime and Delinquency* 27: 364–75.

Christie, Nils

1981 *Limits to pain.* Oxford: Martin Robertson.

Citizens' Inquiry on Parole and Criminal Justice

1975 *Prison without walls.* New York: Praeger.

Clarke, Stevens

1974 Getting 'em out of circulation: Does incarceration of juvenile offenders reduce crime? *Journal of Criminal Law and Criminology* 67: 528–35.

Claster, Daniel S.

1967 Comparison of risk perception between delinquents and nondelinquents. *Journal of Criminal Law, Criminology and Police Science* 58: 80–86.

Clear, Todd R., and George F. Cole

1986 *American corrections.* Monterey, Calif.: Brooks/Cole.

Clear, Todd R., and Kenneth W. Gallagher

1985 Probation and parole supervision: a review of current classification practices. *Crime and Delinquency* 31: 423–43.

Clear, T. R., J. D. Hewitt, and R. M. Regoli

1977 Discretion and the determinate sentence: its distribution, control and effect on time served. Paper presented to the American Society of Criminology, Atlanta.

Clemmer, Donald

1958 *The prison community* (originally published in 1940). New York: Holt, Rinehart and Winston.

Clinard, Marshall B.

1949 The group approach to social reintegration. *American Sociological Review* 14: 257–62.

Cohen, Fred

1983 Probation and parole: procedural protection. In *Encyclopedia of crime and justice,* ed. S. H. Kadish, pp. 1240–46. New York: Macmillan.

Cohen, Jacqueline

1983a *Incapacitating criminals: recent research findings.* Washington: U.S. Department of Justice, National Institute of Justice.

1983b Incapacitation as a strategy for crime control: possibilities and pitfalls. In *Crime and justice* (vol. 5), ed. M. Tonry and N. Morris, pp. 1–85. Chicago: Univ. of Chicago Press.

Cohen, Lawrence E., and James R. Kluegel

1978 Determinants of juvenile court dispositions: ascriptive and achieved factors in two metropolitan courts. *American Sociological Review* 43: 162–76.

Cohen, Stanley

1985 *Visions of social control.* Cambridge, U.K.: Polity Press.

Cole, G. F., R. A. Hanson, and J. E. Silbert

1982 Mediation: Is it an effective alternative to adjudication in solving prisoner complaints? *Judicature* 65: 481–89.

Conrad, John P.

1985 The penal dilemma and its emerging solution. *Crime and Delinquency* 31: 411–22.

Cook, Thomas D., and Donald T. Campbell

1979 *Quasi-experimentation.* Chicago: Rand McNally.

Cook, Thomas D., and Charles S. Reichardt, eds.

1979 *Qualitative and quantitative methods in evaluation research.* Beverly Hills, Calif.: Sage.

Corbett, R. P., and E. A. L. Fersch
1985 Home as prison: the use of house arrest. *Federal Probation* 49: 13–17.

Corrections Corporation of America
1985 Proposal for state of Tennessee. Nashville: Corrections Corporation of America.

Covey, Herbert C., and Mary Mande
1985 Determinate sentencing in Colorado. *Justice Quarterly* 2: 259–70.

Cressey, Donald R.
1955 Changing criminals: The application of the theory of differential association. *American Journal of Sociology* 61: 115–120.
1958 The nature and effectiveness of correctional techniques. *Law and Contemporary Problems* 23: 754–72.
1965 Social psychological foundations for using criminals in the rehabilitation of criminals. *Journal of Research in Crime and Delinquency* 1: 49–59.

Crotty, Norma
1983 The guard's world. In *New perspectives on prisons and imprisonment*, ed. J. B. Jacobs, pp. 133–41. Ithaca, N.Y.: Cornell Univ. Press.

Cullen, Francis T., and Karen E. Gilbert
1982 *Reaffirming rehabilitation.* Cincinnati: Anderson.

Cullen, Francis T., and John Wozniak
1982 Fighting the appeal of repression. *Crime and Social Justice* 18: 23–34.

Currie, Elliott
1973 *Managing the minds of men: the reformatory movement, 1865–1920.* Unpublished doctoral dissertation, University of California-Berkeley.
1985 *Confronting crime.* New York: Pantheon.

Curry, P. M.
1975 Probation and individualized disposition: a study of factors associated with the presentence recommendation. *American Journal of Criminal Law* 4: 31–81.

Dannefer, Dale, and Russell K. Schutt
1982 Race and juvenile justice processing in court and police agencies. *American Journal of Sociology* 87: 1113–32.

Davidson, Theodore R.
1983 *Chicano prisoners: the key to San Quentin.* Prospect Heights, Ill.: Waveland Press.

Davies, Malcolm
1985 Determinate sentencing reform in California and its impact on the penal system. *British Journal of Criminology* 25: 1–30.

Davis, Allan J.
1968 Sexual assaults in the Philadelphia prison system and sheriff's vans. *Trans-Action* 6: 8–16.

Dawson, Robert O.
1966 The decision to grant or deny parole: a study of parole criteria in law and practice. *Washington University Law Quarterly* 1966: 243–303.

Dembo, Robert O.
1972 Orientation and activities of the parole officer. *Criminology* 10: 193–215.

Dershowitz, Alan M.
1971 The law of dangerousness: some fictions about predictions. *Journal of Legal Education* 23: 24–48.

Dewitt, Charles B.
1986 *New construction methods for correctional facilities.* Washington: U.S. Department of Justice, National Institute of Justice.

Dobash, R. P., R. E. Dobash, and S. Gutteridge
1986 *The imprisonment of women.* New York: Basil Blackwell.

Einstadter, Werner
1984 Citizen patrols: prevention or control? *Crime and Social Justice* 21–22: 200–12.

Emerson, Robert M.
1969 *Judging delinquents.* Chicago: Aldine.
1983 Holistic effects in social control decision-making. *Law & Society Review* 17: 425–55.

Empey, Lamar T., and Jerome Rabow
1961 The Provo experiment in delinquency rehabilitation. *American Sociological Review* 26: 679–95.

England, Ralph W.
1955 A study of postprobation recidivism among five hundred federal offenders. *Federal Probation* 19: 10–16.

Erickson, R. J., W. J. Crow, L. A. Zurcher, and A. V. Connett
1973 *Paroled but not free.* New York: Behavioral Publications.

Erwin, Billie S.
1984 *Evaluation of intensive probation supervision in Georgia.* Atlanta: Georgia Department of Offender Rehabilitation, Office of Evaluation.

Espy, Watt
1980a The historical perspective. In *Slow coming dark,* ed. D. Magee, pp. 163–74. New York: Pilgrim Press.
1980b Capital punishment and deterrence: what the statistics cannot show. *Crime and Delinquency* 26: 537–44.

Etzioni, Amitai
1964 *Modern organizations.* Englewood Cliffs, N.J.: Prentice-Hall.

Farrington, David P.
1983 Randomized experiments on crime and justice. In *Crime and justice* (vol. 4), ed. M. Tonry and N. Morris, pp. 257–308. Chicago: Univ. of Chicago Press.

Feeley, Malcolm
1979 *The process is the punishment.* New York: Russell Sage.

Feinman, C.
1980 *Women in the criminal justice system.* New York: Praeger.

Feld, Barry C.
1977 *Neutralizing inmate violence.* Cambridge, Mass.: Ballinger.
1981 A comparative analysis of organizational structure and inmate subcultures in institutions for juvenile offenders. *Crime and Delinquency* 27: 336–63.

Figueira-McDonough, J., A. Iglehart, R. Sarri, and T. Williams
1981 *Females in prison in Michigan, 1968–1978.* Ann Arbor: University of Michigan, Institute for Social Research.

Fisher, H. Richmond
1974 Parole and probation revocation procedures after *Morrissey* and *Gagnon. Journal of Criminal Law and Criminology* 65: 46–61.

Fisher, Sethard
1961 Social organization in a correctional residence. *Pacific Sociological Review* 4: 87–93.

Flanagan, Timothy J., and Edmund F. McGarrell, eds.
1986 *Sourcebook of Criminal Justice Statistics—1985.* Washington: U.S. Government Printing Office.

Flynn, Edith Elisabeth
1973 Jails and criminal justice. In *Prisoners in America,* ed. L. E. Ohlin, pp. 49–88. Englewood Cliffs, N.J.: Prentice-Hall.
1983 Jails. In *Encyclopedia of crime and justice,* ed. S. H. Kadish, pp. 915–22. New York: Macmillan.

Fogel, David
1975 *We are the living proof.* Cincinnati: Anderson.

Fogel, David, and Joe Hudson, eds.
1981 *Justice as fairness: perspectives on the justice model.* Cincinnati: Anderson.

Forst, B., W. Rhodes, J. Dimm, A. Gelman, and B. Mullin
1982 *Targeting federal resources on recidivists.* Washington: INSLAW, Inc.

Fosen, Robert H., and Jay Campbell, Jr.
1966 Common sense and correctional science. *Journal of Research in Crime and Delinquency* 3: 73–81.

Foucault, Michel
1979 *Discipline and punish: the birth of the prison.* New York: Vintage.

Fox, James G.
1982 *Organizational and racial conflict in maximum security prisons.* Lexington, Mass.: D. C. Heath.

Frankel, Marvin E.
1973 *Criminal sentences.* New York: Hill and Wang.

Frazier, Charles E., and John K. Cochran
1986 Official intervention, diversion from the juvenile justice system, and dynamics of human service work. *Crime and Delinquency* 32: 147–76.

Freedman, Estelle B.
1981 *Their sisters' keepers.* Ann Arbor: Univ. of Michigan Press.

Galliher, John F., and James L. McCartney
1973 The influence of funding agencies on juvenile delinquency research. *Social Problems* 21: 77–90.

Gatz, Nick, and Gennaro F. Vito
1982 The use of the determinate sentence— an historical perspective. *Journal of Criminal Justice* 10: 323–29.

Gaylin, Willard
1974 *Partial justice.* New York: Knopf.

Genego, W. J., P. D. Goldberger, and V. C. Jackson
1975 Parole release decision-making and the sentencing process. *Yale Law Journal* 84: 810–903.

Giallombardo, Rose
1966 *Society of women.* New York: Wiley.
1974 *The social world of imprisoned girls.* New York: Wiley.

Gibbons, Don C.
1979 *The criminological enterprise.* Englewood Cliffs, N.J.: Prentice-Hall.

Gibbs, Jack P.
1975 *Crime, punishment and deterrence.* New York: Elsevier.

Gibbs, John J.
1982 Disruption and distress: going from the street to jail. In *Coping with imprisonment,* ed. N. Parisi, pp. 29–44. Beverly Hills, Calif.: Sage.
1983 Problems and priorities: perceptions of jail custodians and social service providers. *Journal of Criminal Justice* 11: 327–38.

Gilman, David
1975 Developments in correctional law. *Crime and Delinquency* 21: 163–73.

Glaser, Daniel
1964 *The effectiveness of a prison and parole system.* Indianapolis: Bobbs-Merrill.
1965 Correctional research: an elusive paradise. *Journal of Research in Crime and Delinquency* 2: 1–11.
1971 Some notes on urban jails. In *Crime in the*

city, ed. D. Glaser, pp. 236–44. New York: Harper & Row.
1973 *Routinizing evaluation.* Washington: National Institute of Mental Health, Center for Studies of Crime and Delinquency.
1985 Who gets probation and parole: case study versus actuarial decision making. *Crime and Delinquency* 31: 367–77.

Glaser, Daniel, and Max S. Zeigler
1974 Use of the death penalty v. outrage at murder. *Crime and Delinquency* 20: 333–38.

Glick, Ruth M., and Virginia V. Neto
1977 *National study of women's correctional programs.* Washington: U.S. Department of Justice, National Institute of Law Enforcement and Criminal Justice.

Goetting, Ann, and Roy Michael Howsen
1983 Women in prison: a profile. *Prison Journal* 63: 27–47.

Goffman, Erving
1961 *Asylums.* Garden City, N.Y.: Anchor.

Goldfarb, Ronald
1975 *Jails.* Garden City, N.Y.: Anchor.

Goldfarb, Ronald L., and Linda R. Singer
1970 Redressing prisoner grievances. *George Washington Law Review* 39: 174–320.

Goode, Erich
1969 Marijuana and the politics of reality. *Journal of Health and Social Behavior* 10: 83–94.

Goodstein, Lynne
1984 *Determinate sentencing and the correctional process.* Washington: U.S. Department of Justice, National Institute of Justice.

Goodstein, Lynne, and John Hepburn
1985 *Determinate sentencing and imprisonment: a failure of reform.* Cincinnati: Anderson.

Gottfredson, Don M.
1970 Assessment of prediction methods. In *Sociology of Punishment and Correction,* 2d ed., ed. N. Johnston, L. Savitz, and M. Wolfgang, pp. 745–71. New York: Wiley.
1983 Probation and parole: release and revocation. In *Encyclopedia of crime and jus-*

*tice*, ed. S. H. Kadish, pp. 1127–35. New York: Macmillan.

Gottfredson, D. M., C. A. Cosgrove, L. T. Wilkins, J. Wallerstein, and C. Rauh
1978 *Classification for parole decision policy.* Washington: U.S. Department of Justice, National Institute of Law Enforcement and Criminal Justice.

Gottfredson, D. M., L. T. Wilkins, and P. B. Hoffman
1978 *Guidelines for parole and sentencing.* Lexington, Mass.: D. C. Heath.

Gottfredson, Michael, and Travis Hirschi
1986 The true value of Lambda would appear to be zero. *Criminology* 24: 213–34.

Gottfredson, M. R., S. D. Mitchell-Herzfeld, and T. J. Flanagan
1982 Another look at the effectiveness of parole supervision. *Journal of Research in Crime and Delinquency* 19: 277–98.

Greenberg, David F.
1972 The special effects of penal measures (treatment, special deterrence, etc.): a descriptive summary of existing studies. Washington: Committee for the Study of Incarceration (staff memorandum).
1974 Much ado about little: the correctional effects of corrections. New York Univ., Department of Sociology (mimeo).
1975a The incapacitative effects of imprisonment: some estimates. *Law & Society Review* 9: 541–80.
1975b Problems in community corrections. *Issues in Criminology* 10: 1–34.
1977a The correctional effects of corrections. In *Corrections and punishment*, ed. D. F. Greenberg, pp. 111–48. Beverly Hills, Calif.: Sage.
1977b Fixed sentencing: the cooptation of a radical reform. Paper presented at the meeting of the American Society of Criminology, Atlanta.
1981 *Crime and capitalism.* Palo Alto, Calif.: Mayfield.
1983 Reflection on the justice model debate. *Contemporary Crises* 7: 313–27.

Greenberg, David F., and Drew Humphries
1980 The cooptation of fixed sentencing reform. *Crime and Delinquency* 26: 206–25.
1982 Economic crisis and the justice model: a skeptical view. *Crime and Delinquency* 28: 601–9.

Greenwood, Peter W.
1983 Controlling the crime rate through imprisonment. In *Crime and public policy*, ed. J. Q. Wilson, pp. 251–69. San Francisco: ICS Press.

Greenwood, Peter W., with Allan Abrahamse
1982 *Selective incapacitation.* Santa Monica, Calif.: Rand Corporation.

Gross, Bertram
1982 Some anticrime proposals for progressives. *Crime and Social Justice* 17: 51–55.

Gross, Seymour Z.
1967 The prehearing juvenile report: probation officers' conceptions. *Journal of Research in Crime and Delinquency* 3: 212–17.

Hagan, Frank E.
1982 *Research methods in criminal justice and criminology.* New York: Macmillan.

Hagan, John
1974 Extra-legal attributes and criminal sentencing: an assessment of a sociological viewpoint. *Law & Society Review* 8: 357–83.
1975 The social and legal construction of criminal justice: a study of the pre-sentencing process. *Social Problems* 22: 620–37.
1983 Making sense of sentencing: a review and critique of sentencing research. In *Research on sentencing* (vol. 2), ed. A. Blumstein, J. Cohen, S. E. Martin, and M. H. Tonry, pp. 1–55. Washington: National Academy Press.

Hagan, John, and Ilene N. Bernstein
1979 Conflict in context: the sanctioning of draft resisters, 1963–76. *Social Problems* 27: 109–22.

Hagan, J., J. D. Hewitt, and D. F. Alwin
1979 Ceremonial justice: crime and punishment in a loosely coupled system. *Social Forces* 58: 506–27.

Hakeem, Michael
1961 Prediction of parole outcome from sum-

maries of case histories. *Journal of Criminal Law, Criminology and Police Science* 52: 145–55.

Haney, C., C. Banks, and P. Zimbardo
1973    Interpersonal dynamics in a simulated prison. *International Journal of Criminology and Penology* 1: 69–97.

Hardesty, Monica, and Jim Thomas
1986    Prisoner litigation: boom or bane? Paper presented at the annual meeting of the American Society of Criminology, Atlanta.

Harris, Jean
1986    *Stranger in two worlds.* New York: Macmillan.

Hartnagel, Timothy F., and Mary Ellen Gillan
1980    Female prisoners and the inmate code. *Pacific Sociological Review* 23: 85–104.

Hasenfeld, Yeheskel, and Paul P. L. Cheung
1985    The juvenile court as a people-processing organization: a political economy perspective. *American Journal of Sociology* 90: 801–24.

Hawkins, Darnell
1985    Trends in black–white imprisonment: changing conceptions of race or changing conceptions of social control? *Crime and Social Justice* 24: 187–209.

Heffernan, Esther
1972    *Making it in prison.* New York: Wiley.

Heidensohn, Frances
1985    *Women in crime.* New York: New York Univ. Press.

Henretta, J. C., C. F. Frazier, and D. Bishop
1986    The effect of prior case outcomes on juvenile justice decision-making. *Social Forces* 65: 554–62.

Hepburn, John R., and Lynne Goodstein
1986    Organizational imperatives and sentencing reform implementation. *Crime and Delinquency* 32: 339–66.

Heumann, Milton, and Colin Loftin
1979    Mandatory sentencing and the abolition of plea bargaining. *Law & Society Review* 13: 393–430.

Hewitt, John D., and Todd R. Clear
1983    *The impact of sentencing reform.* New York: University Press of America.

Hirschi, Travis
1969    *Causes of delinquency.* Berkeley: Univ. of California Press.

Hoffman, Peter B.
1983    Probation and parole: parole guidelines. In *Encyclopedia of crime and justice,* ed. S. H. Kadish, pp. 1234–39. New York: Macmillan.

Hoffman, Peter B., and Lucille K. DeGostin
1974    Parole decision-making: structuring discretion. *Federal Probation* 44: 44–52.

Hoffman, Peter B., and Barbara Stone-Meierhoefer
1980    Reporting recidivism rates: the criterion and follow-up issues. *Journal of Criminal Justice* 8: 53–60.

Hogarth, John
1971    *Sentencing as a human process.* Toronto: Univ. of Toronto Press.

Honderich, Thomas
1982    On justifying protective punishment. *British Journal of Criminology* 2: 268–75.

Hood, R. G.
1971    Some research results and problems. In *The criminal in confinement,* ed. L. Radzinowicz and M. Wolfgang, pp. 159–82. New York: Basic Books.

Horowitz, Irving L., and Martin L. Liebowitz
1968    Social deviance and political marginality: toward redefinition of the relation between sociology and politics. *Social Problems* 15: 280–96.

Horwitz, Allan, and Michael Wasserman
1980    Some misleading conceptions in sentencing research. *Criminology* 18: 411–24.

Huff, R. C., R. A. Ball, and J. R. Lilly
1987    Social and legal issues of home confinement. In *House arrest and correctional policy,* ed. J. Inciardi. Newbery Park, Calif.: Sage.

Hughes, Everett C.
1971    Good people and dirty work. In *The*

*sociological eye* (vol. 1), ed. E. C. Hughes, pp. 87–98. Chicago: Aldine-Atherton.

Hughes, Thomas R., and David M. Altschuler
1982 Juvenile detention facilities: summary report of a second national survey. *Juvenile and Family Court Journal* 33: 3–15.

Hylton, John
1981 *Reintegrating the offender.* Washington: University Press of America.
1982 Rhetoric and reality: a critical appraisal of community correctional programs. *Crime and Delinquency* 28: 341–73.

Ignatieff, Michael
1978 *A just measure of pain.* New York: Pantheon.
1981 State, civil society and total institutions: a critique of recent social histories of punishment. In *Crime and justice* (vol. 3), ed. M. Tonry and N. Morris, pp. 153–92. Chicago: Univ. of Chicago Press.

Inciardi, James A.
1984 *Criminal justice.* Orlando, Fla.: Academic Press.

Irwin, John
1970 *The Felon.* Englewood Cliffs, N.J.: Prentice-Hall.
1977 The changing social structure of the men's prison. In *Corrections and punishment,* ed. D. F. Greenberg, pp. 21–40. Beverly Hills, Calif.: Sage.
1980 *Prisons in turmoil.* Boston: Little, Brown.
1985 *The jail.* Berkeley: Univ. of California Press.

Irwin, John, and Donald R. Cressey
1962 Thieves, convicts and the inmate culture. *Social Problems* 10: 142–55.

Jackson, Patrick G.
1983 *The paradox of control: parole supervision of youthful offenders.* New York: Praeger.

Jacobs, James B.
1974 Street gangs behind bars. *Social Problems* 21: 395–409.
1976 The Stateville counsellors: symbol of reform in search of a role. *Social Service Review* 50: 136–47.
1979 Race relations and the prisoner subculture. In *Crime and justice* (vol. 1), ed.

N. Morris and M. Tonry, pp. 1–27. Chicago: Univ. of Chicago Press.
1983a Town-prison relations as a determinant of reform. In *New perspectives on prisons and imprisonment,* ed. J. B. Jacobs, pp. 99–106. Ithaca, N.Y.: Cornell Univ. Press.
1983b *New perspectives on prisons and imprisonment.* Ithaca, N.Y.: Cornell Univ. Press.

Jericho
1985 The trend to privatization: update and analysis. Washington: National Moratorium on Prison Construction.

Johnson, Perry M.
1978 The role of quarantine in reducing violent crime. *Crime and Delinquency* 24: 465–85.

Johnson, Robert
1981 *Condemned to die: life under sentence of death.* New York: Elsevier.
1987 *Hard time: understanding and reforming the prison.* Monterey, Calif.: Brooks/Cole.

Jurik, Nancy C.
1985 Individual and organizational determinants of correctional officer attitudes toward inmates. *Criminology* 23: 523–39.

Jurik, Nancy C., and Michael C. Musheno
1986 The internal crisis of corrections: professionalization and the work environment. *Justice Quarterly* 3: 457–80.

Kassebaum, G., D. A. Ward, and D. M. Wilner
1971 *Prison treatment and parole survival.* New York: Wiley.

King, Daniel B.
1969 Religious freedom in the correctional institution. *Journal of Criminal Law, Criminology, and Police Science* 60: 299–310.

Kingsworth, R., and L. Rizzo
1979 Decision-making in the criminal courts: continuities and discontinuities. *Criminology* 17: 3–14.

Kitsuse, John I., and Aaron V. Cicourel
1963 A note on the uses of official statistics. *Social Problems* 11: 131–39.

Kleck, Gary
1981 Racial discrimination in criminal sentencing. *American Sociological Review* 46: 783–805.

Klein, Malcolm W.
1979 Deinstitutionalization and diversion of juvenile offenders: a litany of impediments. In *Crime and justice* (vol. 1), ed. N. Morris and M. Tonry, pp. 145–201. Chicago: Univ. of Chicago Press.

Korn, Richard
1971 Of crime, criminal justice and corrections. *University of San Francisco Law Review* 6: 27–75.

Kramer, John H., and Rogin L. Lubitz
1985 Pennsylvania's sentencing reform: the impact of commission-established guidelines. *Crime and Delinquency* 31: 481–500.

Krisberg, Barry, and James Austin
1978 *The children of Ishmael: critical perspectives on juvenile justice.* Palo Alto, Calif.: Mayfield.

LaFree, Gary
1986 Adversarial and nonadversarial justice: a comparison of guilty pleas and trials. *Criminology* 23: 289–312.

Lampman, H. P.
1973 *The wire womb.* Chicago: Nelson-Hall.

Langan, Patrick A.
1985 Racism on trial: new evidence to explain the racial composition of prisons in the United States. *Journal of Criminal Law and Criminology* 76: 666–83.

Langan, Patrick A., and Lawrence A. Greenfeld
1985 *The prevalence of imprisonment.* Washington: U.S. Department of Justice, Bureau of Justice Statistics.

Legal Defense Fund
1985 *Death row, U.S.A.* New York: Legal Defense Fund.

Lemert, Edwin M.
1951 *Social pathology.* New York: McGraw-Hill.
1981 Diversion in juvenile justice: what hath been wrought? *Journal of Research in Crime and Delinquency* 18: 34–46.

Leopold, Nathan, F., Jr.
1958 *Life plus 99 years.* Garden City, N.Y.: Doubleday.

Lerman, Paul
1968 Evaluative studies of institutions for delinquents. *Social Work* 13: 55–64.
1975 *Community treatment and social control.* Chicago: Univ. of Chicago Press.
1980 Trends and issues in the deinstitutionalization of youths in trouble. *Crime and Delinquency* 26: 281–98.
1984 Child welfare, the private sector, and community-based corrections. *Crime and Delinquency* 30: 5–38.

Lerner, K., G. Arling, and S. C. Baird
1986 Client management classification strategies for case supervision. *Crime and Delinquency* 32: 254–71.

Lerner, Mark Jay
1977 The effectiveness of a definite sentence parole program. *Criminology* 15: 211–24.

Levin, Martin A.
1971 Policy evaluation and recidivism. *Law & Society Review* 6: 17–45.

Lilly, J. R., R. A. Ball, and W. R. Lotz, Jr.
1986 Electronic jail revisited. *Justice Quarterly* 3: 231–61.

Link, Christopher T., and Neal Shover
1986 The origins of criminal sentencing reform. *Justice Quarterly* 3: 329–42.

Lipton, D., R. Martinson, and J. Wilks
1975 *Effectiveness of correctional treatment.* New York: Praeger.

Liska, Allen E., and Mark Tausig
1979 Theoretical interpretations of social class and racial differentials in legal decision-making for juveniles. *Sociological Quarterly* 20: 197–207.

Lockwood, Dan
1980 *Prison sexual violence.* New York: Elsevier.

Loftin, C., M. Heumann, and D. McDowall
1983 Mandatory sentencing and firearms violence. *Law & Society Review* 17: 287–318.

Logan, Charles H.
1972 Evaluation research in crime and delinquency: a reappraisal. *Journal of Criminal Law, Criminology and Police Science* 63: 378–87.

# Bibliography

Logan, Charles H., and Sharla P. Rausch
1985a Why deinstitutionalizing status offenders is pointless. *Crime and Delinquency* 31: 501–18.
1985b Punishment and profit: the emergence of private enterprise prisons. *Justice Quarterly* 2: 303–18.

Lombardo, Lucien X.
1981 *Guards imprisoned.* New York: Elsevier.
1982 Stress, change, and collective violence in prison. In *The pains of imprisonment,* ed. R. Johnson and H. Toch. Beverly Hills, Calif.: Sage.

Lundman, Richard J.
1986 *Beyond Probation:* assessing the generalizability of the delinquency suppression effects reported by Murray and Cox. *Crime and Delinquency* 32: 134–47.

McCarthy, Belinda R., and Brent L. Smith
1986 The conceptualization of discrimination in the juvenile justice process. *Criminology* 24: 41–64.

McCleary, Richard
1975 How structural variables constrain the parole officer's use of discretionary powers. *Social Problems* 23: 209–25.
1978 *Dangerous men.* Beverly Hills, Calif.: Sage.
1983 Probation and parole: supervision. In *Encyclopedia of crime and justice,* ed. S. H. Kadish, pp. 1255–60. New York: Macmillan.

McCleary, Richard, and Richard A. Hay
1980 *Applied time series analysis for the social sciences.* Beverly Hills, Calif.: Sage.

McCorkle, Lloyd W., and Richard Korn
1954 Resocialization within walls. *Annals of the American Academy of Political and Social Science* 293: 88–98.

McGarrell, Edmund F., and Timothy J. Flanagan, eds.
1985 *Sourcebook of criminal justice statistics—1984.* Washington: U.S. Government Printing Office.

MacIsaacs, John
1968 *Half the fun was getting there.* Englewood Cliffs, N.J.: Prentice-Hall.

Mahan, Sue
1984 Imposition of despair—an ethnography of women in prison. *Justice Quarterly* 1: 357–83.

Maltz, Michael D.
1984 *Recidivism.* New York: Academic Press.

Mannheim, Herman, and Leslie Wilkins
1955 *Prediction methods in relation to Borstal training.* London: Her Majesty's Stationery Office.

Marquart, James W., and Ben M. Crouch
1985 Judicial reform and prisoner control: the impact of *Ruiz v. Estelle* on a Texas penitentiary. *Law & Society Review* 19: 557–86.

Martin, Susan E.
1983 The politics of sentencing reform. In *Research on sentencing* (vol. 2), ed. A. Blumstein *et al.,* pp. 265–304. Washington: National Academy Press.

Martinson, Robert
1974 What works?—questions and answers about prison reform. *Public Interest* 35: 22–54.
1976 California research at the crossroads. *Crime and Delinquency* 35: 180–91.

Martinson, R. M., G. G. Kassebaum, and D. A. Ward
1964 A critique of research in parole. *Federal Probation* 28: 34–38.

Marx, Gary
1985 "I'll be watching you": reflections on the new surveillance. *Dissent* 32: 26–34.

Marx, Karl
1964 *Selected writings in sociology and social philosophy.* Translated by B. T. Bottomore, edited by B. T. Bottomore and Maximilien Rubel. New York: McGraw-Hill.

Matheny, Kenneth B.
1976 Conditions of jails within the United States. Report prepared for the National Institute of Corrections, Atlanta.

Mattick, Hans W.
1974 The contemporary jails of the United States: an unknown and neglected area of justice. In *Handbook of criminology,* ed.

D. Glaser, pp. 777–848. Chicago: Rand McNally.

Meehl, Paul E.
1954 *Clinical vs. statistical prediction.* Minneapolis: Univ. of Minnesota Press.

Melossi, Dario, and Massino Pavarini
1981 *The prison and the factory: origins of the penitentiary system.* Totowa, N.J.: Barnes and Noble.

Mennel, Robert M.
1973 *Thorns and thistles: juvenile delinquents in the United States 1824–1940.* Hanover, N.H.: University Press of New England.

Messinger, S. L., J. E. Berecochea, D. Rauma, and R. A. Berk
1985 The foundations of parole in California. *Law & Society Review* 19: 69–106.

Messinger, Sheldon L., and Phillip D. Johnson
1978 California's determinate sentence statute: history and issues. In *Determinate sentencing: reform or regression?*, pp. 13–59. Washington: U.S. Department of Justice, National Institute of Law Enforcement and Criminal Justice.

Michalowski, Raymond J.
1983 Crime control in the 1980s: a progressive agenda. *Crime and Social Justice* 19: 13–23.

Miethe, Terance D., and Charles A. Moore
1985 Socioeconomic disparities under determinate sentencing systems. *Criminology* 23: 337–63.

Mileski, Maureen
1971 Courtroom encounters: an observational study of a lower criminal court. *Law & Society Review* 5: 473–533.

Milgram, Stanley
1974 *Obedience to authority.* New York: Harper & Row.

Miller, Lovick C.
1970 Southfields: evaluation of a short-term in-patient treatment center for delinquents. *Crime and Delinquency* 16: 305–16.

Miller, Walter B.
1974 Ideology and criminal justice policy:

some current issues. In *The criminologist: crime and the criminal,* ed. C. Reasons, pp. 19–50. Pacific Palisades, Calif.: Goodyear.

Mills, C. Wright
1942 The professional ideology of social pathologists. *American Journal of Sociology* 49: 165–80.

Minor, W. William, and Michael Courlander
1979 The postrelease trauma thesis: a reconsideration of the risk of early parole failure. *Journal of Research in Crime and Delinquency* 16: 273–93.

Mitford, Jessica
1973 *Kind and usual punishment.* New York: Knopf.

Monahan, John
1983 Prediction of crime recidivism. In *Encyclopedia of Crime and Justice,* ed. Sanford H. Kadish, pp. 1170–77. New York: Macmillan.

Morris, P., and F. Beverly, assisted by J. Vennard
1975 *On license: a study of parole.* New York: Wiley.

Moynahan, J. M., and Earle K. Stewart
1980 *The American jail.* Chicago: Nelson-Hall.

Mullen, Joan
1985 *Corrections and the private sector.* Washington: U.S. Department of Justice, National Institute of Justice.

Murray, Charles A., and Louis A. Cox, Jr.
1979 *Beyond probation.* Beverly Hills, Calif.: Sage.

Nagel, Stuart, and Marian Neef
1981 Changing benefits and costs to encourage lawful and desired behavior. *Crime and Delinquency* 27: 225–33.

Nagin, Daniel
1979 The impact of determinate sentencing legislation on prison population and sentence length: a California case study. *Public Policy* 27: 69–98.

National Advisory Commission and Criminal Justice Standards and Goals
1973 *Corrections.* Washington: U.S. Government Printing Office.

National Center for Educational Statistics
1983–84  *Digest of Educational Statistics.* Washington: U.S. Department of Health, Education, and Welfare.

National Congress on Penitentiary and Reformatory Discipline
1981  Statement of principles. In *Transactions of the National Congress on Penitentiary and Reformatory Discipline,* pp. 541–47. Albany, N.Y.: Weed, Parsons. Reprinted in *Sentencing,* ed. H. Gross and A. von Hirsch. New York: Oxford University Press.

National Council on Crime and Delinquency
1972  A model act for the protection of rights of prisoners. *Crime and Delinquency* 18: 4–13.
1974  Peaceful settlement of prison conflict: a policy statement. *Crime and Delinquency* 20: 1–3.

National Probation and Parole Institutes
1976  *1972 parolees: three-year follow-up and trend analysis.* Davis, Calif.: National Council on Crime and Delinquency Research Center.

Newman, Graeme
1983  *Just and painful.* New York: Macmillan.

Nimick, E. H., H. N. Snyder, D. P. Sullivan, and N. J. Tierney
1985  *Juvenile court statistics 1982.* Washington: U.S. Department of Justice, National Institute for Juvenile Justice and Delinquency Prevention.

Ohlin, Lloyd E.
1974  Organizational reform in correctional agencies. In *Handbook of criminology,* ed. D. Glaser, pp. 995–1020. Chicago: Rand McNally.

Ohlin, L. E., H. Piven, and D. M. Pappenfort
1956  Major dilemmas of the social worker in probation and parole. *National Probation and Parole Association Journal* 2: 211–25.

O'Leary, Vincent, and Daniel Glaser
1972  The assessment of risk in parole decision making. In *The future of parole,* ed. D. J. West, pp. 135–98. London: Duckworth.

O'Leary, Vincent, and Joan Nuffield
1972  *The organization of parole systems in the United States.* Hackensack, N.J.: National Council on Crime and Delinquency.

Orland, Leonard
1975  *Prisons: houses of darkness.* New York: Free Press.

Packer, Herbert L.
1964  Two models of the criminal process. *University of Pennsylvania Law Review* 113: 1–68.

Palmer, Jan, and John Salimbene
1978  The incapacitation of the dangerous offender: a second look. *Journal of Research in Crime and Delinquency* 15: 130–34.

Palmer, John
1985  *Constitutional rights of prisoners.* 3rd ed. Cincinnati: Anderson.

Palmer, Ted
1975  Martinson revisited. *Journal of Research in Crime and Delinquency* 12: 133–52.

Pappenfort, D., D. M. Kilpatrick, and A. M. Kuby
1970  *Detention facilities.* Chicago: Univ. of Chicago, School of Social Service Administration.

Park, James W. L.
1975  The organization of prison violence. In *Prison violence,* ed. A. K. Cohen, G. F. Cole, and R. Bailey. Lexington, Mass.: D. C. Heath.

Partridge, Anthony, and William B. Eldridge
1974  *Second circuit sentencing study.* Washington: Federal Judicial Center.

Patton, Michael Quinn
1980  *Qualitative evaluation methods.* Beverly Hills, Calif.: Sage.

Pearson, Frank S.
1985  New Jersey's intensive supervision program: a progress report. *Crime and Delinquency* 31: 393–410.

Pepinsky, Harold E.
1970  A theory of police reaction to *Miranda v. Arizona. Crime and Delinquency* 16: 379–88.

Petchesky, Rosalind
1981  At hard labor: penal confinement and

production in nineteenth-century America. In *Crime and capitalism*, ed. D. F. Greenberg, pp. 341–57. Palo Alto, Calif.: Mayfield.

Petersilia, Joan
  n.d. *Exploring the option of house arrest.* Santa Monica, Calif.: Rand Corporation.
  1980 Career criminal research: A review of recent evidence. In *Crime and justice* (vol. 2), ed. N. Morris and M. Tonry, pp. 321–70. Chicago: Univ. of Chicago Press.
  1985 Community supervision: trends and critical issues. *Crime and Delinquency* 31: 339–47.

Petersilia, Joan, and Peter W. Greenwood
  1978 Mandatory prison sentences: their projected effects on crime and prison populations. *Journal of Criminal Law and Criminology* 69: 604–11.

Petersilia, J., S. Turner, J. Kahan, and J. Peterson
  1985a Executive summary of Rand's study, "Granting felons probation." *Crime and Delinquency* 31: 379–92.
  1985b *Granting felons probation.* Santa Monica, Calif.: Rand Corporation.

Petersilia, J., S. Turner, and J. Peterson
  1986 *Prison versus probation in California.* Santa Monica, Calif.: Rand Corporation.

Peterson, M. A., and H. B. Braiker (with S. M. Polich)
  1980 *Doing crime: a survey of California prison inmates.* Santa Monica, Calif.: Rand Corporation.

Piliavin, I., R. Gartner, C. Thornton, and R. L. Matsueda
  1986 Crime, deterrence, and rational choice. *American Sociological Review* 51: 101–19.

Plamenatz, John
  1970 *Ideology.* New York: Praeger.

Platt, Anthony M.
  1977 *The child savers.* Chicago: Univ. of Chicago Press.
  1982 Crime and punishment in the United States: immediate and long-term reforms from a Marxist perspective. *Crime and Social Justice* 18: 38–46.
  1984 Criminology in the 1980s: progressive

alternatives to "law and order." *Crime and Social Justice* 21–22: 191–99.

Platt, Tony, and Paul Takagi
  1977 Intellectuals for law and order: a critique of the "New Realists." *Crime and Social Justice* 8: 1–16.

Polk, Kenneth
  1984 Juvenile diversion: a look at the record. *Crime and Delinquency* 30: 648–59.

Polsky, Howard W.
  1962 *Cottage Six.* New York: Russell Sage.

Portes, Alejandro
  1971 On the emergence of behavior therapy in modern society. *Journal of Consulting and Clinical Psychology* 36: 303–13.

Poster, Mark
  1984 *Foucault, Marxism and history.* Cambridge, U.K.: Polity Press.

Pownall, George
  1963 The role of the parole supervision officer. Unpublished doctoral dissertation in sociology, University of Illinois-Urbana.

President's Commission on Law Enforcement and Administration of Justice
  1967a *The challenge of crime in a free society.* Washington: U.S. Government Printing Office.
  1967b *Task force report: the courts.* Washington: U.S. Government Printing Office.

Propper, Alice M.
  1981 *Prison homosexuality: myth and reality.* Lexington, Mass.: D. C. Heath.

Prus, Robert C., and John R. Stratton
  1976 Parole revocation decisionmaking: private typings and official designations. *Federal Probation* 40: 48–53.

Quinney, Richard
  1979 The production of criminology. *Criminology* 16: 445–67.

Radelet, Michael L., and Margaret Vandiver
  1986 Race and capital punishment: an overview of the issues. *Crime and Social Justice* 25: 94–113.

Rafter, Nicole Hahn
  1983 Prisons for women 1790–1980. In

*Crime and justice* (vol. 5), ed. M. Tonry and N. Morris, pp. 129–81. Chicago: Univ. of Chicago Press.

1985 *Partial justice*. Boston: Northeastern Univ. Press.

Rauma, David, and Richard Berk
1982 Crime and poverty in California: some quasi-experimental evidence. *Social Science Research* 11: 318–51.

Reed, John P., and Charles E. King
1966 Factors in the decision-making of North Carolina probation officers. *Journal of Research in Crime and Delinquency* 3: 120–28.

Regnery, Alfred S.
1985 Getting away with murder. *Policy Review* 34: 1–4.
1986 A federal perspective on juvenile justice reform. *Crime and Delinquency* 32: 39–51.

Reiber, Leslie
1985 *Parole in the United States 1980 and 1981*. Washington: U.S. Department of Justice, National Institute of Justice.

Reiman, Jeffrey H.
1982 Marxist explanations and radical misinterpretations. *Crime and Delinquency* 28: 610–17.

Reiman, Jeffrey H., and Sue Headlee
1981 Marxism and criminal justice policy. *Crime and Delinquency* 27: 24–47.

Reuterman, Nicholas A., and Thomas R. Hughes
1984 Developments in juvenile justice during the decade of the '70s: juvenile detention facilities. *Journal of Criminal Justice* 12: 325–33.

Robertson, John A., ed.
1974 *Rough Justice*. Boston: Little, Brown.

Robison, James O., and Gerald Smith
1971 The effectiveness of correctional programs. *Crime and Delinquency* 17: 67–80.

Rogers, Kristine Olson
1972 For her own protection . . .: conditions of incarceration for female juvenile offenders in the state of Connecticut. *Law & Society Review* 7: 223–46.

Rosecrance, John
1985 The probation officer's search for credibility: ball park recommendations. *Crime and Delinquency* 31: 539–54.

Ross, J. G., E. Heffernan, J. R. Sevik, and F. T. Johnson
1978 *Assessment of coeducational corrections*. Washington: U.S. Department of Justice, National Institute of Law Enforcement and Criminal Justice.

Rossett, Arthur, and Donald R. Cressey
1976 *Justice by consent*. Philadelphia: J. B. Lippincott.

Rossi, P. H., R. A. Berk, and K. J. Lenihan
1980 *Money, work and crime*. New York: Academic Press.
1982 Saying it wrong with figures: a comment on Zeisel. *American Journal of Sociology* 88: 390–94.

Rothman, David
1971 *The discovery of the asylum*. Boston: Little, Brown.
1973 Decarcerating prisoners and patients. *Civil Liberties Review* 1: 8–30.
1980 *Conscience and convenience*. Boston: Little, Brown.
1983 Sentencing reforms in historical perspective. *Crime and Delinquency* 29: 631–47.

Rubin, Sol
1971 Needed—new legislation in corrections. *Crime and Delinquency* 17: 392–405.

Rusche, George
1939 *Punishment and social structure*. New York: Columbia Univ. Press.
1980 Labor market and penal sanction: thoughts on sociology of criminal justice. In *Punishment and penal discipline*, ed. T. Platt and P. Takagi, pp. 10–16. Berkeley, Calif.: Crime and Social Justice Associates.

Rutherford, Andrew, and Osman Bengur
1976 *Community-based alternatives to juvenile incarceration*. Washington: U.S. Department of Justice, National Institute of Law Enforcement and Criminal Justice.

Ryan, John Paul
1980 Adjudication and sentencing in a misde-

meanor court. *Law & Society Review* 15: 79–108.

Sacks, Howard R., and Charles H. Logan

1979 *Does parole make a difference?* Storrs: Univ. of Connecticut School of Law Press.

Sarri, Rosemary C.

1974 *Under lock and key: juveniles in jails and detention.* Ann Arbor: Univ. of Michigan, National Assessment of Juvenile Corrections.

Schmidt, Janet

1977 *Demystifying parole.* Lexington, Mass.: D. C. Heath.

Schnur, Alfred C.

1958 Some reflections on the role of correctional research. *Law and Contemporary Problems* 23: 772–83.

Schrag, Clarence

1961 Some foundations for a theory of corrections. In *The prison,* ed. D. R. Cressey, pp. 309–58. New York: Holt, Rinehart and Winston.

Schroeder, Andreas.

1976 *Shaking It Rough.* Garden City, N.Y.: Doubleday.

Schur, Edwin M.

1971 *Labeling deviant behavior.* New York: Harper & Row.

1973 *Radical nonintervention.* Englewood Cliffs, N.J.: Prentice-Hall.

Schwartz, David A.

1984 *Wakenikona v. Olin:* The hands-off doctrine gains further support in prison transfer decisions. *New England Journal on Criminal and Civil Confinement* 10: 433–58.

Schwartz, I. M., M. Jackson-Beeck, and R. Anderson

1984 The "hidden" system of juvenile control. *Crime and Delinquency* 30: 371–85.

Schwitzgebel, Ralph K.

1971 *Development and legal regulation of coercive behavior modification techniques with offenders.* Washington: National Institute of Mental Health, Center for Studies of Crime and Delinquency.

Scott, Joseph E.

1974 The use of discretion in determining the severity of punishment for incarcerated felons. *Journal of Criminal Law and Criminology* 65: 214–24.

Scull, Andrew T.

1977a *Decarceration.* Englewood Cliffs, N.J.: Prentice-Hall.

1977b Madness and segregative control: the rise of the insane asylum. *Social Problems* 24: 337–51.

1981 A new trade in lunacy: the recommodification of the mental patient. *American Behavioral Scientist* 24: 741–54.

1984 *Decarceration.* 2d ed. Cambridge, U.K.: Polity Press.

Sechrest, L., S. O. White, and E. D. Brown, eds.

1979 *The rehabilitation of criminal offenders.* Washington: National Academy of Sciences.

Seidman, David, and Michael Couzens

1974 Getting the crime rate down: political pressure and crime reporting. *Law & Society Review* 8: 457–94.

Sexton, G. E., F. C. Farrow, and B. Auerbach

1985 The private sector in prison industries. In *Research in Brief.* Washington: U.S. Department of Justice, National Institute of Justice.

Shane-DuBow, S., A. P. Brown, and E. Olsen

1985 *Sentencing reform in the United States.* Washington: U.S. Department of Justice, National Institute of Justice.

Shinnar, Shlomo, and Reuel Shinnar

1975 The effect of the criminal justice system on the control of crime: a quantitative approach. *Law & Society Review* 9: 581–611.

Shover, Neal

1975 Criminal behavior as theoretical praxis. *Issues in Criminology* 10: 95–108.

1979 *A sociology of American corrections.* Homewood, Ill.: Dorsey.

1985 *Aging criminals.* Beverly Hills, Calif.: Sage.

Sigler, Maurice H.

1975 Abolish parole? *Federal Probation* 39: 42–48.

# Bibliography

Smith, Joan, and William Fried
1984 *Uses of the American prison.* Lexington, Mass.: D. C. Heath.

Smykla, John D., ed.
1980 *Coed prison.* New York: Human Sciences Press.

Sobell, Morton
1974 *On doing time.* New York: Scribner's.

Spangenberg, R. L., B. Lee, M. Battaglia, P. Smith, and A. D. Davis
1986 *National criminal defense systems study.* Washington: U.S. Department of Justice, Bureau of Justice Statistics.

Spitzer, Steven
1975 Toward a Marxian theory of deviance. *Social Problems* 22: 638–51.
1979 The rationalization of crime control in capitalist society. *Contemporary Crises* 3: 187–206.

Stanley, David T.
1976 *Prisoners among us.* Washington: Brookings Institution.

Stapleton, V., D. P. Aday, Jr., and J. A. Ito
1982 An empirical typology of American metropolitan juvenile courts. *American Journal of Sociology* 88: 549–64.

State of Minnesota
1985 Ombudsman for corrections. In *Correctional institutions*, 3d ed., ed. R. M. Carter, D. Glaser, and L. T. Wilkins, pp. 402–25. New York: Harper & Row.

Stone-Meierhoefer, Barbara, and Peter B. Hoffman
1982 The effects of presumptive parole dates on institutional behavior. *Journal of Criminal Justice* 10: 283–97.

Street, D., R. D. Vinter, and C. Perrow
1966 *Organization for treatment.* New York: Free Press.

Studt, Eliot
1973 *Surveillance and service in parole.* Washington: U.S. Department of Justice, National Institute of Law Enforcement and Criminal Justice.

Sullivan, Dennis C., and Larry L. Tifft
1975 Court intervention in corrections: roots of resistance and problems of compliance. *Crime and Delinquency* 22: 213–22.

Swigert, Victoria Lynn, and Ronald A. Farrell
1976 *Murder, inequality, and the law.* Lexington, Mass.: D. C. Heath.

Sykes, Gresham M.
1956 The corruption of authority and rehabilitation. *Social Forces* 34: 157–62.
1958 *Society of captives.* Princeton, N.J.: Princeton Univ. Press.

Sykes, Gresham M., and Sheldon L. Messinger
1960 The inmate social system. In *Theoretical studies in social organization of the prison*, ed. R. A. Cloward *et al.*, pp. 5–19. New York: Social Science Research Council.

Sylvester, S., J. Reed, and D. Nelson
1977 *Prison homicide.* New York: Spectrum.

Takagi, Paul
1967 Evaluation and adaptations in a formal organization. Unpublished doctoral dissertation in sociology, Stanford University.
1975 The Walnut Street Jail: a penal reform to centralize the powers of the state. *Federal Probation* 34: 18–26.

Takagi, Paul, and James O. Robison
1969 The parole violator: an organizational reject. *Journal of Research in Crime and Delinquency* 5: 78–86.

Thomas, Charles W.
1987 *Corrections in America.* Newbery Park, Calif.: Sage.

Thomas, Charles W., and Shay Bilchik
1985 Prosecuting juveniles in criminal courts. *Journal of Criminal Law and Criminology* 76: 439–79.

Thomas, Charles W., and Robin J. Cage
1977 The effect of social characteristics on juvenile court dispositions. *Sociological Quarterly* 18: 237–52.

Thomson, Randall J., and Matthew T. Zingraff
1981 Detecting sentencing disparity: some problems and evidence. *American Journal of Sociology* 86: 869–80.

Thornberry, Terrence P., and R. L. Christenson
1984 Juvenile justice decision-making as a

longitudinal process. *Social Forces* 63: 433–44.

Tittle, Charles R.
1974 Prison and rehabilitation: the inevitability of failure. *Social Problems* 21: 385–94.
1980 *Sanctions and social deviance.* New York: Praeger.

Tittle, Charles R., and Charles H. Logan
1973 Sanctions and deviance: evidence and remaining questions. *Law & Society Review* 7: 371–92.

Toch, Hans
1977 *Living in prison.* New York: Free Press.

Twentieth Century Fund
1976 *Fair and certain punishment.* New York: McGraw-Hill.

U.S. Comptroller General
1980 *Women in prison.* Washington: U.S. Government Printing Office.

U.S. Department of Justice
n.d. *Survey of inmates of local jails: advance report.* Washington: National Criminal Justice Information and Statistics Service.
1975 *The nation's jails.* Washington: National Criminal Justice Information and Statistics Service.
1977a *Sourcebook of criminal justice statistics.* Washington: National Criminal Justice Information and Statistics Service.
1977b *Children in custody: advance report on the juvenile detention and correctional facility census of 1974.* Washington: National Criminal Justice Information and Statistics Service.
1978 *State and local probation and parole system.* Washington: Law Enforcement Assistance Administration.
1980a *National symposium on children in jail.* Washington: Office of Juvenile Justice and Delinquency Prevention.
1980b *Parole in the United States: 1979.* Washington: Bureau of Justice Statistics.
1982 *Capital punishment 1981.* Washington: Bureau of Justice Statistics.
1983a *Children in custody: advance report on the 1982 census of public juvenile facilities.* Washington: Office of Juvenile Justice and Delinquency Prevention.
1983b *Report to the nation on crime and justice.* Washington: Bureau of Justice Statistics.
1983c *Setting prison terms.* Washington: Bureau of Justice Statistics.
1983d *Tracking offenders.* Washington: Bureau of Justice Statistics.
1984 *The 1983 jail census.* Washington: Bureau of Justice Statistics.
1985a *Capital punishment 1983.* Washington: Bureau of Justice Statistics.
1985b *Felony sentencing in 18 local jurisdictions.* Washington: Bureau of Justice Statistics.
1985c *Jail inmates 1983.* Washington: Bureau of Justice Statistics.
1985d *Prisoners in 1984.* Washington: Bureau of Justice Statistics.
1986a *Capital punishment 1984.* Washington: Bureau of Justice Statistics.
1986b *Children in custody—1982/83: census of juvenile detention and correctional facilities.* Washington: Bureau of Justice Statistics.
1986c *Crime and justice facts, 1985.* Washington: Bureau of Justice Statistics.
1986d *Jail inmates 1984.* Washington: Bureau of Justice Statistics.
1986e *Prison admissions and releases, 1983.* Washington: Bureau of Justice Statistics.
1986f *Prisoners in 1985.* Washington: Bureau of Justice Statistics.
1986g *Probation and parole 1984.* Washington: Bureau of Justice Statistics.
1986h *Public juvenile facilities, 1985: children in custody.* Washington: Bureau of Justice Statistics.
1986i *State and federal prisoners, 1925–1985.* Washington: Bureau of Justice Statistics.

U.S. Parole Commision
1985 *Parole commission rules.* Washington: U.S. Department of Justice.

Van den Haag, Ernest
1975 *Punishing criminals.* New York: Basic Books.

Van Dine, S., S. Dinitz, and J. Conrad
1977 The incapacitation of the dangerous offender: a statistical experiment. *Journal*

*of Research in Crime and Delinquency* 14: 22–34.

Van Maanen, John
1978 The asshole. In *Policing: a view from the street,* ed. P. K. Manning and J. Van Maanen, pp. 221–37. Santa Monica, Calif.: Goodyear.

von Hirsch, Andrew
1976 *Doing justice.* New York: Hill and Wang.
1983 Recent trends in American criminal sentencing theory. *Maryland Law Review* 42: 6–37.

von Hirsch, Andrew, and Kathleen Hanrahan
1979 *The question of parole.* Cambridge, Mass.: Ballinger.
1981 Determinate penalty systems in America: an overview. *Crime and Delinquency* 27: 289–316.

Waldo, Gordon P., and Theodore G. Chiricos
1977 Work release and recidivism. *Evaluation Quarterly* 1: 87–108.

Walker, Samuel
1985 *Sense and nonsense about crime.* Monterey, Calif.: Brooks/Cole.

Waller, Irvin
1974 *Men released from prison.* Toronto: Univ. of Toronto Press.

Ward, David A.
1973 Evaluative research for corrections. In *Prisoners in America,* ed. Lloyd E. Ohlin, pp. 184–206. Englewood Cliffs, N.J.: Prentice-Hall.

Ward, David A., and Gene Kassebaum
1965 *Women's prison.* Chicago: Aldine.

Warren, Carol A. B.
1981 New forms of social control—the myth of deinstitutionalization. *American Behavioral Scientist* 24: 724–40.

Warren, Marguerite Q.
1971 Classification of offenders as an aid to efficient management and effective treatment. *Journal of Criminal Law, Criminology and Police Science* 62: 239–58.

Weeks, H. Ashley
1958 *Youthful offenders at Highfields.* Ann Arbor: Univ. of Michigan Press.

Weimer, David L., and Lee S. Friedman
1979 Efficiency considerations in criminal rehabilitation research: costs and consequences. In *The rehabilitation of criminal offenders,* ed. L. Sechrest *et al.,* pp. 251–72. Washington: National Academy of Sciences.

Wheeler, S., E. Banouch, M. Cramer, and I. Zola
1966 Agents of delinquency control: a comparative analysis. In *Controlling delinquents,* ed. S. Wheeler, pp. 31–60. New York: Wiley.

Whitehead, John T.
1985 Job burnout in probation and parole. *Criminal Justice and Behavior* 12: 91–110.
1986 Gender differences in probation: a case of no differences. *Justice Quarterly* 3: 51–65.

Whitehead, John T., and Charles Lindquist
1985 Job stress and burnout among probation/parole officers. *International Journal of Offender Therapy and Comparative Criminology* 29: 109–19.

Wideman, John E.
1984 *Brothers and keepers.* New York: Penguin.

Wilkins, Leslie T.
1965 *Social deviance.* Englewood Cliffs, N.J.: Prentice-Hall.
1971 The case for prediction. In *The criminal in confinement,* ed. L. Radzinowicz and M. E. Wolfgang, pp. 375–81. New York: Basic Books.

Williams, Vergil L., and Mary Fish
1974 *Convicts, codes and contraband.* Cambridge, Mass.: Ballinger.

Wilson, James Q.
1968 *Varieties of police behavior.* Cambridge, Mass.: Harvard Univ. Press.
1975 *Thinking about crime.* New York: Basic Books.
1983 *Thinking about crime.* Rev. ed. New York: Vintage.

Wolfgang, M. E., R. Figlio, and T. Sellin
1972 *Delinquency in a birth cohort.* Chicago: Univ. of Chicago Press.

Wolfgang, Marvin E., and Marc Reidel
1973 Race, judicial discretion, and the death

penalty. *Annals of the American Academy of Political and Social Science* 53: 301–11.

Wooden, Kenneth
1976 *Weeping in the playtime of others.* New York: McGraw-Hill.

Wright, Erik Olin, ed.
1973 *The politics of punishment.* New York: Harper Colophon Books.

Yeager, Matthew G.
1979 Unemployment and imprisonment. *Journal of Criminal Law and Criminology* 70: 586–88.

Young, Jock
1975 Working-class criminology. In *Critical criminology,* ed. I. Taylor, P. Walton, and J. Young, pp. 63–94. London: Routledge and Kegan Paul.

Zeisel, Hans
1982a Disagreement over the evaluation of a controlled experiment. *American Journal of Sociology* 88: 378–89.
1982b Hans Zeisel concludes the debate. *American Journal of Sociology* 88: 394–97.

Zimring, Franklin E.
1977 Making the punishment fit the crime. Occasional paper no. 12 from the Law School, Univ. of Chicago.

Zimring, Franklin E., and Gordon J. Hawkins
1968 Deterrence and marginal groups. *Journal of Research in Crime and Delinquency* 5: 100–14.
1973 *Deterrence.* Chicago: Univ. of Chicago Press.

# Subject Index

Subject Index

## Subject Index

## Subject Index

# Name Index

Name Index

# Name Index

## Name Index

# Acknowledgments

Adamson, Christopher. 1984. Toward a Marxian penology: captive criminal populations as economic threats and resources. *Social Problems* 31: 437, 440, 442. © 1984 by The Society for the Study of Social Problems. Reprinted by permission of the University of California Press and Christopher Adamson. (**Chapter 10, pp. 148– 149.**)

Bowker, Lee H. 1977. *Prisoner subcultures*, p. 100. Lexington, Mass.: D. C. Heath. Reprinted by permission of Lexington Books. (**Chapter 8, pp. 113– 114.**)

Braly, Malcolm. 1976. *False starts: a memoir of San Quentin and other prisons*, pp. 51–52, 59–60, 147– 148, 157–158, 181–182, 253, 264–265, 342– 343. Boston: Little, Brown. Reprinted by permission of Knox Burger Associates Ltd., agents for the Malcolm Braly estate. (**Panels 3.1, 4.2, 6.3, 8.4, 8.5, 9.1, 9.2, 9.3.**)

Brown, Claude. 1965. *Manchild in the promised land*, pp. 133–134. New York: Macmillan. Copyright © Claude Brown 1965. Reprinted by permission of Macmillan Publishing Company. (**Panel 8.3.**)

Brown, Waln K. 1983. *The other side of delinquency*, pp. 24–25, 122–124, 126–127. New Brunswick, N.J.: Rutgers University Press. Copyright © 1983 by Rutgers, The State University. Reprinted by permission of Rutgers University Press. (**Panels 5.6, 8.1, 8.3.**)

Bunker, Edward. 1981. *Little boy blue*, pp. 37–42. New York: Viking. Reprinted by permission of Watkins/Loomis Agency, Inc., agents for Edward Bunker. (**Panel 5.5.**)

Burkhart, Kathryn W. 1973. *Women in prison*, pp. 24, 57, 90. Garden City, N.Y.: Doubleday. Reprinted by permission of Kathryn Watterson Burkhart. (**Panels 4.3, 5.4, 7.2.**)

Chang, Dae H., and Warren B. Armstrong, eds. 1972. *The prison: voices from the inside*, pp. 49–50. Cambridge, Mass.: Schenkman. Reprinted by permission of Schenkman Books, Inc. (**Panel 5.2.**)

Currie, Elliott. 1973. *Managing the minds of men: the reformatory movement, 1865–1920*, pp. 3, 4, 5. Unpublished doctoral dissertation, University of California-Berkeley. Reprinted by permission of Elliott Currie. (**Chapter 3, p. 35; Chapter 10, p. 145.**)

Currie, Elliott. 1985. *Confronting crime: an American challenge*, p. 278. New York: Pantheon. Reprinted by permission of Pantheon Books, a Division of Random House, Inc. (**Chapter 14, p. 207.**)

Foucault, Michel, 1979. *Discipline and punish: the birth of the prison*, pp. 201–203. Translated by Alan Sheridan. New York: Vintage. Reprinted by permission of Vintage Books, a Division of Random House, Inc. (**Chapter 14, p. 203.**)

Giallombardo, Rose. 1966. *Society of women*, p. 137. New York: Wiley. Reprinted by permission of John Wiley & Sons, Inc. (**Chapter 7, p. 100.**)

Harris, Jean. 1986. *Stranger in two worlds*, pp. 300, 310, 311. New York: Macmillan. Copyright ©

1986 by Jean Harris. Reprinted by permission of Macmillan Publishing Company. (**Panels 6.5, 7.3.**)

Irwin, John. 1970. *The felon,* pp. 157, 165–166, 204. Englewood Cliffs, N.J.: Prentice-Hall. Reprinted by permission of Prentice-Hall, Inc. (**Chapter 9, pp. 132–133.**)

Irwin, John. 1980. *Prisons in turmoil,* pp. 37–38, 39. Boston: Little, Brown. Copyright © 1980 by John Irwin. Reprinted by permission of Little, Brown and Company (Inc.) (**Chapter 10, p. 144.**)

Irwin, John. 1985. *The jail,* pp. 1, 2, 23, 46, 73, 84, 98, 103–105, 115, 118. Berkeley: University of California Press. Reprinted by permission of the University of California Press. (**Chapter 5, pp. 62–64, 70, 72–73.**)

*Knoxville News-Sentinel.* Editorial. November 26, 1977, p. 6. Reprinted by permission of the *Knoxville News-Sentinel.* (**Panel 3.4.**)

Korn, Richard. 1971. Of crime, criminal justice and corrections. *University of San Francisco Law Review* 6: 31–32. Reprinted by permission of the *University of San Francisco Law Review.* (**Chapter 11, pp. 156–157.**)

Leopold, Nathan F., Jr. 1958. *Life plus 99 years,* p. 141. Garden City, N.Y.: Doubleday. Copyright © 1957, 1958 by Nathan F. Leopold, Jr. Reprinted by permission of Doubleday & Company, Inc. (**Panel 6.1.**)

MacIsaac, John. 1968. *Half the fun was getting there,* pp. 69, 204–205. Englewood Cliffs, N.J.: Prentice-Hall. Reprinted by permission of Prentice-Hall, Inc. (**Panels 3.2, 4.1.**)

Melossi, Dario, and Massimo Pavarini. 1981. *The prison and the factory: origins of the penitentiary system,* pp. 143–144. Translated by Glynis Cousin. Totowa, N.J.: Barnes & Noble. Reprinted by permission of Barnes & Noble Books, a Division of Littlefield, Adams & Company, Totowa, N.J. (**Chapter 10, p. 147.**)

National Council on Crime and Delinquency. 1972. A model act for the protection of rights of prisoners. *Crime and Delinquency* 18: 4–13. Reprinted by permission of Sage Publications, Inc. (**Chapter 11, p. 160.**)

Palmer, John. 1985. *Constitutional rights of prisoners.* 3rd ed., p. 23. Cincinnati: Anderson. Reprinted by permission of Anderson Publishing Company. (**Chapter 11, p. 159.**)

Rafter, Nicole Hahn. 1983. Prisons for women 1790–1980. In *Crime and justice* (vol. 5), pp. 135, 148. Edited by M. Tonry and N. Morris. Chicago: University of Chicago Press. Reprinted by permission of the University of Chicago Press. (**Chapter 7, pp. 96, 98.**)

Rafter, Nicole Hahn. 1985. *Partial justice: women in state prisons, 1800–1935,* pp. 49, 187. Boston: Northeastern University Press. Copyright © 1985 by Nicole Hahn Rafter. Reprinted by permission of Northeastern University Press. (**Chapter 7, pp. 97, 105.**)

Rothman, David J. 1980. *Conscience and convenience: the asylum and its alternatives in progressive America,* pp. 5, 44–45. Boston: Little, Brown. Copyright © 1980 by David J. Rothman. Reprinted by permission of Little, Brown and Company (Inc.). (**Chapter 10, pp. 143–144.**)

Rusche, Georg, and Otto Kirchheimer. 1939. *Punishment and social structure,* p. 6. New York: Columbia University Press. Reprinted by permission of Columbia University Press. (**Chapter 10, pp. 146–147.**)

Schroeder, Andreas. 1976. *Shaking it rough,* pp. 29–30. Garden City, N.Y.: Doubleday. Copyright © 1976 by Andreas Schroeder. Reprinted by permission of Doubleday & Company, Inc. (**Panel 6.2.**)

Takagi, Paul. 1967. *Evaluations and adaptations in a formal organization.* Unpublished doctoral dissertation in sociology, Stanford University. (**Chapter 9, p. 131.**)

Wideman, John E. 1984. *Brothers and keepers,* pp. 185, 218. New York: Penguin. Reprinted by permission of Henry Holt and Company, Inc. (**Panel 6.4.**)